THE
$MART
INVESTOR'S
$URVIVAL
GUIDE

THE $MART INVESTOR'S $URVIVAL GUIDE

The Nine Laws
of Successful Investing
in a Volatile Market

CHARLES B. CARLSON, CFA

Currency

New York   London   Toronto   Sydney   Auckland

A CURRENCY BOOK
Published by Doubleday
a Division of Random House, Inc.
1540 Broadway, New York, New York 10036

Currency and Doubleday are trademarks
of Doubleday, a division of Random House, Inc.

Library of Congress Cataloging-in-Publication Data

Carlson, Charles B.
   The smart investor's survival guide : the nine laws of
successful investing in a volatile market / Charles B.
Carlson
      p. cm.
   ISBN: 0-385-50387-3
   1. Investments—Handbooks, manuals, etc.
   2. Portfolio management—Handbooks, manuals, etc.
   I. Title.
HG4527 .C2983 2002
332.6—dc21   2001058289

Book Design by Tina Thompson

PRINTED IN THE UNITED STATES OF AMERICA

First Edition: April 2002

SPECIAL SALES
Currency Books are available at special discounts for
bulk purchases for sales promotions or premiums.
Special editions, including personalized covers,
excerpts of existing books, and corporate imprints, can
be created in large quantities for special needs. For
more information, write to Special Markets, Currency
Books, 280 Park Avenue, 11th Floor, New York, NY
10017, or email specialmarkets@randomhouse.com.

10 9 8 7 6 5 4 3 2

To Denise,
my first and my last

ACKNOWLEDGMENTS

Writing a book is rarely a solitary endeavor. This book is no exception. I'd like to thank my editor, Roger Scholl, and my agent, Wes Neff, for their unlimited patience, uncompromising guidance, and unconditional support.

I'd also like to thank David Wright, who provided a lot of the heavy lifting when it came to crunching numbers for this book, and Tanya Yzaguirre, who created the charts for the book.

Three additional people I'd like to thank are Chris Miles, Steve Gittelson, and Bill McGuire, my editors at *Bloomberg Personal Finance* magazine. Indeed, a lot of the ideas and concepts that went into Chapter 7 ("Making the Hard Decision—Knowing When to Sell") sprung from my work with Chris and Bill over the years in putting together my "Stock Selector" column for *Bloomberg Personal Finance.*

Finally, I'd be remiss if I didn't give a special thank-you to Avis Beitz and Robert Evans. Avis and Bob have been with me since the start of my writing life some two decades ago. Avis has proofread each of my seven books. If there are better proofreaders in the business, I've yet to meet them. Thanks, Avis. Bob has been my boss at Horizon Publishing for the better part of those two decades and has supported me immensely in my publishing efforts. If there are better bosses on the planet than Robert, I've yet to meet them. Thanks, Bob.

CONTENTS

Preface . . . . *xi*

Introduction . . . . *xv*

Chapter One
LAW #1: KNOW YOUR "ENEMY"—UNDERSTANDING VOLATILITY *1*

Chapter Two
LAW #2: IN TURBULENT MARKETS, INVEST IN THE EYE OF
THE STORM *23*

Chapter Three
LAW #3: RIDE OUT THE TURBULENCE THROUGH ASSET AND
TIME DIVERSIFICATION *47*

Chapter Four
LAW #4: RIDE OUT VOLATILE MARKETS WITH EASY HOLDS *65*

Chapter Five
LAW #5: HANDLE STORMY MARKETS BY CREATING AN
ALL-WEATHER PORTFOLIO *103*

Chapter Six
LAW #6: USE DOLLAR-BASED INVESTING PROGRAMS TO
INVEST REGULARLY *125*

Chapter Seven
LAW #7: MAKING THE HARD DECISION—KNOWING
WHEN TO SELL *159*

Chapter Eight
LAW #8: THE IMPORTANCE OF SIMPLICITY IN A VOLATILE
WORLD *191*

Chapter Nine
LAW #9: STAY IN THE EYE WHEN THE STORM MOVES—
TOOLS FOR DETECTING MARKET SHIFTS *207*

Chapter Ten
IT'S GAME TIME *235*

Appendix A
DIRECT-PURCHASE PLANS *239*

Appendix B
THE "EASY-HOLD" STOCK LIST (1,500 COMPANIES) *253*

Appendix C
"EASY-HOLD" STOCKS BY INDUSTRY *279*

Appendix D
THE TOP 150 "EASY-HOLD" STOCKS *291*

Appendix E
THE "EASY-HOLD" MUTUAL FUND LIST (1,200 FUNDS) *295*

Appendix F
THE TOP 100 "EASY-HOLD" MUTUAL FUNDS *313*

Index *315*

PREFACE

A few years ago I went on a fishing trip with my father, brother, and brother-in-law. The four of us chartered a boat, the *Challenger*, out of Islamorada in the Florida Keys.

While I wouldn't call us expert fishermen, all of us grew up fishing ocean waters at least a few times each year, so we understood (or at least thought we understood) the schizophrenic nature of the sea.

When we arrived at the *Challenger*'s dock around 6 A.M. that Sunday morning, our craft was one of only a few preparing for the day's catch. According to our captain, Rob Dixon, a big storm the previous night had riled up things to the point that most of the other boats were staying home.

I remembered being awakened by the storm—it was one of those nasty ones that never quite graduated to hurricane status. As I told my dad, any storm that could chase my brother from the hotel hot tub was no small storm.

The *Challenger*, with the six of us on board, including Captain Dixon and his first mate, left the dock around 7 A.M. Almost immediately the undulating waters from the storm's wake lifted and dropped the *Challenger* with such rhythmic violence that simply standing required the balance of a Cirque de Soleil performer. Although no one said anything, I'm sure the thought crossed each of our minds that perhaps the day might have been better spent doing cannonballs in the hotel pool.

The hot-tub king was the first victim of the seasickness gods, assuming the fetal position inside the ship's hole after only about 20 minutes into our journey. I wasn't exactly feeling chipper myself, but I was hanging on, still looking forward to the day's activities and praying that the angry seas would calm.

They wouldn't.

After another 20 minutes or so—and with the volatility of the ocean's EKG intensifying—I felt that awful, paralyzing shroud that comes over you when you know you've lost the battle with the seasickness gods and can do nothing but await their judgment. My punishment was hastened by witnessing my brother-in-law—a graduate of the U.S. Naval Academy and someone who had been around boats and the ocean all his life—lose his private battle (along with his breakfast).

Seeing the Annapolis kid go down was the catalyst that tripped my own peristaltic adventure.

At about 9 A.M.—a mere two hours into the ordeal—Captain Dixon decided to take pity on us and suggested we shorten our trip from a full day to a half day. That meant getting back to dock around noon instead of 4 P.M.

Talk about your good news/bad news.

On the one hand, cutting four hours off the trip was the governor's pardon I and the rest of my "fishermen" were seeking. Yet, going in at noon meant another three hours of performing the "grab-my-sunglasses-and-bend-over-the-ship's-railing-without-falling-in" move I had perfected by this time.

Mustering all the strength I could, I shouted back to Captain Dixon, "Eleven-thirty."

Thus, a deadline had been set. Deals could now be cut with our stomachs—"You hang in there for another couple of hours, and this all will be over." Of course, our stomachs didn't believe us and continued to carry out their own agendas until the *Challenger* touched dock at around 11:30.

If you've never been seasick, you'll never understand just how bad you feel, or the almost instant relief that occurs when foot hits dock. It's the craziest thing, but what ails you leaves almost the second you touch terra.

As we straggled off the boat and down the dock to our car, the four of us started to laugh uncontrollably. We laughed at the hot-tub king, who emerged from the boat's womb looking as pale as skim milk. We laughed at the Annapolis kid, who broke his lifelong record of never getting sick on a boat. We laughed at my father, who, at one particularly rough stretch, was on his hands and knees shouting to the gods of the sea (and I'm not making this up), "I have nothing left to give."

And we laughed at me, whose formerly white T-shirt now looked like a Rorschach print.

To this day, when the four of us get together, we start giggling

about what a trip we had that day on the *Challenger*. The funny thing
is, we would go back tomorrow and do it again. Why? One reason is
that, to a man, we're not very bright. The big reason, however, and
what I've failed to tell you up to this point, is that we *caught fish like
crazy* that day. All sorts of fish: Barracuda. Bluefish. Dolphin fish (no,
not Flipper, but a type of ocean fish). Shark. It was one of the best
fishing trips—in terms of catching fish—we've ever had.

Now I know you bought this book to learn about investing, not
fishing. But when I began to think about writing the book, my fishing
story kept popping into my head. Actually, my fishing story truly is a
metaphor for the stock market in recent years, a story of big undula-
tions, rampant second-guessing, and plenty of casualties.

And a story of big opportunities (after all, we did catch lots of fish).

Indeed, coping with angry seas is much like coping with angry
markets:

- *One way to survive choppy waters is to avoid them altogether.*
  This is an approach we could have taken in Florida—simply stay
  on land. Investors can avoid choppy markets, too, by staying on
  the sidelines and out of the market. There are pluses and minuses
  to this approach, but it is an approach that works if your main
  objective is to eliminate risk altogether.

- *Another way to survive choppy waters is to get a bigger boat.*
  Indeed, the deck of an aircraft carrier would have been much
  calmer than the deck of the *Challenger*. That's because the aircraft
  carrier's giant surface diffuses the ocean's volatility. Likewise, an
  investor can ride out market volatility by diversifying a portfolio
  across many stocks and asset groups.

- *One way to survive an angry ocean is to stay close to shore.* But
  staying close to shore would likely have limited the amount and
  size of our catch. An investor can stay "close to shore" during
  volatile markets, venturing primarily into only defensive, low-risk
  stocks and bonds. Such an approach will limit the upside, however—the "big catch," if you will.

- *Experience matters.* The only two people on the boat who didn't
  get sick were Captain Dixon and his first mate. That's not surpris-

ing, since they're on water nearly every day of the year. They are used to the manic nature of the seas. They know what to expect. They have developed coping mechanisms that allow them to function even during the roughest of seas. In effect, they frame the ocean's volatility entirely differently than do those with less experience with rough seas. And because of that viewpoint, they weather volatility much better. As an investor, you have the ability to frame market conditions in a variety of ways. For example, some people view dramatic market downturns as dangerous events. Smart investors, however, who have lived through volatility and are not afraid of it view market choppiness and even bear markets as opportunities to pick up stocks on the cheap. Again, it's all about point of view.

If there is a lesson to take away from this book, it is the following: Investors can survive volatile markets. True, making money in choppy markets isn't easy. It requires patience. Courage. Discipline. It demands that you strip emotion from the investment process—something much easier said than done when stocks are cascading and your 401(k) plan is shrinking by the minute. It requires a recognition that getting rich in the market does not mean you have to swing for the fences but that you can do quite nicely taking your 10 percent a year. It may mean sitting idly by and watching your friends rack up big gains—if only momentarily—in high-risk stocks.

But make no mistake—smart investors can not only survive, but thrive, in volatile markets.

This book shows you how.

INTRODUCTION

The math of the stock market can be punishing at times.

Take the years 1999 and 2000. In 1999, the Nasdaq Composite registered its biggest gain ever, rising 85 percent. In 2000, that same Nasdaq Composite did an about-face, falling a record 39 percent.

Up 85 percent in one year, down 39 percent the next. Just by looking at the numbers, one would think that investors who had invested in the Nasdaq Composite at the beginning of 1999 and held through 2000 would still be well ahead of the game despite the 39 percent decline in 2000. After all, if you average the performance of the two years, it comes out to a gain of 23 percent per year (85 percent minus 39 percent divided by two years) for the Nasdaq Composite.

Ah, if the math were only that simple.

My guess is that most of you would be surprised to learn that an investor who bought the Nasdaq Composite at the beginning of 1999 and held through the 2000 decline would be sitting with only a scant gain. That's because the 39 percent decline took back nearly all of the 85 percent gain of the previous year.

Here's another example. Let's say you own a stock that climbs 100 percent in year 1, declines 50 percent in year 2, advances 100 percent in year 3, and declines 50 percent in year 4. If you add up the advances and declines over the volatile four-year period, you have an average annual return of 25 percent (200 percent minus 100 percent divided by 4). Yet how much money did you actually make during that four-year period?

The answer: *Zero.*

Do the math. Let's say you started with a $50 stock. In year 1, the stock rose 100 percent to $100. In year 2 the stock declined 50 percent to $50 per share. And the same round-trip was recorded in years 3 and 4, leaving you back where you started in year 1—a $50 stock.

Like I said, the math of the stock market can be punishing.

Now indulge me for one last example. Let's say that during the four-year period you were alternating 100 percent gains with 50 percent losses, your friend's portfolio went up 10 percent in year 1, 8 percent in year 2, 9 percent in year 3, and 9 percent in year 4. When you average those returns, they come out to a measly 9 percent per year (36 percent divided by 4). But what actually happened to your friend's money? Over the four-year period, his investment grew *41 percent.* (If you don't trust my math, start with a portfolio of $100 and run the numbers. You'll wind up at the end of year 4 with a portfolio valued at $141—a 41 percent gain.)

While a 41 percent gain in four years may not be your idea of big market performance, there's no disputing that 41 percent is better than zero percent.

So what does all this mean? Actually, several things. First, when somebody tells you that they are "averaging" 30 percent a year on their investments, ask to see the computation. Chances are, that "average" number is the result of some funny math. *Nobody* truly averages 30 percent a year on their investments over a several-year period.

Second, volatility is a double-edged sword for investors. When volatility works to the upside (such as the big gain in the Nasdaq in 1999), it's great. But when volatility occurs on the downside, it can be devastating.

Third, slow and steady usually wins the race on Wall Street. You don't need outsized returns to create wealth in the stock market. If you have enough time, you can do quite well earning a decent though unspectacular return each year.

Finally, a big key to stock market success is avoiding the big loss.

That doesn't mean that, as an investor, you play "not to lose." Playing not to lose, as any coach will tell you, usually means you don't win. You become too tight, too defensive, too cautious.

You play not to lose in the stock market by staying on the sidelines and keeping your money in money market funds or Treasuries. True, by staying on the sidelines you eliminate volatility from affecting your investments. Over time, however, inflation will chew you up, and you will lose.

No, I think investors can still play offense during volatile markets while, at the same time, limiting the likelihood of the big loss.

That, in essence, is the aim of this book—to show you how to play to win on Wall Street without losing your shirt during rough markets.

Before an investor can survive and even thrive during volatile markets, it's important to understand this enemy called "volatility." Indeed, volatility may be one of the more misunderstood words in market vernacular. By understanding volatility—what it is and isn't, how it's measured, why it's been so prevalent in recent years, and how volatility provides opportunities for long-term investors—an investor is better prepared to invest during a climate of big price swings. Chapter 1 provides everything you ever wanted to know about *volatility*.

During big storms, the quiet place is the eye of the storm. In the eye is safety, coherency, calm, rationality. As an investor in turbulent markets, you want to find the eye of the market—that place in which you can operate free from the storm's fury and influence. Chapter 2 discusses the second law of investing in volatile markets—*Finding the Eye*. This chapter looks at the metaphor of the storm's eye as it relates to the markets—how the eye is formed, how it changes, and how investors can find the eye during turbulent markets.

I know some of you are now saying, "There's no way I could have avoided the market collapse in 2000, despite what you say." The short answer to that statement is the following: "Wrong." I've seen enough investor portfolios over the last year or so to know that much of the pain from the volatile markets of 2000 and 2001 was self-inflicted.

Take a look at your own portfolio. What stocks do you own? Did you, like everybody else, chase the hot stocks that were posting scorching gains in 1998 through early 2000—technology stocks and anything with "dot-com" at the end? Such investors loaded up on the priciest, fastest-charging stocks in the market. That strategy may have worked for a while, but it failed miserably in 2000 and 2001 when these stocks tanked. Could you have avoided all of the 39 percent decline in the Nasdaq Composite in 2000, the 50-percent-or-more declines in tech stocks, and the 80-percent-or-more declines in Internet stocks? You may not have avoided the carnage altogether (after all, having some technology representation in a portfolio makes perfect sense), but you could have eased the pain substantially simply by following time-tested strategies.

Remember "diversification"? Nobody wanted a diversified portfolio in the late 1990s. Diversification was for chumps. Diversification meant you underperformed the market. Diversification meant you didn't keep pace with the blistering returns of your friends and coworkers. No, diversification was the third rail of investing, and "smart" investors stayed as far away from diversification as possible.

Hindsight is 20/20, and no doubt diversification seems like a good idea now that the market has crumbled. But diversification was a good idea in 1998, 1999, and early 2000 even when the Dow and the Nasdaq were soaring. True, one's portfolio wouldn't have been on jet fuel during that period, but investors still would have been producing decent results without incurring big risks—risks that came back to bite investors in 2000 and 2001.

Diversification is essential if an investor is going to survive turbulent markets. For that reason, Chapter 3 discusses a variety of techniques and strategies for *diversifying* a portfolio *within* asset classes, *across* asset classes, and across *time*. All three forms of diversification work hand in hand to reduce the risk of a portfolio and are necessary for the investor who wants to play offense during rocky markets without taking on too much risk.

A lot of Wall Street experts have written that one casualty of the market's volatility over the last two years is the concept of "buy-and-hold" investing. After all, investors who bought and held the likes of Cisco, Yahoo!, Amazon, or many other stocks got their heads handed to them. Buy and hold doesn't work anymore. It's an out-of-date method for dealing with today's supercharged, crazy markets.

I maintain the problem isn't so much with the strategy of buying and holding stocks. I think the problem lies with how investors implemented a buy-and-hold investment approach.

For example, implementing a buy-and-hold strategy with certain types of stocks is akin to creating an apple pie with pears. The recipe doesn't work. Certain investment styles demand certain stocks. This is one lesson traders learn in a hurry. Traders don't want to own sloth-like, slow-moving, low-volatility stocks. They want to own high-action, high-octane, volatile stocks. Those are the stocks that provide the price swings that allow traders to, well, trade.

A buy-and-hold strategy may not be the best strategy for such volatile stocks. That's not to say that buying and holding volatile stocks won't work over time. The problem is that volatility often causes investors to flee the stocks at the worst time. Remember, buy and hold doesn't mean that you never sell a stock—and that when you do sell, you do so because the fundamentals underlying a company's performance have changed.

For most long-term buy-and-hold investors, it's better to own stocks that show slow, steady gains year-in, year-out. I call such stocks "easy holds," because they don't force investors to make too many decisions. Rather, easy holds are the Energizer bunnies of the stock market—they don't move too fast, but they just keep going, and going, and going. When investing in turbulent markets, easy-hold stocks can help your portfolio weather the storm without causing you to lose sleep. Chapter 4 explores the fourth law of surviving volatile markets: matching your stock selection with your investment style, whatever that style is. The chapter discusses the factors that go into identifying *the right stocks for the right investment style.* For buy-and-hold investors, that means consistent earnings growth and stock-price stability. The chapter will highlight some of my favorite easy-hold stocks and mutual funds. And in what is certainly one of the center-piece features of the book, I provide easy-hold ratings on nearly 3,000 stocks and mutual funds, for both buy-and-hold investors and those with a shorter time horizon who want a percentage of their portfolio invested in less volatile stocks.

Portfolio construction is one of those things that most people think they do very well. The problem is, most people are wrong.

Proper portfolio construction is more than just a numbers game. In fact, I've seen portfolios with 20 stocks and five mutual funds that are less diversified than a portfolio with six well-chosen stocks.

The science of portfolio construction goes well beyond slapping together various assets. It involves understanding how stocks and bonds relate to one another and the overall market. It means understanding how your portfolio's sector weightings compare to benchmarks, such as the S&P 500. It requires knowing the risk level of your portfolio relative to expected returns. It suggests knowing where to go to "stress-test" a portfolio to see how it holds up under certain scenarios.

Chapter 5 explores these and other issues when it comes to *creating the perfect portfolio* for choppy markets. The chapter concludes with my All-Weather Portfolio for volatile markets.

Any of you who have read my previous books know I'm an advocate of the buy-and-hold school of investing. Actually, what I'm a fan of isn't merely buy and hold, but "buy and hold *and buy some more.*"

Indeed, this last piece of the puzzle is very important. It's not enough to buy and hold investments. You have to be willing to step up to the plate and buy stocks during volatile market periods.

The problem with buying during declining markets, however, is that it is really hard to do. Declining markets cause you to question your investment abilities. Declining markets shake your confidence. Declining markets make you cautious. Declining markets freeze you in your tracks. Declining markets give you the false impression that, if you just wait, you'll be able to buy everything at much lower levels.

The upshot is that you have a million reasons not to buy during declining markets, so you don't. Consequently, you never "buy low."

In fact, what usually happens is that instead of buying low, you chase stocks after they have rebounded and jumped sharply higher.

To take advantage of the opportunities that volatile markets present investors, you must be willing to buy even when times look the darkest. The trick, then, is to come up with a way, a program, a strategy for forcing yourself to buy stock even when everyone (including you) says you shouldn't. Ideally, you want a method that reduces the barriers, that makes it palatable for you to invest.

One way investors would be more willing to invest during volatile markets is if they could invest relatively small amounts of money. Which is a more likely scenario:

1. Dumping $10,000 into the market when it is falling like a rock? Or . . .

2. Spacing that $10,000 over a few months by investing $1,000 a month for 10 months (or $2,000 for five months)?

My guess is that most investors would say that it is much more palatable to feed smaller amounts of money into the market during rocky periods than to drop a big chunk of change and risk further declines. The problem: How can you invest such small amounts of money?

Fortunately, the advent of "dollar-based" investment vehicles—investments built around the concept of investing dollars, not buying shares—makes it extremely easy to funnel small amounts of money into the markets on a regular basis.

What are these dollar-based investment programs? Mutual funds were probably the first vehicles that framed the investment process in terms of investing dollars, not buying shares. After all, how many people even know how many shares of a fund they own? Not many. Rather, most people have a dollar figure in their head and invest accordingly.

Over time, new dollar-based investment programs emerged. Favorites of mine are dividend reinvestment plans (DRIPs). These are programs that allow investors to buy stock directly from companies—without using a broker—in amounts as small as $10 in some cases.

A more recent take on dollar-based investing are the new types of online brokerage firms that buy both full and fractional shares for investors while permitting investments of as little as $20 a crack.

And perhaps the most popular dollar-based investment vehicle—the 401(k) plan—has literally opened the door to Wall Street for millions of small investors.

The upshot is that investors now have many different investment vehicles to use to buy during rocky markets, investment vehicles that are easy on the pocketbook and more palatable from a risk standpoint. Chapter 6 explores the various *dollar-based investment vehicles* and shows how these programs have an important role in allowing investors to navigate stormy markets.

An important rule of survival in difficult markets is knowing when to cut and run. Indeed, ask someone who owned Cisco at $80 and rode it all the way down to $11 about selling, and you'll get an earful.

The fact is that volatile markets put a premium on knowing when to sell. Unfortunately, volatile markets are also the time investors tend to be reactive rather than proactive. A reactive investor sells a stock because it is declining. A proactive investor has a game plan for buying and selling and follows that plan in a disciplined way.

Investing during volatile markets means checking your emotions at the door and making the hard decisions in a disciplined, consistent fashion. Chapter 7 explores perhaps the hardest decision of all: *knowing when to sell stocks.* The chapter provides clear-cut guidelines for dumping stocks, as well as signals that should help embolden an investor to buy during declines.

Crazy markets create confusion. Why is my stock dropping? Why are investors selling even though earnings are rising? Is that stock a great buy now that it has fallen 50 percent?

In confusing market periods, when stocks are flying all over the place, the successful investor is one who has streamlined and simplified his or her approach to managing investments.

The eighth law of investing in volatile markets is keeping an investment program simple. Simplicity reduces confusion and makes for more sound judgments. This is key, because the consequences of a bad decision are accentuated during volatile markets. Simplicity also increases the probability that you'll be ready to seize opportunities that present themselves—often very briefly—during volatile markets.

In Chapter 8, I identify, explain, and solve *potential problems facing investors in managing portfolios.* Along the way, I'll offer a variety of information and tools for monitoring your portfolio as well as ways to simplify your record keeping, especially as it relates to taxes.

I believe a storm is a useful metaphor for framing a discussion of volatile markets. Storms have centers of calm and tranquillity. So, too, do stormy financial markets have their "eyes," those pockets of calm and tranquillity. As an investor, what you want to do is find the eye of the storm.

Of course, as any meteorologist will tell you, storms shift; eyes move. Volatile markets have shifting "eyes" as well. Indeed, what makes sense from an investment standpoint at one moment can shift dramatically in fairly short order. What's important for investors to learn is how to identify shifting markets.

Chapter 9 discusses the ninth and final law of investing in volatile markets: *staying in the eye when the storm shifts.* In this chapter, I'll identify changes that can lead to quantum shifts in the investment landscape and offer advice on how to adjust investment strategies accordingly.

Volatility is a double-edged sword. When volatility in the markets is to the upside, everyone's happy. In fact, when stocks are rising at a rapid clip, investors don't call it "volatility." They call it "doing what the market is supposed to do—go up lots!" It's only when stocks go down, down, down that investors drag out the "V" word and use it disparagingly.

I can't tell you whether stocks will experience that good kind of volatility or that bad kind of volatility over the next few months or years. My sense is that stocks will do what stocks always do—trend higher over time. However, my guess is that the path will be very uneven, with big swings in either direction. And that volatility will certainly cause some investors to second-guess whether they should be an investor at all.

Make no mistake. The stock market is still the greatest tool on earth for *anyone* to create wealth. It would be a crime for you to get chased out of the market simply because you feel ill equipped to handle the volatility. The aim of the tenth and final chapter is to pull a lot of the elements discussed in this book into a "to-do" list for investors who want to stay in the game.

Investing during volatile markets is not always fun. It is not always immediately profitable. But if you plan on reaping the long-term returns of the market, you'll have to be comfortable playing in markets that at times will feel out of control, without rhyme or reason.

What you are now holding in your hands is your battle plan for doing business in the volatile markets of today and tomorrow.

Good luck.

THE
$MART
INVESTOR'S
$URVIVAL
GUIDE

Chapter One

Law #1:
Know Your "Enemy"—
Understanding Volatility

Those who cannot remember the past are condemned to repeat it.

—George Santayana

C'MON, ADMIT IT. For most of you, your portfolio got slaughtered in 2000 and 2001. A millennium mauling. At best, it went into a serious retraction.

Remember all those tech stocks that made you think "early retirement" in 1998 and 1999? They suddenly turned against us in 2000. Yahoo!, Broadcom, Sun, Amazon. Hundreds of stocks falling 50 percent, 70 percent, even 90 percent. And many others going belly-up.

And most of 2001 wasn't much better. Those hoped-for rebounds in the techs never materialized. And many stocks that held up reasonably well in 2000 decided to take the plunge in 2001, too.

And just when you thought things couldn't get worse, they did.

September 11.

The Saturday after the terrorist attacks in New York City and Washington, D.C., I was scheduled to speak to a gathering of individual investors in Chicago. I didn't give too much thought to my scheduled talk immediately following that tragic Tuesday. I, like everyone else in America, had freeze-framed my own life to focus on this national horror.

But as the weekend drew closer, I began to wonder whether there would be any speech at all. Many gatherings were being canceled throughout the country in the wake of the awful tragedies; not many people wanted to talk about stocks just days after such unprecedented destruction to our country's collective psyche.

Truth be told, I wasn't sure if I wanted to talk about stocks either.

So when I received a call on that Friday from the individual who had asked me to speak, I was expecting to hear from her that my gathering had been canceled or postponed.

Instead, what I heard was the following: "We have been getting a very strong response."

That my talk was still on surprised me; that many people wanted to venture into the country's third-largest city—where skyscrapers would serve as reminders that what happened in New York could easily have happened in Chicago—to talk about stocks surprised me even more.

But I was surprised only for a moment. *Life really does go on*, I thought to myself.

Actually, life can't help but go on. Life is what all of us do. *We live.*

And living, ultimately, is not a spectator sport.

That's why people showed up for my talk. That's why I showed up. That's why you showed up at work on the Wednesday and Thursday and Friday following the attack. That's why you took your clothes to the cleaners, dragged your garbage to the curb for pickup, ran your kids to soccer practice, played with your grandkids after church on Sunday.

Life goes on.

To be sure, I know there were people who came to my talk who probably felt guilty about attending. After all, it doesn't seem right that anyone should care about something as "trivial" as a stock portfolio when thousands of people are suffering physically and emotionally. But you know what? It's OK to care about your stock portfolio. Or your job. Or your pet. Or your refrigerator that's on the blink. Or your car that's running rough. That's all about the process of living, of moving from one day to the next and to the next and to the next.

Yes, there is an investment message in all of this. Much is being made about how our own private worlds will be changed forever. I'm not so sure about that. That process of living is tough to disrupt for long.

Whenever I'm confronted with the notion that bad times are irreversible, I think back to how people must have felt during the Civil War. Think about that period of history for a moment. A nation under siege *from itself*. States against states. Families against families.

And yet our nation survived.

As it will this time.

But while I'm optimistic about the long-term prospects for the market and, indeed, our country, I can't help but feel that the roller-coaster existences investors have been living over the last few years will become the norm, not the exception. I say this not as an alarmist, but as a realist.

Yes, volatility is unsettling. Yes, volatility can be destructive. But volatility can also be harnessed and used to your advantage. But you need to get back in the game, to deal with volatility head-on.

I know many investors who are numb to what has happened in the world and the stock market over the last two years. They sit with portfolios that they thought were sure things in the late '90s but now are huge question marks.

And they just don't know what to do.

Don't feel too bad. I guarantee you that the guy sitting in the office next door, the woman in the cubicle down the hall, the car-pool colleague who has stopped talking about all the money he was making in the market, your golfing buddy who never seemed to get around to buying that boat he was coveting—all of them got chewed up over the last two years.

How do I know? From my perch as editor of several financial newsletters and CEO of a money-management company, I see lots of portfolios every year. And what I have been seeing a lot of over the last two years are portfolios where the owners eschewed diversification. Portfolios where the owners chased hot stocks in 1998 and 1999 only to get smoked in 2000 and 2001. Portfolios where the owners didn't have a clue what their portfolio companies really did. (Seriously, do you honestly know what a router is or does?)

And the pros were just as bad. Indeed, mutual-fund managers, fearing for their jobs and tired of hearing from their shareholders that not owning tech was stupid, caved and bought the highfliers.

Heck, some of the most acclaimed investors of our generation got fed up missing out on the party and started buying tech—right at the top.

Like everyone else, I was not immune to the tech bug either. I bought tech and Internet stocks that, in hindsight, I had no business buying. And I held some stocks (Lucent comes painfully to mind) way too long, even when problem signs were evident.

Fortunately, however, I didn't own just tech. I also owned banks and restaurants and information-services companies and oil stocks and drug companies and financial-services companies and drugstore chains and consumer-products companies and payroll-processing companies. In other words, I had a reasonably diversified portfolio of some 25 stocks and several mutual funds. Consequently, while I got hurt in 2000 and 2001, I didn't suffer the kind of mind-boggling losses that many pure technology investors did.

In fact, investors who saw their portfolios plummet over the last two years may be surprised to realize that some areas of the stock market actually hung in there pretty well. While much attention was given to the Nasdaq Composite's record decline of 39 percent in 2000, the Dow Jones Industrial Average fell only 6 percent for the year. Other major indexes showed similar resiliency. The S&P 500 fell 10 percent in 2000; and if you excluded telecom and technology stocks in the S&P 500, that index would have actually *increased* 6 percent in 2000. The Russell 2000, an index of small-cap stocks, dipped just 4 percent in 2000. And the Dow Jones Utility Average skyrocketed 45 percent in 2000.

I know this may be hard to believe, but more stocks on the New York Stock Exchange actually advanced than declined in 2000.

And while the Nasdaq Composite continued its nosedive in 2001—down 21 percent—the Dow turned in a much better year, declining a scant 7 percent.

The upshot is that even with certain market indexes and individual stocks registering huge price swings, investors could still have survived—and even thrived—in 2000 and 2001 with the right game plan.

Now, I realize that talking about how you could have avoided getting stomped in 2000 and 2001 doesn't help you much today. After all, you can't relive the past, you can't undo your mistakes.

Fortunately, Wall Street is the land of second chances. I once worked for a man who compared Wall Street to horse racing, "with a new race running every day," he'd say. That's the beauty of investing. Second chances do exist. Fresh opportunities come along every day. Despite the pounding you may have taken in 2000 and 2001, if you are like most investors, you probably have a good 10, 20, maybe 30 years or more of investing ahead of you. That's more than enough time to make serious money in the market, more than enough time to make the last two years a dim memory.

In order to do that, however, you have to stop managing your portfolio using a rearview mirror. I can't tell you how many people I talk to who still believe that tech stock they bought at $100 and now trades for $20 will get back to $100 "in a couple of years." Sorry, but that's not going to happen.

Do the math. A stock that falls 80 percent from its high (for example, falling from $100 per share to $20 per share—and there are plenty of technology stocks that have done just that) needs to go up *fivefold* in order to return to its previous level. Stocks don't increase fivefold (that's *400 percent* for those of us who are mathematically challenged) in just a couple of years. In fact, most stocks don't increase fivefold in a decade; most never do.

Until investors give up this fantasy about seeing technology stocks regain their glory days in relatively short order, they will never be in the right mind-set to do the things necessary to get their portfolios positioned for better market times

I know that it's brutally difficult to stop looking backward and start looking forward. Looking forward may mean admitting mistakes, and nobody likes to do that. Looking forward may mean selling stocks today that could come back to haunt you tomorrow. Looking forward may mean locking up big losses.

But in order to move forward, to position your portfolio for the next 20 years—*and to avoid making the same mistakes*—you have got to let go of the past and chalk it up to an expensive learning experience that will pay dividends over the next decade and beyond.

What's important now is to learn from your mistakes, get a good game plan, and position your portfolio for the future.

This book shows you how.

But before I discuss tactics and strategies for succeeding in volatile markets, it is important to understand this animal called volatility. To conquer this "enemy"—or at least coexist with it profitably—you need to learn as much about it as possible.

UNDERSTANDING VOLATILITY— NINE ESSENTIAL LESSONS

Lesson #1: Volatility is not permanent.

Volatility is derived from the word *volatile*. It may surprise you, but Webster's has no fewer than five definitions for *volatile*.

Definitions 1 through 3 bear little resemblance to what you probably think *volatile* means. Definition 1 is "passing through the air on wings; having the power to fly." Definition 3 is "airy, lighthearted, lively."

It is only after the first three definitions that Webster's gives the more familiar definitions—"easily surprised or irritated; characterized by wide price fluctuations."

But it is the last definition from Webster's that I find most intriguing—"difficult to capture or hold permanently."

It is that definition that is perhaps the most telling and relevant for investor behavior in recent years. Investors ignored the fact that the tremendous volatility to the upside we experienced in 1998 and 1999 would be "difficult to capture or hold permanently." They assumed it would last forever. Such is not the nature of volatility. Thus, we come to our first important lesson concerning market volatility:

"Directional" volatility cannot be permanent.

Volatility, by definition, is not a permanent state. To assume that volatility is the new "steady state" redefines volatility.

In short, "permanent volatility" is an oxymoron.

Now, I know what some of you are saying. "Out of one side of his mouth, Carlson says volatility is here to stay. Out of the other side of his mouth, he says that volatility is not permanent. What gives?"

Actually, there is a critical distinction between permanent volatility (which does not exist) and the *likelihood* of volatile market periods increasing in regularity in the future. I have little doubt that big market swings will occur with greater frequency in the years ahead, and I'll discuss those reasons in a moment. But an investor must never believe that this big swing, this volatility, is the new permanent state of things.

Volatility in one direction (up or down) won't last forever. That's a good thing when thinking about bear markets; that's not so good when thinking about bull markets.

Once an investor understands that volatility to the upside or downside is not a steady state or some new paradigm for the market (as market experts often claim during such periods of elongated volatility), you will avoid making the crushing mistakes (chasing winners, concentrating portfolios in just a few stocks, ignoring risk for the sake of higher expected returns) that investors made during the late '90s.

Lesson #2: Volatility cuts both ways.

People are optimists by nature. Focus on the positive, ignore the negative. We usually don't consider the eventual and often inevitable reactions from our actions, especially if those actions are being positively reinforced.

Unfortunately, our willingness to extrapolate short-term trends into permanent states often colors our investment judgment. Prior to 2000, the Dow, S&P 500, and Nasdaq Composite had reeled off five consecutive years of nearly 20-percent-or-better annual returns.

To put those percentages into perspective: A $10,000 investment that grows 20 percent per year for five years grows to nearly $25,000—a 150 percent gain.

Since many individuals came to the markets for the first time during that five-year time frame, they had no reference point from which to understand that markets *just don't go up 20 percent a year for five years*. These investors didn't understand that what happened from 1995 to 1999 was truly an anomaly in the market. A six-sigma event. One giant outlier in the history of market movements.

In short, 1995–1999 was a period of unprecedented *upside volatility*.

For many investors, however, especially market newcomers, 20-percent-or-better gains weren't abnormal; they were expected. And the market's volatility didn't concern anyone, since the volatility was all to the upside. After all, how could 50 percent or 100 percent gains in a stock in a few months—or even a few days in some cases—be a bad thing?

Of course, what investors failed to understand is that volatility cuts both ways. Newton's laws. What goes up quickly comes down quickly; for every action there is an equal but opposite reaction.

Applying the laws of gravity and physics to the market may be a stretch, but in reality, big market movements over the years have had this pendulum effect. Why? One reason is that, in the short run, the stock market runs as much, and perhaps even more, on emotion as it does on reason. How else do you explain an Internet stock losing money hand over fist, with annual sales of less than $5 million, being valued by Wall Street at $5 billion or more? That value is not based on reason. It's based on emotion, on herd mentality, on one giant group-think that the Internet was going to revolutionize everything. And as we've seen, when that group-think changes, when all of a sudden the Internet is not Utopia but a killing field, valuations come swinging back violently in the opposite direction.

Fire up Yahoo! Finance (or any of your favorite stock-charting services) and check out the chart patterns of any of those favored technology and Internet stocks. What you see is eerily similar—stock prices exploding from a base in 1998, peaking in early 2000, and coming right back down to the 1998 levels. One giant round-trip, with zero value creation. A big bubble. That's the pendulum in action—for every action there's an equal but opposite reaction.

A lot of what I talk about in this book concerns market volatility and how it affects investors. I consider the market's volatility to be the biggest influence on investor behavior over the last seven years. Market volatility, coupled with the power of the Internet, spawned a new type of individual investor: the day trader. Market volatility fueled stock bets in thousands of companies possessing little more than an idea and other people's money. Market volatility caused investors to replace time-tested ways of valuing stocks with investment metrics that today sound downright silly. (Remember things like "mind share" and "eyeballs" and "Web site stickiness"?)

Market volatility caused many investors to do something when they should have done nothing. And, especially today, market volatility causes many investors to do nothing when they should be doing plenty to prepare their portfolios for the future.

Lesson #3: The factors driving volatility in recent years will continue to generate huge swings in stock prices over time.

There's no denying that while volatility is not permanent, it is becoming more commonplace in the financial markets. Here are just a few of the reasons volatility has and will continue to dominate the markets.

Investor Nation

Today, roughly 50 percent of U.S. households are invested in the stock market in some way, shape, or form. Many reasons exist for this "investor nation." For starters, it has never been easier to access the stock market. Dividend reinvestment plans, mutual funds, retirement programs such as IRAs and 401(k) plans, online discount brokers— all of these investment vehicles have torn down the roadblocks on Wall Street and allowed even those with modest bankrolls to get in the game.

In fact, to say we (that's individual investors like you and me) have a big stake in the game understates our importance. *We are the game.*

The huge and growing presence of individual investors accelerates volatility for the simple reason that there is much more money now coming into the market. Investors often forget that stocks are like any other commodity; they are driven by supply and demand. Yes, I know that earnings and revenue and financial statements and insider buying and chart patterns and a whole lot of fundamental and technical stuff influence *demand* for stocks. But what ultimately affects stock prices is simple dollars—how much money is flowing into or out of stocks and the market. Given that market volatility is often driven by the herd mentality—1998 and 1999 was a perfect example of this herd mentality at work in the tech sector—the bigger the herd (as a result of millions of new players), the greater the volatility.

Another way individual investors are influencing market volatility is by trading on information geared toward institutional investors. Let me explain.

An equity analyst told me that one of the big reasons that markets have become more volatile is the "repackaging" of research information for individuals. "Up until about two years ago, our customer was solely institutions," says this analyst. "That was important in that institutional investors cannot get in and out of stocks on a dime because of the big positions they take. Thus, we have to take a long-term view on stocks."

The game changed, however, when investment banks—the providers of information to institutional investors—began merging with retail brokers. Indeed, you had deals such as Morgan Stanley merging with Dean Witter, Salomon and Smith Barney merging under the Citigroup banner, and other similar deals. Consequently, research that had been focused on the institutional market began to be repackaged for individual investors, too. The upshot is that, according to the analyst, "research geared primarily for institutions is now being used by retail investors. But it's not really geared toward them. Retail investments can jump in and out of the market. Institutions can't."

What is the effect of this jumping in and out by individual investors? "Stocks that disappoint now move rather sharply. We (the analysts) like a stock at $100 that disappoints, and the stock gets killed to $50 because individuals sell. We downgrade, and the stock rebounds and makes us look bad. Information hits much more quickly and violently."

Given that we haven't seen the end of mergers between investment banks and retail brokers, the factors creating an environment in which retail investors are trading based on research geared for institutions is likely to accelerate.

Frictionless Markets

Another factor that drives volatility is the frictionless movement of money in the system. We have created financial markets where literally millions and, indeed, billions of dollars can move from one investment to the next as quickly as the punch of a computer key.

My guess is that you've witnessed such frictionless movement if you've ever owned a stock that missed its earnings estimate and fell 25 percent in a single day. Chances are the stock actually lost most of its value in seconds following the announcement. Why? Because thousands of sellers placed orders that were executed literally in the blink of a computer screen. Money out, off to a new home.

When you have tons of money sloshing around a financial system that can be shoveled quickly into virtually any investment, it is not surprising that you see such wide price swings across asset classes and individual securities. And the seamlessness with which money moves throughout our global financial system is only likely to accelerate in the years ahead as technology improves.

It's interesting that technology is not the only factor paving the way for rapid movement of money. The reduction in transaction costs in virtually every trading market in the world has sped up the flow of money in and out of investments. Think about it. The ability to trade stocks for literally pennies does not provide much of a hurdle if you want to dump and run on an investment. And since there still seems to be movement toward even lower transaction fees, my guess is that the friction in the markets caused by transaction costs will disappear altogether.

Increased Globalization of Financial Markets

Not only has the number of players been increasing in the U.S. markets, but the number of investors has been growing throughout the world with the advent of emerging stock markets. I would expect that trend to continue as capitalism—a relatively new concept in many parts of the world—goes through its growing pains to a point where reasonably well-functioning capital markets emerge.

Granted, this is not something that will happen overnight. But certainly in our lifetime you will see flourishing financial markets in virtually every part of the globe.

This globalization is important as it relates to volatility. Increased globalization means increased interdependency of financial markets. We already see this to some extent. What happens in the United

States drives markets throughout the world. And what happens throughout the world—you may recall the international currency crisis in 1998 and its impact on the U.S. market—affects markets in the United States. Now compound that volatility with more mature capital markets in Africa, Latin America, and Asia, and it's easy to see how volatility will accelerate.

Internet and the Movement of Information

As technology and reduced transaction costs have created frictionless movement of money in the financial system, the Internet and other technology have created the frictionless movement of that other important catalyst of volatility—information.

As noted earlier, it used to be that information was the property of a chosen few, and the rest of us had to wait until the next day's *Wall Street Journal* to find out what was happening in the financial markets.

Those days are long gone.

Today, not only do we get information that was formerly available only to institutional investors, but the information hits the market immediately and is dispersed in such a way that anyone with a computer and modem can know what is happening with any stock almost instantly. The rapid dissemination of information also means that such information gets factored into the price of the investment almost immediately. As noted earlier, that's why you see such huge price movements in stocks that come out with bad news.

In the past, what would happen is that the stock might decline 25 percent, but the decline would probably occur over a few days or even weeks as the full story trickled out to the market. Nowadays, the 25 percent decline occurs in minutes, and sometimes in seconds, as all market participants get the news and react almost simultaneously.

That all market players—big and small—get the news at the same time has as much to do with regulatory changes as it does with new technology and communications. In October 2000, the Securities and Exchange Commission implemented Regulation FD (Fair Disclosure). "Reg FD" is the SEC's attempt to level the playing field between Wall Street and Main Street when it comes to information flow from corporate America.

In a nutshell, Reg FD says that companies can't play "I've got a secret" with a chosen few of their favorite Wall Street analysts. If a company has something to say of a material, nonpublic nature, the firm has to tell everybody at the same time. In that way, no individuals would be privy to information beforehand and be able to make a profit or avoid a loss at the expense of those kept in the dark.

Reg FD was a response to companies making "selective disclosures" of a material nature to Wall Street analysts.

Now, Wall Street firms will never admit that their analysts were in bed with companies. Nor will they admit that their analysts and the companies were doing anything wrong when it came to selective disclosure. In effect, the practice had gained an undeserved legitimacy simply because everyone was doing it. That's probably one reason the SEC felt compelled to create a separate regulation focused on selective disclosure.

How widespread was the practice of companies and analysts playing footsie when it comes to information? Here's one example of the analyst-company coziness. According to member surveys of the National Investor Relations Institute, 87 percent of the group's corporate members reviewed draft analyst reports at the request of the analysts. In effect, nearly nine out of 10 companies traditionally have had the opportunity to sign off on the very same research reports that are supposed to provide an unbiased and independent evaluation of the company.

Yet, as hard as Reg FD came down on analysts, the regulation was also an indictment of the company's role in the selective-disclosure game. The SEC understood how companies benefit from maintaining close relationships with analysts. Companies have information. Analysts want information. If you have something I want, I'm going to give you something in return for what I want. Thus, companies share information selectively in hopes of currying favor—and favorable reviews—with analysts. In turn, analysts write favorable reviews in order to curry favor and remain in the information loop. It's this cycle of secrecy and biasness that the SEC wanted to stop.

Not surprisingly, Wall Street analysts have been the biggest complainers concerning Reg FD. One complaint centers on Reg FD increasing market volatility. The thinking here goes something like this: Since analysts aren't able to receive guidance from companies, •

the likelihood increases that companies will surprise analysts. And surprises fuel volatility.

There's some truth to this statement. Having all market players privy to the same information at the same time does mean more immediate buying and selling in response to the news, and that can mean more volatility.

However, it's not like there weren't earnings surprises and huge volatility *before* Reg FD. To be sure, the stocks may have been sliding a bit prior to the earnings surprise, as analysts in the know (as a result of selective disclosure) were dumping ahead of the news. Still, is a 30 percent decline in five days better than a 30 percent decline in one day? The answer: only for people selling early, which is why analysts like selective disclosure.

The ability for even small market players to be on even ground with the pros in terms of receiving information is a good thing. In fact, it makes the market and individual securities more efficiently priced.

But here is the paradox of efficient markets: The more efficient the market, that is, the more quickly new information is reflected in the stock price—the more volatile (at least in the short run) the movement of prices. In effect, as our markets move to a more level playing field for all participants, that increased efficiency means quicker, more dramatic adjustments to new information.

Terrorism—The New Battlefield

September 11, 2001, is one of those days that you'll never forget. You'll always remember where you were when you heard that a plane had slammed into one of the World Trade Center towers. And you'll always remember the disbelief you had when a second plane slammed into the other Trade Center tower and a third plane crashed into the Pentagon.

Such acts of unmitigated horror weren't supposed to happen on U.S. soil. Sure, we see acts of terrorism all of the time. In the Middle East. In Northern Ireland. But never in the United States.

Until September 11, 2001.

The impact of that day is still being felt throughout the United States and, indeed, throughout the world. Not to mention on Wall Street.

In a world where war between countries is replaced by war with various amorphous "cells" of terrorists—individuals who belong to no country and travel among us anonymously—the financial markets truly are at risk.

Markets hate uncertainty. Terrorism is the antithesis of certainty. One never knows when the next strike will occur. One never knows who the real enemy is. That is the world that all of us now live in—a world where anything can happen anywhere at any time.

Obviously, such geopolitical conditions in the United States and throughout the world make the markets a much more tenuous place to do business. Witness what happened to the major exchanges when the stock market finally reopened on September 17. The Dow Jones Industrial Average registered its largest single-day point drop in history, falling nearly 685 points. The Nasdaq Composite plummeted nearly 7 percent. And individual sectors took big hits, especially the airline stocks. Indeed, airline issues such as Delta Air Lines, American Airlines, and United each fell 39 percent or more on the Monday following the tragedy.

Will there be more terrorist attacks in the United States? We certainly cannot rule them out. Actually, the fact that the possibility exists is more than enough to keep the market on edge and volatility high. Indeed, every plane crash, every explosion, will always be viewed first through the prism of terrorism. And that reference point cannot help but fuel greater volatility in the financial markets.

Earnings Volatility Leads to Equity Volatility
Stock prices follow earnings. This relationship may not hold up in the short run. Over the long run, however, a stock price will follow the trend of a company's profits.

Given this tight correlation between stock prices and corporate earnings, it's not surprising that volatile corporate profits lead to volatile stock prices. Just look at all those technology stocks that rode the roller coaster higher in 1998 and 1999 and crashed in 2000 and 2001. In most cases, what you see is tremendous growth in technology earnings in 1998 and 1999, followed by disastrous earnings for technology companies in 2000 and 2001.

We live in a world of increasingly short product cycles, of technological innovation happening in nanoseconds, of old-line industry leaders being replaced by upstarts, of whole industries becoming obsolete. What is happening in corporate America, in a word, is change.

And while change is good—indeed, necessary for vibrant capitalism—change brings uncertainty, especially in corporate cash flows and, ultimately, in earnings. That is one of the by-products of this "new economy"—massive change.

Stock prices are merely a reflection of this massive change. And the speed of change is only going to accelerate in the decades ahead.

Lesson #4: Volatility is not necessarily good or bad for investors.

Ask 10 investors about market and stock volatility, and nine of them will tell you that high volatility is bad. Now ask those same 10 people if it was good to be an investor during 1998 and 1999, and all 10 will answer you in the affirmative.

That's one of the many paradoxes of volatility. When volatility works to the advantage of investors—as was the case in the second half of the '90s, when annual market returns were almost double the long-run average—investors love it. In fact, investors don't think of such periods as being "volatile"; in some cases, investors view such periods as the norm.

But when investors talk about volatility, it usually has a negative undercurrent, as in "Boy, that's a volatile stock. It *fell 30 percent* in one day!"

Actually, volatility is neither good nor bad for the market. It is simply a part of doing business in the market, a measure of risk. How investors react to volatility is what truly matters. Do you let volatility freeze you from doing the right thing? Do you take advantage of market volatility to increase positions in favored stocks? Do you avoid volatile stocks even though their inclusion in your portfolio might actually *reduce* your portfolio's overall volatility?

Successful investing is all about knowing what to fear and what to embrace. Volatility is not necessarily the enemy of investors. In fact, volatility can be an investor's best friend in certain circumstances (just ask any options or futures trader).

The trick is not reacting to volatility but developing a plan to exist profitably with volatility. That, in essence, is what this book will show you.

Lesson #5: Buy-and-hold investing can and does work in volatile markets—with the right stocks.

I've fielded a lot of media calls over the last six months concerning the death of buy-and-hold investing in an age of volatile markets. Most callers point to the huge declines in such stocks as Lucent, Cisco, Motorola, and many other technology stocks as evidence that buy-and-hold investing doesn't work.

Actually, volatile markets and buy-and-hold investing are not mutually exclusive. The trick is knowing what stocks are best suited for this strategy. Chapter 4 talks at length about matching investment style with stock selection. What's worth discussing now are the following two points:

1. **To be a buy-and-hold investor, you need to do three things—buy, hold,** *and buy more.* That last part is how you cope with volatile markets. A buy-and-hold investor needs to add to positions when volatile markets knock down stock prices. Admittedly, this can be a risky strategy, especially when a stock goes from $80 to $50 to $20 to $10 and you've been buying all the way down. (Actually, only time can tell whether that strategy backfires. Indeed, five years from now, people who were buying Cisco or Lucent all the way down may be awfully glad they did. We'll see.) Thus, not only must you be willing to buy and hold and buy more when markets and stock prices decline, but you also must . . .

2. **Match investment style with stock selection.** To buy an Internet stock—a company with little track record, in many cases with no profits, and with an ever-changing business model—and expect to hold on to that stock forever seems a bit silly. Yet people who bought Pets.com and held it all the way to bankruptcy will blame their folly on a buy-and-hold strategy. Obviously, some stocks are cut out for a buy-and-hold strategy; others are not. Knowing which stocks are and aren't is important, especially in volatile markets.

Again, it's not fair to blame the "failure" of buy-and-hold investing on volatility. In fact, buy-and-hold investing is still an extremely effective way to invest, if properly executed. And it is still a very viable strategy even if market volatility accelerates.

Lesson #6: Volatility is more relevant to investors with short-term time horizons than long-term time horizons.

Time heals all wounds. This is especially true in the stock market. Time can cover a multitude of investment sins. Indeed, my guess is that someone who is in his or her twenties or thirties will look back on the difficult market period of recent years with barely a memory of the trials and tribulations.

Ask someone in his or her seventies, however, and you'll see that what has happened over the last 24 months has had a profoundly negative and perhaps lasting impact on their investment experience. Understanding how volatility impacts investors differently depending on their investment time horizons makes a big difference in how you approach volatility within an investment program.

Volatility is a measure of short-term market risk. In the short run, investments may be extremely volatile. Jeremy Siegel, in his best seller *Stocks for the Long Run*, writes that stocks overall have risen as much as 67 percent and fallen nearly 39 percent over any given year. That's a huge spread in potential returns. That, indeed, is volatility.

Over time, however, price movements tend to smooth out a bit. Siegel estimates that over 10-year holding periods, stocks have risen nearly 17 percent and fallen 4 percent. For 20-year holding periods, stocks have risen nearly 13 percent on the high end and 1 percent on the low end. Look at that last statistic again. What that says is basically this: If you are willing to hold stocks for at least 20 years, you are pretty sure of generating a positive return over that time frame. And if you are willing to hold stocks for at least 30 years, be aware that the worst 30-year period in the market since 1802 still generated a positive return of nearly 3 percent.

What all of this means is simple. The longer your time frame, the less volatile your market returns. Said differently, the longer you own stocks, the less risky they become. That's why an investor with a short-term horizon must be extra careful during volatile market periods. Indeed, a big hit in any given year has much greater repercussions if you don't have many years to make up for the decline. Likewise, a pasting in any one year is probably of no lasting consequence if it is merely a blip in an investment program with a long-term horizon.

Lesson #7: Tools to measure market volatility are based on historical prices and may not hold up well going forward.

Volatility is often measured in terms of standard deviation of returns. In a nutshell, the greater the deviation around averages, the greater the volatility.

Another measure of volatility is beta. A stock's beta reflects the volatility of an investment relative to the market. For example, a stock with a beta of 1.2 means that, historically, the stock has outperformed the market (which carries a beta of 1) by 20 percent during up markets and underperformed the market by 20 percent during downturns.

Note that in each case volatility scores are based on what has happened in the past. In short, the past is used to measure expected volatility.

Granted, the past is often a pretty good yardstick for how something will behave in the future. Still, the world does change. Industries that may have been sleepy and dormant could awaken in the future with new technology. This is exactly what happened to a variety of industries that were jolted by the growth of the Internet. Retailing, for example, became a much more volatile investment sector with the advent of the Amazons and eBays. Of course, many of these Internet "e-tailers" ultimately went out of business or failed to live up to their early promise. Still, their emergence created ground-moving changes in their respective industries.

This is especially important when looking at expected volatility of an investment. Investors who have insight into dramatic sea-changes in industries, especially those where volatility had been pretty much nil, will have a huge advantage in the investment game. Indeed, early recognition of how the Internet was going to shake up many markets led those early seers to huge gains in many Internet stocks.

Bottom line: Things change. Volatility levels can change. Don't forget that when evaluating certain investment sectors.

Lesson #8: There is such a thing as "selective" volatility.

To say that stocks are volatile is to paint with too broad a brush. Yes, many stocks have been volatile over the last two years. How volatile? Check out these stats:

- According to money manager Grantham Mayo, a major stock fell 20 percent or more in a single day (relative to the market) in 2000 on almost 500 occasions. That number compares to an average of just 18 between 1962 and 1995.

- In the first four months of 2001, the average daily move in the S&P 500 was 1.2 percent, roughly twice the historic average going back to 1940.

- In 2000, the Nasdaq Composite registered its worst one-year decline ever (down 39 percent for the year). However, the year also saw nine of the 10 largest one-day percentage *increases* in the index. These record percentage gains include the single largest one-day percentage increase in the Nasdaq Composite history— 10.48 percent on December 5, 2000.

And yet during this period of unprecedented volatility, as I noted in the introduction, there were "eyes" within the storm. Consider these statistics:

- Despite record decline for the Nasdaq Composite in 2000, the S&P 500 fell a much more subdued 10 percent.

- Other market indexes had much milder years than the Nasdaq Composite. The Dow Jones Industrial Average fell just 6 percent in 2000, and the Russell 2000 fell a meager 4 percent.

The fact is that it is usually a mistake to use volatility as a comprehensive term. If you owned technology stocks the last two years, certainly your results have been volatile. If you owned a diversified portfolio of stocks, however, your returns have not deviated too far from the expected range of returns in the market.

What this "selective" volatility means is that there are usually places to hide during even the most volatile market periods. These are the "eyes" of the storm. A significant portion of this book is devoted to showing investors how to find the eye and how to detect shifts in the eye during changing market conditions.

Lesson #9: You can make money in volatile markets.

While the Nasdaq Composite fell 39 percent in 2000, the Dow Jones Utility Average rose 45 percent. While Amazon fell nearly 80 percent in 2000, Bristol-Myers Squibb rose 15 percent. While Merck & Co. fell 37 percent in 2001, competitor Johnson & Johnson rose 12 percent.

Just because markets and stock prices are volatile doesn't mean you can't make money on Wall Street. In any kind of market, there are always winners. True, more winners exist in bull markets. But bear markets aren't without opportunities for profits as well.

Of course, the key is betting on the right investments. I'll show you how to find the winners in tough markets later in this book.

Chapter Two

Law #2:
In Turbulent Markets,
Invest in the Eye of the Storm

There's always a bull market.

That may be hard to believe after seeing the shrinkage in your 401(k) plan over the last two years. However, the fact is that there were bull markets in 2000 and 2001. In utility stocks. In real estate investment trusts. In bonds. In health care stocks. In regional banks. In cash.

Of course, chances are pretty good that you didn't participate in these bull markets if you stocked your portfolio with the winners of the '90s—technology, telecom equipment, Internet. We all know what happened to those stocks.

Now, second-guessing yourself over the investment vehicles you owned in the last few years is not a very productive exercise. But I think it is important to point out that even during severe market declines, there's always a bull market for certain investments. Or, at the very least, a much tamer bear market.

So if that market sweet spot always exists, how do you find it? In short, how do you find the "eye" of the market storm?

UNDERSTANDING THE EYE

The eye of a hurricane is one of nature's great wonders. There, at the center of 100-mile-an-hour fury, is this spot of calm. Peace. Safety.

True, the eye of the hurricane is often the smallest part of the storm. And getting to the eye means passing through some pretty nasty stuff. In fact, the most violent part of a hurricane is the "eye-wall," the area that separates the eye from the storm. In a level 5 hurricane (hurricanes are rated on a scale from 1 to 5, with 5 being the most severe), the winds in the eyewall may exceed 150 miles per hour.

The storm's eye is an excellent metaphor for what investors must do during stormy market periods. Find the eye. Get to the calm. Play in the space where you won't get hurt.

The interesting thing about the eye, as it applies to markets, is that sometimes investors don't want any part of the eye. Go back to 1998 and 1999. Make no mistake, there was a storm, a *violent* storm, brewing in the markets. The wild ride for stocks was very much like the fury that accompanies a hurricane.

The difference, however, is that this hurricane was like your favorite roller coaster—thrilling, exciting, fun, but not destructive. Your portfolio swooped and turned and pitched and soared. But while the storm raged, you usually found yourself (and your portfolio) lifted to higher ground by the fury.

As long as you were being lifted higher, you wanted no part of the eye. Indeed, the eye was boring. The eye was safe. Investing in the eye meant the bullish winds didn't carry you higher.

In the last two years, however, the trajectory of the storm changed. What was exciting and thrilling and stomach churning became destructive. Suddenly, the eye wasn't such a bad place to be.

As an investor, you need to decide just how much excitement you can tolerate. In other words, you need to determine just how far outside the eye you want to go.

TRADE-OFFS WHEN INVESTING IN THE EYE

If you decide that you want to invest in the eye, understand that this decision has trade-offs. Investing in the eye is a less risky way to invest. That may seem like a good thing during down markets. However, as discussed, investing in the eye will cost you when the market storms higher.

Indeed, you can't have it both ways—low risk and high returns. You may think you can. I can't tell you how many investors I talk to who believe 15 percent annual returns with low risk are not only possible, but also the norm. These investors think that holding a portfolio of 50 percent stocks and 50 percent bonds can achieve the same returns as a portfolio invested totally in stocks.

In our money-management business, we ask clients to complete a questionnaire pertaining to their risk tolerances, investment goals, and expectations. When clients are asked about their investment objective, most say that they want reasonable growth with a bit of income. In other words, most investors prefer a fairly conservative portfolio with a bent toward growth. That is hardly a portfolio trying to hit home runs.

Yet, when asked what they believe such a portfolio should return each year, the answer is often in the 15 percent to 20 percent range.

The problem with that answer is that 15 percent to 20 percent annual returns are incompatible with a conservative growth approach. Remember: Despite the huge gains of the second half of the 1990s, the stock market's long-run average annual return (and this includes dividends) is approximately 11 percent. And that is a portfolio 100 percent invested in equities. If stocks, on average, rise 11 percent per year, you shouldn't expect to achieve a higher rate of return with a portfolio that takes lower risk (a lower-risk portfolio might hold bonds and cash, for example).

Bottom line: If you choose to stay in the eye, you will be reducing expected portfolio returns over time. That may be an acceptable trade-off, especially for investors nearing the end of their investment time horizon. But don't expect to run at the front of the herd during bull markets. It's not going to happen.

FINDING THE EYE

So you've made the decision that investing in the eye is the safest place to be. You don't need oversized portfolio gains. The last few years have taught you that you derive more pain from losses than you do pleasure from gains. You're now committed to a slower, steady approach, one that avoids the big loss.

Where do you go?

The bulk of this book lays out ways to reduce risk during volatile market periods. Asset diversification. Time diversification. Proper portfolio construction. Successful selling.

What I'd like to cover now are more "macro" themes when it comes to investing in the eye. Investors should incorporate these ideas into their investment-selection process when implementing diversification and allocation strategies.

LIQUIDITY

Liquidity, in essence, is the amount of money pushing through any market.

For example, the amount of money chasing stuff at an estate sale doesn't compare to the amount of money being pushed through the New York Stock Exchange on any given day.

Understanding the level of liquidity of any market is crucial to success when participating in that market. Why? Because liquidity ultimately determines the ease of buying and selling an investment. That's important, especially during volatile markets.

A by-product of volatile markets is uncertainty. In uncertain times, investors want the ability to transact quickly and efficiently. After all, in volatile markets, when circumstances are changing rapidly, you want the flexibility to buy and sell investments quickly and without affecting the price.

Now, one could argue that the last thing you want to do during volatile markets is buy and sell with great rapidity. Still, ask any investor what he or she treasures most during volatile markets, and one of the things that will be near the top of the list is flexibility. Flexibility to respond quickly to changes in opinions about certain investments.The flexibility to raise cash quickly if need be.

Liquidity provides flexibility, especially in fast-changing markets. Since liquidity is highly prized during uncertain market times, investors usually migrate toward the most liquid investments and away from illiquid investments when markets are in flux. For example, say you are buying a house in a community of just 1,000 residents. The community is in the middle of nowhere; the closest town is 100 miles away.

How much liquidity do you think there is in that market for the house? In other words, how many buyers and sellers are making bets on the house?

Obviously, such a home probably will not have many suitors. Because of so few potential buyers, two things will likely happen to the house. First, it will probably be on the market for a fairly long period of time. Second, in order to find a buyer, it is quite likely that the seller will have to reduce the price over time.

Now let's throw one more ingredient into the mix. Say this town's only industry is mining. Now let's say that the mining industry hits the skids. What will happen to the market for that already difficult-to-sell property? Simple. Any liquidity that was in the market will likely vanish.

Notice what happens in a market that lacks lots of buyers and sellers. First, the ability to sell is impinged. Second, the selling price may be impinged as well. Third, any liquidity in the market can dry up rather quickly when an exogenous event (such as weakness in the mining industry, in our example) hits the market.

How do you determine the amount of liquidity in a stock? Think of the stock market as a market of products, just like your local supermarket. Sitting on the shelves of the stock market are boxes of IBM, cans of Wal-Mart, frozen packages of Oracle, cartons of Veritas Software, bottles of eBay, and so on. Supply and demand for each of these stocks may vary dramatically. Indeed, there may be 1 billion boxes of IBM on the shelves—reflecting demand for IBM boxes and the amount of supply—but only four million cartons of Veritas Software. Thus, the liquidity of each product may differ dramatically.

Here are some important factors to consider when evaluating just how easy it is to buy and sell a particular investment:

- Number of outstanding shares

A market for a stock is driven by the supply of stock available and demand for the stock. IBM has more than 1.7 billion shares outstanding. That's a lot of potential supply of stock that can come into the market. On the other hand, JPS Industries, a small maker of products for the roofing and glass markets, has only 9 million shares outstanding. Obviously, the fact that the supply of IBM stock is much greater than the supply of JPS Industries's stock should make IBM's market much more liquid. You can find out the amount of outstanding shares by looking at a company's quarterly and annual reports. These reports may be obtained from the company or by going to the SEC Web site at www.sec.gov.

- Percentage of shares held by corporate insiders

It is not enough to know the number of outstanding shares. What you are trying to get a handle on is the number of shares that actually trade in the market. The number of actual tradable shares is referred to as a stock's "float."

The amount of the float may be a dramatically different number from the amount of outstanding stock if corporate insiders own lots of shares. What is a corporate insider? Top executives, board members, and large shareholders. These investors are required to file their trading moves with the SEC. Thus, it is easy to track the buying and selling of company stock by its insiders. However, the fact is that corporate insiders generally do not trade their shares that frequently. While insider shares do represent stock that could come into the market, one should not depend on insider shares to boost supply during highly volatile markets.

Obviously, the greater a stock's float, the more liquid the shares. Float statistics may be found at the Yahoo! Finance Web site—

www.finance.yahoo.com. At the Web site, put in the stock's symbol. What will pop up is a quote for the stock as well as a box containing a number of additional links—"News," "Profile," "Chart," "Research," "Insider," and "Messages." Click on the "Profile" link and scroll down to the various statistics near the bottom of the page. On the left-hand side you'll see the number of shares in the company's float.

For example, when you punch in "IBM" at the site and click on "Profile," you'll see that IBM's float is 1.71 billion shares. The size of IBM's float swamps the 1.4-million-share float of JPS Industries.

The Yahoo! Finance site is also useful for keeping track of insider buying and selling of company shares. To find out what insiders are doing, just click on the stock's "Insider" link.

• Average daily trading volume

A good measure of liquidity is the average daily trading volume of a stock. IBM, with its 1.7 billion shares outstanding, has average trading volume of roughly 7 million shares. That is the number of shares that trade hands each day. JPS Industries, with its 1.4-million-share float, has an average trading volume of just 2,600 shares. Thus, on average, the daily trading volume for IBM is roughly 2,600 times greater than that for JPS.

Why should you care about the daily trading volume? In volatile markets, you always want a quick escape route. And you want that escape route to have the least impact on a stock's price. This latter point is very important. If you are selling something, you can find a buyer eventually, as long as you are willing to continue cutting the price. The problem is that in markets with few buyers, you may have to cut the price to the bone. You don't want to have to do that with your stocks. That's why liquidity matters during rocky market periods. With liquid stocks, you usually can sell without having to mark down your selling price. Indeed, I can sell IBM pretty easily, even in volatile markets. And I can sell without having much of an impact on the stock price. The same might not be said for JPS Industries. Indeed, to draw buyers for these shares, I may have to reduce my selling price fairly dramatically.

Bottom line: In volatile markets, particularly markets moving sharply lower, you don't want to be stuck in investments with little liquidity and where the lack of liquidity is forcing a dramatic mark-down in prices to draw buyers.

Another reason to monitor average daily trading volume is that volume increases may indicate increasing demand for the stock. For example, a stock whose average trading volume jumps from 5,000 shares to 50,000 shares over the course of a few weeks is clearly a stock that is gaining attention from investors. This may be an early signal that interest, and perhaps demand, for the stock is rising. If a stock is moving higher on increasing trading volume, demand for the stock is rising.

To find out the average trading volume of a stock, use the Yahoo! Finance site. When you go to the site, input the stock symbol and hit Enter. You'll be taken to a page showing a quote of the stock along with a box containing a variety of links. One of those links is "Chart." Click on this link and you'll see a chart of the stock. If you scroll down under the chart, you'll see an "Avg Vol" number. This is the average daily volume for the stock.

To see whether daily trading volumes are changing, Yahoo! Finance allows you to see historical daily trading volumes. Return to the Yahoo! chart of the stock. If you scroll down under the chart and the table, you'll see a line on the right-hand side of the page—"His-torical Quotes" and a choice of daily, weekly, or monthly quotes. Click on these links and you'll be asked to enter the dates of interest.

• Spread between the "bid" and "ask" price

The problem with illiquid markets is that you may have trouble selling into an illiquid market without reducing your price dramati-cally. One way to get a feel for just how easy it is to sell an investment without impacting the price is by examining a stock's "bid-ask spread."

Think of the bid-ask spread as the range of prices at which buyers and sellers are willing to buy and sell. For example, let's say you want to sell your TV for $100, but the few buyers who have shown an interest are willing to pay only $50. In this example, the bid-ask spread is $50 (the buyer "bid" price) to $100 (your "ask" price).

As you can see from this example, the bid-ask spread is affected by the liquidity of the market. The easier it is to buy and sell something, the more narrow the spread between the bid and the ask price.

This principle applies to stocks and other investments. A stock with a very liquid market, with lots of buyers and sellers, will have a narrow range between the bid and ask price. For example, the spread between the bid and ask prices for IBM is generally as little as one-eighth or one-sixteenth of a point. That is a very small margin when you're talking about a stock with a price of more than $100 per share. That narrow spread speaks to the ample liquidity in IBM's stock.

Now look at JPS Industries. Remember that JPS Industries has a very small float—less than 2 million shares. I've seen the spread between the bid and ask prices for this $5 stock to be as high as one dollar. That is, the bid price is $4.80, or a whopping 17 percent less than the ask price of $5.80. In other words, a seller would have to reduce his or her price 17 percent in order to match up with a buyer. It is not unusual for stocks with small floats and small average daily trading volume to have bid-ask spreads of 50 cents or more.

Keep in mind that bid-ask spreads change constantly, widening and narrowing based on market conditions and investor interest. The important fact, however, is that illiquid stocks generally have wide spreads, and those wide spreads will widen even further during volatile markets.

VOLUME LEADERS

To give you an idea of the most liquid stocks in the market, here are the stocks that are perennially the most actively traded stocks on the New York Stock Exchange and Nasdaq Composite:

New York Stock Exchange Most Actives

AOL Time Warner	IBM
AT&T	Lucent
Citigroup	Motorola
Exxon Mobil	Nortel Networks
GE	Pfizer

Nasdaq Composite Most Actives

Applied Materials	Microsoft
Cisco Systems	Oracle
Dell Computer	QUALCOMM
Intel	Sun Microsystems
JDS Uniphase	WorldCom

Now, what should jump out immediately is that many of these most actively traded stocks didn't exactly weather the market's storm over the last two years. In fact, several of these stocks were abused by sellers, with some falling 70 percent or more.

That brings up an important point. Just because a stock is liquid doesn't mean it won't decline during down markets. However, what is important to understand is that investors who took a beating on these stocks held on to them because they *wanted* to hold, not because they *had* to hold as a result of an illiquid market and no buyers.

This is an important distinction to grasp. "Liquid" is not the same as "safe." Indeed, you don't invest in liquid stocks because these stocks will hold up better than other stocks when markets decline. You invest in liquid stocks during volatile markets to increase your flexibility in case you need to transact quickly and efficiently in the market.

Go back to the international currency crisis of a few years ago. A lot was written about various hedge funds and other investment groups being devastated by the global currency problems. One well-documented case is the firm Long-Term Capital Management. This company, comprised of Ph.D.s and Nobel Prize winners, was making bets all over the globe in fairly illiquid investments. As long as the markets were reasonably calm and sane, Long-Term Capital Management made money hand over fist for its investors. But when the international currency crisis hit, liquidity in its markets dried up. In short, there were no buyers. Long-Term Capital was stuck with its positions, and when those positions started to go against them, the losses piled up.

Long-Term Capital is a perfect example of the dangers of owning illiquid investments when markets stop functioning.

What markets are the most liquid?

- Cash.

- Large-capitalization stocks. A company's market capitalization is the number of outstanding shares times the stock price. For example, IBM's market capitalization is roughly $200 billion. That number is found by taking the number of outstanding IBM shares and multiplying it by the stock price. Think of a company's market capitalization as its price tag on Wall Street. That is, if you were going to buy the whole company, the price tag is the current market cap. Market capitalizations over $8 billion are considered "large-cap."

What markets are illiquid?

- Certain bond markets can be fairly illiquid. For example, bonds in foreign companies may be difficult to sell during volatile markets.

- "Micro" cap stocks. These are stocks with market capitalizations of less than $200 million.

- Foreign stocks purchased on foreign exchanges. Many foreign exchanges lack the liquidity of U.S. exchanges. This lack of liquidity will be accentuated during global economic crises.

Thus, to maximize liquidity during rocky periods:

- *Keep equity investments focused on market caps above $1 billion.* That's not to say that you shouldn't own smaller companies. However, you don't want a portfolio that is overweighted in small-cap and micro-cap stocks during volatile periods. These stocks will be difficult to sell without impacting the stock price.

- *In the corporate bond arena, stay with larger corporate issuers and non-exotic bonds.* The more exotic the bond, the less liquid the market.

- *Cash always works well in volatile markets.* Although the return on cash will pale next to the return of stocks and bonds over the long term, cash always holds up well during uncertain markets.

- *Don't get trapped in investments such as limited partnerships, private equity, venture capital, and the like.* Liquidity in these markets is very, very limited. Just how bad can things get for these investments during declining markets? Just ask any venture capitalist about investments made in 1999 and early 2000. Chances are, the private value of many of these investments has declined 70 percent or more. And the biggest problem is that there is nobody to sell the stuff to when markets tank.

- *Stay away from "exotic" investments.* The more exotic the investment, the more illiquid. The following is a good test for determining how exotic an investment is: Can you find a price quote for the investment in your local paper? This sounds rather basic, but it works pretty well. Because of limited space, local newspapers usually print the prices of only the most popular investment. If you can't find the price of an investment in your local paper, think twice about owning it from a liquidity standpoint. And if you can't find the price each day in *The Wall Street Journal,* that is an even greater red flag concerning the investment's liquidity.

DIVIDENDS AND INTEREST

During market storms, what is a major casualty? A big casualty of the stormy markets of 2000 and 2001 was the certainty of capital gains.

In an environment in which the ability to produce consistent capital gains is called into question, where can you look for some certainty for at least a portion of your portfolio? Said differently, what type of investment returns provide the most certainty during difficult market periods?

To answer that question, you need to understand that any investment's total return depends on two factors: price appreciation (capital gains) and income thrown off by the investment (dividends and interest).

For example, a stock that rises 10 percent in a year and pays dividends that yield 5 percent provides a total return of approximately 15 percent for the year. A stock's dividend yield is the amount of dividends paid over 12 months divided by the stock price. Let's say a stock pays 25 cents per share per quarter, or $1 per share in annual dividends. If the stock is trading for $20 per share, the dividend yield is $1 divided by $20, or 5 percent. Think of that 5 percent yield as you would the 5 percent interest rate on your money market account or 5 percent rate on your corporate bond. The dividend yield represents the percentage of your investment that is returned in cash flow. In this example, the yield represents roughly one-third of the investment's return for the year.

Now ask yourself this question: Which one of these components of total return is more dependable and less subject to market vagaries—dividends or capital gains?

Obviously, the cash flow from dividends (and interest on bonds and cash investments) is much more predictable and less volatile than returns generated by investment appreciation potential.

It stands to reason, therefore, that during volatile markets, when certainty of returns is an especially prized commodity, investors will migrate to those investments offering at least some modicum of income via dividends and interest.

Dividends and interest can be extremely powerful weapons in generating portfolio returns over time. For example, since 1926 the S&P 500 has appreciated approximately 6.4 percent annually; with dividends reinvested, it has returned 11 percent annualized.

The beauty of dividend income is that it's the "bird in the hand." You don't have to rely exclusively on the investment rising in price.

True, companies do cut or omit dividends periodically. Still, dividend income is a fairly certain stream of return for investors, especially if you focus on financially sound companies.

Despite all this good stuff about dividends, investors avoided dividends like a proctology exam during the 1990s. The thinking went something like this: "Who cares about getting 2 percent in dividend income when I can generate 30 percent returns by buying growth stocks?"

In short, because stocks were rising so quickly, the appeal of dividends (or should I say dividend-paying investments) was greatly reduced.

Another reason investors want capital gains and not dividend income is that dividend income is taxed at a higher rate. Investors must pay taxes on dividends each year at their ordinary tax rate. That means that if you are in the highest tax bracket, you lose nearly 40 cents in taxes for every $1 in dividends. On the other hand, taxes on capital gains (if the investment is held at least 12 months) will cost you, at most, 20 cents for every $1 in capital gains.

Bottom line: If you have a choice between $1 in capital gains and $1 in dividends, taxes dictate that you would rather have the $1 in capital gains. And that's what people wanted in the '90s.

Of course, as we discovered the hard way, stocks don't rise 35 percent per year forever. Sometimes they *decline* 35 percent. Or more. And in an environment of declining stock prices, that "measly" 2 percent or 3 percent yield doesn't look so measly.

I've been talking about dividend yield, but the same stability and predictability of returns goes for interest payments on bonds, cash, and other liquid investments. Yes, bonds do default. However, the probability of receiving interest payments is high if investments are focused on financially secure issuers of debt. And on Treasury securities, receiving your interest payments is, indeed, assured.

Now, don't misconstrue my point about dividends and interest. I am a firm believer in investing for growth, especially if your time frame is more than just a few years. And you invest in growth by buying growth stocks, many of which may pay little or nothing in dividends. However, the last few years have shown two things:

1. If you are depending solely on price appreciation in every aspect of your portfolio, you may get stung periodically, and even get seriously hurt in a few instances.

2. Having dividend income can help cushion the blow significantly.

For that reason, I try to mix up things in my portfolio. While I have some stocks that pay few or no dividends—Microsoft, for example—I also have plenty of stocks that pay decent dividends, such as Exxon Mobil and Popular.

DIVIDEND YIELD VERSUS DIVIDEND GROWTH

Of course, not all stocks that pay dividends are the same. Some dividend-paying stocks have high yields (4 percent to 15 percent); others have lower yields. I think when most people talk about dividend stocks, they generally think of higher-yielding stocks. Yet Intel, not your typical "income" stock, also pays a dividend.

Thus, investors have many choices when it comes to buying stocks that pay dividends.

What should investors' preference be when it comes to choosing dividend stocks? For starters, understand that stocks with high dividend yields behave differently than do stocks with low dividend yields. Stocks with high dividend yields generally will hold up better during down markets than stocks with low yields. (What is a "high" yield? A rule of thumb is any yield that is at least $2^1/2$ times the yield on the S&P 500. Thus, if the S&P 500 is yielding 2 percent—you can find the yield on the S&P 500 and many other market indexes each week in *Barron's*—a high yield would be 5 percent or more.) Conversely, stocks with high dividend yields underperform the market during most bull markets.

Because of the difference in behavior during bull and bear markets, owning stocks with high yields and low yields enhances the diversification of a portfolio.

Still, if you had to prefer one factor when choosing dividend-paying stocks, the key metric to consider would be dividend *growth*, not current yield. This is especially true if you hold stocks for a long period of time.

With Dividend Growers, You Can
Have Your Cake and Eat It, Too

For some income-oriented investors, dividend yield is all that matters. But you need to consider the big picture. That means considering a stock's potential for price appreciation and dividend growth. Over time, investors usually win out by focusing on a stock's total return. And total return can be enhanced significantly over time by a fast-growing dividend.

For example, an investment in a single share of a $100 stock yielding 6 percent would generate $120 in dividend income over a span of 20 years, assuming no growth in the dividend or share price. So, after 20 years, your principal (which remains $100) plus your dividend income would total $220.

Now consider a stock that yields just 2.5 percent but increases its dividend and share price by 5 percent annually. Buying one share for $100 and holding it for 20 years turns into $348. That $348 includes your $100 principal, about $83 in dividend income, and some $165 in capital appreciation.

The upshot is that a growing dividend stream can add considerably to an investment's total return over a long period of time. That's why, all things equal, companies that pay rising dividend streams are more attractive investments.

The table below lists 20 companies that have achieved five-year annualized total returns of at least 10 percent and dividend growth of at least 3 percent.

Company (Ticker)	Five-Year Dividend Growth (Annualized Rate) (%)
Alltel (AT)	6
Commerce Group (CGI)	38
Cullen/Frost Bankers (CFR)	22
Exxon Mobil (XOM)	3
First Midwest Bancorp (FMBI)	13
First Virginia Banks (FVB)	10
Jefferson-Pilot (JP)	12
John Nuveen (JNC)	12
Lincoln National (LNC)	6
Marsh & McLennan (MMC)	14
McGraw-Hill (MHP)	9
Mercantile Bankshares (MRBK)	12
Merck & Co. (MRK)	15
Old Republic International (ORI)	19

Philip Morris Cos. (MO)	11
Price (T. Rowe) (TROW)	26
Public Storage (PSA)	11
SBC Communications (SBC)	4
Synovus Financial (SNV)	22
Westamerica Bancorp (WABC)	25

Source: Dow Theory Forecasts

PREFERRED STOCKS, BONDS, AND TREASURY SECURITIES

Again, stocks are not the only investment vehicle that throws off income. Other dividend- and interest-bearing investments include preferred stocks, corporate bonds, municipal bonds, and treasury securities. Each of these investments can enhance the diversification of a portfolio, reduce portfolio risk, and provide a shelter during a market storm. I talk more about these assets in Chapter 3.

RECESSION FIGHTERS

Stock prices follow earnings. The relationship between stock prices and earnings is not always a straight line. You may have periods when stock prices decline despite rising profits. Likewise, you may have skyrocketing prices for a time without any corporate profits. Internet stocks were the shining examples of this last scenario. However, over time, the value of stocks is derived by the earnings-generating capacity of the underlying company. Looked at a different way, you own a stock because you want a portion of a growing stream of earnings. It's really that simple. Thus, the value of the company should rise as its profits rise.

Now, if stock prices are dependent on earnings, what is a leading cause of stock declines? You guessed it. Falling earnings.

Look at some examples from the tech massacre to see just how linked stock prices are to earnings. JDS Uniphase was the poster child for earnings growth in 1998 and 1999. The company, a maker of fiber-optic networking equipment, saw skyrocketing demand for its products. That demand drove per-share profits up sevenfold from fiscal 1997 through fiscal 2000. Not surprisingly, the stock price followed profits higher, with JDS Uniphase stock rising from a low of $2 (adjusted for splits) in 1997 to a high of $153 in 2000.

Rising earnings equals rising stock price. Pretty simple equation.

Unfortunately for JDS Uniphase, stock prices not only follow earnings higher, but also lower when earnings decline. Check out what happened to JDS Uniphase stock. After peaking at $153 in 2000, the stock retreated to $5 in 2001—a decline of 97 percent. I know we all sometimes throw numbers around without really focusing on what they mean. And with lots of tech stocks getting crushed in recent years, we've become comfortably numb to such dramatic drops. But think about what a 97 percent decline in the stock price of JDS Uniphase means.

In a nutshell, in less than 24 months, Wall Street stripped some *$135 billion* from the value of the company. That's a staggering decline in value in a relatively short period of time. An overreaction on Wall Street's part? Only time will tell. But when you look at what happened to JDS Uniphase's corporate profits in fiscal 2001, the decline makes more sense.

Indeed, in fiscal 2001, JDS Uniphase lost a record-setting *$56 billion.*

I talk about JDS Uniphase more in Chapter 7 ("Making the Hard Decision—Knowing When to Sell"), but what's important to understand now is the fact that JDS Uniphase's stock price truly did follow profits. Up, up, up, as profits expanded. Down, down, down, as profits disappeared.

If profits matter, then what is the cause of most major market declines? Ultimately, big bear markets result from widespread weakness in corporate profits. And widespread declines in corporate profits usually occur during economic downturns or recessions.

Therefore, a big part of riding out investment storms is being in stocks of companies where profits are resilient during economic downturns.

Take a look at the following table, which shows sector perform-

Sector Performance (ranked by total return)

Economic Sector	1985–1987	1988–1990	1991–1993	1994–1996	1997–1999	2000–2001*
Consumer staples	1	2	8	6	6	6
Basic materials	2	10	6	7	11	8
Health care	3	1	10	2	4	4
Communications services	4	3	7	8	2	10
Utilities	5	5	9	10	10	1
Consumer cyclicals	6	8	2	11	3	9
Capital goods	7	6	5	4	5	7
Energy	8	4	11	5	8	2
Financial services	9	9	1	3	7	3
Technology	10	11	4	1	1	11
Transportation	11	7	3	9	9	5

* March 31

Sources: Morningstar, Inc., Vanguard Group, Wilshire Associates, Investor's Business Daily

ance for periods dating back to 1985. What jumps out immediately is the feast-or-famine nature of many industry groups.

For example, the technology sector is either at the top of the heap (as it was in 1994–1996 and 1997–1999) or at the bottom of the heap (as it was in 1985–1987, 1988–1990, and 2000–2001). Clearly, the feast-or-famine performance of the technology sector since 1985 demonstrates the volatility of this group.

On the other hand, capital-goods stocks are rarely at the top or the bottom of the heap but somewhere around the median each year. Of course, that may seem like a good thing, but who wants to own stocks that are, well, just middling year in, year out?

Obviously, what you want to own are stocks that do well across both bullish and bearish market periods, stocks that do well during economic boom times as well as economic downturns.

Now return to the table. What sector has demonstrated the most consistently superior performance since 1985? I'd have to cast my lot with health-care stocks. Indeed, in only one period (1991–1993) did the group fail to be in the top half of sector performance. And in the down period, the group was pushed lower by an exogenous event— the "Hillary" health-care-reform scare. Not surprisingly, as concerns over health-care reform passed and investors concentrated once again on the group's strong fundamentals, health-care stocks rose nicely.

Clearly, health-care stocks represent excellent recession fighters and have demonstrated the ability to weather economic storms extremely well.

What other sectors hold up reasonably well during tough economic times? Not surprisingly, consumer staples have achieved relatively consistent performance since 1985. The group has finished among the top six sectors every year except 1991–1993, and the group has never been in the cellar.

Another way to compare these groups is by looking at their performances during their best years and their worst years.

Check out the graph on the next page. One way to measure volatility is by looking at the standard deviation of returns. That's a fancy way of saying look at the spread of returns. What sectors have experienced big spreads in returns? Once again, technology is out in front. The group's best year since 1991 was 1999, when technology stocks rose more than 120 percent. The worst year was 2000, when technology stocks declined more than 30 percent. Other groups with big spreads from positive to negative returns in any one year are precious metals and telecommunications.

Now look at health care. What the table shows is a nice trade-off between positive and negative returns. The group's best year was 1991, when the group rose by more than 60 percent. The worst year for the group was 1992, when health-care stocks declined about 10 percent.

What can you learn from these tables and charts? One lesson is that not all sectors run to extremes, either to the upside or the downside. Indeed, health-care stocks have shown the ability to produce market-beating returns during both up periods and down periods. That's what you call an "easy-hold" sector. That is, the group's per-

Best/Worst Returns, 1991–2000

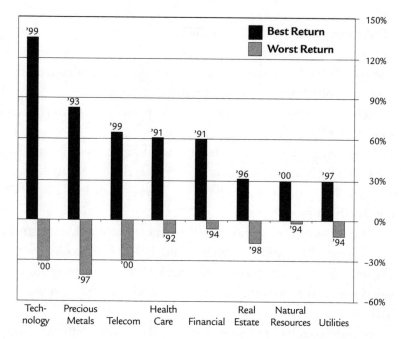

Sources: Morningstar, Inc., Vanguard Group, Wilshire Associates, *Investor's Business Daily*

formance during good and bad times makes it easy to hold the stocks.

Conversely, some groups are better suited for trading. Technology, for example, is not an easy-hold sector. Stocks in the technology sector tend to run to extremes, and it is important that investors understand the movement of the groups when deciding what to buy and how long to hold.

Bottom line: If you are trying to reach the eye of the storm, certain industry sectors are more conducive than others for weathering volatile markets. At the top of the list is health care, followed by consumer staples and financial services. These groups, especially health care, have steady product demand regardless of economic conditions. That consistent demand usually leads to consistent earnings.

Groups that will likely be buffeted during stormy markets include technology and consumer cyclicals. Earnings for these groups tend to be very sensitive to economic conditions and thus will tail off sharply during recessions or economic slowdowns.

LOW-VOLATILITY INVESTMENTS

The final piece in finding the eye of the storm is understanding the expected volatility of various investment groups.

Volatility, as we've discussed, is the expected spread in returns for a particular asset class.

What investment classes have the most expected volatility? At the top of the list, not surprisingly, are stocks and stock mutual funds.

What investment classes have the least expected volatility? Cash. Bonds. Treasury securities.

Of course, within stocks and fixed-income investments are varying degrees of volatility. As we've seen, health-care stocks are generally less volatile than technology stocks. Utility stocks tend to be less volatile than telecom stocks. Common stocks are more volatile than preferred stocks.

Within fixed-income investments, some distinctions are especially important. First, short-term bonds are less volatile than long-term bonds. That is, long-term bonds react more aggressively to interest-rate movements than do short-term bonds. Also, low-coupon-paying bonds are more volatile than high-coupon-paying bonds when it comes to interest-rate fluctuations.

Another important point is that foreign bonds are likely to be more volatile than U.S. corporate bonds due to such factors as liquidity and political risk.

In the eye of the storm, less volatile issues will generally weather the fury better than volatile investments. We saw that in 2000 and 2001 when cash and other fixed-income investments handily outperformed most equities.

Of course, investing in low-volatility investments, while paying dividends during market choppiness, will also keep you from outperforming the market when stocks rally. That's why it is crucial that you understand your risk/reward tolerances and investment time horizon when developing a plan to weather market volatility.

Conclusion

The rest of this book talks about ways to create and manage a portfolio to minimize the pain and maximize the opportunities presented by volatile markets. Underlying a lot of what is discussed will be these four "macro" concepts—liquidity, dividends/interest, recession fighters, and low-volatility investments. If you understand and remember these concepts, you'll be light-years ahead of other investors when it comes to investment selection during difficult market periods.

Law #3:
Ride Out the Turbulence Through Asset and Time Diversification

---

D-I-V-E-R-S-I-F-I-C-A-T-I-O-N. Fifteen letters. Funny—given how people viewed diversification a few years ago, I thought it was a four-letter word.

Diworsification

Diversification in the late '90s was for chumps. To diversify meant to underperform. Smart investors leveraged up portfolios by concentrating in those stocks that were on the move: techs; telecoms; Internet companies.

I can remember getting letters from people frustrated because they were making "only" 20 percent on their diversified portfolios when their neighbors were pulling down annual gains of 50 percent or more.

Diworsification, it was called.

Of course, people who didn't diversify discovered the dangers of concentrated portfolios. And the people who diversified were awfully glad they had.

PORTFOLIO INSURANCE

Diversification is like insurance. When you don't need the insurance, you moan and groan about paying the annual premium.

When you need the insurance, you're glad you paid those premiums.

When you diversify, you buy a bit of insurance for your portfolio against catastrophes. Of course, as is the case with any insurance, diversification will cost you. Indeed, by definition, diversification reduces risk. And reducing risk reduces expected returns of the portfolio. That's the trade-off.

But if a portfolio is diversified properly, the trade-off of lower expected returns for lower expected risk doesn't have to be huge. This chapter and Chapter 5 discuss diversification and asset allocation and how these concepts are used to create the perfect "all-weather" portfolio.

WHY DIVERSIFY?

If you always knew what investments would do well and what investments would flop, you wouldn't need to diversify. You'd make a whole lot more money putting all your dough into that stock, mutual fund, or bond that skyrockets.

Indeed, if you knew what investment would be the best performer, you'd be foolish to put your money anywhere else.

The problem is that you don't know *anything* for certain when it comes to the stock market. Sure, everyone thought that tech stocks were the best investments in 1998 and 1999, and they were. But everyone also thought that tech stocks would continue to be the best investments in 2000. But they weren't. Not by a long shot.

That's the point of diversification. You don't know with complete certainty what groups will be leading and lagging the market at any point in time. Since you don't know where the next leaders will come from, a prudent approach is to own a bunch of investments across a bunch of industry groups and asset classes. In that way, you're sure to avoid owning all of the groups getting killed and increase your chances of owning groups and investments that are doing well.

I'm sure there is nothing particularly earth-shattering here. Most investors understand the fundamental basis of diversification.

But if investors understand the basis for diversification, why didn't most of them diversify their portfolios in recent years? The answer is that diversifying is like dieting. Nobody wants to diet. Nobody wants to limit the good stuff while adding food to your menus that is less appetizing, less sexy.

And most people don't diet seriously until there is a real risk to their health.

The same goes with diversification. Why own a boring utility stock when a portfolio of technology stocks is much sexier. Why own the bond fund when foreign stock funds are raging and making money hand over fist. Bottom line: Many investors didn't diversify because they were afraid to lose out on the big gains being afforded those who didn't diversify.

See the problem? Investors became greedy. They became fixated on maximizing short-term gains without any thought to risk. All of a sudden, that 10 percent or 15 percent annual return—you know, the return where your money doubles every five to seven years—wasn't good enough. You could get double that by not diversifying.

Of course, the lessons of the last two years show that diversification is not for chumps. In fact, diversification makes perfect sense, especially during turbulent market periods.

But how does one diversify a portfolio? What follows are four ways to diversify a portfolio.

I. Diversify Within Asset Classes

Diversification does not and should not mean the same thing to every investor. Diversification has an entirely different meaning to a 25-year-old than to an 85-year-old. Indeed, a diversified portfolio for each of these investors may look dramatically different. That's a key point to understand about diversification: One size does not fit all.

A 25-year-old should be investing primarily for long-term growth.

An 85-year-old should be investing primarily for preservation of capital.

How should the 25-year-old and the 85-year-old diversify? In my opinion, the diversification should be primarily *within* asset classes. For the 25-year-old, that means diversification within equities. For the 85-year-old, that means diversification within fixed-income investments.

Too often investors regard all stocks as being the same when it comes to diversification. They are not. Indeed, individual stocks have dramatically different risk/reward profiles. The same goes for fixed-income investments. Long-term corporate bonds have a different risk profile than do money market accounts.

These distinctions within asset classes must be made when diversifying a portfolio. The lists below give an idea of just how different investments within asset classes can be:

Stocks/Stock Mutual Funds

Common stocks	Foreign small-cap stocks
Preferred stocks	Large-cap mutual funds
Growth stocks	Mid-cap mutual funds
Value stocks	Small-cap mutual funds
Dividend stocks	Growth equity funds
Large-capitalization stocks	Value equity funds
Mid-capitalization stocks	Large-cap growth funds
Small-capitalization stocks	Mid-cap growth funds
High-beta (volatility) stocks	Small-cap growth funds
Low-beta (volatility) stocks	Large-cap value funds
Foreign growth stocks	Mid-cap value funds
Foreign value stocks	Small-cap value funds
Foreign large-cap stocks	Index funds
Foreign mid-cap stocks	Exchange-traded funds (ETFs)

Cash/Fixed-Income Investments

Short-term bonds	Guaranteed investment contracts (GICs)
Intermediate-term bonds	Convertible bonds
Long-term bonds	Zero-coupon bonds
Corporate bonds	Certificates of deposit

Municipal bonds   Passbook savings accounts

Ginnie Mae bonds   Savings bonds

Junk bonds   Treasury inflation-protected bonds (TIPs)

Money market funds   "I" (Inflation) savings bonds

Foreign bonds

Real Estate

Residential real estate   Apartments

Commercial real estate   Time shares

Industrial real estate   Real estate investment trusts

Hard Assets

Precious Metals   Ostrich farms

Collectibles   Thoroughbred horses

Coins   Show dogs

Art

Given the many different types of securities within the same asset classes, an individual who wants to invest exclusively in equities (the 25-year-old, for example) still has ample ways to diversify a portfolio.

Indeed, even within equities, returns and volatility have varied over the years. For example, look at the difference in risk/return between large-cap and small-cap stocks:

	Average Annual Return (1926–2000) (%)	Standard Deviation (i.e., volatility) (%)
Large-company stocks	11.0	20.2
Small-company stocks	12.4	33.4

And the same goes for fixed-income instruments:

Long-term corporate bonds	5.7	8.7
Long-term government bonds	5.3	9.4
Intermediate-term bonds	5.3	5.8
U.S. Treasury bills	3.8	3.2

Source: Ibbotson Associates, Chicago

Perhaps an easy way to understand how different equities perform differently during market environments is to look at the return numbers for the major indexes in 2000. While the Nasdaq Composite (fueled largely by large-cap technology stocks) fell 39 percent during the year, the Dow Jones Industrial Average (driven by industrial stocks) declined only 6 percent.

Obviously, had you owned Dow-type stocks in a portfolio, it would have helped cushion the blow from the blowups in other stocks.

This brings up an important point. A well-diversified equity portfolio has representation across a variety of stocks. Unfortunately, most of the portfolios I've seen in recent years—even those with 20 or more individual stocks—had their equity holdings focused in one segment of equities: large-capitalization growth stocks, often largely technology.

Even investors who believed they were diversified because they owned six different mutual funds didn't realize that the six funds all invested basically in the same stocks.

Given this extreme focus in one equity area (large-cap growth), it was little wonder portfolios were obliterated when this sector turned down.

We will talk more about the science and art of portfolio building in Chapter 5. Right now, what's important to understand is that you have a lot of different building blocks at your disposal, even within the same asset class.

The goal is to use them well.

II. DIVERSIFICATION ACROSS ASSET CLASSES

A second level of diversification involves holding investments *across* asset classes.

Why hold investments from different asset classes? Because the essence of portfolio diversification is to include investments that don't correlate with one another.

Let's return to the performance numbers for stocks and bonds. What we see, not surprisingly, is that bonds have lower historical volatility than stocks. To be sure, over a long period of time, stocks outperform bonds. But some investors don't have a long time. And others don't have the fortitude to invest for the long term. That means bonds can provide a nice stabilizer to a portfolio, even if it does mean accepting lower returns over the long term.

Bonds and stocks are not the only asset classes. Indeed, you can diversify a portfolio by including real estate, not to mention hard assets (gold, collectibles, etc.). These investments generally correlate differently with stocks and bonds.

Actually, most people have a fairly large exposure to real estate via their home. In fact, real estate is the largest asset in most people's portfolios. Fortunately, while real estate may not exhibit the same appreciation as equities, real estate usually doesn't have the wild gyrations that stocks have (that is, unless you live on either coast).

What determines how much of each asset class you hold in a portfolio? Certainly investment time horizon is a key determinant. The longer the investment time horizon, the more equities you should hold in your portfolio. The shorter the time horizon, the more fixed-income investments you should hold.

Another factor is risk tolerance. Most people believe they are risk takers. Being a risk taker implies a certain "macho" personality. Indeed, risk often means danger. Cool guys—athletes, fighter pilots, astronauts, card sharks, firemen, policemen—are risk takers. Yeah, we're all risk takers, right?

Actually, most people do everything they can to avoid risk. Why? Because risk means uncertainty. We don't like uncertainty. We like predictability. Taking risks means accepting uncertain outcomes. That goes against human nature.

That's why determining your comfort level when it comes to risk is easier said than done. Assessing your level of risk aversion truly requires you to consider your personal make-up objectively, and looking inward objectively is not the easiest thing to do.

For example, you may like to think you are a risk taker, but does your lifestyle reflect any risk taking? Have you been in the same job for more than 10 years, or do you rarely last more than a year or two at a job before moving on? Have you lived in the same house for 10 years, or do you change houses every three years? And what about your hobbies. Do you bungee jump? Skydive? Or is your idea of a vacation lounging in a hammock? And how comfortable are you with debt? Risk takers generally feel very comfortable having lots of debt. People uncomfortable with risk are usually uncomfortable with debt.

To be sure, these are all qualitative ways to assess your risk tolerance. But risk cannot be measured with a thermometer. Determining your risk tolerance is going to be rather inexact. Still, all investors have had a good acid test for their risk tolerance in the last four years. In that time, all of us have truly seen the highs and the lows when it comes to the stock market and our portfolios. Thus, we have some reference point to understand our own feelings toward risk.

If you want a more quantitative way to measure your risk tolerance, try this test.

One of the first things a client of our money management business does is fill out a questionnaire. The questionnaire asks the question, "Do you consider yourself a risk taker?" Many people answer in the affirmative. However, when the questionnaire solicits specific yes/no answers to certain probability scenarios, what comes out is that most people have a much greater aversion to risk than they admit.

For example, how would you answer this question? *You have $5,000. You have a 70 percent chance of doubling the $5,000 to $10,000, and a 30 percent chance of losing the entire $5,000. Would you take the bet?*

We ask this question of new money-management clients as part of getting a true read on their risk tolerance.

A person who is truly a risk taker would accept this bet in a heartbeat. After all, probability says that the expected payoff of this bet is $7,000. (To find the expected payoff of any probability scenario, simply multiply the odds times the payoff and add up the amounts. In this example, 70 percent multiplied by $10,000 is $7,000, and 30 percent multiplied by zero equals zero. Thus, the sum of the probabilities is $7,000.)

Because $7,000 is greater than the starting stake of $5,000, probability says you should take the bet. However, nearly all of our clients admit that they would not take the bet.

What would you do? That's an important question to ponder. Indeed, when figuring out your risk tolerance, you need to determine whether the pain you feel when you lose money is greater than the pleasure you feel when you make money.

That's not an easy question to answer. But you need to answer this question at the onset of an investment program. You cannot answer this question midway through the game, because your answer will be skewed by what is happening in the market at that time.

Go back to the late '90s. Everybody seemed to value the pleasure of a dollar gained more than the pain of a dollar lost simply because nobody was losing money. Likewise, in 2000 and 2001, many people felt that saving a dollar was better than reaching for another dollar of gains.

The point is that assessing risk is critical to developing the proper diversification in an investment portfolio. More important, once that risk tolerance is struck, you need to stick with it, even when market conditions are making you want to change your mind. Trust me. You'll always become more/less risk averse at precisely the wrong time.

In Chapter 5, we'll talk more specifically about how to combine investments across asset classes to create the appropriate portfolio based on a person's risk/reward parameters.

III. Weighting and Rebalancing of Assets

An important component of proper diversification is appropriate weighting of the investments in portfolios.

One area where I find many investors' portfolios lacking is how investments are weighted in the portfolio. For example, a prospective money-management client came to me with a portfolio in which three stocks comprised 80 percent of the entire portfolio. Actually, this is not all that unusual. You may even have such a portfolio.

Having a portfolio concentrated in just a few stocks can occur over time for several reasons. First, you may be an employee of a company that gives its workers a discount on company shares purchased through the employee stock purchase plan. So you bought stock with your extra dollars. And maybe your company's stock is an investment option in the 401(k) plan. Or the company's contribution to the plan is paid for in company stock and then you buy more stock. And, fortunately, the stock has done well over the years, much better than the other stocks in your portfolio. And you never sold any of the stock because to do so would create a huge tax bill. (Some employees are restricted from selling shares of stock in the company in their 401(k) plans, which is another matter.) So you held all the shares to the point that they make up a big part of your portfolio.

Happens all the time.

But is it good diversification practice to have so much of your money in just one or two stocks? Clearly you are assuming a higher level of risk whenever you concentrate your wealth in a few stocks.

To be sure, many of the largest fortunes in this country were made off the backs of a single stock. Microsoft. Berkshire Hathaway. Indeed, had Bill Gates or Warren Buffett said, "Boy, I need to sell a lot of my holdings for diversification purposes," neither would be nearly as rich today.

Nevertheless, for every Microsoft or Berkshire Hathaway there is a Bethlehem Steel or Xerox that has gone dramatically south.

Whether one stock should make up 10 percent of a portfolio, 20 percent, 2 percent, or 80 percent could be argued ad infinitum by financial planners and investment advisers. Obviously, if the stock goes up, you can never own enough; if the stock declines, you can never own too little. The point is that you need to understand that if you are trying to weather volatile markets, simply buying and owning a bunch of stocks across asset classes is not enough. How those investments are weighted in the portfolio means everything.

Coupled with weighting is rebalancing. Investors rebalance to keep investment weightings in a portfolio consistent. Rebalancing is one of those concepts that, if you think about it, makes little sense. Indeed, rebalancing means selling your winners and buying your losers. Why? Because the stocks that become a larger part of your portfolio are usually those that have performed the best. These are the investments that exceed their target weightings. Conversely, the weighting in portfolio losers will fall below the desired weighting, forcing investors to buy more to up the weighting.

You don't need to go overboard with rebalancing a portfolio.

Indeed, constantly rebalancing a portfolio to keep weightings in perfect alignment will generate many transactions. And many transactions generate transaction fees and possible tax liabilities.

A more realistic approach to rebalancing is examining your portfolio weightings every 12 months or so and making adjustments if weightings have gotten out of whack by 5 to 10 percentage points.

Again, the idea isn't to fine-tune your weightings down to five decimal points. Rather, the idea is to rebalance whenever you feel overly exposed to any one investment or industry sector.

IV. TIME DIVERSIFICATION

While diversification usually refers to investing in a variety of assets—stocks, bonds, real estate, and so on—in order to lower portfolio risk, you can also diversify across *time*. How? By spreading investments over a period of time, perhaps monthly.

Investing every month is a form of *time diversification*. When you invest monthly, you limit your risk of buying at market peaks. You also assure yourself of periodically buying near market low points.

Dollar-Cost Averaging

An easy way to implement time diversification in an investment program is by using "dollar-cost averaging." Dollar-cost averaging (DCA) takes emotion out of the investment process. Dollar-cost averaging requires you to make regular contributions to your investments, regardless of market levels.

For example, let's say you own my fund, the Quaker Horizon Dow 30 Plus Fund. A dollar-cost averaging strategy dictates that you contribute the same amount of money to the fund over some regular time interval, usually monthly. That means every month, you buy $100 (or $500 or $1,000 or whatever you can afford) of the fund. If the market is high, your $100 investment buys fewer fund shares; if the market is down, your $100 buys more fund shares.

Using a dollar-cost averaging strategy, your average cost of an investment will always be less than the average of the prices at the time the purchases were made. This is significant, for it means that dollar-cost averaging can make you money even if your investments, over time, show no net positive change.

Let's look at a series of 12 monthly investments made using a DCA strategy:

Month	Amount Invested	Cost Per Share	Shares Bought
January	$500	$35	14.29
February	$500	$40	12.50
March	$500	$43	11.63
April	$500	$50	10.00
May	$500	$41	12.20
June	$500	$34	14.71
July	$500	$32	15.63
August	$500	$31	16.13
September	$500	$30	16.67
October	$500	$26	19.23
November	$500	$29	17.24
December	$500	$35	14.29

Total Investment: $6,000
Number of shares purchased: 174.52
Average cost per share: $34.38
Profit per share (at current $35 price): $0.62 (1.8 percent gain)

Notice that even though the stock price started and ended the period at $35 per share, you now sit with a profit. You have this profit because dollar-cost averaging forced you to buy when the stock dipped below $35. That's one strength of DCA. It forces you to buy when stocks decline. Everyone wants to buy low. Few have the guts to do so. DCA provides a way to buy at or near the lows.

What this example also shows is that market declines are a long-term investor's friend if that investor uses DCA.

If you plan to dollar-cost average, be aware of the following:

- Make your investments at the beginning of the month rather than the end. This distinction may not sound like much. Over time, the difference can add up. For example, if you invest $500 per month—and you invest at the *end* of the month—and earn 11 percent per year, you'll have $788,072 at the end of 25 years. If you invest the $500 at the beginning of the month, over 25 years you'd earn an additional $7,200.

- Dollar-cost averaging can be disastrous if you DCA in a stock that goes from $100 to $2 and never recovers. Choose your DCA investments wisely. Don't dollar-cost average in small, speculative stocks or second- and third-tier technology companies. These stocks rarely come back after being crippled. Do dollar-cost average in blue-chip stocks that are leaders in their industries and have solid finances. For example, I would feel comfortable dollar-cost averaging in any of the "easy-hold" stocks I review in Chapter 4.

- Don't be afraid to modify your dollar-cost averaging program to take advantage of big sell-offs in favored stocks. I do this occasionally with my investments. However, don't tweak your DCA plan too much based on your perceptions of value. After all, that defeats the whole purpose of dollar-cost averaging.

- Dollar-cost averaging works best with low-cost/no-cost investment vehicles. If you use a full-service broker and pay $100 or more per transaction, dollar-cost averaging gets very expensive. Focus on no-load mutual funds with low expenses. Buy stock using low-cost discount brokers. I like to use dividend reinvestment plans to dollar-cost average. DRIPs have few or no fees. Most DRIPs also permit investments with as little as $25 to $100.

Dollar-Cost Averaging Versus Lump-Sum Investing

One question that is often asked relative to dollar-cost averaging is the following: Am I better off putting all my money into the market at once or spacing out my investments via dollar-cost averaging?

Of course, the choice between investing via dollar-cost averaging and lump-sum investing may be no choice at all for many of us. Indeed, rarely do we have lump sums to invest. Our money comes to us in chunks, over time, via our paycheck.

Nevertheless, some occasions occur—a pension rollover, an inheritance, or proceeds from the sale of property—when you must decide how to invest a sizable chunk of money.

What should you do?

Actually, history has shown that you are better off getting your money into the market as quickly as possible. Why? Remember that the market has an upward bias over time. To maximize the upward bias, you should have as much money as possible in the market. By spreading out your investments, you are keeping some money out of the market.

From a practical standpoint, however, I find that most investors just can't bring themselves to lump-sum invest. This is especially the case during volatile markets. That's why I'm a big fan of dollar-cost averaging. It makes investing during difficult market periods much more palatable. I believe this point is so important to successfully weathering volatile markets that I devote a whole chapter (Chapter 6) to the notion of strategies and investment vehicles that will help you invest regularly, even during ugly markets.

How quickly should you get a lump sum into the market? Assuming that these funds are destined for the equity portion of a portfolio, a prudent approach would be to focus on dollar-cost averaging the money into the market over a 12 to 18-month period, putting equal amounts in the market each month.

Value Averaging

Another form of time diversification, and a variant on dollar-cost averaging, is value averaging. Value averaging says that, instead of making the same dollar investment each month in a stock or mutual fund, you vary the amount invested so that the value of the portfolio increases by a fixed sum or percentage each interval.

For example, let's say that, instead of investing $500 each month, you want the value of your investment to rise by $500 each month. In month 1, the value of your investment rose $200. Under value averaging, you would add $300 to the investment to achieve your plan of having the investment increase $500 each month.

Now, let's say that the investment rose $700 in a given month.

Since you want the investment to rise $500, you would sell $200 worth of the investment.

Conversely, let's say the value of the investment dropped $200 in a given month. Since you want the value of the investment to rise $500 each month, you would contribute $700 for that month—$200 to offset the loss plus $500 to increase the value of the portfolio.

An easy way to compare value averaging with the basic dollar-cost averaging is to think in the following terms:

- With dollar-cost averaging, you know how much you'll invest, but you don't know what the value will be at the end of your investment horizon.

- With value averaging, you know how much your portfolio will be worth at the end of your investment horizon, but you don't know how much it will cost out of your pocket.

When examined in these terms, it's easy to see that value averaging is a more aggressive strategy than dollar-cost averaging. The total amount you invest is not constrained, as it is under dollar-cost averaging. This is a negative for many investors. Another negative of value averaging compared with dollar-cost averaging is that the strategy could create more transaction costs, since you may have to sell shares to stay within your parameters. The selling also creates tax consequences. Finally, value averaging requires more monitoring than does a basic dollar-cost averaging program.

Which method is appropriate for you? It depends to a large extent on how much time you want to spend monitoring your portfolio, how aggressive you want to be (remember that value averaging is more aggressive, since there is no cap on how much you invest to maintain the system), and how much you can afford to invest. If you invest $25 or $50 in a particular investment each month, it's easier to dollar-cost average. However, if you invest $1,000 or more a month, value averaging may be more attractive to you.

Time Diversify by Extending Holding Periods

Another aspect of time diversification is extending your investment holding periods. Remember, the key point of diversification is reducing portfolio risk—that is, portfolio volatility. Investment returns are more volatile the shorter the time frame.

For example, in any one year, stocks can be extremely volatile. As we've seen earlier, annual returns for stocks have ranged from a positive 66 percent to a negative 39 percent. That's a huge spread in potential one-year returns. That's why stocks are potentially extremely volatile in the short run.

As you extend the holding periods for stocks, however, volatility of returns decreases. In fact, according to Jeremy Siegel, in *Stocks for the Long Run,* there has not been a 20-year time frame in the market in which stocks did not produce a positive return.

The importance of time diversification cannot be overstated, especially when your current view of the market is rather bearish. Indeed, during difficult market periods, most investors tend to be reactive. They change investment approaches after the fact, after they've already been crushed.

The problem with being reactive is that your timing is usually wrong. You sell stocks after the market has already declined. Or you buy aggressively after the market has already skyrocketed. These are natural reactions to short-term market movements.

By understanding that market movements tend to smooth out over time, you should be less reactive as an investor. And being less reactive should help your portfolio.

Why does investment volatility tend to smooth out over time? One reason is that the natural trend for most investments is higher. The stock market, on average, rises two out of every three years. Of course, that doesn't mean stocks *always* rise two out of three years. But when you look out over time, stocks generally move higher on a fairly consistent basis.

Thus, whenever you have a market decline in any one year, long-run averages say that higher markets will usually follow the decline. The gains tend to smooth out the one bad year.

This "pendulum" effect in the market is fairly well documented. Look at the chart on the next page showing the annual returns of large-cap stocks since 1926. What you should notice are several things:

Large Company Stock Returns, 1926–2001

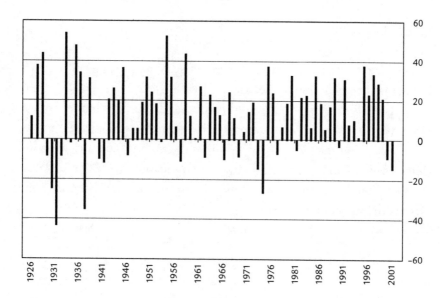

Source: Ibbotson Associates, Chicago

1. There are a lot more up years than down years. In fact, since 1926, there have been 54 years when large-cap stocks advanced versus 22 years when large-cap stocks declined.

2. In years when the market registered big moves to the upside or downside, a reversal of the trend usually occurred in short order.

3. The longest streak of consecutive down years was four.

The other thing that you should notice, and what should give you some pause as you look out over the market's probable returns over the next few years, is the following: Since 1982, large-cap stocks have declined only three times (1990, 2000, and 2001). While that doesn't necessarily mean that stocks can't rip off another long streak of gains, it does suggest that the pendulum effect could continue its swing back to the negative side in the short run.

CONCLUSION

Although diversification may not be as sexy as putting all of your investment eggs in one basket, diversification works, especially when markets decline. What you should take away from this chapter is that many ways exist to diversify a portfolio—within asset classes, across asset classes, with asset weightings and rebalancing, and, finally, with time diversification. Using all the diversification weapons at your disposal should go a long way toward helping you survive and even thrive during volatile markets.

Chapter Four

LAW #4:
RIDE OUT VOLATILE MARKETS
WITH EASY HOLDS

MUCH HAS BEEN written over the last two years about the death of "buy-and-hold" investing. Indeed, look at all the people who bought Cisco at $40, held it all the way to $82, and rode it all the way back down to $15. Or the people who bought Yahoo! at $50, then rode it to $224 and back down to $8.

Clearly, buy-and-hold is antiquated and is not appropriate for today's high-octane markets, right?

I suppose the easy answer is "Yes." Buy-and-hold investing has lost its effectiveness. Today's markets demand a more active approach to portfolio management, an approach that calls for taking quick gains and moving on to the next investment.

Of course, the easy answer is often the wrong answer.

For starters, you can't judge the success or failure of any investment strategy, especially a buy-and-hold approach, after just two years. Markets run in cycles. Saying buy and hold doesn't work because it failed to protect investors in 2000 and 2001 is like saying value investing doesn't work because it didn't work in 1998 and 1999, or growth investing doesn't work because it didn't work in 2000 and 2001.

It is intellectually dishonest to pick a small period in time to judge anything, including investment styles.

Another reason you should be careful about trashing a buy-and-hold philosophy is that the strategy was misused by investors on three levels.

First, a buy-and-hold investment strategy doesn't mean investors aren't allowed to sell. There's nothing in a buy-and-hold investment strategy that says you must ride down losers simply because you are a buy-and-hold investor. That's foolish. To be sure, buy-and-hold investors should sell stocks sparingly. Still, things change, and sometimes the reasons you bought a stock no longer are valid. When that happens, you should sell the stock, whether you intended to hold the stock for the long term or not.

Bottom line: Don't blame buy-and-hold investing for not selling a stock that should have been sold. When stocks are no longer worth owning, you should sell. Period. For more on knowing when to sell, see Chapter 7.

Second, successful buy-and-hold investing actually has three components: buying, holding, and *buying more* over time. Buying more over time is especially crucial to a successful buy-and-hold strategy. In any long-term investment strategy, you must be willing to step up to the plate and buy favored stocks when they decline. This is the only way you maximize the opportunities presented by a buy-and-hold philosophy.

For example, let's say you truly love a certain stock that you have made a core holding of your portfolio. And you have bought and held the stock over the years. If your plans really are holding the stock for five or 10 years, then you must be willing to take advantage of stocks that pull back. That's the leverage of a long-term investing strategy—buying favored stocks when they go on sale so you can expand your positions at favorable prices.

I think one of the fundamental flaws with how most investors conduct a buy-and-hold investment strategy is that they are reluctant to step up to the plate and buy stocks that are in decline. Their long-term investment strategy becomes overwhelmed by the short term. They let near-term events dictate their actions. Thus, many investors doom a buy-and-hold investment strategy from the start because of their unwillingness to perform all three crucial elements of the strategy—buy, hold, and *buy more over time.*

Now I know what many of you are thinking. "Are you telling me, Chuck, that I should be buying more stock in [put your favorite technology disaster stock here] now because that's what I should be doing as a long-term investor?" Actually, that may be precisely what you should be doing, *depending on the stock.*

But that last part—*depending on the stock*—is extremely important and gets me to my third point of how a buy-and-hold investment strategy has been misused by millions of investors.

Simply put, investors failed to match strategy with stock selection.

MATCH STYLE AND SELECTION

Many approaches exist for investing in the markets. Some investors trade stocks in rapid-fire fashion. Others hold stocks forever. Some investors buy only stocks that have already gone up. Others focus their buys exclusively on the list of stocks making new lows.

Now, I believe some styles of investing are more conducive than others to success. Still, I concede that there are many different ways to be successful in the markets.

What is important to understand is that smart investors have an approach. That is, smart investors have a disciplined, consistent way of looking at the markets. Smart investors also understand that it is not enough to have an approach or a style; ultimately you must mesh that style with the investment-selection process.

Take your typical trader. Traders live for volatility. After all, no trader wants to own a stock that flat-lines for three or six months. Traders need action, they need movement; and they need movement *now.*

Because a trader has adopted this approach to making money, it is imperative that the trader focus on those stocks that are likely to give him or her the most chance for success as a trader. Thus, traders want volatile stocks. They want stocks that undergo big price swings on a daily basis. Because traders need volatility, smart traders look at a variety of volatility-related factors when considering what stocks to trade: a stock's beta, standard deviation, earnings consistency, and so on.

Actually, as much as market observers decry the ill-conceived investing strategies of day traders—and I have been among their crit-

ics over the years—the one thing day traders got right was this important concept of matching investment style with stock selection. Most
day traders weren't trading Exxon or GE or Johnson & Johnson. They
were trading Yahoo!, Broadcom, Veritas Software, stocks that com-
pressed decade-like price movements into months or even weeks.

Now, don't misconstrue what I'm saying. I'm not advocating a
day-trading style of investing. What I'm saying is that day traders
understood their strategy and chose those stocks that gave them the
best chance of success. The fact that most day traders failed miserably underscores the difficulty of trading stocks. But at least day
traders did what they should have done based on their investment
style—focus on the crazy stocks.

The big mistake of many investors in the last two years is that
they claimed to be buy-and-hold investors, yet they invested in the
"crazy" stocks. In other words, these investors, after choosing an
investment approach, failed to put the second important piece in
place—proper stock selection to match investment style.

Think about your own investment experience. My guess is that
you believe yourself to be a buy-and-hold investor, or, at the very
least, an investor who tends to hold stocks longer than lunchtime. My
experience has been that most individual investors fall into that
camp. You know this by looking at the amount of trading activity
you've done over the years. This may come as a surprise, given all the
attention paid to the hyperkinetic trading patterns of investors in the
'90s, but the majority of individual investors make just four to eight
trades per year. That averages out to about one or two trades every
three months. That's not much trading, which means that, by and
large, you hold the investments you buy.

Now go through your portfolio and see what you own. If it's like
the portfolios I see, you probably have a fair number of highly
volatile stocks left over from the tech-craze days.

What's wrong with this picture? Obviously, when selecting these
stocks, you didn't consider whether they were appropriate for a buy-
and-hold strategy. You bought the stocks because, quite frankly,
everyone else was buying them, prices were skyrocketing, and you
were sick and tired of being left behind.

I know—I bought some of these stocks for the same reason.

To be sure, you also bought some of these stocks because they were industry leaders and had rapidly growing sales and profits. But you probably never considered whether these stocks were appropriate for your buy-and-hold investment approach.

And as it turned out, many weren't.

Of course, the essence of portfolio diversification is including investments in the same portfolio that are not highly correlated with one another. In other words, you don't want a portfolio of stocks that behave exactly the same.

Doesn't that mean you should own volatile stocks in a portfolio to offset your more sedate holdings? Yes, but the problem with investor portfolios in recent years, including portfolios held by self-proclaimed long-term investors, is that the sedate stocks weren't included. It was usually made up, in large measure, of hot growth stocks. And when those hot growth stocks did exactly what they were supposed to do—experience lots and lots of price volatility—it wreaked havoc on the psyche of those long-term investors.

Bottom line: Smart investors survive difficult markets because they don't forget to match investment style with stock selection. Thus, if you believe in a long-term, buy-and-hold strategy, you must align that strategy with stocks that give you the best chance for success.

Easy Holds

Slow and steady often wins the race on Wall Street. Avoiding the big loss in any given year can have as much of a positive impact on your portfolio over time as holding the stock that goes up a lot for two years only to be cut down big time in year three.

Over the years I've made the following argument in my newsletters and books. I would rather have a stock that goes up 11 percent a year, year in and year out, than a stock that goes up 100 percent in four months.

I know that sounds nonsensical, but hear me out.

A stock that goes up 11 percent per year doesn't require me to make any decisions. It is truly an "easy hold." As you'll see, easy-hold stocks are the perfect stocks for long-term investing since they fit nicely with a style of not frequently trading stocks. You don't get flushed out of easy-hold stocks prematurely. After all, nobody gets itchy wanting to take profits in a stock that goes up 11 percent in one year.

On the other hand, the stocks that force your hand are the ones flying around, up 100 percent in four months, down 40 percent in two weeks, up 30 percent in a week, down 60 percent in six months. Those are the stocks that drive you crazy, the ones that keep you up at night.

The ones that usually force you to make a decision.

And one thing I've come to know about investing: The more decisions you make, the more apt you are to be wrong.

The other point about easy-hold investments is that they can make you rich over time. That's the beauty of these stocks. They'll never impress your friends with their plodding performance. You'll rarely see these stocks at the top of the leader board in any given month or year. But rest assured—these stocks can make you rich.

Do the math. A stock that rises 11 percent per year doubles every $6^{1}/_{2}$ years or so. That doesn't sound too impressive until you look out over 20 years. Over 20 years, a stock rising 11 percent per year will double three times. That means a $10,000 investment in the stock will grow to $80,000.

Look at that math one more time: $10,000 becomes approximately $80,000 in 20 years at 11 percent per year.

Now, I don't want to sell you on the idea that finding stocks that rise 11 per year, each and every year, is a slam dunk. Still, 11 percent per year is the average annual performance of the market since 1926. So we're not talking about pie-in-the-sky numbers here.

Of course, if you could find that stock that rises 24 percent per year for 20 years, you would be much, much richer. (For the record, a stock that rises 24 percent per year for 20 years turns a $10,000 investment into more than $700,000.)

However, the chances of hitting such a home run are quite slim. Worse, by attempting to swing for the fences, you'll take on so much risk with your investments that the odds are much greater that the investment will eventually blow up. (Witness what has happened to a lot of investor money in the Internet stocks.) And let's face it—even if you did find a stock that went up 24 percent per year for 20 years, what is the likelihood that you would have stuck around for that 20 years? You would be long gone after year three or four.

What all this means is that long-term buy-and-hold investors do best owning stocks that fit the strategy, and the best stocks for that strategy are easy holds.

Investors should note that easy-hold stocks can fit virtually any investment style. For example, growth investors should be able to supplement a high-octane, high-growth portfolio with easy-hold stocks in a variety of growth sectors—health care, technology, information services. True, sectors that experience the highest earnings growth also tend to be extremely volatile. Still, I consider myself a growth investor. That is, I try to buy companies that are growing revenue and earnings at rates better than the overall economy. But even though I like growth stocks, I still like the idea of owning growth stocks that fit well with a long-term investment approach. In short, I like to own easy-hold growth stocks. Fortunately, there are plenty of easy-hold growth stocks from which to choose, as you'll see later in this chapter.

But what if you are a "value" investor? Value investors buy stocks that are undervalued based on a variety of value criteria—price/earnings ratios, book values, etc. Value stocks have been in vogue in the last two years after being out of favor for most of the '90s. Actually, value investors have a plethora of easy-hold stocks from which to choose. Indeed, one of the characteristics of easy-hold stocks is that they tend to hold up relatively well during market downturns. Value stocks are generally defensive holdings, which means they, too, hold up well during down markets.

But how do you find easy-hold stocks? In other words, what are the criteria investors should use to find these stocks?

FINDING EASY HOLDS

If you could construct the perfect buy-and-hold stock, a stock that would be a solid hold to ride out market volatility, what would that stock look like?

- You want a stock that has demonstrated the ability to show reasonably consistent price performance regardless of market conditions. That is, you want a stock where the standard deviations of returns from year to year are not hair-raising.

- You want a stock where fundamentals (profits, sales, finances) are reasonably steady and predictable from one year to the next.

- You want a stock that, while not likely to be on the leader board in any given year, still is not a consistently sluggish performer. In other words, you don't want your easy holds to be easy holds because the stocks go nowhere. You want easy holds that still have decent long-term growth prospects.

- Since you are investing for several years, you want easy holds with the financial strength necessary to stay in the game for the long term.

- Since valuation does matter, you want easy-hold stocks that are not necessarily screaming bargains but are still fairly priced relative to their growth prospects.

In short, what you want from an easy hold is steady performance during bull markets, price resiliency (relative to the overall market) during bear markets, solid finances, and the ability to register decent though not spectacular growth over the long term.

In an attempt to quantify some of these qualitative factors, I (with the help of my colleague David Wright) have put together the following 15 "easy-hold criteria" for evaluating stocks:

Relative Strength Versus Russell 3000 Index—One Year

This factor looks at the price performance of a stock divided by the price performance of the Russell 3000 Index over the past year. The Russell 3000 Index is a broad measure of the market, incorporating both large and small stocks. All things being equal, stocks with strong relative strength tend to continue their winning ways.

Relative Strength Versus Russell 3000 Index—Five Years

This factor measures the performance of a stock compared to the return for the broad Russell 3000 Index over the past five years. This is a measure of consistent stock performance; a high relative-strength score here means a stock has done well over the long haul.

Beta

Beta measures a stock's volatility relative to the performance of the S&P 500 Index. A stock with a high beta is likely to have greater price swings versus the S&P 500. In contrast, low-beta stocks have a tendency to rise or fall in price more slowly than the S&P 500. Beta is also a gauge of market risk, which is the underlying risk built into stocks.

Revenue Growth—Three Years

This is annual percent change in revenue for the past three years. Investors should favor stocks of companies generating sales growth from increased volumes—not just price hikes or deep discounting.

Earnings Per Share Growth—Three Years

This is the annual percent change in earnings per share for the past three years. Investors should favor stocks of companies posting steady earnings growth and growth from increased revenue rather than by cost-cutting or investment gains.

Equity Per Share Growth—Three Years

Equity per share (also known as book value per share) is what is left after subtracting liabilities and preferred stock from a company's assets. Evaluating equity growth over time can help gauge how effectively a company is increasing retained earnings.

Return on Equity Versus Industry—One Year

Return on equity (ROE) is the ratio of net income to the average shareholders' equity needed to produce those profits. Shareholders' equity represents the investor's stake in the net assets of a company. When a company posts a high ROE, that suggests it is efficiently using the funds shareholders have provided.

Earnings Growth Variability

This metric measures a company's ability to generate consistent profit growth over time. The higher the variability of earnings around a company's long-term earnings trend line, the more uncertain investors are of a company achieving its growth target. And variability in earnings growth can lead to huge volatility in stock price.

Revenue Growth Variability

This metric measures a company's ability to deliver steady revenue growth over time. The higher the variability of sales around a company's long-term revenue trend line, the more uncertain investors are of the company's achieving its revenue forecasts.

Bear Market Performance

This factor evaluates the monthly performance of a stock during bear markets. In contrast to other risk measures, such as standard deviation, the factor measures volatility only during market downturns. A market downturn is considered any month the S&P 500 Index dips more than 3 percent.

Worst Stock Price Performance

This factor represents a stock's worst consecutive three-month performance during the past five years. A good downside risk measure, the factor can shed light on a stock's short-term volatility.

Standard Deviation—Three Years

A traditional way of measuring risk, this factor gauges how much (in either direction) stock prices have varied. A high standard deviation indicates volatile performance. In general, investors demand higher total returns from more volatile stocks.

Price/Sales Relative to Five-Year Average

This is calculated by dividing a stock's price by a company's trailing 12-month sales per share and comparing that number to the five-year average. Typically, the lower the price/sales ratio, the better the chance a stock is undervalued or is trading at depressed levels.

Price/Earnings Relative to Five-Year Average

This metric is calculated by dividing a stock's price by a company's trailing 12-month earnings per share and comparing that number to the five-year average. The ratio gives investors an idea of how much they are paying for a company's profits. Usually, the lower the price/earnings ratio, the choppier the growth record.

Price/Earnings Versus the S&P 500 Index

This metric looks at a stock's price/earnings ratio relative to the S&P 500's P/E multiple. Value stocks typically have below-market P/E ratios. The idea is that a value stock is considered cheap by the market and is usually viewed as a more conservative holding. Growth stocks, which have accelerating sales and profits, usually trade at more lofty P/E ratios.

What I like about these 15 criteria is that they do a nice job of capturing

- how well a stock has behaved during up and down markets relative to the market and other stocks

- the underlying quality of the company's fundamentals

- the relative value of the stock

I also like the fact that the criteria look back over not only the last year, but also the last five years. That's important. Factors that look at short time periods can be misleading. However, given the tremendous variety in markets (growth versus value, bull market versus bear market) over the last five years, looking at metrics over that five-year period can be extremely useful in determining a stock's easy-hold qualities.

RUN THE NUMBERS

Armed with these criteria, Dave and I set out to give easy-hold ratings to all of the stocks in the Russell 3000. Since some of the stocks either had no data available or have not been around for five years, the number of stocks actually rated was reduced to around 1,500.

Each company received a percentile rank for each of the 15 factors. The ranks were then averaged. Finally, the equal-weighted averages were ranked, with 100 being the highest possible score.

Keep in mind that the final score is the stock's percentile rank. In other words, a stock with an easy-hold rating of 95 means the stock scores better than 95 percent of the 1,500 stocks rated.

To see how well your stocks scored in our easy-hold rating system, check out Appendix B. In addition to an alphabetical listing of stocks and their easy-hold ratings, a list of the best easy-hold stocks (Appendix D), along with breakdowns by industry groups (Appendix C), are provided.

TOP EASY HOLDS—STOCKS

The following are reviews of some of my favorite easy-hold stocks. All of these stocks ranked in the top quartile of our easy-hold rating system. These stocks all represent excellent building blocks for an easy-hold portfolio.

Alltel (AT)—Telecommunications—Alltel is an interesting play in the telecom sector. The firm has exposure to the long-distance, local, and wireless markets. The firm's niche is in more rural areas. This niche has limited competition in its major markets. Business has held up extremely well relative to that of its peers. The wireless business, in particular, has been a good growth area for the firm. The company also has a growing business in information services, including services for the financial-services industry. Telecom stocks have been slaughtered over the last two years, although Alltel has given a relatively good account of itself. These shares represent a solid easy-hold play in a sector that is down but should rebound nicely over the next five years. *Easy-Hold Rating: 91*

Automatic Data Processing (ADP)—Business/Computer Services— Here's the big reason Automatic Data Processing rates so high on our easy-hold scale—40 consecutive years of higher earnings. That's right—40 straight years of earnings growth. The company has achieved such an impressive growth record by virtue of its market-leading position in payroll-processing and tax-filing services for corporate America. Other services include back-office record-keeping services for the brokerage community, as well as services for auto and truck dealerships. As you would expect, such a strong record of growth has led to a strong stock performance. Automatic Data Processing stock has gone up roughly fivefold over the last decade. These shares are never cheap; the stock usually sports a price/earnings ratio well above the market average. Still, you don't buy such quality cheaply. *Easy-Hold Rating: 92*

*BISYS Group (BSYS)—Data Processing—*BISYS provides outsourcing services for financial institutions. Services include check-imaging applications, brokerage services, mutual fund record-keeping services, and bank-automation tools. The firm also provides various services for the insurance industry. BISYS has been a big beneficiary of the trend in corporate America to outsource data-processing and billing services. Per-share profits have risen nicely in the last five years, and further growth in the bottom line is expected. Long-term acquisitions and new products should drive revenue and profits. BISYS stock has marched steadily higher over the last five years, and I expect these shares to continue to do well. For investors looking for a play in the financial-services sector, these shares hold ample appeal. *Easy-Hold Rating: 90*

Datascope (DSCP)—Medical Equipment—Datascope is probably not a household word for many investors, but the company's performance over the years takes a backseat to no company. The firm manufactures cardiac-assist products, such as intra-aortic balloon pumps. The firm also makes monitors that measure heart rate, blood pressure, and oxygen levels. Per-share profits have risen every year since 1990. The company's stock price has trended higher over the last eight years. The company is on the small side relative to other firms listed here; annual sales are less than $400 million. That size makes these shares an interesting takeover candidate. Finances are solid, with no long-term debt. The stock should produce steady returns for investors over the next several years. *Easy-Hold Rating: 91*

Duke Energy (DUK)—Electric Utility—One of the top easy-hold groups is the electric utility sector. Primarily because utilities tend to hold up reasonably well during market downturns, many electric utilities score in the top quintile in the easy-hold ratings. One of the best utilities in the market is Duke Energy. The company provides electricity services to more than 2 million customers in North and South Carolina. Duke's nonutility businesses, especially its wholesale power unit, have solid growth potential. In fact, it is excitement over nonutility businesses that has helped Duke trade more like a growth stock since the beginning of 2000. The company's international operations provide another avenue for growth. Because Duke is becoming more like a growth stock— per-share profits should rise in double digits this year—you could see these shares become a bit more volatile going forward. Still, the stock provides an excellent way to gain exposure to the utility sector without sacrificing too much in terms of growth. Duke Energy offers an easy way to buy the stock. Indeed, any investor may buy shares directly from the company, without a broker, via the firm's direct-purchase plan. (More on direct-purchase plans is provided in Chapter 6.) This applies to the initial purchase as well as subsequent purchases. Minimum initial investment is $250. For enrollment information for Duke Energy's direct-purchase plan, call (800) 488-3853. *Easy-Hold Rating: 98*

Duke Realty (DRE)—Real Estate Investment Trust—I've never been a big fan of real estate investment trusts. Still, during volatile market periods, REITs tend to hold up very well. While I wouldn't want a portfolio composed entirely of REITs, these investments provide nice ballast during stormy markets. One of my favorite REITs is Duke Realty. The company was formed via the 1999 merger of Duke Realty and Weeks Corp. The company is one of the largest mixed office/industrial real estate companies in the United States. The fully integrated company owns interests in more than 109 million square feet of properties across the Midwest and the Sun Belt. Duke Realty stands above its competition on several fronts. The company has an impressive record of double-digit growth in funds from operations per share. The firm has accomplished this impressive growth record during good and bad times in the real estate market. Another impressive statistic is that the firm has increased its dividend every year since 1993. The stock provides a good choice for dividend yield and reasonable appreciation. And you can buy the stock directly, the first share and every share, without paying any purchase fees. Minimum initial investment is $250. Enrollment information for the company's direct-purchase plan may be obtained by calling (800) 278-4353. *Easy-Hold Rating: 97*

Equifax (EFX)—Business Services—Equifax provides a variety of marketing and credit-information services. The company has benefited from low mortgage rates and the refinancing boom of the last few years. I'm a big fan of information-services companies because of their high profit margins and ability to generate new products from their massive information database. Equifax expanded its operations with the addition of R. L. Polk in 2000. I look for high-single-digit/low-double-digit growth on an annual basis. I own Equifax and expect it to continue to make me money. The company's easy-hold rating puts the stock in the top 5 percent of all rated companies. Equifax allows investors to buy the first share and every share directly from the company. Minimum initial investment is $500. For enrollment information, call (888) 887-2971. *Easy-Hold Rating: 95*

Exxon Mobil (XOM)—Oil—I've owned Exxon for roughly 10 years and have found these shares to be the quintessential easy hold. The company's consistent results and the stock's steady performance have made these shares the perfect complement to a growth portfolio. What is especially impressive is that Exxon Mobil has remained consistent despite huge swings in oil prices. Exxon's big global presence and diversified business lines have shielded Exxon from volatility in any one region or sector of the energy business. A rising dividend stream enhances appeal. While there may be oil stocks that show bigger gains during cyclical upswings in the group, it's tough to find an oil stock that will provide consistently steady returns through strong or weak periods in the industry. Exxon Mobil allows you to buy the first share and every share directly, without a broker and without any fees. The firm also offers an IRA option in its direct-purchase plan. Minimum initial investment is $250. For enrollment information, call (800) 252-1800. *Easy-Hold Rating: 77*

*Gannett (GCI)—Publishing—*Gannett publishes about 400 newspapers. The flagship publication is *USA Today*. Other prominent dailies include *Detroit News* and *Arizona Republic*. The firm also owns more than 20 network-affiliated television stations. Earnings are affected periodically from a slowdown in the economy or a sluggish ad market. However, Gannett is one of the better-managed companies in its business. The stock held up relatively well over the last 12 months, a testament to its status as a top easy-hold stock in the publishing sector. While a prolonged slump in the ad market will be felt in the company's bottom line, I would have no problem holding the stock in a portfolio for its long-term growth potential. *Easy-Hold Rating: 88*

*General Electric (GE)—Conglomerate/Electric Equipment—*Remember that a big part of being an easy-hold stock is consistency—that is, consistency in earnings and sales growth, consistency in stock performance, consistency in valuation relative to the market. When you think in those terms, one stock that would be tough to exclude from any top easy-hold list is General Electric. This sprawling conglomerate—with operations in such fields as broadcasting (NBC), finance (GE Capital), airplane engines, and electrical equipment—has one of the most impressive earnings and sales records of any major corporation. A lot of that success is due to the company's take-no-prisoners attitude when it comes to its markets. Indeed, GE plays only in markets in which it is either one or two. Thus, unless the firm can dominate a market—and earn the high returns that such domination brings—it doesn't waste its time or corporate resources. To be sure, the company is in a transition stage now that revered leader Jack Welch is no longer running the company. But GE is deep in terms of management talent and should be able to weather the change in management just fine. While I don't see the stock providing the type of oversized gains that we saw for much of the 1980s and 1990s, I do expect the stock to continue to outperform the overall market in the long term. General Electric permits investors to buy stock directly from the company, the first share and every share. Minimum initial investment is $250. For enrollment information in the company's direct-purchase plan, call (800) 786-2543. *Easy-Hold Rating: 85*

*Guidant (GDT)—Medical Technology—*Guidant is one of the world's largest medical-device companies. The firm offers a range of products, including stents to treat vascular diseases. Guidant had been a very fast grower until 2001, when increased competition hindered growth. However, Guidant has a record of developing in-demand products, and strong research and development should fuel further product development. Guidant usually trades at a premium price/earnings ratio. Thus, anytime you can buy the stock at a market price/earnings ratio, you should take advantage of the opportunity. The stock traded for more than $75 in 2000 and has the ability to post substantial gains for investors. Guidant permits investors to buy the first share and every share directly from the company, without a broker. Minimum initial investment is $250. For enrollment information, call (800) 537-1677. *Easy-Hold Rating: 96*

*Harley-Davidson (HDI)—Transportation Equipment—*Here's an Easy Rider that's an Easy Hold. Harley-Davidson has demonstrated impressive resiliency despite market conditions. In fact, the stock has achieved a higher high every year except one since 1990, and that includes 2000 and 2001. Demand for its motorcycles shows no signs of slowing, and the firm has done a good job of meeting the voracious demand by boosting production. Harley-Davidson is an interesting play on strong brands, the increase of leisure time for baby boomers, and the propensity for Americans to do more on-ground travel. The stock is never cheap. Still, these shares are a suitable holding for any portfolio. *Easy-Hold Rating: 76*

Johnson & Johnson (JNJ)—Health Care/Household Products—For a glimpse at Johnson & Johnson's staying power during rough markets, just look at what the stock did during 2001. Indeed, during a very difficult market period for most stocks, including health-care issues, Johnson & Johnson forged to new all-time highs. Pushing the stock higher were solid gains in net income and revenue for the company. Johnson & Johnson's diversified base in the health-care sector—the firm does big business in everything from medical-technology products to pharmaceuticals and over-the-counter remedies—has helped the bottom line hold up better than competitors. Finances are quite strong and should afford further acquisitions. Johnson & Johnson has been extremely effective in making growth via acquisitions work over the last decade. For a broad-based play in the health-care sector, you'd be hard-pressed to find a more consistent player than Johnson & Johnson. This stock has made a higher high every year but one (and the year it failed, it missed by less than $1) since 1993. *Easy-Hold Rating: 78*

Johnson Controls (JCI)—Automotive Parts—Johnson Controls has operations in two areas. Its automotive systems group supplies heating systems, interior systems, and batteries to auto companies. This unit comprises roughly three-quarters of total sales and profits. The company's controls group provides lighting, security, fire protection, and heating and cooling systems for commercial buildings. What sets Johnson Controls apart is its consistent earnings record and steady upward trend in the stock price—both practically unheard of for a company in seemingly cyclical industries. While growth could slow with a soft economy, I would expect earnings to rebound nicely as demand recovers in its primary markets. With an easy-hold score of 87, Johnson Controls represents an attractive way to play the auto sector without the volatility. Johnson Controls offers a direct-purchase plan for investors. Minimum initial investment is $250. For enrollment information, call (800) 524-6220. *Easy-Hold Rating: 87*

Microsoft (MSFT)—Computer Software—Technology stocks don't have a reputation for being easy holds. Indeed, the roller-coaster ride that many techs have given investors over the last four years has no doubt left a bad taste in the mouths of buy-and-hold investors. Having said that, some technology stocks are a lot better than others in terms of providing relatively easy holds for buy-and-holders who want representation in the tech sector. Within the techs, Microsoft ranks quite well as an easy hold. One reason is that the stock's market-leading position and strong finances—the firm has some $36 billion in cash assets—give it support during rocky periods for the tech sector. During tough markets, the strong usually get stronger. I suspect Microsoft will come out of this technology slowdown a much stronger company, which bodes well for long-term capital gains. *Easy-Hold Rating: 87*

Patterson Dental (PDCO)—Health Care—Patterson Dental distributes dental supplies. The firm also offers related services, such as equipment installation, maintenance, and equipment financing. The company has expanded into the market for veterinary products. The firm's marketing and distribution is spearheaded by more than 1,000 direct-sales reps and equipment specialists. Per-share profits have risen every year since the company went public in 1992. Double-digit growth in sales and earnings should continue. The stock has split three times since 1993. Patterson Dental stock has posted a higher high every year since 1992. Finances are solid, with no long-term debt. The stock provides a nice niche play in the health-care sector. *Easy-Hold Rating: 93*

Pfizer (PFE)—Drugs—With the addition of Warner-Lambert, Pfizer is the second-largest drug company in the world. During a time when many drug companies are finding products under siege from generic competitors, Pfizer is solidifying its position as the top growth play in the drug sector. Leading products include Norvasc (cardiovascular), Zoloft (antidepressant), Viagra (impotence), Diflucan (antifungal), Celebrex (rheumatoid arthritis), Zyrtec (antihistamine), and Aricept (Alzheimer's). As far as patent protection, nine of the firm's 10 leading products have significant remaining patent protection in the United States, with expirations ranging from 2004 through 2017. The company will spend some $5 billion on research and development this year. That spending should continue to add to the firm's impressive stable of drugs, including eight medications with annual sales of at least $1 billion. The firm should turn in 20-percent-plus growth over the next several years. Not only is Pfizer an easy hold, it's also an easy buy. Indeed, the company allows any investor to buy even initial shares directly, and Pfizer doesn't charge a penny in commission. For enrollment information, call (800) 733-9393. *Easy-Hold Rating: 83*

Philadelphia Suburban (PSC)—Water Utility—Philadelphia Suburban does the impossible every day—turn water into gold. Indeed, this leading water utility has an excellent track record of earnings growth, and I expect profits to continue to move higher over the next several years. It is important to understand that water is an increasingly precious commodity in many parts of the country. I expect that the increased demand for water over the next several years will put water suppliers like Philadelphia Suburban in a strong position. One kicker to these shares is their takeover potential. Vivendi, a French conglomerate with water businesses, owns roughly 18 percent of Philadelphia Suburban and could decide to buy the company down the road. To be sure, I don't expect Philadelphia Suburban to lead the market during strong rallies. I do, however, expect these shares to provide solid total returns over the next several years and regard the stock as a good diversifier for a portfolio. Investors should note that Philadelphia Suburban has an extremely investor-friendly direct-purchase plan. Minimum initial investment is $500. The firm does not charge a penny in commission. Stock purchased with reinvested dividends will receive a 5 percent discount. For enrollment information, call (800) 205-8314. *Easy-Hold Rating: 78*

Popular (BPOP)—Banking—Popular has banking outlets in Puerto Rico, surrounding Caribbean and Latin American countries, and the United States. I like several things about Popular. First, I'm impressed with the firm's consistent earnings record. The company has posted higher per-share profits every year since 1991. The strong and steady profit growth has fueled rising dividends. Indeed, the dividend has doubled since 1996. Another attraction is the firm's niche in a growing market segment. Not only is the Hispanic population grow-ing at a rapid rate, but also income levels in the Hispanic community should trend upward. This is good news for Popular, which is the banker of choice for this increasingly powerful economic group. Regional banks usually provide decent staying power during rocky markets. Popular offers one of the better plays in the group. I own these shares and recommend them for conservative growth accounts. Popular's stock may be bought directly, the first share and every share. Minimum initial investment is $100. Popular doesn't charge a penny in commission. Even better, shares purchased with reinvested dividends will receive a 5 percent discount. For an enrollment form, call (877) 764-1893. Be warned that the individual answering the phone will probably speak Spanish. Don't hang up. The individual also understands English, so make your request for information about the direct-purchase plan. You might find it easier to obtain an enrollment form from the company's Web site—www.popularinc.com. In fact, most companies that have direct-purchase plans make the enrollment information available on their Web sites. *Easy-Hold Rating: 86*

Southwest Airlines (LUV)—Airlines—In an industry where it is notoriously difficult to make a buck, Southwest Airlines has done it better than any other company. An attention to costs, solid labor rela-tions, and a well-conceived expansion program have helped the com-pany post an impressive earnings record. Wall Street has rewarded this consistent performance, as the stock has trended higher over the last decade. Southwest Airlines has felt the effects of a decline in air-line traffic that occurred following the September 11, 2001, terrorist attacks. However, it is not unusual for strong companies to get even stronger during industry crises. That should be the case with South-west Airlines. While I'm not a huge fan of most transportation issues due to the cyclical nature of their business, having some representa-tion in the group is a good idea. Southwest Airlines offers the best easy hold in the transportation sector and would be a good holding in any portfolio. *Easy-Hold Rating: 80*

SunGard Data Systems (SDS)—Computer System/Software—Sun-Gard's largest segment in terms of revenue (73 percent) and profit (66 percent) is its application software for investment support systems. The company also provides various Internet services for corporations. SunGard processes roughly 70 percent of all Nasdaq trades and provides infrastructure services to markets on a global basis. This global reach is important given the likelihood of further growth in foreign markets over the next decade. Per-share profits have risen every year going back to 1985. The company has grown via strategic acquisitions that have helped to fill out its product line in the investment applications area. I've had dealings with this company over the years and have found the firm and its employees to be extremely competent and especially savvy when it comes to operating a business for profit. I would have no problem owning this stock in a growth portfolio. *Easy-Hold Rating: 90*

Sysco (SYY)—Food Services—The biggest nightmare for investors is uncertainty. That's why Wall Street pays a big premium for companies that produce consistent results quarter after quarter after quarter. One firm that has consistently met Wall Street's expectations is Sysco. The company is the leading provider of food and related products to the food-service industry. Sysco has posted record revenue and profits every year for more than two decades. Such consistent top-line and bottom-line growth has helped the stock post a higher high every year except one since 1994. In other words, even if you bought Sysco at its highest level each year over the last eight years, you still would have made plenty of money. Two financial ratios that are especially telling when evaluating a company are operating profit margins and return on equity. Sysco's operating margins have risen steadily over the last decade and are near 6 percent. Margins are razor thin in this industry, so Sysco's ability to boost margins reflects the strength of management and leadership position in its markets. Return on equity is over 27 percent, up from 17 percent in 1993. I know the food-service industry does not have lots of sex appeal. However, Sysco's track record of growth holds up well against most companies. *Easy-Hold Rating: 84*

Wal-Mart Stores (WMT)—Retailing—When it comes to retailing, it is tough to beat Wal-Mart Stores. The firm continues to crank out impressive sales-growth numbers even when the rest of the retailing sector is floundering. The firm continues to expand its supercenter store concept by double-digit numbers on an annual basis. Growth here, coupled with further international expansion, should help profits grow nicely over the next several years. In fact, profit growth could even accelerate over the next couple of years—no small feat for a company the size of Wal-Mart (more than $200 billion in sales annually). Wal-Mart stock has been marking time in the last few years. That sideways trading pattern may not be all that exciting until you put it into the context of what has been happening to the rest of the market. To be sure, these shares are not likely to provide the huge gains that investors experienced early in the company's growth cycle. Still, as far as easy holds go in the retailing sector, Wal-Mart is one of the best. Wal-Mart Stores offers a direct-purchase plan for investors. Minimum initial investment is $250, although Wal-Mart will waive the minimum if an investor agrees to monthly automatic investments (via electronic debit of a bank account) of at least $25. For enrollment information, call (800) 438-6278. *Easy-Hold Rating: 80*

Walgreen (WAG)—Drugstores—One of my all-time favorite stocks is Walgreen. The company is the largest player in the drugstore sector. Walgreen gives you a nice combo play on retailing and health care. The firm fills roughly 11 percent of the nation's retail drug prescriptions. Given the aging of America, there's plenty of growth ahead in this sector. The firm has posted record profits and sales for more than 25 years, and that growth record should stay intact for the foreseeable future. Long-term growth should be fueled by the company's online pharmacy presence. I've owned these shares for years and have been very happy with their performance. Walgreen offers a direct-purchase plan for investors. Initial shares may be made with a minimum of just $50. For enrollment information, call (800) 286-9178. *Easy-Hold Rating: 93*

Waters (WAT)—Measuring Devices—An attractive way to invest in sexy industries is to buy the company that makes the "picks and shovels" for that industry. Waters is the "arms supplier" for biotechnology companies. The firm is the largest supplier in the world of high-performance liquid chromatography instruments. These products are used to identify and analyze the components of a variety of chemicals and materials. Drug companies use Waters's products to help identify protein characteristics in patients' cells and thus improve testing. Given the long-term growth potential of the biotechnology sector, Waters should see its products remain in demand. This stock may be more volatile than the typical easy-hold stock. However, within the high-technology medical sector, the stock scores very well. These shares represent a solid holding within a diversified portfolio of easy holds. *Easy-Hold Rating: 79*

Top Easy Holds—Mutual Funds

I realize that many investors prefer owning mutual funds to owning individual stocks. Also, in most 401(k) plans, the only investment options are mutual funds. Thus, it is important that buy-and-hold investors have some way to evaluate the easy-hold attributes of mutual funds.

To that end, Dave and I came up with a variety of easy-hold criteria for mutual funds. Again, as was the case with individual stocks, the perfect easy-hold mutual fund would be one that

- provides acceptable returns during strong markets and good relative price resiliency during down markets

- limits volatility of returns from one year to the next

- ranks well relative to its peers in risk-adjusted returns

With these qualitative concepts in mind, David and I put together 11 criteria on which to evaluate the "easy-hold" attributes of domestic equity funds. The source for this information is Morningstar (www .morningstar.com).

Relative Performance Versus Group Average

This metric evaluates a fund's performance versus the risk-free Treasury bill and peer-group averages. Funds that consistently underperform the T-bill rate do not reward investors for taking on risk.

Relative Performance Versus Asset Class—Three Years

Similar to the factor listed above, this factor evaluates a fund's performance versus the risk-free Treasury bill and major asset class (stock funds). Funds that consistently trail T-bills and the market are considered laggards.

Load-Adjusted Total Return—One Year

A fund's 12-month total return adjusted for front-end loads (up-front sales charge) and deferred loads (back-end sales charge).

Load-Adjusted Total Return—Three Years

A fund's three-year total return adjusted for front-end loads (up-front sales charge) and deferred loads (back-end sales charge).

Sharpe Ratio

This ratio is used to gauge risk-adjusted return. It is calculated by dividing a fund's excess total return (return minus the T-bill rate) by its three-year standard deviation. The higher the Sharpe ratio, the better a fund's risk-adjusted performance.

Beta

Beta measures a fund's sensitivity to the overall market. Low-beta funds have less market-related risk than do high-beta funds.

Alpha

Alpha is used to measure the value added (or subtracted) by a portfolio manager. It is calculated as the difference between a fund's actual total return and its expected performance, given its level of risk as measured by beta. A positive alpha figure indicates that the fund has performed better than its beta would predict.

Standard Deviation—Three Years

This factor is used to evaluate a fund's total risk or volatility. A high standard deviation implies greater volatility over time. Moreover, the higher the standard deviation, the more uncertain an investor is of achieving a desired return.

Yield

This is the sum of a fund's trailing 12-month income distributions divided by its net asset value per share. For stock funds, income refers only to dividends from common stocks.

Bear Market Performance

This factor evaluates the monthly performance of a fund during market downturns. In contrast to other risk measures, such as standard deviation, the factor measures volatility only during bear markets. For stock funds, a market downturn is considered any month the S&P 500 Index dips more than 3 percent.

Expense Ratio

This is the percentage of fund assets consumed by management fees, 12b-1 fees, and other costs incurred by a mutual fund. High expenses can be a huge drag on fund performance. Cheaper funds have an easier time outperforming the market over time.

Armed with these criteria, David and I rated some 1,200 mutual funds to determine their easy-hold status. The scores represent percentile rankings, with 100 being the highest score. The results of these ratings are provided in Appendix E. In addition to an alphabetical listing of funds, the best easy-hold funds are listed in Appendix F.

Please note that the funds are all domestic equity funds. We did not rate foreign mutual funds. Also, we excluded funds that held less than 60 percent of assets in equities. We also excluded funds with very high minimum initial investments. We did include load and no-load funds.

The following are reviews of 10 top-rated easy-hold funds. The fund's stock symbol and Morningstar-style category are provided, along with a contact telephone number.

American Century Equity Income (TWEIX)—Mid-Cap Value— American Century seeks current income first, with capital appreciation as a secondary objective. Typically, the fund invests at least 65 percent of assets in stocks. The fund managers look for companies with favorable dividend-paying histories and capital-appreciation potential. They also screen for undervalued, leading companies that have temporary issues impacting the price of their shares. The financial sector, which includes insurance companies, banks, and brokerage firms, represents one of the fund's largest sector bets. The fund also has a sizable stake in industrial stocks. The fund, which yields better than 2 percent, may be appropriate for investors who seek income along with long-term growth. The fund ranks among the top one-third of its category for five-year annual return. American Century Equity Income, which started in 1994, is a no-load fund. The minimum initial investment is $2,500, and $1,000 to open an IRA. The fund offers an automatic investment plan. For enrollment information, call (800) 345-2021. *Easy-Hold Rating: 100*

Clipper (CFIMX)—Large-Cap Value—Clipper invests mostly in large-cap value stocks. The management team looks for dominant companies generating healthy cash flow in industries that are out of favor. The managers adhere to a disciplined value approach, focusing on stocks that appear mispriced relative to a company's underlying intrinsic value. Stocks are sold when their share price hits that intrinsic value. If a position is sold and no other opportunities are available with a meaningful margin of safety, the proceeds are put into cash or bonds. Management concentrates on their best ideas subject to reasonable portfolio diversification. Thus, the fund usually invests in only 20 to 35 stocks. Most stocks are held for the long haul, resulting in low portfolio turnover. Clipper, which opened its doors in 1984, is a no-load fund. The minimum initial investment is $5,000, and $2,000 to open an IRA. The fund offers an automatic investment plan. For enrollment information, call (800) 776-5033. *Easy-Hold Rating: 100*

*Dodge & Cox Stock (DODGX)—Large-Cap Value—*Dodge & Cox stock invests in a broadly diversified portfolio. The fund focuses on stocks that appear to be temporarily undervalued by the market but have solid prospects for long-term growth. The management team screens for future earnings growth, cash flow, and financial strength. And while the fund holds mostly large-company stocks, mid-cap stocks account for roughly one-third of the portfolio. The fund maintains a sizable stake in industrial and financial stocks. Dodge & Cox adheres to a buy-and-hold approach. That strategy helps keep portfolio turnover low. And the fund's expense ratio is far below category averages. The fund, left behind when technology stocks soared, nonetheless has notched solid long-term gains. Dodge & Cox Stock, which opened its doors in 1965, is a no-load fund. The minimum initial investment is $2,500, and $1,000 to open an IRA. The fund offers an automatic investment plan. For enrollment information, call (800) 621-3979. *Easy-Hold Rating: 99*

*Fidelity Low-Priced Stock (FLPSX)—Small-Cap Value—*Fidelity Low-Priced stock normally invests in stocks trading at $35 or less at time of purchase. That strategy leads to hefty exposure to small- and medium-sized companies. At any given time, the portfolio manager may be buying growth stocks, value stocks, or both. Recently, the fund's solid relative performance is due largely to its focus on companies that have continued to grow earnings even in a difficult economic environment. The fund's technology position consists of companies with recurring service revenues, particularly in the area of business outsourcing. Moreover, the fund's emphasis on current profitability enabled it to avoid most of the Internet-related meltdowns. Fidelity Low-Priced Stock, which opened to investors in 1989, charges a 3 percent load. The minimum initial investment is $2,500, and $500 to open an IRA. The fund offers an automatic investment plan. For enrollment information, call (800) 544-8888. *Easy-Hold Rating: 99*

*Jensen (JENSX)—Large-Cap Growth—*Jensen offers a relatively low-risk play on large-cap growth stocks. The median market value of the stocks in the portfolio surpasses $15 billion. Jensen has held up well in choppy markets, buoyed by the downside protection of owning blue chips. A diverse collection of companies results in fairly broad industry diversification. Top holdings are giants such as Automatic Data Processing, Clorox, and Equifax. Typically, the fund buys companies with solid track records of delivering good growth and high returns on equity. Thanks to modest technology holdings, the fund soared 20 percent in 2000, compared to a loss of 14.5 percent for the average large-cap growth fund. Jensen, which opened in 1992, is a no-load fund. The minimum initial investment is $1,000 for both regular accounts and IRAs. The fund offers an automatic investment plan. For enrollment information, call (800) 221-4384. *Easy-Hold Rating: 93*

Mairs & Power Growth (MPGFX)—Mid-Cap Blend—Longtime portfolio manager George Mairs III focuses on companies with reasonably predictable profits, high returns on equity, and solid market positions. Because Mairs believes that smaller companies generate somewhat higher returns over time, small- and mid-caps make up a healthy chunk of the fund. Mairs usually keeps the portfolio fully invested in stocks. Portfolio turnover is very low, which makes the fund reasonably tax friendly. Stocks are held for relatively long periods to allow for compounding to build wealth. Mairs & Power Growth, which opened to investors in 1958, is a no-load fund. The fund is not available in every state. The minimum initial investment is $2,500, and $1,000 to open an IRA. The fund offers an automatic investment plan. For enrollment information, call (800) 304-7404. *Easy-Hold Rating: 99*

Meridian Value (MVALX)—Mid-Cap Blend—Meridian Value offers solid long-term performance and modest volatility. The fund shuns stocks with stretched valuations. Instead, Meridian holds stocks that have already been knocked down and seem poised for a recovery. The stocks that make the cut usually have a catalyst for growth. The fund invests mostly in small and mid-sized companies. Currently, the fund favors stock in such sectors as services, technology, and health care. The fund ranks among the top 5 percent of mid-cap funds for five-year performance. The fund has had no down years since inception. Its best year, 1999, saw a 38 percent gain. Meridian Value, which started in 1994, is a no-load fund. The minimum initial investment is $1,000, and $1,000 to open an IRA. The fund offers an automatic investment plan. For enrollment information, call (800) 446-6662. *Easy-Hold Rating: 98*

Oakmark Equity & Income (OAKBX)—Domestic Hybrid—Oakmark Equity & Income invests for high current income as well as preservation and growth of capital. The fund is mostly made up of U.S. stocks (roughly 60 percent of assets) and bonds (30 percent). The fund is appropriate for investors who want stock exposure yet desire the downside cushion of bonds. The portfolio is heavy on small and mid-sized companies. Comanagers Clyde McGregor and Edward Studzinski are value investors. They look for companies trading at a discount to the business value. McGregor and Studzinski avoid market timing. The managers believe that, over time, a stock's price will rise to reflect the value of the underlying company. The fund has never had a losing year. Oakmark Equity & Income, which began in 1995, is a no-load fund. The minimum initial investment is $1,000 for both regular accounts and IRAs. The fund offers an automatic investment plan. For enrollment information, call (800) 625-6275. *Easy-Hold Rating: 100*

Pennsylvania Mutual (PENNX)—Small-Cap Value—Pennsylvania Mutual seeks long-term capital appreciation by investing primarily in small- and micro-cap companies. The fund defines small-cap as companies with market values of less than $2 billion. Micro-cap companies typically have market values below $400 million. Pennsylvania's long-term track record is impressive—total returns have been positive in 25 of the last 28 years. To mitigate risk, the fund holds relatively smaller positions in a larger number of securities. The fund sports a below-average portfolio turnover. The 10 largest holdings usually make up about 15 percent of total assets. Top sectors include industrials, financials, and technology. At just over 1 percent, the fund's expense ratio is far below peer averages. Pennsylvania Mutual, which opened its doors in 1962, is a no-load fund. There is a 1 percent redemption fee. The minimum initial investment is $2,000, and $500 to open an IRA. The fund offers an automatic investment plan. For enrollment information, call (800) 221-4268. *Easy-Hold Rating: 100*

T. Rowe Price Small-Cap Value (PRSVX)—Small-Cap Blend— T. Rowe Price Small-Cap Value seeks long-term capital growth by investing mostly in companies with market values of less than $1 billion. Micro-cap stocks make up a large portion of the portfolio. The stocks selected are considered undervalued as measured by assets, earnings, cash flow, or business franchises. Portfolio manager Preston Athey also looks for companies with above-average dividend yields relative to their peers and solid finances. Athey lets his winners ride—the fund does not sell a stock just because a company's market value has topped $1 billion. The fund's 10-year annual total return ranks among the top one-third of small-cap funds. T. Rowe Price Small-Cap Value, which opened in 1988, is a no-load fund. The minimum initial investment is $2,500, and $1,000 to open an IRA. The fund offers an automatic investment plan. For enrollment information, call (800) 638-5660. *Easy-Hold Rating: 99*

EASY HOLDS—FIXED-INCOME INVESTMENTS

I think most investors believe that the entire spectrum of "fixed-income" investments—corporate bonds, Treasury securities, municipal bonds, zero-coupon bonds, junk bonds—are all easy-hold investments. To be sure, fixed-income investments don't usually have the risk (as measured by volatility of returns) of stocks. However, risk levels do differ within the fixed-income universe.

There are four primary risk measures to consider when examining fixed-income investments:

- Credit risk

- Interest-rate risk

- Reinvestment risk

- Inflation risk

Credit risk refers to the risk of a default on the investment. When a company or government entity issues a bond, there is always the possibility that the entity will not be able to pay interest or repurchase the bond at the time of maturity. For many companies, the possibility is remote. For others, however, default risk is very real. Obviously, the greater the risk of default, the more an investor needs to be compensated for the risk of default by receiving a higher coupon on the bond. That's why "junk" bonds—bonds issued by corporations with poor credit—pay much higher yields than bonds issued by corporations with strong finances. If you want to reduce credit risk, focus on corporate or municipal bonds with AA ratings or better.

Interest-rate risk refers to the sensitivity of bond prices to changes in interest rates. Here's an important lesson when investing in bonds: When interest rates rise, bond prices fall, and vice versa. Now, how much bond prices fluctuate depends on two factors: the maturity of the bond, and the coupon rate on the bond. All things equal, the shorter the maturity of the bond, the less vulnerable the bond is to interest-rate movements. Thus, short-term bonds (bonds with maturities of less than three years) are less sensitive to interest-rate movements than are long-term bonds (bonds with maturities of at least 15 years). Also, bonds with high coupon rates are less vulnerable to interest-rate movements than are bonds with low coupon rates.

Understanding the relationship between interest rates and bond prices is critical when selecting easy-hold investments in the bond sector. For example, a 20-year zero-coupon bond is going to be extremely sensitive to interest-rate movements (long maturity, zero coupon rate).

If you want to protect against interest-rate risk, stick with fixed-income investments with short-term to intermediate-term maturities. That means maturities of eight years or less.

Reinvestment risk pertains to the risk incurred with having to reinvest the principal and cash flows from fixed-income investments. To understand reinvestment risk, think of the money you earn on your one-year certificate of deposit. Let's say the yield is 4 percent, which means you'll earn $40 in interest on the $1,000 one-year CD. Now, a year goes by and the CD matures. Unfortunately, rates on new CDs have fallen to 3 percent. Thus, if you buy another one-year CD, you'll receive only $30 per year in interest payments.

As you can see, reinvestment risk depends partly on the maturity of the fixed-income investment. The longer the maturity, the longer you "lock up" the coupon rate.

One way to handle reinvestment risk is by "laddering" fixed-income investments. Laddering refers to buying fixed-income investments of varying maturities—short term to long term. In that way, you stagger when your fixed-income investments mature and reduce the impact of reinvestment risk on your portfolio.

Inflation risk is a risk common to all fixed-income investments. Inflation erodes the value of the fixed stream of cash flows thrown off by fixed-income investments.

For example, let's say you own a bond that pays a 5 percent coupon rate for the next 15 years, and you bought the bond at par ($1,000). That means you'll receive $50 per year in interest on this bond for the next 15 years. The problem with this and every other bond payment, however, is that inflation will erode the purchasing power of that fixed income stream. In fact, let's say inflation averages 5 percent per year for that 15-year period. What will happen to the *real* purchasing power of that $50 interest payment? It will erode dramatically.

The ill effects of inflation are what create this paradox when it comes to bond investments. On the one hand, the volatility of bonds is much lower than that of stocks. On the other hand, while your bond investment is sitting still, in reality it is losing money due to the stealth attack from inflation.

Inflation risk is perhaps the most dangerous risk to long-term fixed-income investments. To reduce inflation risk, consider the new breed of easy-hold fixed-income investments with inflation protection.

TIPS

Treasury inflation-protected securities (TIPS) are an option for investors who want to wring most inflation and default risk from the bond component of their portfolios. TIPS offer investors a chance to buy a security whose value will not be eroded by inflation if the securities are held in a nontaxable account and the inflation index used by the U.S. Treasury is an accurate reflection of inflation.

TIPS have almost no default risk, like all debt backed by the full faith and credit of the U.S. government. The securities typically have nominal yields below those offered on other Treasury fixed-income securities of comparable maturities. In an inflationary environment, real returns can be higher for TIPS than for Treasury securities not indexed to inflation.

Key TIPS features include:

- The securities are sold in January, July, and October. Maturities are 5, 10, and 30 years. The Treasury Department issues the securities through its TreasuryDirect system and through the TRADES commercial book-entry system, where financial institutions or government securities brokers or dealers hold the securities on investors' behalf.

- The securities are sold in multiples of $1,000. Competitive bidding before the security's issue determines the fixed interest or coupon rate. Competitive bids are accepted, starting with the lowest yield and continuing to the highest yield needed to cover the announced offering amount.

- A noncompetitive bid will buy securities at the yield established at the auction. Noncompetitive bids can be for $1,000 to $5 million.

- The principal amount of the security is adjusted for inflation, but the inflation-adjusted principal is not paid until maturity.

- Semiannual interest payments are based on the inflation-adjusted principal at the time the interest is paid. The nominal interest rate is set at auction and remains fixed throughout the term of the security.

- The index for measuring the inflation rate is the nonseasonally adjusted U.S. City Average All Items Consumer Price Index for All Urban Consumers (CPI-U), published monthly by the Bureau of Labor Statistics. The Secretary of the Treasury can substitute an "appropriate alternative index" for the CPI-U under certain circumstances, such as if the CPI-U is discontinued or materially altered.

- The U.S. Treasury will resell the securities on the secondary market for investors. The Treasury obtains quotes from different brokers and provides the best price offered. The fee is $34 for each security sold.

- The securities are exempt from state and local taxes, but federal income taxes apply. In any year when the accrued inflation compensation goes up, the increase is considered reportable income, even though the investor does not receive the inflation-adjusted principal until maturity.

- Generally, the interest is taxable when received.

- At maturity, the securities will be redeemed at the greater of their inflation-adjusted principal or par amount at original issue. In other words, if deflation occurs, the value of the security will not drop below the par amount at which the security was issued.

The primary risks faced by an investor in these securities are the following:

- The market price for an inflation-indexed bond can change because of shifts in the real interest rate prevailing in the market.

- Income taxes reexpose TIPS to inflation risk. In fact, with sufficiently high inflation and taxes, it is possible that an indexed bond can have negative after-tax real returns. For this reason, the securities are best held in a nontaxable account.

- The inflation adjustments might not match real inflation in the economy. And the method for calculating the CPI could be changed or the U.S. Treasury Department could decide to use another index to calculate the bonds' inflation-adjusted coupon and principal payments.

Visit www.treasurydirect.gov for more information and to purchase TIPS.

I Bonds

"I bonds" are inflation-adjusted 30-year savings bonds. Like inflation-indexed Treasury securities, I bonds provide a guaranteed return above inflation. You must hold them at least six months, and you'll be penalized three months' interest if you sell within five years. The fixed rate is set twice a year—May 1 and November 1.

One big advantage of I bonds is that interest grows tax deferred until the bonds are sold. This differs from TIPS, which require the holder to pay taxes each year on both the interest you receive and the stepped-up value as a result of inflation (if TIPS are held outside a tax-preferenced account, such as an IRA). There's a $30,000-per-person annual limit on I bond purchases. For further information and to purchase I bonds, visit www.savingsbonds.gov.

FIXED-INCOME MUTUAL FUNDS

If you prefer to hold fixed-income investments via a mutual fund, you have plenty of top choices for easy holds. The Vanguard fund family has two bond fund holdings that represent excellent choices for easy-hold investors. *Vanguard Short-Term Corporate Fund* (VFSTX) a no-load fund, invests in short-term investment grade bonds. It may not invest more than 30 percent of its assets in debt securities rated BBB. Thus, credit quality is quite good. Ian MacKinnon, Vanguard's bond guru, has been managing the fund since 1982. The annual expense ratio is a minuscule 0.25 percent. Because of the short-term maturities of the investments, this bond fund holds up nicely when interest rates rise. In fact, the fund offers an attractive alternative to most money market funds.

The *Vanguard Total Bond Market Index* (VBMFX) is another easy-hold investment in the fixed-income arena. The fund seeks to replicate the total return of the Lehman Brothers Aggregate Bond Index. One attraction of the fund is its diversified holdings of fixed-income investments, including government and corporate securities. The average maturity of the fund is around eight years, making this a solid play for investors who want to stretch maturities a bit without going out more than 10 years.

All Vanguard funds may be purchased directly, without a broker. For purchasing information on these two funds, call (800) 662-7447.

CONCLUSION

A key part of weathering market volatility is being in the types of investments that have the ability to ride out the storm intact. Easy holds are those types of investments.

If you prefer a long-term buy-and-hold investment strategy, it is important that you remember to match that strategy with the proper investments. This chapter and Appendix B through Appendix F should go a long way toward providing choices for an easy-hold portfolio.

And even if you're an investor who prefers a more active approach to investing, you might still find easy-hold stocks suitable for at least a portion of your portfolio.

But what if you have no interest in buying and holding stocks? What if you just want high-action, high-volatility stocks to trade? Interestingly, you can still use our easy-hold ratings. Indeed, low-ranking stocks in our easy-hold scoring system will be those that tend to show extreme volatility. As a trader, you want volatile stocks. Thus, if you are looking for trading ideas, focus on stocks scoring in the bottom half of the easy-hold ratings.

Chapter Five

Law #5:
Handle Stormy Markets by
Creating an All-Weather Portfolio

A **COMMON MISTAKE** individual investors make is assuming that building a portfolio is purely a numbers game. All you need to do is buy 15 or 20 stocks, throw in a couple of mutual funds for good measure—and, presto! You have a diversified portfolio ready to weather any market storm.

You're probably laughing. Nobody puts together a portfolio like that, right?

Actually, many individual investors have constructed portfolios based solely on the number of components. No consideration given to diversification across industries. No consideration given to weightings of the individual components. No consideration given to the amount of overlap between fund holdings, as well as the overlap between fund holdings and individual stocks held.

In other words, simply buy a bunch of stocks and funds and call it a portfolio.

Of course, investors who built portfolios in this fashion found out just how leaky those portfolios were when market storms erupted.

It's been said that investing is as much art as science, and it's true. However, if there is one investment area where some science should be applied, it is in the construction of portfolios. This chapter focuses on the portfolio-construction process with an eye toward creating an "all-weather" portfolio capable of withstanding volatile markets.

THE RIGHT ALLOCATION

The first step in building a portfolio is developing the proper allocation of assets. In other words, you need to determine the percentage weighting of assets in the total portfolio.

The two biggest determinants of asset allocation are risk tolerance and investment time horizon. In basic terms, the more risk-averse you are as an investor, the greater the portion of bonds/cash versus stocks you should have in a portfolio. Also, the shorter the time horizon, the larger the percentage of the portfolio should be devoted to bonds/cash.

Now, what if I am a 45-year-old risk taker who plans to invest for the next 25 years? What asset allocation should I consider?

Given your lengthy investment time horizon and ability to handle risk, your portfolio should be well-stocked with stocks and/or stock mutual funds. Here would be a reasonable allocation:

Stocks—70 to 80 percent
Bonds—10 to 20 percent
Cash—0 to 10 percent

Now, what if I am a recently retired 65-year-old, with no large financial responsibilities, $1 million in an IRA rollover, and a good monthly pension? In this case, you probably want to achieve some growth (primarily to offset inflation) and also preserve your assets. A reasonable allocation would be:

Stocks—35 to 50 percent
Bonds—25 to 40 percent
Cash—10 to 25 percent

What's a good rule of thumb for setting an allocation? One that works pretty well is the following: Subtract your age from 110, and that is the percentage of your portfolio that should be in stocks. Split the remainder between bonds and cash.

Based on this rule of thumb, a 70-year-old could have as much as 40 percent of his or her portfolio in stocks. Of course, not all 70-year-olds are alike. Financial obligations, health factors, monthly cash-flow needs, the amount of assets—all of these factors will drive investment allocation decisions. But as a benchmark, this rule of thumb works pretty well.

Here are some additional model portfolio allocations given investor risk profiles and investment objectives:

Preservation of Capital (most suitable for investors with an extremely limited investment time horizon, an extremely low tolerance for risk, and a limited need for growth given his or her financial position, obligations, etc.):

Stocks—15 to 25 percent
Bonds—40 to 50 percent
Cash—25 to 35 percent

Current Income (most suitable for retirees who require income from their investments to supplement other income flows):

Stocks—30 to 40 percent (and much of that will be in stocks that pay dividends)
Bonds—45 to 55 percent
Cash—10 to 15 percent

Income and Growth (most suitable for investors who give equal weighting to generating income and growth from investments—this might apply to individuals nearing retirement):

Stocks—40 to 50 percent
Bonds—40 to 50 percent
Cash—0 to 10 percent

Long-Term Growth (most suitable for investors who are 15 years or more from retirement):

Stocks—70 to 80 percent
Bonds—15 to 25 percent
Cash—0 to 5 percent

Aggressive Growth (most suitable for investors with at least a 25-year investment time horizon and who are comfortable assuming a higher level of risk):

Stocks—80 to 100 percent
Bonds—0 to 10 percent
Cash—0 to 10 percent

Is there one all-weather allocation that will work for a wide range of investors? I'm a little leery of trying to give a one-size-fits-all allocation. However, the allocation closest to what I consider an all-weather mix would be the following:

All-Weather Allocation

Stocks—67 percent
Bonds—25 percent
Cash—8 percent

Again, the most important part in setting the proper allocation is how you answer the following two questions:

- What is your risk tolerance?

- What is your investment time horizon?

Once you have answered those important questions, you should be able to create an asset allocation that meets your needs.

A useful tool in helping you determine the proper asset-allocation mix is offered by SmartMoney.com (www.university.smartmoney .com/Departments/TakingAction/AssetAllocation/). By answering several questions about your financial position, this tool will provide an asset allocation for you.

Keep in mind that many asset-allocation tools will not be able to measure very well your aversion to risk. Thus, use allocations suggested by this and other tools as benchmarks, not absolutes.

CONSIDER ALL OF YOUR ASSETS IN THE ALLOCATION PROCESS

Don't forget that when you are allocating assets, take into account all of your assets.

For example, many people have a variety of portfolios—a 401(k) plan, an IRA, several stock accounts, annuities, and so on. Keep in mind that all of these assets represent your investment portfolio. You'll need to reflect all of these assets in your allocation.

What is the best way to combine various portfolios for asset-allocation purposes? My guess is that while you may have a variety of portfolios, the portfolios have similar risk/return attributes and investment time horizons. If that is the case, you should consider all of the portfolios as one big portfolio for allocation purposes.

What that means is that just because you may have 100 percent of your 401(k) plan in stocks, you may not be overweighted in stocks in that account if the rest of your assets are spread across bonds and cash. Don't look just at the allocation of individual portfolios. Look at how all of your assets are allocated when developing an asset-allocation mode.

How your assets are allocated is perhaps the single most important factor in how your portfolio will perform over time. That's why it was so tragic to see people who had entirely inappropriate portfolio mixes get hammered when the market declined. Many of these people failed to consider either their tolerance for risk or their investment time horizons. They rolled the dice that the gains of the 1990s would continue. Unfortunately, they crapped out.

Thus, when setting an allocation, choose wisely. It will make a huge difference in how your portfolio behaves, especially during tumultuous market periods.

WHAT'S THE RIGHT NUMBER?

Once you've established the proper allocation, the next step is to choose the investments for each of the asset areas.

The two big questions here are:

• What?

• How many?

That is, what are the best stocks/bonds to own? And how many of each should I own?

When it comes to bonds, I generally use bond mutual funds. To be sure, individual bonds have some advantages over bonds in that you'll get the principal back on individual bonds if you hold to maturity (assuming no default). That is not guaranteed with bond funds. However, my experience has been that individual bonds often lack the desired liquidity for individual investors. Perhaps more important, individual investors generally lack the financial resources to diversify properly among a variety of bonds.

If you do buy individual bonds, I suggest you concentrate on high-quality bonds (AA rated or better) and keep the bulk of the maturities to less than 15 years. Also, consider owning at least 10 to 15 different bonds in a portfolio.

If you choose a bond mutual fund, the picking is a bit easier. The Vanguard fund family (800-662-7447) offers a variety of attractive bond funds across the credit-risk and maturity spectrum. Bond funds I would consider from Vanguard include the Short-Term Corporate Bond Fund and the Total Bond Market Index Fund. For more aggressive investors, you could put a little bit of money into the Vanguard High-Yield Corporate Fund.

In terms of percentages, I would be inclined to put 40 to 45 percent of the bond portion of a portfolio in the short-term bond fund, 40 to 45 percent in the Total Bond Market Index Fund, and 10 to 20 percent in the High-Yield Bond Fund. Again, these percentages relate to the bond side of the portfolio, not the entire portfolio.

For example, let's say you choose an overall portfolio allocation that is 60 percent stocks and 40 percent bonds. Within that 40 percent bond allocation, the aforementioned percentages apply. Thus, here's how that translates to the overall portfolio:

If the portfolio's bond allocation is 40 percent, then . . .

- *Vanguard Short-Term Corporate*—16 to 18 percent of the entire portfolio. (This range is found by multiplying the 40 percent bond allocation by 40 to 45 percent allocation for Vanguard Short-Term Corporate.)

- *Vanguard Total Bond Market Index*—16 to 18 percent of the entire portfolio.

- *Vanguard High-Yield Corporate*—4 to 8 percent of the entire portfolio.

To summarize, a portfolio in which the asset allocation is 60 percent stocks and 40 percent bonds should have up to 18 percent in each of the Vanguard Short-Term Corporate and Vanguard Total Bond Market Funds and up to 8 percent of the portfolio in the Vanguard High-Yield Corporate Fund.

What about the 60 percent in stocks? How many individual stocks and/or mutual funds should make up that 60 percent? And what stocks from what industries should be selected?

NOT TOO MANY, NOT TOO FEW

Two types of portfolio risk exist:

- The risk of the overall market (called "systematic" risk)

- Company risk (called "unsystematic" risk)

Systematic risk is the risk you run from owning any stock when the overall market declines. Since most stocks have some correlation to the broader market, it is impossible to diversify away systematic risk from a portfolio of stocks.

How do you lower systematic risk? This is done basically by portfolio allocation—stocks versus bonds versus cash. Also, some stocks are less correlated to the market than others, so spreading a portfolio of stocks across various industry groups will reduce systematic risk.

It is unsystematic risk—the risk of individual companies—that equity investors hope to eliminate by diversifying across stocks. In fact, if investors diversify properly across stocks, investors can greatly reduce or even eliminate company risk—the risk that one poor stock will significantly drag down the whole portfolio.

Now, some investors don't believe math is the only way to reduce unsystematic risk. You can also do it through good stock picking. Everyone's shining example of someone who reduces unsystematic risk while still holding a small portfolio is Warren Buffett. Arguably the most successful investor of our time, Buffett usually owns fewer than two dozen stocks, yet his portfolio has been able to weather nicely the rare blowups in any one stock.

Of course, not all of us are Warren Buffett. Not all of us have his acumen (not to mention the time and resources) for stock picking. Furthermore, I'm sure that many investors believed that they had eliminated unsystematic risk in their portfolios by picking such quality stocks as Cisco and Oracle, only to see that unsystematic risk rear its ugly head when these stocks blew up.

The upshot is that, yes, if you pick stocks like Warren Buffett, you can reduce unsystematic risk just by picking good stocks. But my guess is that you are not Warren Buffett, which means you need math on your side when it comes to reducing unsystematic risk in a portfolio.

The other reason the number of stocks in a portfolio has increased in importance is that—and I know this won't shock anyone who has seen his or her tech stocks lose 80 percent of their value—individual stocks have become more risky over the last several years.

A study done by researchers John Campbell, Martin Lettau, Burton G. Malkiel, and Yexiao Xu looked at the time period from July 1962 to December 1997. What they found was that volatility at the firm level (i.e., individual companies) has increased dramatically over that time period. In fact, the researchers found that from 1962 to 1997, firm-level volatility increased *30 times* for a typical company. While the researchers found that firm-level volatility had risen in large companies, the bulk of the increase was due to the large number of smaller companies coming into the market.

What this and other research clearly shows is that individual stocks are riskier now than in the past.

If stocks individually are riskier now than ever before, it implies that diversification across a number of stocks is more necessary now than ever. Furthermore, the old belief that you should own 10 to 15 stocks to be properly diversified may need to be reexamined in light of the increased risk of individual stocks.

I have to admit that I've never been a fan of having 60 stocks in a portfolio. For one, that many stocks are hard to follow both from an investment standpoint and from a record-keeping standpoint. Furthermore, most investors don't have 60 great investment ideas, so holding that many stocks tends to water down your best ideas.

Having said that, however, I have begun to believe that holding 10 to 15 stocks may not be enough. Indeed, with the increase in volatility of individual stocks and the need for broader representation across a variety of sectors as well as stock classifications (large-cap, mid-cap, small-cap, growth, value, U.S., foreign), it is tough to get all the diversification across equities that is needed in just 10 to 15 stocks.

So, if 60 stocks are too many for individual investors to follow, and 15 too few in order to be properly diversified, what's the right number? Well, in my company's managed-account business, we generally hold 24 to 40 stocks in client portfolios, depending on the amount of money in the portfolio devoted to equities. In my personal portfolio, I own about 25 stocks. But I also own a number of mutual funds, especially in my 401(k) plan.

Thus, I think a fairly workable number for stocks in a portfolio is probably in the neighborhood of 25 to 35 individual stocks, especially if you balance those holdings with mutual funds.

Does that mean that if you own just 10 or 15 stocks you should get to 25 or 30 stocks in a hurry? Not necessarily. However, you should be aware that by owning 10 or 15 stocks, you are taking on greater risk today—as a result of the increasing volatility of individual stocks—than you may have been assuming just a decade ago.

If that increased risk puts you out of your comfort zone, then you probably need to diversify across more individual stocks. An alternative would be to include mutual funds in your portfolio mix. Later in this chapter I'll put together an all-weather portfolio for most investors that brings together individual stocks as well as mutual funds.

WHAT SECTORS?

Now that you've allocated across asset classes, it's time to allocate within asset classes. We've already allocated within the bond sector with the Vanguard funds. What about stocks?

You'll want to accomplish two things when allocating within stocks:

1. You want to make sure you are not overexposed in any one industry sector. Ask any investor who loaded up on technology stocks in the late '90s just how painful concentration in one industry sector can be.

2. You want to make sure you are not overexposed in any one stock. While some people believe you shouldn't have more than 10 percent of a portfolio in one stock, I'm a bit more pragmatic. Indeed, I think an investor with a 20- or 30-year time horizon would be OK with a single stock making up 20 percent of a portfolio. Conversely, an investor in his or her sixties would be taking a big risk by having one stock comprise more than 20 percent of their portfolio. I try to keep individual stock weightings to 2 percent to 15 percent of the portfolio. I think this works for most portfolios.

While it seems reasonably clear what constitutes too much exposure to one stock, how can an individual investor gauge when one industry sector seems too heavy in a portfolio?

A reasonably good benchmark to use for industry portfolio weightings is the Standard & Poor's 500 Index.

Using a benchmark to evaluate sector weightings makes sense on several counts. For starters, your ability to add value to the investment process depends to a great extent on your ability to make sector bets. That is, in order to beat the performance of an index, such as the S&P 500, you'll have to do a good job not only on stock selection, but also on sector allocation.

Remember—you should invest in individual stocks only if you think you can add value and, in the end, outperform your index benchmark. Admittedly, it's tough to beat the S&P 500 year in, year out. Quite frankly, most investors don't. Still, I don't believe that's a reason not to try with individual stocks. One thing is for sure: Investing in individual stocks is a whole lot more fun than owning index funds. Besides, you can always add index funds to provide ballast to a portfolio of stocks.

The problem is that most investors who think they can beat the S&P 500 don't understand how important sector bets are in the equation. For that reason, it pays to know how your portfolio is situated across industries relative to some benchmark.

Fortunately, the Internet provides a number of tools to compare your portfolio's sector weightings to that of the S&P 500. One useful tool in this regard is found on the Morningstar Web site—www.morningstar.com. At the Web site's home page, scroll down until you come to "Investing Tools." Under "Investing Tools" click on "Instant X-Ray." You'll be taken to a page where you can input the stock symbols and dollar value of holdings in your portfolio. After you have completed loading your portfolio, click on "Show Instant X-Ray" at the bottom of the page. What you'll see is a nice diagnostic sheet on the composition of your portfolio. The X-Ray will tell you the percentage of your portfolio in large-cap, mid-cap, and small-cap stocks; and the percentage of the portfolio in growth, value, and blend stocks. The X-Ray will also tell you the sector weightings of your portfolio versus the sector weightings in the S&P 500. You'll be able to see in what sectors your portfolio is overweighted or underweighted relative to the benchmark.

Knowing how your portfolio compares in its sector weightings allows you to understand better the reasons for divergence in performance between your portfolio and the benchmark. This tool also allows you to run sensitivity tests to see how adjustments to various equities (in terms of dollar weighting in the portfolio) would affect the sector composition of the portfolio.

The point of comparing industry weightings versus a benchmark is not so much to alter your portfolio to match the benchmark weightings. After all, if you want sector weightings that match the index, it'd be a whole lot easier just buying the index. Rather, knowing how your portfolio compares will allow you to gauge your sector weightings and decide how the portfolio is positioned relative to your expectations for sector performance, volatility, and so on.

WHAT STOCKS?

The last piece of the puzzle is the actual selection of the individual stocks.

Keep in mind that sector weightings are only part of the equation when it comes to portfolio risk. Indeed, you can have sector weightings that match a benchmark, but portfolio performance could be dramatically different given what stocks you choose to hold in those sectors.

For example, a portfolio with a 20 percent weighting in technology via four stocks—Veritas Software, Verisign, Intuit, and Broadcom—will have a risk/return profile different from a portfolio with the same 20 percent weighting in four dramatically different technology stocks—IBM, Microsoft, Applied Materials, and Intel.

So how can an investor judge the risk/reward parameters of individual stocks? Chapter 4 and Appendix B provide a useful tool—our easy-hold ratings—in evaluating the potential volatility of stocks.

Another useful tool is offered by RiskGrades (www.riskgrades.com).

RiskGrades Brings Professional Portfolio Tools to Main Street

What is the risk of each of your portfolio holdings?

What is the risk of the entire portfolio?

Quite frankly, most individual investors have no idea how risky their portfolios are. One reason is that determining portfolio risk often requires the math skills of Pascal, not to mention the pocketbook of Bill Gates, to buy the necessary software to perform such chores.

Fortunately, the days when only institutional investors had access to high-powered portfolio tools are over. Indeed, thanks to RiskGrades (www.riskgrades.com) individual investors now have no excuse for not knowing the risk level of their portfolios.

In order to use RiskGrades, you'll have to register. Registration is free. Once you have registered, you'll be able to use the plethora of risk-evaluation tools on this amazing site.

One useful tool is the site's RiskGrade scores on individual stocks. At the site's home page, click on "Get A RiskGrade" at the top right-hand side of the page. You'll be asked to enter a stock symbol. Punch in the stock symbol, hit "go," and RiskGrade will produce a RiskGrade score on the stock.

While some pretty high-powered math goes into computing this risk score, the system basically computes two items:

- A calculation is made based on how much variation there is in the asset's price, making the most recent history more important than outdated observations.
- The asset's volatility is compared to the volatility of a basket of global equities.

The ratio of these two volatilities results in the RiskGrade measure. The lower the score, the lower the risk. Cash, for example, receives a RiskGrade score of 0. For very speculative investments, the RiskGrade score could be higher than 1,000.

What's especially nice about RiskGrade is that you can compute the risk score for entire portfolios, including portfolios that hold a variety of asset classes (stock funds, bonds, etc.). You can receive a portfolio risk score and see how the portfolio's risk compares to the risk of an appropriate benchmark, such as the S&P 500 or Nasdaq Composite. RiskGrade also allows you to run "what if" scenarios on your investments to see how changes in investments and their weightings affect risk levels.

An especially neat feature is the ability to see how your portfolio would have performed during certain market crises, such as the Gulf War, Black Monday, the dot-com blowup, or the Asian crisis.

Another thing I like about this site is that it is user friendly and converts a lot of the information into easy-to-understand charts and tables. Best of all, you get all this *free.*

If you are serious about applying science to portfolio building—and you should be, given the importance of properly constructed portfolios to long-term financial success—you won't find a better tool on the Web than RiskGrades.

MUTUAL FUND DIVERSIFICATION

Just as you can own 10 stocks and have terrible diversification (all the stocks are in the same industry, for example), so, too, can you own 10 mutual funds and have terrible diversification.

Mutual funds have very different risk/return parameters. A mutual fund that focuses exclusively on Japanese securities will behave very differently from a mutual fund that buys large-cap value stocks.

Remember that proper portfolio diversification is understanding how assets correlate to one another. Stocks that are strongly correlated will behave similarly. Stocks that are weakly correlated will behave differently.

When you set up portfolios, you need to know how assets are correlated. The same goes for mutual funds. Are the funds you are buying correlated? Do the funds own virtually the same stocks? Or will the funds perform differently depending on market conditions?

How can you tell how mutual funds are expected to correlate? Once again, the Internet provides an extremely useful resource for information on fund correlations. One excellent site is offered by SmartMoney.com (www.smartmoney.com/fundbuilder). At this site, you can enter the investment style of your funds and the percentage exposure to that style in your portfolio. The "Portfolio Graphic Equalizer" will show you the portfolio's return and volatility over the last five years. You can then play "what if" scenarios by adjusting the portfolio weightings based on the fund's investment style. When you play around with the Portfolio Graphic Equalizer, you'll quickly see how you can influence the risk/return profile (based on historical numbers) by altering the mix of funds.

Another way to gauge the risk of a portfolio of funds is to use RiskGrade. Indeed, in addition to equities, you can generate RiskGrade scores on individual funds as well as a portfolio of funds. You can even derive a risk score for a single portfolio consisting of stocks, funds, and bonds.

THE ULTIMATE ALL-WEATHER PORTFOLIO

Armed with various Internet tools, I thought it would be useful to construct an ultimate "all-weather" portfolio for a typical buy-and-hold investor.

For our all-weather portfolio, let's start with our all-weather allocation:

Stocks/Stock mutual funds—67 percent
Bonds/Bond mutual funds—25 percent
Cash—8 percent

As is the case with any portfolio that attempts to minimize risk, you do give up a bit in terms of long-term growth. Indeed, the fact that 33 percent of the portfolio is not in stocks will hinder the portfolio's potential returns over the long term.

However, what we're trying to do with this portfolio is strike an acceptable combination of reasonable return without huge swings in portfolio value, something that is important in today's volatile market. This asset allocation should achieve that goal.

Now that we have our asset allocation, what stocks and funds?

A good starting point for stocks for the portfolio is the list of favorite easy-hold stocks provided in Chapter 4. I've selected the following 20 easy holds, covering a variety of industry sectors:

Alltel (AT)—Telecommunications
Automatic Data Processing (ADP)—Computer Services
Duke Energy (DUK)—Electric Utility
Duke Realty (DRE)—Real Estate Investment Trust
Equifax (EFX)—Information Services
Exxon Mobil (XOM)—Energy
General Electric (GE)—Conglomerate
Guidant (GDT)—Medical Technology
Harley-Davidson (HDI)—Leisure/Transportation
Johnson & Johnson (JNJ)—Health Care
Johnson Controls (JCI)—Industrial/Automotive Parts

Microsoft (MSFT)—Technology
Pfizer (PFE)—Pharmaceuticals
Philadelphia Suburban (PSC)—Water Utility
Popular (BPOP)—Banking
Southwest Airlines (LUV)—Airline
Sysco (SYY)—Foodservices
Wal-Mart (WMT)—Retailing
Walgreen (WAG)—Drugstore
Waters (WAT)—Instruments

Keep in mind that if this portfolio had a larger equity exposure, you would probably want to hold at least 25 to 35 stocks. However, with an equity exposure of 67 percent, 20 stocks (especially since I'm also including a few equity mutual funds) is more than enough.

To these stocks, I'm adding three equity mutual funds:

Meridian Value (MVALX)—Mid-Cap Blend
Pennsylvania Mutual (PENNX)—Small-Cap Value
UMB Scout WorldWide (UMBWX)—Foreign Stock

Why these funds? For starters, these funds plug some holes in that they give the portfolio overseas exposure as well as more exposure to small- and mid-cap stocks. Second, all three funds have outstanding track records.

I must now weight these equity investments. Since the equity portion of my all-weather portfolio amounts to 67 percent, the weightings across the 20 stocks and three mutual funds must add up to 67 percent.

For the 20 individual stocks, I would weight them equally at 2 percent of the portfolio. That leaves 27 percent for the three funds. I would weight the UMB Scout World Wide at 11 percent of the entire portfolio, and the Meridian Value and Pennsylvania Mutual Funds at 8 percent each.

For the bond allocation, I'm using three funds, all from the Vanguard fund family:

Vanguard Short-Term Corporate (VFSTX)
Vanguard Total Bond Market Index (VBMFX)
Vanguard High-Yield Corporate (VWEHX)

Why these three funds? First, they are from the same fund family, so keeping track of them should be easy. Second, fees are extremely low on these funds, which is critical when choosing bond funds. Third, these three funds give nice representation across a variety of bond groups and credit ratings. The Short-Term Corporate is very low risk. The Total Bond Market Index gives broad coverage across the entire spectrum of fixed-income investments. The Vanguard High-Yield provides exposure to the junk-bond sector. I know this may sound scary, but infusing a portfolio with some high-yield bonds provides a way to improve diversification.

For weightings for the three bond funds, I'm putting 10 percent in the Vanguard Short-Term Corporate, 10 percent in the Vanguard Total Bond Market Index, and 5 percent in the Vanguard High-Yield Corporate.

For the 8 percent cash component of this portfolio, I'm using Vanguard's Money Market Fund.

So there you have it—Carlson's All-Weather Portfolio. The portfolio consists of 20 stocks, three equity mutual funds, three bond funds, and a money market account—a total of 27 different investment vehicles.

I like several things about this portfolio:

- The number of investments (27, including the money market account) is manageable from a record-keeping and portfolio-monitoring standpoint.

- The portfolio, with 40 percent of the allocation to individual stocks, should be friendlier, from a tax standpoint, than a portfolio invested strictly in funds. Indeed, with individual stocks, you decide when to incur a tax liability. With funds, the fund manager decides.

- The stock holdings juice up the fun factor. (After all, stocks are more fun than funds.)

- The portfolio does not require an arm and a leg to initiate. Indeed, many of the stocks may be purchased in fairly small amounts directly from the companies via their dividend reinvestment plans. Dollar-based online brokerage firms offer another avenue for buying these stocks in small increments. And the mutual funds have reasonable minimums. Thus, an investor with $50,000 or more should be able to carve out this portfolio reasonably well. If you have fewer dollars, say $5,000 to $20,000, you should still be able to piece together much of this portfolio given that twelve of the stocks (Duke Energy, Duke Realty, Equifax, Exxon, GE, Guidant, Johnson Controls, Pfizer, Philadelphia Suburban, Popular, Wal-Mart, and Walgreen) may be purchased directly with minimum initial investments of $500 or less; four stocks (Alltel, Harley-Davidson, Johnson & Johnson, and Sysco) have traditional dividend reinvestment plans that have small minimums once investors become eligible to join the DRIPs by owning at least one share; and the mutual funds have reasonable minimums as well.

- The portfolio provides broad coverage across and within asset classes without having 100 or more investments to buy and track. Thus, portfolio diversification should be excellent.

PUTTING THE PORTFOLIO THROUGH ITS PACES

If this is supposed to be an all-weather portfolio, what is its risk profile?

Fortunately, we can see just how risky this portfolio is using RiskGrades. When I load the stock and fund symbols into RiskGrades, I'm told the following about my all-weather portfolio (I assume a portfolio of $50,000):

- As I suspected, the portfolio risk score is only 41 versus 77 for the S&P 500 Index. Remember, however, that the reduced risk will impact expected portfolio returns over time. Still, volatility of this portfolio is expected to be only half as much as the S&P 500.

- One reason for the portfolio's low risk is its underweighting in some fairly volatile industry sectors, such as technology. Indeed, this portfolio's technology weighting is roughly half that of the benchmark S&P 500. Now, if technology stocks skyrocket over the next few years, that will cost this portfolio. However, my guess is that you will not see again the technology boom period of 1998 and 1999.

Another question you should be asking is the following: How would this portfolio have fared during some of the more difficult times in the market?

Again, RiskGrade allows us to answer that question using its "Event Study" feature:

- *Black Monday* (October 16, 1987, to October 19, 1987)—During this market debacle, the all-weather portfolio declined 11 percent relative to a 20 percent decline in the S&P 500 and 13 percent decline in the Nasdaq Composite.

- *Gulf War* (August 1, 1990, to August 30, 1990)—Once again, our all-weather portfolio would have held up much better than other indexes, declining just 5 percent versus a 10 percent decline for the S&P 500 and a 13 percent decline for the Nasdaq Composite.

- *Russian Crisis* (August 18, 1998, to October 8, 1998)—The all-weather portfolio declined 6 percent versus a 13 percent decline in the S&P 500 and a 23 percent decline in the Nasdaq Composite.

- *Dot-Com Bomb* (March 24, 2000, to April 14, 2000)—Once again, the all-weather portfolio lived up to its billing, falling just 4 percent while the S&P 500 declined 11 percent and the Nasdaq Composite fell a whopping 33 percent.

Of course, keep in mind that all this back-testing of this all-weather portfolio is just that—back-testing. Past results are not always indicative of future returns. Only time will tell whether this all-weather portfolio indeed remains a good portfolio for volatility-shy investors. However, given that the portfolio has an ample bond exposure and big easy-hold exposure in its stock and fund components, I'm betting it will continue to stand up well during rocky markets.

CONCLUSION

If you take nothing away from this chapter but one thing, let it be this: Spending time thinking about portfolio creation is time well spent. I know everyone usually focuses on individual investment selection. But it's how you put individual investments together into a cohesive portfolio that will ultimately prove the success or failure of your investment program.

Take the time to answer the necessary questions:

- What is my investment objective?

- What is my time horizon?

- What is my tax situation and how does that affect my asset allocation?

- Do I plan to buy and hold?

- What do I value more, saving a dollar in losses or gaining a dollar in gains?

- Am I covering my bases across and within asset classes, or am I putting all of my bets on just a few investments?

- How does the industry weighting in my portfolio compare to a benchmark, such as the S&P 500?

- How can I go about putting together this asset mix in the most cost-efficient and time-efficient way?

- What is the risk of my portfolio relative to a benchmark index?

- What rebalancing needs to be done each year to make sure my objectives and risk parameters are still in line?

I can tell you that those investors who suffered the biggest losses in recent years are those who didn't ask themselves these questions.

If you didn't make that mistake with your portfolio, don't start now. Dig in and make sure you are not incurring too much risk for too little potential reward. And if you did make that mistake with your portfolio, now's the time to get it right.

Chapter Six

Law #6:
Use Dollar-Based Investing
Programs to Invest Regularly

SMOKERS KNOW they shouldn't smoke. Alcoholics know they shouldn't drink. Gamblers know they shouldn't gamble. Yet cigarettes and alcohol are trillion-dollar industries. And Las Vegas has no problem luring pigeons to its parlors every day.

Why is it that we humans do things (smoke, drink, gamble) we know we shouldn't, yet don't do things (exercise, diet) we know we should?

I think the answer is that what's good for you is not always what's easy. Exercise is hard work. Dieting is tough stuff. The trick, of course, is figuring out a way to break the bad habits and replace them with good ones. How does that process occur? Some people break bad habits cold turkey. Stop the bad stuff today, start the good stuff tomorrow.

However, I think you'll find that many behavior-modification experts believe a gradual approach is more effective. We ease out of bad habits and ease into good ones. The process takes longer but usually is more lasting.

I think most people would buy the idea that a good habit in dealing with volatile markets is to capitalize on the volatility when stocks get crushed. How? By buying stocks on sale.

Yet getting investors to behave in their own best interest and buy during volatile markets can be quite difficult. Why? Because you have tons of reasons *not* to buy stocks when the market is tanking:

- By not buying, you save yourself the pain of further declines.

- By not buying, you'll eventually be able to buy those stocks even more cheaply.

- By not buying, you will avoid looking stupid to your friends and family members who believe only chumps should be buying stocks right now.

- By not buying, you've put off making any decisions—and who likes to make decisions?

Unfortunately, by not buying, you've also lost a golden opportunity to position your portfolio for gains down the road.

It's no coincidence that the Chinese symbol for "crisis" is also the symbol for "opportunity." I've always said that you get rich during bear markets—you just don't realize it until later. While volatile, ugly markets are painful and confusing, they are also filled with opportunities for those looking ahead more than a few months or even a few years.

Think about it. Everyone wanted to buy Cisco in early 2000 when the stock traded for more than $80 per share.

Nobody wanted to buy Cisco in 2001 when it traded for $11.

In 1999 and early 2000, investors were falling over themselves to buy many Nasdaq stocks trading in triple digits with triple-digit price/earnings ratios. Twelve months later, you couldn't give away many of these same Nasdaq stocks.

Wall Street is the only market in the world where merchandise has more buyers when prices rise and fewer buyers when merchandise is in the bargain bin.

To be sure, not every highflier that gets its wings clipped is a good buy at reduced prices. However, if you liked a stock at $100, and the reasons you liked the stock still hold, shouldn't you be buying all you can at $10?

But that's not how most investors think. Most investors think that a stock that's $100 is worth buying because it's, well, $100 and everyone is buying. A stock that's $10—one that no one wants—is damaged goods.

Smart investors take advantage of volatile markets in two important ways:

- *Smart investors step up to the plate to buy, even if everyone is shouting "sell."* Now, I know it is easy to say that investors should buy during bear markets. The rebuttal is often the following: "Buy with what? I don't have any money. I just lost it in the market!" Of course, sometimes you don't have fresh funds to take advantage of price dips. More likely, however, you probably have at least part of your investment program on autopilot. For example, most people invest via a 401(k) program with funds taken automatically from their paychecks. During bear markets, the temptation is great to put those investments into cash. However, smart investors don't try to time the market aggressively. Instead, they take advantage of declines to buy stock with their fresh 401(k) dollars. You may have to endure a prolonged period of time when that dollar-cost averaging in stocks works against you. However, studies show that you actually do better over time if the market undergoes periodic declines and you maintain a regular investment program The reason is that declines provide opportunities for your dollars to buy more shares. Even if you get nervous and move some of your funds to cash or bonds, make sure that you are putting at least something into stocks or stock mutual funds during the rough patches.

- *Smart investors use volatile markets to upgrade portfolios.* A common mistake investors make during market downturns is that they look backward, not forward. Investors fixate on lost profits, on what they should have done. This takes their eyes off what they should be doing to make money going forward. You cannot undo the past. Smart investors don't miss the future by looking at the past. They take their lumps, learn their lessons, and do what they can to position their portfolios for the market's inevitable upturn. That means smart investors use volatile markets to trim their deadwood and buy those stocks that they always wanted to own (if they got cheap enough). That's the beauty of bear markets: All the stocks that you told yourself you would love to own can usually be bought at prices that you would have killed for during the previous bull market.

Bottom line: Nobody can tell you with certainty the perfect time to buy stocks. Nobody knows with certainty when a market has bottomed. What I do believe can be said with a high degree of certainty is that five years from now, stocks will trade higher than they do today. I can't guarantee that, but history says that'll be the case. That's why you need to keep putting money into the market, even if it is just a modest amount, during ugly market periods.

Over time, you'll be glad you did.

DOLLAR-BASED INVESTING MAKES BUYING EASIER

Tell me which is easier—investing $30,000 in one shot during a declining market (presuming you have $30,000 to invest), or investing $3,000 per month for 10 months? I'm not necessarily saying which is *better* to do, mind you. I'm asking which is *easier*—$30,000 now or $3,000 a month for 10 months?

That's easy. It's a whole lot easier cutting a check for $3,000 during rocky market periods than investing $30,000. With $3,000, you don't have nearly as much at risk as if you plowed in $30,000.

Look at that choice one more time—$3,000 versus $30,000. Notice one of the options isn't zero. You have to make an investment. That's critical when framing investment decisions. You can't leave yourself an out, a zero. You have to put some money into the market.

If you make it mandatory that you invest at least something on a regular basis, even if it is a relatively small amount, you shift the process from "to buy or not to buy" to "how much to invest." That's significant in altering behavior. You are now forced to buy, even if it is just a little.

Now, the second step in the process is the following: If I agree to invest, but only if I can invest in a way that allows me to kick in small amounts of money (that's so I can sleep at night), what investment vehicles are going to allow me to invest that way?

Enter dollar-based investing vehicles.

WHAT IS DOLLAR-BASED INVESTING?

I think one of the most empowering developments in the financial markets in the last 20 years is the advent of *dollar-based investing* vehicles.

What are dollar-based investing programs? These are programs predicated on dollar investing, not share investing. In other words, investment decisions are made based on how many *dollars* to invest, not how many *shares* to buy.

This distinction may sound trivial. It isn't. In fact, investing in dollar terms frames the entire investment decision process in a whole new light.

Be honest. If you had no other options but to invest through a stockbroker, how would you invest? Would you call up your local stockbroker and say, "Bill, buy me six shares of Intel"? Probably not. Why? Because who wants to look like a nickel-and-dime player with his or her broker? *Nobody* calls up a broker and buys a lousy six shares.

And forget about your broker buying fractional shares for you. It's a whole share or no share. Don't have enough to buy a whole share of stock? See you later!

Unfortunately, if all the money you have is $500 or $1,000, and you feel compelled to buy at least 100 shares via the broker, what type of stocks are left for you to buy? Cheap stocks.

And that's my point. By focusing on the number of shares your investment dollars can buy, you shift the investment decision-making process to the price of the stock rather than the quality of the investment. You buy 100 shares of a $5 stock because that's all you can afford. Second, buying stocks based on per-share price is nonsensical. Companies have a great deal of discretion to make the per-share price anything they want. One way companies "manipulate" the per-share price is via stock splits. If a company believes its $100-per-share stock price is too high to draw interest from individual investors, presto!—a 2-for-1 stock split brings the per-share price down to $50.

Or if a stock is trading at a low price that is scaring off investors (lots of big, institutional investors, for example, aren't permitted to buy penny stocks), the company can undergo what's called a "reverse" stock split to boost the per-share price. In a reverse stock split, a company reduces the number of outstanding shares while boosting the per-share price.

For example, let's say a stock is selling for 80 cents per share. The company decides it needs to boost the per-share stock price in order to (1) avoid being delisted by the exchange; (2) eliminate the stigma of being a "penny stock"; and (3) increase the stock price to lure interest from institutional investors whose charters, in many cases, do not allow them to buy penny stocks. Thus, the firm implements a 1-for-10 "reverse" stock split. Magically, the stock now trades for $8 per share. Of course, no value is created. Had you owned 100 shares prior to the reverse stock split, you now own 10 shares. The total value of your holdings is still only $80. But the per-share stock price has jumped sharply.

Bottom line: Buying a stock based on its per-share price makes about as much sense as buying a stock because you think the stock symbol is cute. Neither has anything to do with the fundamentals of the company. Yet when the investment decision process is framed in buying shares, the per-share price carries a lot of weight in the minds of most investors.

The beauty of dollar-based investing is that the decision-making process is focused exclusively on the *best* investment, not the cheapest (in terms of per-share price) investment:

• You have only $500? No problem—you can invest that $500, and you can invest *all* of it. Full *and* fractional shares.

• Want to buy a blue-chip stock with that $500? No problem. You have literally hundreds from which to choose.

• Want to buy a top-rated mutual fund? Again, you have plenty from which to choose.

• Want to use that $500 to invest tax-free in a Roth IRA? Go right ahead.

- And do you want to invest that $500 (or $50 or even $5) in a 401(k), where your investment reduces your taxes, grows tax-deferred, and is matched (at least a portion of it) by your employer? Welcome aboard.

Think about that for a moment. With dollar-based investing, *no* investment is outside your consideration. Dollar-based investing truly has leveled the playing field to allow *anyone* to get in the game—in good, high-quality blue-chip investments—regardless of the size of his or her pocketbook.

And the icing on the cake? In most dollar-based investment vehicles, the cost of admission is sometimes *zero,* and always extremely competitively priced. In fact, in some cases, dollar-based investing vehicles allow small investors to buy investments more cheaply than big institutional investors who are investing millions of dollars at a crack. Talk about empowering!

And the benefits of dollar-based investing are truly magnified during volatile markets. Indeed, dollar-based investing provides a palatable vehicle to funnel money into the market on a regular basis. That's a huge benefit, especially since an important defense for tough markets is using the market's weakness to your advantage and buying.

I can't think of any other investment product better suited to allowing investors to do what they should do during rough markets—accumulate quality stocks on declines—than dollar-based investing.

DOLLAR-BASED INVESTING OPTIONS

Dollar-based investing vehicles take many forms, but the common thread is that investors invest to buy both full and fractional shares.

Mutual Funds

Perhaps the best-known dollar-based investment is a mutual fund. Mutual funds have been around for roughly 80 years. Scudder claims to have started the first no-load mutual fund in the 1920s.

The premise of a mutual fund is very simple: Let's take a few dollars from you and you and you and you; bundle the money together; buy a basket of stocks; and manage that basket by buying and selling stocks in the basket over time. The advantages for investors are several:

- *The ability to make a relatively small investment.* Many mutual funds have $1,000 minimums, and a few fund families (Invesco Fund and T. Rowe Price Funds come to mind) will allow investors to get started with as little as $50 per month.

- *The ability to achieve portfolio diversification with a small amount of money.* Buying 20 or 30 individual stocks is rather difficult with just $500. But a $500 investment in a mutual fund literally gives you "ownership" in all the stocks in the fund. In some cases, that may mean your $500 investment is spread across 100 or 200 individual stocks. This instant diversification is a huge selling point with fund investors.

- *The ability for "small" investors to have professional management.* Mutual funds allow even an investor with $50 or $500 to have investment experts manage their investment. That type of access to the brightest minds on Wall Street was traditionally reserved for only the very wealthy. Mutual funds changed all that.

- *The ability to invest without a sales charge and for very little fees.* The advent of no-load funds—"no load" meaning no up-front sales charge—as well as index funds and their minuscule annual management fees meant that small investors could have virtually all of their money working for them. This is significant. Indeed, even what might be considered a small commission by historical standards—say, the $29.95 per trade Schwab charges online traders—would still be a hefty percentage of a $100 or even $500 investment. Mutual funds provided not only unprecedented access for individual investors but also unprecedented efficiency and economy.

Given these advantages, it is not surprising that mutual fund investing took off in the 1980s and 1990s.

To be sure, mutual fund investing is not perfect. While many funds provide low-cost investing, some funds are not bashful to charge an annual fee amounting to 2 percent or more of an investor's assets. That means investors with $50,000 in a fund lose $1,000 or more per year in fees.

And mutual funds aren't great vehicles for controlling taxes. Indeed, when you own a mutual fund outside of a tax-exempt account (such as an IRA or 401(k) plan), you give control of your tax destiny to the fund manager. It is the fund manager who decides when to realize gains on investments, and that could mean a tax liability for you at the end of the year. Worse, in some cases fund investors must pay a tax on capital gains distributed during the year, even though the investor is actually holding a paper loss in the fund.

For example, the Van Wagoner Micro-Cap Growth Fund recorded a loss of more than 18 percent in 2000. Yet, shareholders of the fund still had to pay taxes on a capital-gains distribution of $4.50 a share.

Finally, mutual funds, with their professional management, still don't guarantee top results. It's estimated that in any given year, two-thirds or more of actively managed funds won't beat their benchmarks. In other words, most fund investors would have done better simply owning an index, such as the S&P 500, than buying a fund that attempts to outperform the index. Little wonder that a major growth area in fund assets over the last decade has been in so-called "index" funds—mutual funds that mimic popular indexes. After all, if you can't beat 'em, join 'em, and that's what millions of investors have done in moving money into index mutual funds.

Even with these shortcomings, mutual funds offer a solid vehicle for dollar-based investing. In fact, nearly all mutual funds make it extremely easy to implement a regular, dollar-based investment program via automatic monthly investments. These programs allow you to put your investing on autopilot by having the mutual fund electronically withdraw a predetermined amount of money from your checking account each month. And in some cases, funds may waive their minimum if an investor agrees to invest as little as $50 or $100 per month via automatic monthly investment.

Following are three prominent fund families that offer automatic monthly investment programs with low minimums. For a prospectus and enrollment information, call the toll-free number.

Fund Family	Minimum Automatic Monthly Investment	Phone Number
Dreyfus	$100	(800) 782-6620
Invesco	$50	(800) 525-8085
T. Rowe Price	$50	(800) 638-5660

For more information about mutual funds, including ratings on literally thousands of funds, check out www.morningstar.com.

Dollar-Based Investments for Retirement

It's one of the ironies of investing. The investment program that presumably has the longest time horizon—your retirement investments (401(k) plans and IRAs)—usually are the ones that concern you the most when the market takes a nosedive.

Logic would dictate that retirement programs, with their 20- and 30-year time frames for investors, would be least sensitive to the day-to-day, week-to-week, even year-to-year fluctuations in the market.

Of course, it doesn't work that way. Obviously, the importance of retirement funds and what a financially secure retirement represents—financial freedom; independence from the nine-to-five grind; days filled with golf, tennis, naps, cocktails, vacations—is what makes investors get extra itchy when these funds take a big tumble.

Fortunately, most retirement investing is done via dollar-based investment programs. For that reason, weathering market volatility with these funds is much easier simply because investors have the ability to maintain regular investment programs that are easy on the pocketbook and easy on the psyche.

What are some of these dollar-based retirement vehicles?

401(k) Plans

How's this for an investment deal:

- Every dollar you invest comes "off the top." In other words, every dollar you contribute to this investment vehicle lowers your income and, therefore, your income taxes.

- Every dollar you invest in this vehicle grows tax-deferred.

- Chances are that your contribution will generate "free money" in the form of a match by your employer.

- You don't have to sit down and write a check every time you want to invest. The money is taken automatically from your paycheck— the ultimate in no-muss, no-fuss investing.

- You can invest as little as 1 percent of your salary. That means if you make $500 a week, you can invest as little as $5—*five bucks!*— and your $5 investment will be spread over a variety of investments that you choose.

- Even investments of just $5 are still managed professionally.

What's not to like, right?

Actually, there's *a lot* to like when it comes to 401(k) retirement plans, especially the fact that the investment in 401(k) plans is made with pretax dollars. This is a huge benefit.

Do the math. If you are in the 28 percent tax bracket, every dollar you contribute to your 401(k) plan reduces your income-tax bill by 28 cents. Another way to look at the contribution is the following: A $1,200 contribution ($100 per month) to your 401(k) plan is the equivalent of investing $1,536 ($1,200 times 1.28) outside your 401(k) plan since that contribution would be made with after-tax dollars.

401(k)s and 403(b)s (a 403(b) plan is a similar retirement program for nonprofit entities) have opened the door to investing for literally millions of individuals. When you think about that empowerment, that accessibility for people with even modest incomes, it is not surprising that 401(k) and 403(b) plans were established as dollar-based investing programs. It goes back to that simple truth: When people think about investing in terms of their monthly budget—how much to spend on food, shelter, and investments—what falls out of that process is not some share-based amount of investing ("Let me see—I think I'll buy 18.927 shares in my 401(k)."). No, what falls out of that process is a dollar amount ("I can afford to kick in $400 a month to my 401(k) plan."). That's how most people think about investing. That's one reason 401(k) plans have become so popular—easy entry, no gatekeepers (i.e., brokers), low minimums, tax advantages, *and the ability to invest in dollar amounts.*

Because of all the advantages of the 401(k) plan and the fact that it is a dollar-based investing scheme, these programs stand at the frontlines as a major weapon for investing during volatile markets.

Remember: 401(k) plans are no-muss, no-fuss investments. You literally put them on autopilot. That's important, because that means you'll be more likely to invest in your 401(k) even during rocky market periods. And that's one of the big tactics for dealing with volatile markets—investing during the bad as well as the good times. A 401(k) plan makes it easy for you to do that.

I also think 401(k) plans are important for surviving and thriving during lousy markets because they are truly a more palatable way to invest. The small minimums associated with 401(k) plans reduce the hurdle of investing that may be present if you are forced to invest larger dollar amounts every time you venture into the market.

Bottom line: If you aren't doing everything you can to max out your 401(k) plan, you are wasting your time investing elsewhere. I say this with one qualifier: Max out your plan *provided* you have decent investment options from which to choose. If your only options are a guaranteed income contract, a bond fund, and your company's stock, maxing out your plan may not be a good idea. If your company's investment options are rather limited in scope and don't give you a broad choice among various equity classes— large-cap, small-cap, mid-cap, international, growth, income, balanced, and so on—as well as bond classes—short-term, intermediate-term, long-term—express your concern to the plan administrator. I can tell you that plan administrators (I'm the trustee for my company's 401(k) plan, so I know of what I speak) are very receptive to suggestions about investment options. Trustees and plan administrators have a fiduciary responsibility to provide an adequate number of choices.

New 401(k) Contribution Limits

If your plan options are acceptable, the next step is to invest as much in the plan as possible. Fortunately, the 2001 tax bill made it possible to stash even more cash in your 401(k) plan. And for individuals age 50 and older, your deal just got even better in the way of "catch-up" contributions.

Here's the new contribution schedule for qualified retirement plans, such as 401(k) and 403(b) plans:

Year 2002—$11,000 annually (up from $10,500 in 2001)
Year 2003—$12,000 annually
Year 2004—$13,000 annually
Year 2005—$14,000 annually
Year 2006—$15,000 annually
Year 2007 and beyond—contribution limits adjusted for inflation in $500 increments

An added kicker is available to "older" taxpayers (age 50 and older). These taxpayers can contribute a "catch-up" contribution of an additional $1,000 in 2002, $2,000 in 2003, $3,000 in 2004, $4,000 in 2005, and $5,000 in 2006. Thus, in 2006, an investor 50 years or older will be able to contribute up to $20,000 ($15,000 ceiling plus $5,000 catch-up contribution) to a 401(k) plan.

All-Weather 401(k) Portfolio Allocation

Of course, it's one thing to decide to invest the max in your 401(k); it's another thing to know where to invest. I know a lot of you reading this want some simple, straightforward allocation that you can set now and come back to 15 years from now. In effect, you want an all-weather 401(k) allocation.

In Chapter 5, we discussed an allocation for an all-weather portfolio and even laid out specific stocks and bond funds for this portfolio. Of course, since your 401(k) options are not unlimited, you probably won't be able to replicate the all-weather portfolio laid out in that chapter. Therefore, I thought it would be useful to provide a broader "all-weather" allocation that could be used when creating a 401(k) portfolio.

Keep in mind that any allocation that purports to be all-weather has its shortcomings. One shortcoming is the likelihood of young investors having too large an exposure to bonds.

If you are on the risk-averse side, still licking your wounds from 2000 and 2001, and want an allocation for your 401(k) plan that you can sleep with tonight, tomorrow, a year from now, and a decade from now, here goes. Remember, I don't know what options are in your 401(k) plan, so I'm using asset types and classes. My guess is your 401(k) plan offers an investment option to fill each of these style boxes.

- *Bond/Cash investments*—If possible, choose a diversified bond fund offering with maturities across the spectrum of short-term, intermediate-term, and long-term. If one of your options is a bond index fund, choose that one. **30 PERCENT OF YOUR PORTFOLIO**

- *International stocks*—If you have more than one international fund from which to choose, select the most diversified fund across many countries. Avoid single-country funds. I know international stocks have not exactly set the world on fire in the last few years. Still, you cannot ignore the fact that roughly 60 percent of the total world's equity is outside the United States. **10 PERCENT OF YOUR PORTFOLIO**

- *Large-cap stocks*—Large-cap stocks have market capitalizations (market capitalization is the stock price per share times the number of outstanding shares) of $8 billion or more. My guess is that your investment options include an index fund, such as an index fund that mimics the S&P 500. This would be a worthwhile choice for this portion of your assets. An alternative is to divide the portion devoted to large-cap stocks between a large-cap growth fund and a large-cap value fund. If you're not sure which funds fall in those style categories, talk to your 401(k) plan administrator. **40 PERCENT OF YOUR PORTFOLIO**

- *Mid-cap stocks*—Mid-cap stocks fall in the range of market capitalizations of approximately $2 billion to $8 billion. Mid-cap stocks enhance the diversification of this portfolio since the performance of mid-cap stocks does not correlate exactly with the performance of large-cap stocks. Hopefully, your 401(k) plan offers a growth and value fund in the mid-cap sector. If not, choose the mid-cap fund in the mix with the smallest assets. In that way, the fund will likely stay more true to its focus on mid-cap stocks. A mid-cap fund that has been successful and has garnered lots of assets from investors may not be able to stay true to its investment approach. That's because the fund manager may not be able to put that money to work in mid-cap stocks due to the inability to buy and sell these stocks without impacting prices. What happens next is "style shift"; the fund manager starts buying larger companies with greater trading liquidity. When you set this allocation, you don't want the funds shifting styles; you want them focused on their respective style areas. All things equal, a small (in terms of assets under management) mid-cap fund has a better chance of avoiding style shift than a large mid-cap fund. 10 PERCENT OF YOUR PORTFOLIO

- *Small-cap stocks*—Small-cap stocks have market capitalizations below $2 billion. You own small-cap stocks for the same reason you own mid-cap stocks—small-cap stocks increase the diversification of your portfolio. Also, studies have shown that, over time, small-cap stocks tend to outperform large-cap stocks, although at a higher risk level. You might be thinking that small-caps are too risky to have in an all-weather portfolio. Actually, it is a mistake to look at the riskiness of the asset class by itself. Yes, small-cap stocks are more volatile. However, within a portfolio of other assets, you can actually reduce the volatility of the portfolio by including small-cap stocks. That's exactly what we're doing here with small-cap stocks. Most 401(k) plans have a small-cap fund option. If your plan has a small-cap growth and a small-cap value fund, split the money. If your fund has a small-cap index fund, choose that. 10 PERCENT OF YOUR PORTFOLIO

Remember: You are building a portfolio that you can live with through market ups and downs. That means giving up some gains when markets soar to have better protection when markets decline.

Of course, if your crystal ball was infallible, you would simply shift assets back and forth between the "hot" sectors and the "cold" sectors. But trust me—you won't be able to do this successfully over time. That's why I like this portfolio—it doesn't force you to chase hot investment styles. It is an approach that should serve most investors well over the next several years.

One point worth mentioning is the following: Invariably the percentage allocations in this portfolio will change from month to month and year to year. Indeed, one investment sector (perhaps large-cap stocks) will do better than another, which will mean that, in this example, the percentage of assets in the all-weather 401(k) portfolio designated for large-cap stocks (40 percent) may become 50 percent or higher.

The question: How often should you rebalance your portfolio (*rebalance* is a fancy term for buying and selling investments to restore your appropriate asset allocation) to keep the percentages in line with your initial allocation?

Given that 401(k) plans are tax-preferenced accounts—you don't pay capital gains when you buy and sell investments in the 401(k) plan—you do have the luxury of being able to rebalance your portfolio as frequently as you want. However, I would be reluctant to rebalance more than, say, once a year or once every 18 months. The reason for this 12- to 18-month time frame is that asset classes generally have bullish/bearish periods lasting at least 12 to 18 months. You don't want to get into the bad habit of rebalancing on a daily basis. What that will do is cause you to sell potential 12-month winners. I would rather let each asset class have an opportunity to perform for at least a 12-month period. At the end of the 12 months, I would sell off the winners and buy more of the losers. In this case, rebalancing does force you to put more money into asset classes when they are down, which is exactly what you should do but often don't have the courage to do.

Finally, remember that your 401(k) plan is not a savings account. It is a retirement account. Don't raid it to buy cars, toys, vacations, and so on. If you draw on your 401(k) plan before age 59$^{1}/_{2}$, you'll likely pay penalties along with taxes.

Also, if you change jobs and must move your 401(k) plan, make sure your 401(k) funds are rolled over directly either into the 401(k) of your new employer or to a self-directed IRA account. You don't want to take possession of these funds. You want your former employer to send the funds directly to your new designate.

IRAs—Traditional and Roth

Another favorite vehicle for retirement saving is the individual retirement account. And, not surprisingly, the mass appeal of this product stems to a large extent from IRAs being dollar-based investment vehicles.

There are two types of IRAs—traditional and Roth. The traditional IRA lets individuals set aside money in an investment or investments of their choice. In order to make contributions to a Roth or traditional IRA, you must have earned income. Money contributed to a traditional IRA grows tax-deferred. You pay taxes when the money is withdrawn. You must begin withdrawing money from an IRA at age 70$^1/_2$.

Under certain circumstances, money contributed to a traditional IRA may be tax-deductible:

- If you are not covered by a qualified retirement plan at your place of employment, your contribution to a traditional IRA is deductible regardless of your income. For example, if you make $150,000 per year at your job, yet you are not covered by a qualified retirement plan, you can make a deductible contribution to a traditional IRA.

- If you are covered by a qualified plan, you may still be able to deduct contributions to a traditional IRA. For 2002, a full deduction is available to individuals with adjusted gross incomes below $34,000 (single filer) or below $54,000 (married, filing jointly). For incomes between $34,000 and $44,000 (single filer) and $54,000 and $64,000 (married, filing jointly), partial deduction of contributions is permitted. For incomes above $44,000 (single filer) and $64,000 (married, filing jointly), no deductible contributions are permitted. However, you can still make nondeductible contributions to an IRA regardless of your income.

The Roth IRA is one of the best dollar-based investment programs available to investors:

- Money contributed to a Roth IRA grows tax-deferred and is withdrawn *tax-free.* In other words, if your Roth IRA grows to $2 million, you will never pay a dime in taxes when you start to make withdrawals. This is a big advantage over the traditional IRA, which taxes withdrawals. In order to withdraw your money tax-free, your account has to have been open at least five years and your withdrawal occurs either after you reach age 59^1/$_2$ or due to disability, death, or if the money is used for expenses under the "first-time home buyer" rule.

- Anyone is eligible to contribute to a Roth IRA as long as they meet certain income requirements. Single individuals with an adjusted gross income of up to $95,000 ($150,000 for couples filing jointly) can make a full contribution. Partial contributions are allowed for individuals whose adjusted gross income is between $95,000 and $110,000 ($150,000 and $160,000 for couples filing jointly).

- Unlike the traditional IRA, you can make contributions to a Roth IRA after the age of 70^1/$_2$ as long as you have earned income.

- Unlike the traditional IRA, you are not required to make withdrawals beginning at age 70^1/$_2$. In fact, you are never required to withdraw the money. If you leave your Roth IRA to your heirs, your beneficiaries do not have to pay taxes on the money either. The ability to leave tax-free income to your heirs makes the Roth an interesting estate-planning tool.

- You can contribute to a Roth IRA as well as a traditional IRA if you have earned income, but the total cumulative contributions cannot exceed the annual contribution limit, which we'll discuss in a moment.

- You can contribute to a Roth IRA even if you contribute to a 401(k) plan.

- Virtually any stock or mutual fund is eligible to be held in a Roth IRA.

The biggest downside to a Roth IRA is that the contribution is never tax-deductible. Also, if you withdraw your money before your account is five years old, your earnings may be subject to federal income taxes plus a 10 percent penalty.

So which IRA is the best—traditional or Roth? All things equal, the Roth IRA, because money is withdrawn tax-free, is the better choice, especially for individuals who cannot make deductible contributions to a traditional IRA because of their income levels.

So if I have a traditional IRA, shouldn't I convert it to a Roth IRA? Perhaps, although whether conversion makes sense for you depends on a variety of things. First, you can convert a traditional IRA to a Roth IRA only if your adjusted gross income in the year of conversion is less than $100,000.

Second, when you convert a traditional IRA to a Roth IRA, you will likely give yourself a tax hit. The size of the tax liability depends on whether you are converting deductible or nondeductible IRA funds. If you convert IRA funds that were tax-deductible upon contributions, the entire amount is considered ordinary income for tax purposes.

For example, if you convert a deductible IRA of $60,000 to a Roth IRA, you'll have to pay taxes on the full $60,000. If you are in the 28 percent tax bracket, that's a tax hit of $16,800.

If you convert a traditional IRA in which contributions were not tax-deductible, only the earnings are subject to tax, not the contributions that were made with after-tax dollars.

When should you convert?

- If you have a lot of time until retirement to make up for the tax hit you'll take when you convert, conversion makes sense.

- If you expect to be in a higher tax bracket when you retire, conversion makes sense.

- If the amount in your traditional IRA is small, conversion makes sense.

- If you can pay the taxes without robbing the account, conversion makes sense.

Several Web sites, including www.financenter.com, offer "Roth Conversion Calculators" to help you decide whether it makes sense for you to convert. At www.financenter.com, scroll to the bottom of the page to "Retirement Center" and click on the link. You'll be taken to a page where you can click on "Analyzers."

New Contribution Limits for Traditional, Roth IRAs

Uncle Sam, via the 2001 Tax Bill, is now letting you stash more cash in your traditional or Roth IRA. Here is the new schedule of contribution limits. (Remember: You and your spouse can each contribute the maximum each year):

- Years 2002–2004: $3,000 annually

- Years 2005–2007: $4,000 annually

- Year 2008: $5,000 annually

- Year 2009 and beyond: Contribution limits are adjusted for inflation in $500 increments.

And, similar to the new 401(k) contribution limits, older taxpayers (age 50 and older) can contribute an additional $500 a year in "catch-up" contributions starting in 2002 and $1,000 over the cap starting in 2006.

SEP IRA

Another type of IRA is the SEP IRA. The SEP IRA allows self-employed individuals to establish an individual retirement account. Contributions to the SEP IRA are in dollar amounts, thus making them yet another dollar-based method for saving for retirement.

SEP IRAs have several attractions:

- If you have self-employed income, contributions to your SEP IRA are tax-deductible.

- The contribution limits for a SEP IRA may exceed those of a traditional or Roth IRA. Indeed, under most circumstances, you can invest up to 15 percent of your income in a SEP IRA, with a cap at $30,000 per year.

- You can contribute to a SEP IRA with income generated from self-employment even if you also are enrolled in a 401(k) plan at your primary employer.

- SEP IRAs are easy to establish and require minimal paperwork to maintain. The convenience of opening and contributing to these plans is a big advantage over other, more complicated self-employed retirement programs, such as KEOGH.

- You can open up a SEP IRA at virtually any mutual fund family or brokerage firm.

- You can invest in virtually any investment (bonds, stocks, mutual funds) with your SEP IRA contribution.

SEP IRAs carry restrictions and penalties similar to those of traditional and Roth IRAs when it comes to withdrawals prior to age $59^1/2$.

Investment Options for Traditional, Roth, and SEP IRAs

The beauty of traditional, Roth, and SEP IRAs is that they provide lots of flexibility in terms of investment options. As mentioned, you can open any of these IRAs at any brokerage or mutual fund firm. And you can stock your portfolio with virtually any investment you want.

Of course, having lots of choices is a double-edged sword. Lots of choices are empowering, but also confusing. What funds? What stocks?

Let's return to my all-weather portfolio featured in Chapter 5. You can replicate this all-weather portfolio in virtually any IRA.

DIVIDEND REINVESTMENT PLANS/ DIRECT-PURCHASE PLANS

Up to this point, I've focused on dollar-based investing via mutual funds. Dollar-based investing is also possible via individual stocks. One way to dollar-based invest in individual stocks is a vehicle that is near and dear to my heart: dividend reinvestment plans.

As many of you know, I've done a lot of work on DRIPs over the last decade. I write a monthly newsletter on the subject (*DRIP Investor*). I've written two best-selling books on the subject (*Buying Stocks Without a Broker, No-Load Stocks*). I give 10 to 20 speeches a year on the subject. I've given literally hundreds of media interviews on the subject.

In short, I've spent the better part of the last decade of my professional life extolling the virtues of dividend reinvestment plans.

Why have I spent so much time and energy on this topic? Simple. DRIPs remain among the most powerful investment vehicles available for bringing Wall Street to Main Street.

I know from my own experience just how powerful these programs can be. Indeed, I began investing in DRIPs in the early '90s. I had dabbled in mutual funds prior to that and had tried my hand with a few stocks I bought via a broker. But I didn't really have an organization, a theme to my investing outside of my retirement accounts. In many cases, I bought cheap stocks because I could afford to buy only cheap stocks via a broker. Consequently, I bought a lot of junk.

For example, I bought warrants in an electric utility that went bankrupt. Yes, I know electric utilities don't go bankrupt. This one did. Public Service New Hampshire. Look it up. First utility since the Great Depression to go belly up. And I owned warrants in it. Why? Because the warrants were cheap. Forget the fact that they expired worthless. I could afford a round lot of them.

I also bought stock options. Calls and puts. You buy call options as a bet on a stock's rising. You buy put options as a bet on a stock's sinking. Options have a finite life, however, which means you not only have to be right on the direction of the underlying stock, you have to be right on the time frame. I was rarely right on both accounts. So why did I buy stock options? Because you could buy a couple of options for a few hundred bucks. They were cheap. Forget the fact that most options expire worthless. I bought them because I could afford them.

To be sure, not all my early investments were dogs. However, what I found was that the investments I bought because I could afford to buy 100 shares or more rarely provided any meaningful return and usually ended up costing me most if not all of my money.

And then I discovered DRIPs.

It's funny, but when I first heard about DRIPs, it was one of those "Wow!" experiences. *Let me get this straight,* I thought. *I can buy stocks directly from a company, without a broker, in amounts as little as $10, and pay little or nothing in commissions? And I can buy blue chips, not just crummy companies?*

It was truly an epiphany.

When I think back to when I got started in DRIPs, what stands out as key was the fact that I could now invest in dollar amounts, not share amounts. No longer was my investing mind-set shackled to buying in shares. I could now buy in dollar amounts, often as little as $10 or $25.

That shifted how I viewed investing by 180 degrees. I began focusing on quality, not quantity. I bought the best stocks I could find—my first two DRIP investments were Exxon and Procter & Gamble, stocks I had never thought of buying because I couldn't afford to buy 100 shares—and didn't worry about the per-share price. I bought whether the stock was up or down, whether the market was running with the bulls or hibernating with the bears.

For me, DRIPs represented a sort of savings account, a way of taking, literally, pocket change and buying blue chips.

Even today, when I can afford to buy 100 shares or more of any stock, I still use DRIPs. Why? Because the reasons I liked them more than a decade ago still hold true for me today.

DRIP Nuts and Bolts

I don't want to bore you with all the nitty-gritty details of DRIPs—my guess is that most of you are familiar with these plans via my other books and newsletters—but a brief primer is in order for newcomers to the market reading this book.

DRIPs are programs, offered by approximately 1,100 publicly traded companies, that allow investors to buy stock directly from the company, *without a broker.*

Investors buy stock from companies in two ways:

- First, instead of receiving dividend checks, investors have the company reinvest dividends on their behalf to purchase additional shares.

- Second, most DRIPs permit investors to send money directly to the company to buy additional shares. In many cases, these "optional cash payments" may be as little as $25 or $50. If you have deeper pockets, most DRIPs permit investments of up to $100,000 or more per year.

DRIPs offer four main benefits for investors:

- Many DRIPs charge no fees to purchase shares in their plans, and DRIPs that do charge fees usually have fees that are much lower than even the lowest online brokerage firm.

- In more than 8 percent of all DRIP plans, you can buy stock at a *discount* to the market price. These discounts are usually in the 3 to 5 percent range. I don't know of any other investment that allows investors to buy stock at 95 cents or 97 cents on the dollar. It's instant profit.

- DRIPs allow investors to buy both full and fractional shares of stock. If, for example, your $50 investment isn't enough to buy a full share of stock, the DRIP will sell you a fractional share, and that fractional share is entitled to a fractional part of the dividend. In short, DRIPs allow you to buy high-priced stocks on the install-ment plan, a little bit at a time.

- DRIPs offer a lot of flexibility for any investor to mold an invest-ment program *in high-quality stocks* based on his or her financial situation. If you have a lot of money, you can invest a lot. If you have a little money, you can invest a little. If you don't have any money in a given month, you are not obligated to invest.

There are two types of DRIPs. The first type is the traditional DRIP, which requires investors to already be a shareholder of the company in order to participate in the plan. The usual share require-ment in traditional DRIPs is just one share. Coca-Cola, for example, requires that you own at least one share of Coca-Cola stock in order to enroll in the plan, and that share must be registered in your own name, not the broker name (also known as the "street" name).

Obviously, DRIPs that require prior share ownership present the problem of how to get that first share. Brokerage firms offer one avenue for getting the first share. However, newcomers to investing may not have a broker or may feel uncomfortable choosing one.

Another way to obtain the first share is the "buddy system." Let's say a friend owns stock in a company in which you would like to join the DRIP. Your friend could transfer a share of stock from his or her account to your name, and presto! You're now a registered shareholder. Transferring stock is easy. All you need to do is obtain a "stock power" form from a brokerage firm or any financial institution. Fill out the form and get a "medallion signature guarantee" stamp on the form. You should be able to obtain a medallion signature guarantee at a bank in your area. Once you have completed the form and obtained the stamp, send it to the company's DRIP administrator, also known as the transfer agent. Your friend should include a letter stating that he or she is transferring a share of stock to you and, if possible, would like to have you directly enrolled in the DRIP.

Of course, the obvious shortcoming to this solution is that your friend may not own a stock in which you are interested.

Fortunately, a number of companies are taking their DRIPs to the next level by allowing individuals to make even their initial purchase of stock directly. These "DRIPs on steroids" are often referred to as "direct-purchase plans." I call them "no-load stocks" because you buy directly, without a broker, much the same way you buy a no-load mutual fund.

The minimum initial investment in more than half of the more than 600 direct-purchase plans now available is $250 or less. Once you've made the initial investment, subsequent investments can be made with as little as $50 or $100 in most plans.

In addition to allowing you to buy your initial shares directly, direct-purchase plans provide a number of other features in common with no-load mutual funds:

- Most direct-purchase plans permit investors to invest via automatic monthly debit of their bank account. These plans are excellent for helping to maintain a regular investment program.

- A number of direct-purchase plans have IRA (individual retirement account) options built directly into the plans. For example, *Exxon* (800-252-1800) allows investors to buy even initial shares directly from the company. Minimum initial investment is just $250, and subsequent investments may be as little as $50. Exxon permits investment via automatic electronic debit of your bank account. Furthermore, Exxon has an IRA option built into its plan.

In other words, you can invest directly with Exxon, without a broker and without any purchase fees, and earmark those investments for an IRA that Exxon administers for you. Exxon charges a small annual fee to administer the IRA.

- A growing number of plans allow you to sell your shares over the phone. Telephone redemption is a big departure from earlier DRIPs, which required you to submit your sell instructions in writing.

To participate in a direct-purchase plan, you'll need to obtain the enrollment information and a plan prospectus (the prospectus provides all of the details of the plan). This material is available by calling the company or downloading the information the company's Web site. Once you obtain the enrollment form, fill it out and return it along with your check for the initial investment. That's all there is to it. After the initial investment, you are free to make optional cash investments. The stock certificates are held by the company but are always available upon request.

Before you invest in DRIPs, it's important to know the plans' shortcomings:

- You won't have the precision over the buy and sell price that you have through a broker. Most DRIPs buy stock either once a week or once a month. If you like a stock's price today, it could be higher or lower by the time the shares are purchased for you in the plan. I don't consider this that big a deal since I hold DRIPs for a long time. However, if you want exact control over the buy and sell price, these plans may not be for you.

- If you invest in, say, five different DRIPs, you will receive account statements from each company. These statements provide all the information you need for tracking your shares for tax purposes. However, there is no such thing as a single consolidated statement in the DRIP world.

- Some DRIPs have been implementing fees. These fees may include a one-time enrollment fee of $5 to $15 and per-transaction fees of $1 to $10. Make sure you know all of the details of the plan, including fees, before investing. The plan prospectus provides information on fees and other plan specifics.

Also be aware that DRIPs may differ dramatically from one company to another. Although most DRIPs require shareholders to own only one share in order to enroll, others may require investors to own as many as 50 shares in order to be eligible. Some DRIPs may charge commissions and fees, while others will invest commission-free. Other differences include the timing and frequency of optional cash purchases, the availability of services such as IRAs and automatic monthly investment, and so on. How do you find out about the particulars? Call the company, talk to the shareholder services department, and get a copy of the plan prospectus, which provides all of the details concerning the plan. Remember: It is important to know the specifics of the plan, especially eligibility requirements, before investing in the stock. You don't want to buy one share of stock only to find out afterward that you need 10 shares in order to enroll in the DRIP.

One final point worth mentioning concerns DRIPs and record keeping. Companies and their transfer agents do their best to help dividend reinvestment plan participants keep track of their investments. Investors receive statements, usually after each investment with dividends and optional cash payments. Make sure you keep track of this information, especially your cost basis for each purchase of stock. This information is essential when you sell shares and need to determine your cost basis for tax purposes. Also, at the end of the year, companies send 1099 forms showing the amount of dividend income that was reinvested during the year. This information is important, since such dividends are taxable income each year even though the dividends were reinvested to purchase additional shares.

For a complete list of all U.S. and foreign companies (that's right, more than 300 foreign companies allow U.S. investors to buy stock directly, the first share and every share), see Appendix A, beginning on page 239.

Recommended DRIPs/Direct-Purchase Plans

In Chapter 4, I discussed the concept of easy-hold stocks and why easy holds represent excellent holdings for weathering market volatility. Many easy-hold stocks offer dividend reinvestment plans. Three easy holds that allow investors to make initial purchases directly are *Exxon Mobil, Pfizer,* and *Popular.* For investors who want to get their feet wet investing in direct-purchase plans, these three companies represent excellent stocks for a "starter portfolio." None of the three charges a penny in fees on shares purchased through the plan.

- *Exxon Mobil* (XOM) is perhaps the premier player in the energy group. I own the stock and recommend these shares for any portfolio. Minimum initial investment is $250. Subsequent investments may be as little as $50. There are no fees on the buy side. Exxon offers an IRA option, including the Roth IRA. For enrollment information to buy the stock directly from the company, call (800) 252-1800.

- *Pfizer* (PFE) is one of the best stocks in one of the best groups for long-term investors. The company has a well-stocked product stable (Viagra, Celebrex, Zoloft, Lipitor). With research and development outlays of some $5 billion annually, Pfizer should remain on the cutting edge of groundbreaking developments in the drug sector. If you are building a portfolio, you need a quality drug stock as a core holding. Pfizer represents such a holding. Minimum initial investment is $500. Subsequent investments may be as little as $50. There are no fees on the buy side. For enrollment information, call (800) 733-9393.

- *Popular* (BPOP) is a regional bank headquartered in Puerto Rico. The firm has produced steady earnings growth over the years. One reason is that the company's primary customer base is growing at a rapid rate. Indeed, Popular's markets are primarily Hispanic communities in the United States and Puerto Rico. This fast-growing ethnic group should help Popular continue to deliver solid earnings growth. I own Popular and regard it as an attractive place to deploy new funds. The company has a user-friendly direct-purchase plan. Minimum initial investment is just $100. There are no fees on the buy side. Subsequent investments may be as little as $25. The plan offers a 5 percent discount on shares purchased with reinvested dividends. For enrollment information, call (877) 764-1893. When you call that number, you'll likely hear someone speaking Spanish. DON'T HANG UP. The phone person also understands English and can take your mailing information. If you prefer, you can download the enrollment form at the company's Web site—www.popularinc.com.

THE NEW DOLLAR-BASED BROKERS

By and large, brokerage firms deal in shares: You buy 100 shares of this stock, 50 shares of that stock, 500 shares of this low-priced stock, or one million shares if you are a big institutional buyer.

Shares. Shares. Shares.

Interestingly, this wasn't always the case. In fact, back in the 1950s, the New York Stock Exchange offered the "Monthly Investment Plan." The program worked like this: Individuals could invest as little as $40 every three months to buy shares in some 1,200 New York Stock Exchange stocks, common and preferred. An investor could sign up for the program at any member firm. All trades went through the brokerage firm, which received a small fee. The commission, according to a 1961 brochure, was a flat 6 percent of the investment when the amount invested was $100 or less. For the minimum $40 investment, the charge was $2.26. For investments of more than $100, the 6 percent commission gradually decreased until, with an investment of $1,000—the monthly maximum investment permitted in the plan—the commission was $14.85, or 1.5 percent of the amount invested. Investors could make simultaneous payments into a number of stocks with a single check. Another feature of the program permitted participants to have their dividends reinvested for additional shares. Participants were also able to sell their shares through the plan for a small fee. There were no contracts or start-up fees, nor did participants have to agree to contribute every month or every quarter. It was easy to enroll. Investors could either contact a brokerage firm or use an enrollment form that was included in the introductory brochure.

Great plan, right? True "dollar-based" investing via a brokerage firm. A perfect way for the small investor to access the market.

Unfortunately, the Monthly Investment Plan died out over time. I suspect the demise of the plan was due to brokerage firms tiring of taking such small orders for small fees.

I mention the Monthly Investment Plan because the brokerage world has experienced a "back-to-the-future" move over the last two years with the emergence of a new breed of broker, one that emulates the Monthly Investment Program. A new breed of broker that emphasizes dollar-based investing.

SHAREBUILDER

Sharebuilder (www.sharebuilder.com) offers a dollar-based investment approach. Investors may buy full and fractional shares of stock. There is no minimum amount needed to establish an account.

Sharebuilder has two pricing plans:

- Per-trade fee of $4.

- "All-You-Can-Build" plan for $12 per month. That is, unlimited trades for $12 per month.

Sharebuilder buys stock only once per week. The firm also offers real-time trades for $15.95 per trade.

Sharebuilder also offers IRAs.

Sharebuilder is strictly an online service, which means you'll need Internet access to trade.

FOLIO*fn*

FOLIO*fn* (www.foliofn.com) is another broker offering dollar-based investing.

Actually, FOLIO*fn* has positioned itself as a hybrid between a mutual fund and a brokerage firm. The company's business is built around "folios"—a group of securities that you can purchase in a single transaction.

Unlike a mutual fund, where an investor owns shares in the fund, not the stocks held in the fund, investors via FOLIO*fn* actually own the individual stocks in their personal folio.

FOLIO*fn* offers a number of prepackaged folio products that investors can purchase with a single transaction. These "ready-to-go" folios generally have 20 to 30 securities and cover such major indexes and investment sectors as the Dow Jones Industrial Average, the 50 largest stocks in the S&P 500, a global folio of stocks from various regions of the world, folios based on investment styles (income, growth, aggressive, conservative), as well as sector folios concentrating on such industries as banks, biotechnology, and computer hardware.

FOLIO*fn* allows you to place orders to purchase shares of your folios in dollar amounts. Trades are made twice daily.

A big advantage of investing via FOLIO*fn* versus a traditional mutual fund is control over your taxes. In a mutual fund, the fund manager determines when gains or losses are realized. The fund holder has no say concerning tax liabilities. When you invest in folios via FOLIO*fn*, however, you are actually buying the individual stocks in the folio. Therefore, you can control when you sell stocks in your folios, which means you control when you incur tax liabilities.

In short, FOLIO*fn* combines benefits of mutual fund investing (diversification, simplicity) with advantages of stock investing (tax management, corporate voting rights), while eliminating many of the disadvantages of both.

One downside to FOLIO*fn* is that the program may not be very cost-friendly until you've accumulated a healthy level of assets. The monthly fee for one folio is $14.95. For three folios (each folio may hold up to 50 stocks) the monthly fee is $29.95, or $359.40 per year. If you choose to pay up front for a full year, it costs $295.00. If you want more than three folios, each additional folio costs $9.95 a month or $95.00 a year.

At the monthly fee of $29.95, you would need roughly $36,000 in your account to get your annual expenses for the program down to 1 percent of your assets. Thus, if you are new to the investing game and investing on a shoestring budget, FOLIO*fn* may not make a lot of sense.

FOLIO*fn* also offers market order trades for $14.95. You may also sell stocks or an entire folio over the phone. The firm charges an additional $45 for broker-assisted trades.

What Is This SIPC?

I know investing via new brokerage firms, such as Sharebuilder and FOLIO*fn*, may be somewhat daunting for investors. Fortunately, all NASD-registered brokers, including Sharebuilder and FOLIO*fn*, are "SIPC insured."

"SIPC insured" is one of those phrases thrown around in the financial world. But do you really know what it means? My guess is that most investors probably don't know what the SIPC is or how it works. I think it is worthwhile here to provide a brief primer on the SIPC, direct from the horse's mouth:

The Role of Securities Investors Protection Corporation

SIPC is your first line of defense in the event of a brokerage firm failure. No fewer than 99 percent of eligible investors get their investments back from SIPC. From its creation by Congress in 1970 through December 2000, SIPC advanced $391 million in order to make possible the recovery of $3.8 billion in assets for an estimated 443,000 investors.

When a brokerage is closed due to bankruptcy or other financial difficulties, the Securities Investor Protection Corporation steps in as quickly as possible and, within certain limits, works to return to you cash, stock, and other securities you had at the firm. Without SIPC, investors at financially troubled brokerage firms might lose their securities or money forever or wait for years while their assets are tied up in court.

What SIPC Covers and What It Does Not

SIPC is not the FDIC. The Securities Investor Protection Corporation does not offer to investors the same blanket protection that the Federal Deposit Insurance Corporation provides to bank depositors.

How are SIPC and the FDIC different? When a member bank fails, the FDIC insures all depositors at that institution against loss up to a certain dollar limit. The FDIC's no-questions-asked approach makes sense because the banking world is "risk averse." Most savers put their money in FDIC-insured bank accounts because they can't afford to lose their money.

That is precisely the opposite of how investors behave in the stock market, in which rewards are possible only with risk. Most market losses are a normal part of the ups and downs of the risk-oriented world of investing. That is why SIPC does not bail out investors when the value of their stocks, bonds, and other investments falls for any reason. Instead, SIPC replaces *missing* stocks and other securities where it is possible to do so . . . even when the investments have increased in value.

SIPC does not cover individuals who are sold worthless stocks and other securities. SIPC helps individuals whose money, stocks, and other securities are stolen by a broker or put at risk when a brokerage fails for other reasons.

How We Help: What You Need to Know About SIPC

Understanding the rules is the key to protecting yourself and your money.

- *When SIPC gets involved.* When a brokerage firm fails, SIPC usually asks a federal court to appoint a trustee to liquidate the firm and protect its customers. With smaller brokerage firm failures, SIPC sometimes deals directly with customers.

- *Investors eligible for SIPC help.* SIPC aids most customers of failed brokerage firms.

- Investments protected by SIPC. The cash and securities—such as stocks and bonds—held by a customer at a financially troubled brokerage firm are protected by SIPC. Among the investments that are *ineligible* for SIPC protection are commodity futures contracts and currency, as well as investment contracts (such as limited partnerships) that are not registered with the U.S. Securities and Exchange Commission under the Securities Act of 1933.

- *Terms of SIPC help.* Customers of a failed brokerage firm get back all securities (such as stocks and bonds) that already are registered in their name or are in the process of being registered. After this first step, the firm's remaining customer assets are then divided on a pro rata basis with funds shared in proportion to the size of claims. If sufficient funds are not available in the firm's customer accounts to satisfy claims within these limits, the reserve funds of SIPC are used to supplement the distribution, up to a ceiling of $500,000 per customer, including a maximum of $100,000 for cash claims. Additional funds may be available to satisfy the remainder of customer claims after the cost of liquidating the brokerage firm is taken into account.

- *How account transfers work.* In a failed brokerage firm with accurate records, the court-appointed trustee and SIPC may arrange to have some or all customer accounts transferred to another brokerage firm. Customers whose accounts are transferred are notified promptly and then have the option of staying at the new firm or moving to another brokerage of their choosing.

- *How claims are valued.* Typically, when SIPC asks a court to put a troubled brokerage firm in liquidation, the financial worth of a customer's account is calculated as of the "filing date." Wherever possible, the actual stocks and other securities owned by a customer are returned to them. To accomplish this, SIPC's reserve funds will be used, if necessary, to purchase replacement securities (such as stocks) in the open market. It is always possible that market changes or fraud at the failed brokerage firm (or elsewhere) will result in the returned securities having lost some—or even all—of their value. In other cases, the securities may have increased in value.

Source: www.sipc.org

CONCLUSION

During tough markets, little things matter big time.

How well you take advantage of market declines to buy stocks on sale has huge long-term ramifications for your portfolio.

How much you're paying in brokerage commissions and mutual fund fees can be the difference between a winning and losing portfolio.

If your investment program is not set up to minimize transaction costs and maximize your opportunities for regular investment, you are ignoring one of the most important rules for surviving and thriving during rough market periods. Dollar-based investing programs—mutual funds, 401(k) plans, IRAs, DRIPs/direct-purchase plans, and dollar-based brokers—offer convenient, easy, flexible, and low-cost ways to funnel money into the market.

Chapter Seven

Law #7:
Making the Hard Decision—
Knowing When to Sell

WHAT'S YOUR biggest regret as an investor?

My guess is that you wish you had sold your Cisco when it was $80 rather than riding it down to $11. Or sold your Lucent at $70. Or your Yahoo! at $200.

You are not alone. Quite frankly, I regret not selling some of my holdings that skyrocketed only to go into the Dumpster.

If only we had sold, right? Well, don't beat yourself up too bad. The hardest part of investing—by far—is knowing when to sell. Sell too early, and you can lose out on huge profits. Sell too late, and you can lose out on huge profits.

Admittedly, I'm not a big fan of selling stocks, for several reasons:

- When you sell an investment, you create a taxable event. I hate paying taxes, especially on my investments. And deferring taxes on investments has a powerful impact on your returns over time.

- When you sell, you're faced with another decision: What to do with the money? This reinvestment risk is very real. You could choose to keep the money in cash, but cash does not beat stocks over the long run. You could buy another investment, but that investment could just as easily decline in value. Even if the investment performs as well as the investment you sold, you're still behind if you take into account taxes.

• When you sell, you incur transaction fees. While transaction fees have come down sharply over the past decade, the fees still chip away at your investment capital.

AVOID THE BIG LOSER

Still, while I'm not a big fan of selling, I'm not a big fan of losing 70 percent of my money by riding down a stock that I should have dumped. That's the problem with not selling investments. You always risk having the big loser. And that big loser can wreak havoc on a portfolio.

I read a story of a successful investor who, when one straight-to-the-point novice asked what this man's secret of investment success was, replied simply, "Don't lose."

We've already talked a bit about the math of the markets and how cruel it can be when you're on the wrong side of a market move. Take a stock that plummets from $100 to $20. That's a decline of 80 percent.

But for that stock to return to $100 per share, the price would have to rise *400 percent.*

Now, take a portfolio that declines 50 percent (and many portfolios have declined 50 percent or more over the last two years). The math here is quite simple. In order to recoup your loss, the portfolio must increase 100 percent.

If you think about that in terms of time, the number of years required to recoup the loss (based on the stock market's historical annual return of approximately 11 percent) is nearly seven. In other words, based on historical market returns, a 50 percent decline in your portfolio shaves roughly seven years off your investment program.

Now, while nobody wants to lose seven years off an investment program, you can afford to play catch-up if you have an investment time horizon of at least 20 or 30 years, especially if you are willing to invest more money when stocks are down.

However, if you are someone in his or her fifties or sixties, the cost of losing big is even steeper. You just don't have enough time to make up the lost years as a result of one big hit.

Sadly, that's what has happened to too many investors in the last two years. People who should have been structuring their investment portfolios to match their investment time horizon ignored prudent diversification and allocation rules. Instead, they kept shooting for the moon. The strategy certainly paid off in 1998 and 1999, when stocks were skyrocketing. But the strategy backfired in 2000 and 2001.

Bottom line: To everything there is a season, including selling. Volatile markets put an even greater premium on selling, as violent market moves can reduce capital gains in a surprisingly short period of time.

WHEN TO SELL

Fine, you say. The importance of selling is fairly obvious. But I still haven't answered the all-important question: *When should you sell?*

To me, selling becomes a pretty logical exercise if you remember this fundamental tenet: Sell when the reasons you bought no longer hold true.

Pretty simple statement. *Sell when the reasons you bought no longer hold true.* Yet, it is also a powerful statement. Indeed, the statement is your road map for selling stock. What I like about this simple statement is that it does not limit your reasons for selling. It does, however, make you crystallize those reasons.

For example, suppose you bought a stock because it was going up. I'm not saying this is a good reason to buy a stock. But it was certainly the reason a lot of investors used to buy Internet stocks in 1999. "Stock going up. I better buy."

Am I being flippant here? Surely, investors didn't buy a stock simply because it was going up? Actually, lots and lots of investors bought stocks simply because they were going up. It's called momentum investing, and it ruled the day during 1998 and 1999.

Let's face it. How many people really understood what most of these technology companies made? Very few. How many people really took the time to dig into the firm's fundamentals, its finances, its competitors' fundamentals, its competitors' finances?

Even fewer.

So if you really didn't know that much about the company, why did you and so many other people own technology stocks? *Because they were going higher!*

Now, if the reason you bought was because the stock was going up, when should you sell?

When the stock is going down!

I know many of you are saying, "Duh." But think about it for a moment. On its way from $120 to $6, JDS Uniphase traded at $100, $90, $80, $70 . . . What was it doing? *It was going down.*

When the stock started to go down, people who bought simply because it was going up should have sold. Unfortunately, many did not.

I know I've simplified things here a bit, but not much. Yes, it is a bit ambiguous to say that you should have sold when the stock went down. Down to where?

Actually, a sell rule based on the stock "going down" could have been refined to be extremely useful. For example, if you bought the stock because it was going up, you could have set the following rule: *I will sell the stock when it declines by 15 percent.* Or 20 percent. Or 25 percent. The more volatile the stock, the more leeway you should give the stock.

But if you buy a stock strictly because it is going up fast, you should never lose more than 25 percent on your money.

Sell Rule #1: If you buy stocks simply because they are going up—and many people made lots of money picking stocks with this single criterion—the best sell rule is to sell when the stock starts going down.

That means setting a limit on the amount of decline you are willing to bear. True, nobody wants to lose 15 percent on their investment. But by limiting your decline to 15 percent, you'll never hold the stock that declines 80 percent. Also, remember to keep raising your sell limit as the stock price rises. One last point about this rule that bears mentioning is the following: The more complicated a company and its business, the better to use some hard-and-fast sell level. Why?

Because the more complicated the business, the less likely you really understand the business and will know when things are turning down. I think that is, essentially, what happened to a lot of the investors who owned technology stocks. The businesses were so complicated, and the markets moved so suddenly, that it was very difficult to tell when business conditions changed. Not impossible, mind you (as you'll soon see), but difficult. If you own such companies and come to realize that you really don't understand what makes them tick, you probably should set a sell limit to avoid taking the big bath. Consider limiting declines on such stocks to 15 to 25 percent.

It is easy to limit a decline in your investments by using "limit orders." A limit order allows you to buy or sell a stock at a specific price. For example, let's say you own a stock that is trading for $55. You don't want the stock to decline below $52. Thus, you put a limit order with your broker saying you want to sell if the stock reaches $52. This type of limit order is called a "stop order"; you'll be "stopped out" of the stock if it reaches $52. With most limit orders, you can make the order "good 'til canceled" or "good for day." Limit orders provide a nice tool for helping investors protect profits.

You can also use limit orders on the buy side. Say a stock is trading for $50. You think $50 is too much for the stock, but you'd be willing to buy the stock for $45. You can enter a "limit order" with your broker saying that you'll buy the stock at $45. Limit orders to buy are useful for stocks on your watch list that you want to buy but only if the stock declines to a certain price.

FOLLOW THE FUNDAMENTALS

Now, I know many of you have more scientific reasons for buying a stock than simply because it is going up. Many investors buy because they like the fundamentals of the company, especially the firm's earnings and sales growth. Actually, buying a company with strong fundamentals usually is a good way to make money. After all, stock prices eventually follow earnings. Picking stocks that have strong and consistent earnings-growth records should get you into more winners than losers.

Of course, company fundamentals change. Look at Cisco Systems's earnings from the second quarter of fiscal 2001 to the third quarter of 2001. In the fiscal second quarter, Cisco's per-share profits rose a healthy 38 percent to 18 cents per share. Three months later, Cisco reported a per-share *loss* of 17 cents. Clearly, fundamentals had changed. And those changes adversely affected the stock price.

If you buy stocks based on fundamentals, you better know when the fundamentals are changing. This is especially true when you buy stocks trading at very high price/earnings multiples.

A stock's price/earnings ratio looks at the stock's per-share price ("price") divided by the company's 12-month per-share earnings (the "earnings" in the ratio). A company with a stock price of $50 and 12-month earnings of $2 per share has a price/earnings (P/E) ratio of 25 (50 divided by 2).

The price/earnings ratio is really a popularity index for the stock. A high price/earnings ratio means the stock is very popular. The trouble is that popularity on Wall Street can change about as quickly as your daughter's favorite boy band. And the consequences of guessing wrong on a stock with a high price/earnings ratio are usually much more severe than guessing wrong on a deflated, low price/earnings ratio stock.

During the late '90s, much was written that price/earnings ratios didn't matter anymore. Evaluating stocks based on P/E ratios didn't work because P/E ratios were irrelevant to the "new economy" stocks. So investors ignored price/earnings ratios and zeroed in on strictly growth measures—revenue and earnings growth, growth in "click-through" rates, growth in "eyeballs" coming to the Web site.

Growth. Growth. Growth.

The problem is that growth is only one side of the equation. Investors need to be aware of the price they are paying for that growth, and whether that price makes sense. Unfortunately, most investors ignored this part of the equation.

To be sure, focusing exclusively on growth and ignoring value was a pretty successful way to pick stocks in 1998 and 1999. However, when the pendulum swung in the direction of value and away from growth in 2000 and 2001, many of these growth investors were ill equipped to detect important changes affecting the growth patterns of these high-flying growth stocks.

In other words, the people who bought Cisco at a price/earnings ratio of 100 didn't know the company well enough to see that business was deteriorating. Thus, when the growth stopped at Cisco, growth investors were left holding the bag.

The upshot is that if you pay a premium (in the form of a high price/earnings ratio) to buy a growth stock, you better be sure you'll be able to detect when the growth story has concluded.

Obviously, when growth stocks stop growing, the lack of growth will show up in the company's revenue and earnings results. However, if you wait until earnings decline, you'll get killed. That's because stock prices anticipate. In other words, stock prices will start their descent before the problems show up in the bottom line.

Thus, in order to avoid getting crushed when growth stocks stop growing, you'll have to detect changes in growth *before* the problems show up in earnings. This brings us to our next sell rule. . . .

Sell Rule#2: If you buy a stock (especially a pricey, high-P/E stock) because of strong earnings and revenue momentum, sell when the operating fundamentals that drive earnings and sales deteriorate.

What are these key operating fundamentals? Below I discuss 12 of the most important operating metrics you absolutely need to monitor in order to stay on top of your growth stocks.

Is it difficult monitoring these ratios? Actually, with the Internet and the easy availability of company financial statements, running the numbers on companies has never been easier. Still, this is the "work" part of investing, and many individuals aren't used to doing work when it comes to their investments. But I guarantee you, by looking at these 12 operating indicators, you will have a much better understanding of your companies and greater conviction in your sell decisions.

(*Author's Note:* A lot of the concepts and examples discussed here have appeared in my "Stock Selector" columns in *Bloomberg Personal Finance*. I'm biased, but my column and, indeed, the rest of *Bloomberg Personal Finance* magazine offer lots of information, tools, and techniques to make you a better investor. Check out a copy at your newsstand or online at www.bloomberg.com.)

1. INVENTORY TURNOVER RATIO

What ultimately creates successful businesses? I maintain it's the following:

Successful companies make stuff customers want NOW.

Fortunately, investors can capture how quickly a company sells its inventory by examining one simple yet extremely powerful financial tool—the *inventory turnover* ratio. The inventory turnover ratio is determined by taking the company's cost of goods sold divided by average inventory. Another way to look at the inventory turnover ratio is to convert it to a "days to sell inventory" number. You derive this number by taking 365 divided by the inventory turnover ratio. For example, if a company's turnover ratio is 3.6, it sells its inventory every 100 days (365 days divided by 3.6).

The financial numbers to compute the inventory turnover ratio and "days to sell inventory" are available in company 10-Q and 10-K reports. These reports are easily obtained by visiting the Securities and Exchange Commission's Web site—www.sec.gov.

A falling inventory turnover ratio means the days to sell inventory is increasing. That could mean the company's products are becoming obsolete. And if the company's products are becoming obsolete, it will eventually show up in the form of declining profits.

By looking only at the inventory turnover ratio, investors would have had plenty of advance notice of many technology companies hitting the wall. One shining example is Lucent Technologies. Despite a stock price that was skyrocketing, Lucent began to show wear and tear as early as 1998. Indeed, after several years of good inventory turnover numbers, the trend reversed in the December 1998 quarter. The number of days to sell inventory started to jump to a point that, five quarters later, the time it took Lucent to sell inventory jumped approximately 23 percent.

Another red flag was that at the same time days to sell inventory was rising, the company's backlog of business was dropping. The poor backlog and inventory turnover numbers were clearly showing that Lucent had too much stuff that customers did not want and was having an increasingly difficult time meeting demand for the stuff customers did want.

Keep in mind that these warning signs were flashing throughout 1999, when the stock traded as high as $84.

Of course, Lucent's inventory turnover problems eventually caught up with the company. Earnings plunged in 2000 and 2001. The stock plunged, too, plumbing a low of $5 in 2001.

While the inventory turnover ratio is a relevant metric for any company, it is especially pertinent for technology companies for several reasons:

- Product obsolescence kills technology companies. If a technology company is taking longer to sell inventory—something you can tell by looking at the inventory turnover ratio—it could be that its products are falling behind that industry's technological curve.

- Acquisitions have become a way of life for many fast-growing technology companies. In fiscal 1999 Lucent made 16 acquisitions. By looking at the number of days to sell inventory, you may gain some insight into the firm's ability to mesh the acquired product lines. For example, if a serial acquirer is seeing its inventory turns decline, it could be symptomatic of several problems, not the least of which is that the company is buying companies with old technology.

Inventory turnover, like most financial ratios, is best used as a comparison tool. For example, knowing Lucent's inventory turnover ratio is important. Putting that inventory turnover ratio in some industry context is critical. Thus, it is always useful to compare inventory turnover ratios of competitors, especially in technology markets.

The final point I want to make about the inventory turnover is that it is best used in conjunction with a company's gross profit margins (gross profit divided by revenue) and its receivable turnover ratio (sales divided by accounts receivables). After all, a company can move product simply by cutting prices or granting overly generous credit arrangements. However, reducing prices will show up in the company's gross profit margins, and Wall Street doesn't like to see declining gross profit margins. Wall Street also doesn't like to see lengthening collection periods.

Ideally, what you want to see is a company's profit margin rising, its receivable turnover ratio staying steady, and its days to sell inventory declining. A worst-case scenario is to see both shrinking inventory and receivable turns and declining profit margins.

Interestingly, this was exactly what was happening to Lucent. For example, in the December 1999 quarter—the quarter when the days to sell inventory hit its highest level ever—the gross profit margin declined from 53 percent in the year-earlier quarter to under 47 percent, and Lucent's collection period jumped to its highest level ever. Those were additional red flags that presaged the stock's massive decline in 2000.

Bottom line: If you know nothing about a company other than how quickly it moves inventory (especially relative to its competitors), you would probably be able to make a reasonably intelligent decision about that company's stock. The inventory turnover ratio allows you to run that diagnostic on any company you want.

2. ACCOUNTS RECEIVABLE TURNOVER

Ask any business owner what are the three most important ingredients for a successful venture, and I guarantee you one of the three will be having customers who pay their bills on time.

Indeed, for many companies, sales are not a problem. Getting customers to pay for the stuff, however, can be a huge problem. In fact, a big cause of extinction among small businesses, in particular, is the inability to turn sales (in the form of accounts receivables) into cash in a timely fashion.

Whether a company is a small shop or a multibillion-dollar conglomerate, the lesson remains relevant: It's cash flow that ultimately matters. You can have all the sales you want. But if you can't turn sales into cash, forget about it. Without cash, you can't pay overhead. You can't pay salaries. You can't pay suppliers. Without cash, a company ultimately can't survive.

Fortunately, any investor can analyze how well a company turns receivables into cash by examining the company's *receivables turnover* ratio.

To compute a firm's annual receivables turnover, divide net annual sales by average account receivables (average receivables is the beginning period receivables plus the ending period receivables divided by two). The result shows how many times a company turns over its receivables in the course of a year. To turn receivables turnover into the average collection period, simply divide 365 by the receivables turnover.

For example, a company that turns over its receivables nine times a year has an average collection period of 40 days (365 divided by 9). I like to use collection period—also known as days receivable—because this is a more intuitive number for comparison purposes. Again, these numbers (as well as the numbers for all the metrics discussed in this chapter) are available in the company's 10-Q and 10-K reports.

Now, I realize that every company where receivables turnover is declining (and, thus, the average collection period is increasing) is not a company destined for Chapter 11 proceedings. Nevertheless, lengthening collection periods could signal several underlying problems:

- Lax or overly generous credit policies (a company may relax credit policies in order to gain business)

- Receivables write-offs

Wall Street is not a fan of either of these developments and usually severely penalizes companies with collection problems. Thus, tracking a company's receivables turnover may provide the type of early warning sign that allows you to head for the exit ahead of sellers.

A good example of a company in which receivables turnover deteriorated long before the stock tanked is BMC Software. BMC provides software products that help companies improve the productivity and efficiency of their mainframe computers. BMC Software's stock had been an investor favorite, rising from $30 to $82 in 1999. Interestingly, the stock's rise occurred at the same time that BMC was showing a deterioration in its ability to turn receivables into cash. From the end of 1998 to the end of 1999, BMC's days receivable expanded from 52 days to 69 days, or more than 32 percent. In other words, it was tak-

BMC Software

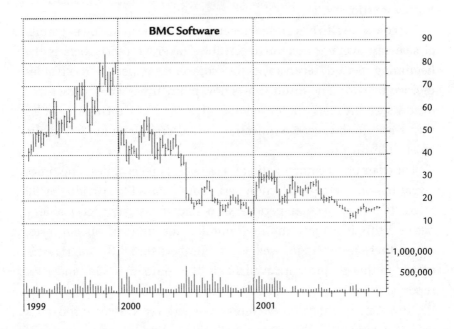

ing BMC more than two months to turn receivables into cash. And the collection problem worsened in 2000. BMC's average collection period at the end of the September 2000 quarter was up to 90 days—a 73 percent increase from December 1998 levels.

BMC's stock price, which had bucked this negative receivables trend in 1999, was beaten up badly in 2000. The stock fell from $85 to $16. A slowdown in sales and earnings fueled selling in these shares. Clearly, demand among its customers was waning. Interestingly, to an investor who had been tracking the decline in BMC's receivables collection, the decline in customer demand was not a surprise. After all, if BMC's customers were taking longer to pay, chances are their business was slowing as well.

Receivables turnover was especially useful in detecting overly generous credit policies in the telecom sector. Indeed, many telecom stocks got crushed when it became obvious that some of the telecom companies were funding the purchases of their equipment by less-than-financially-stellar customers. However, had investors taken the time to track telecom companies' receivables turnover, the evidence of these overly generous credit policies would have been evident well in advance of the stocks' declines.

Remember: Receivables don't pay the bills. Cash does. That's why it's crucial to know how well your companies turn receivables into dollars.

3. Cash Ratio

Too often stock investors miss the forest for the trees. Indeed, stock investors tend to focus on such things as earnings, dividends, chart patterns, insider trading, and so on. Now, these factors all can shed light on a stock's situation. However, certain ratios cut right to the heart of the matter.

One of those is a company's *cash* ratio.

Ask any business owner what's the first financial statement he or she reviews. Trust me. It is not the income statement, which is what most stock investors look at first. No, business owners look at the balance sheet first. Why? Because the balance sheet shows how much cash the company has.

And cash is what allows a business owner to live and fight another day. Simple as that.

If you don't believe me, just ask any of the CEOs of the hundreds of defunct Internet companies. The cause of their extinction wasn't a lack of revenue. In many cases revenues were growing at triple-digit rates. And, believe it or not, the problem wasn't really a lack of profits. After all, these companies didn't have profits when they were out hiring every computer geek they could find, buying the coolest hardware, and spending lavishly on launch parties.

No, what closed the doors was that these companies simply ran out of other people's money and couldn't get their hands on more.

Think of your own finances. How difficult would it be to run a household without cash? Impossible, right?

Fortunately, monitoring a company's liquidity position can be done easily by examining the "cash" ratio. This ratio examines a firm's cash assets (cash and marketable securities) relative to the company's short-term liabilities, such as accounts payable and current portion of notes payable. Both of these items are found in the company's balance sheet.

For example, let's say a company has cash and marketable securities of $50 million and short-term liabilities of $10 million. The cash ratio would be 5 ($50 million divided by $10 million).

When using cash ratios to compare companies from different industries, make sure you understand the cash requirements of each industry. For example, a company in the restaurant sector—a business in which raw materials and finished goods are quickly turned into cash—doesn't require a lot of cash in the bank to drive its business. Conversely, a firm in the growth phase of its business will require lots of cash to fund marketing, capital expenditures, staff expansion, and the like. To new, growing companies, having lots of cash is critical for success and, in fact, survival.

The best way to use the cash ratio, as is the case with most financial ratios, is in terms of trends for a particular company. For example, a growing company where the cash ratio is declining steadily from quarter to quarter may be a firm heading for a cash crunch.

As an investor, it's not enough to know that cash levels have changed; you need to know why they changed. If you want a handle on the ebb and flow of a company's cash position, you must examine the company's statement of cash flows, which accompanies all financial statements. This is perhaps the most overlooked part of the financial statement. Yet it is must reading for understanding what is happening to a firm's cash levels.

One stock I've written about in my *Bloomberg Personal Finance* column is Palm, the maker of the popular handheld personal digital assistants (PDAs). Palm is a good example of a fast-growing company facing a potential cash crunch.

Palm went public in March 2000 when it was spun off from 3Com. The initial public offering and private placements of stock raised $1.1 billion, swelling the company's cash coffers.

Palm's early days as a public company were fast and furious. Revenue increased roughly fourfold from 1998 to 2000. And unlike most other technology upstarts, Palm was profitable, earning 11 cents per share in 2000. And Palm still had lots of cash at the end of the March 2001 quarter—about $595 million.

Good story, right?

Actually, if you looked at Palm's quarterly balance sheets and cash flow statements since the initial public offering, what you see are cash levels and the cash ratio shrinking rather rapidly. And the worst part is that profits have now shifted into the red. In effect, Palm is in a "cash-burn" mode. That means the firm is burning cash faster than it is recouping the money in terms of profits and cash flow from operations.

A company cannot burn cash forever. Palm could try the debt or equity markets to raise additional funds. But given Palm's currently depressed stock price and Wall Street's lack of interest in throwing more money at emerging technology companies, an equity or debt offering appears unlikely. The firm can conserve cash by cutting costs. Not surprisingly, Palm is cutting its workforce dramatically. Another solution for its cash ills is returning the bottom line to the black. But given increased competition in handheld devices and sluggish demand for all things technology, it is not a slam dunk that profits will be coming back anytime soon. Ultimately, the final solution to a cash crunch would be a sale of the company—a very real possibility if profits and cash don't begin stabilizing over the next 12 months.

To be sure, nearly everyone agrees that the next great "new thing" in technology is the movement toward handheld devices. Thus, Palm's market should expand at a healthy clip over the next decade. Unfortunately, Palm will have to be rather adept at stretching a dollar if it is going to be around over the next decade.

One last point I want to make here is that lots of cash may not necessarily be a good thing for a company. Indeed, a company hoarding cash may be one lacking any real opportunities to put that cash to work in its business. As an investor, you don't necessarily want your stocks to be surrogate money market accounts. Presumably, you want them to be using the cash to fund growth.

Thus, if you invest in what you believe to be a growth stock, make sure that growth stock is still truly a growth story. How the company handles its cash may provide insight on this front.

4. DAYS PAYABLE

Paying bills is one of those things you don't want to do too early or too late. Companies are the same way. Ultimately, the goal of bill paying is achieving an optimal balance between preserving cash and financial flexibility and remaining in good financial standing with your creditors. In effect, you want to maximize the supplier's interest-free loan right up to the point this interest-free loan becomes very expensive vendor financing.

You can have a good understanding of a company's bill-paying ways by calculating its *days payable* ratio. Days payable is the average number of days it takes a company to pay its accounts payable. To compute days payable, you'll need several items from the company's financial statements:

$$\text{Days Payable} = \frac{\text{Average Acounts Payable}}{(\text{Cost of Goods Sold}) \times 365}$$

Admittedly, this appears to be a rather complicated formula. However, the numbers are all readily available from a company's 10-Q or 10-K report.

What I especially like about using days payable is that it makes comparisons extremely easy when looking at companies within the same industry. After all, which company would you rather own?

- The company that pays its bills consistently on time (30 to 45 days) and thus has good supplier relationships. Or . . .

- A company in the same industry in which days payable is twice as high and deteriorating from quarter to quarter.

When evaluating a company's days payable numbers, it's usually helpful to examine the company's financial position as well. Has the company taken on more debt? Has the firm's "interest coverage"—a ratio that is found by dividing earnings before interest and taxes (EBIT) by interest expense—been declining over the last few quarters?

A firm that is having trouble paying its bills may be a firm with deteriorating finances.

5. SALES PER EMPLOYEE

You can learn a lot about the productivity of a company's workforce, not to mention a firm's growth prospects, by examining *sales-per-employee* numbers.

Consider Coca-Cola, everyone's favorite growth stock for much of the 1980s and 1990s. However, in the face of tough markets, Coca-Cola handed out pink slips in 2000, the first time anyone could recall layoffs at the soft-drink giant. While the news probably came as a shock to some workers, the job layoffs were not surprising to anyone who had been tracking Coca-Cola's sales per employee. Since 1996, revenue per employee for the soft-drink giant plunged from more than $718,000 to $529,000—a decline of 9 percent a year.

Coca-Cola's answer to the decline in revenue per employee was to cut staffing. Interestingly, Coca-Cola's decision to reduce head count in the wake of falling sales per employee had a signaling effect with investors. The job cuts indicated that the company did not perceive future growth opportunities to be adequate to absorb its current level of staffing. In other words, by cutting head count, Coca-Cola conceded that the glory days of 8 percent volume growth were a thing of the past, at least for a while. Not surprisingly, Coca-Cola stock lost a lot of its fizz with growth investors in 2000.

Perhaps the greatest value of the sales-per-employee metric is its use in comparing companies within the same industry. Presumably, industry competitors face similar issues when it comes to employee recruitment, employee wages and benefits, and so on. Companies from the same industry also face similar macro industry conditions. Because of these similarities, looking at sales per employee provides insight into how companies are doing relative to their peers.

Sales per employee can also be useful in gaining insight into how effectively a company is managing rapid growth. For example, many technology companies, such as Cisco Systems and JDS Uniphase, went on buying sprees in 1998 and 1999. Those acquisitions brought on lots of new employees for these firms. In the case of JDS Uniphase, head count exploded from fewer than 600 employees in fiscal 1997 to approximately 19,000 by the end of the June 2000 quarter.

The huge expansion in JDS Uniphase's workforce created a variety of risks for the company, not the least of which was a dilution of its high-quality, high-productivity workforce. Not surprisingly, when JDS Uniphase's markets tanked in 2001, the firm was forced to shed thousands of these workers.

A company's most important assets are its employees. If you buy that statement—and you should—then you owe it to yourself as an investor to monitor the productivity of a company's employees. The sales-per-employee number allows you to do just that.

6. BOOK-VALUE GROWTH

If you want to invest like Warren Buffett, you better get very familiar with this metric. Indeed, the growth in *book value per share* is one of Buffett's most important metrics for evaluating a company. Why? Because companies should ultimately trade at their "intrinsic value." And no metric provides better insight into a company's intrinsic value than book value.

Now, I'll be the first to admit that intrinsic value is a pretty slippery concept to nail down. One problem is that accounting vagaries and stock-valuation alchemy (remember those goofy justifications given for why Internet stocks were undervalued at one hundred times sales?) can allow you to value a company at any price you want.

Nevertheless, at the end of the day, an important part of the real value of any company, according to Buffett, is the level and growth of retained earnings. Retained earnings are dependent primarily on a company's net income and the dividend-payout ratio. For example, all other things equal, a company that earns $1 million and pays out half of its profits in dividends will have retained earnings of $500,000. Great companies generate high and growing retained earnings.

As a stock investor, you want to own companies where retained earnings are rising. After all, an increase in retained earnings means the intrinsic value of the company is rising. Intuitively, increased value should translate to higher stock prices.

If retained earnings truly matter, a simple way to measure the growth of this metric is book value per share.

The usefulness of book value has always been a bit controversial in investment circles. I will concede that book value, looked at in a vacuum, has its limitations as a benchmark for where a company's stock price should trade. Nevertheless, looking at *trends* in a company's book value per share can be especially enlightening. That's because the change in book value per share does a nice job of capturing the change in a company's retained earnings. And that is meaningful and relevant to the stock price.

In fact, logic argues that, over time, growth in book value per share should cause a proportionate increase in share price. After all, if the intrinsic value of the company (as a result of retained earnings) grows, the market cap of the company should grow in kind to reflect that growth in value.

Of course, things don't always work out dollar-for-dollar on Wall Street. Still, plenty of striking correlations exist concerning the relationship of stock price performance and growth in book value. Indeed, some of the most impressive performers in the stock market prior to 2001 were also those stocks registering big percentage gains in book value per share. For example, from 1997 through 2000, Veritas Software stock rose 1,058 percent; the company's book value per share over the same time frame rose 1,418 percent.

What about stock prices of companies where book value per share was flat or declining from 1997 through 2000? Interestingly, Campbell Soup's book value per share plummeted 90 percent for the three-year period ended December 2000. Not surprisingly, Campbell's stock fell 40 percent over the same period.

Again, it's important to keep in mind that rarely will you see a dollar-for-dollar correlation in the movement of a company's book value per share and its stock price. However, companies that boost book value per share are much more likely to see rising stock prices than are those where book value per share is flat or falling.

Understand that I'm not so much concerned with whether a company is trading at two times book value or five times book value or ten times book value. You could argue all day whether those ratios and comparisons matter. What I will argue is that growth in book value seems to correlate with stock price performance.

7. CAPITAL EXPENDITURE RATIO

Smart investors bet on companies with the financial wherewithal to reinvest aggressively back into the business. One simple way to measure a firm's ability to fund capital expenditures is by looking at the *capital expenditure ratio.*

This ratio compares a company's cash flow from operations to its capital expenditures. To calculate the capital expenditure ratio, divide cash flow from operations by capital expenditures. Cash flow from operations and capital expenditures are found on a company's statement of cash flow.

A capital expenditure ratio that exceeds 1 indicates that a firm has cash left over after payment of capital expenditures. That's important, since the firm may also have to fund interest and dividend payments from cash flow.

As is true of any financial metric, looking at the capital expenditure ratio in a vacuum can lead to misleading interpretations. For example, it is not always the case that big capital expenditure ratios—say, 5 or more—belong to companies with attractive stocks. A firm where the capital expenditure ratio is abnormally high may be a firm that has cut capital spending dramatically and is simply milking its business. These companies, in effect, are in liquidation modes—often not the best investment choices.

Conversely, low capital expenditure ratio does not always indicate a firm in financial trouble. For example, some industries require big capital expenditures every three or four years. Thus, in those years where capital spending is high, you might see an unusually low capital expenditure ratio. But the ratio usually bounces back the next year as capital expenditure needs subside.

For that reason, it is useful to compare capital expenditure ratios across companies from the same industry. Likewise, you want to examine the trend in a company's capital expenditure ratio from quarter to quarter.

8. FIXED-ASSET LEVERAGE RATIO

If you were buying a company, one of the first questions you would ask is how efficient is the company's fixed-asset base in generating revenue.

In other words, does this business require lots of fixed assets— plants, equipment, and so on—to generate revenue? And do these fixed assets continually need replacing?

Fortunately, stock investors can evaluate the efficiency of a firm's fixed assets by examining *fixed-asset leverage ratio.*

To compute the fixed-asset leverage ratio, divide a company's annual sales by the average (of the last two periods) amount of fixed assets—property, plant, and equipment. For example, a firm with revenue of $5 billion and plant, property, and equipment of $1 billion on its books has a fixed-asset leverage ratio of 5.

The fixed-asset leverage ratio is an extremely useful tool for making macro investment decisions on which industries to include in a portfolio. Let's say you are considering equity investments in two industries—railroads and software. The average fixed asset-leverage ratio for four leading railroad companies—Burlington Northern Santa Fe, CSX, Norfolk Southern, and Union Pacific—was 0.52 in 2000. That is, railroads, on average, generated 52 cents in revenue in 2000 for every dollar of plant, property, and equipment.

Compare that to the fixed asset-leverage ratios of four leading software companies—Microsoft, Oracle, PeopleSoft, and Siebel Systems. The average fixed-asset leverage ratio of these four companies was 12 in 2000. Translated: These four software companies, on average, generated $12 in revenue for every dollar of plant, property, and equipment.

When you look at the respective fixed-asset leverage ratios for these two industries, it's easy to see why software companies trade at much higher price/earnings multiples than do railroads. Railroads require huge outlays for its fixed assets to keep running. Software, on the other hand, is almost the perfect business—lots of revenue from a relatively small asset base. That means lots of fixed-asset leverage, which usually translates to big profit margins. Indeed, most railroads have net-profit margins in the 8 percent range—not bad, but nowhere near the 41 percent net profit margin for Microsoft in 2000. And 2000 was considered a relatively slow year for the software giant.

As is the case with most financial ratios, perhaps the most powerful use of the fixed-asset leverage ratio is as a tool to compare companies within the same industry. For example, few industry sectors have been hit as hard as personal computer manufacturers. Three major players in the sector—Compaq, Dell, and Gateway—have felt the brunt of Wall Street's disdain for PC producers.

Now, let's say you have the itch to pick a rebound play in the computer sector. Where do you place your bet? If you look at the fixed-asset leverage ratios for the three companies, the answer is pretty simple. Dell Computer's fixed-asset leverage ratio in 2000 was an off-the-chart 36. To put that number in perspective, it is approximately three times the ratios turned in by Compaq (13) and Gateway (12).

Clearly, no firm in the PC market has been as adept as Dell in generating sales from its base of fixed assets. What that means is that once demand picks up in the PC sector, Dell's ability to leverage its fixed assets should lead to outsized profits relative to Compaq and Gateway.

9. R&D AS A PERCENTAGE OF SALES

Some companies have the luxury of being able to sell the same product year after year after year. These companies, however, are the exceptions. Indeed, most companies must constantly innovate. That is especially the case in technology and health-care markets, where product life cycles can be especially short.

With a company's success or failure determined increasingly by its ability to beat competitors to the next new thing, how much a firm spends on finding that next new thing becomes an extremely important metric for investors to consider.

A simple way to evaluate a firm's ability to stay at the leading edge of product development is by looking at its *research and development* outlays.

To be sure, just because a company spends a lot of money on research and development doesn't mean that it is spending its money productively. One way to check on the success of a company's research-and-development spending is to look at the firm's net profit margin. Higher research-and-development spending should lead to new proprietary products with patent protection and, therefore, higher profit margins.

For example, Amgen, the biotechnology company, spends roughly 23 percent of its annual revenue on research and development. One would hope that such large outlays would pay off with above-average profit margins. That's exactly the case with Amgen. The firm drops 31 cents to the bottom line for every dollar in revenue. Clearly, the company is getting a nice return on its hefty R&D spending.

Tracking R&D spending as a percentage of revenues can help detect companies that are boosting profits merely by cutting research outlays. From 1996 to 2000, Eastman Kodak's net income inched up $120 million to $1.4 billion. But Kodak spent $244 million less on R&D in 2000 than in 1996. In short, Kodak boosted profits not by addition (i.e., greater sales), but by subtraction (lower expenses). Boosting profits by cutting research spending and other expenses is not an enduring formula for profit growth, which partly explains why Kodak's stock price has floundered over the last five years.

One final reason I like to look at R&D spending as a percentage of sales is that it is an effective "tiebreaker" when considering two companies in the same industry. The R&D tiebreaker is especially useful in industries, such as health care, where many of the players are suitable portfolio holdings.

One health-care firm that scores well on the R&D front is Pfizer. The company spends 15 percent of annual sales on research and development. That amounts to $5 billion annually on R&D. That spending supports more than 150 projects in 19 therapeutic areas. And Pfizer has shown an ability to spin R&D dollars into sales. Indeed, in 2000, the company had eight drugs with revenues greater than $1 billion. The company expects that, over the next two years, its product pipeline will yield no fewer than seven new important products. Those new products should help sustain the company's industry-leading revenue and earnings growth rates.

10. Same-Store Sales Comparisons

One way to measure the sustainability of certain consumer-oriented concepts (retailing and restaurants come quickly to mind) is by examining the company's same-store sales figures.

Investors can be deceived into thinking a restaurant chain, for example, is doing a good job merely by looking at overall sales growth. However, growing total sales is easy in the restaurant business—just add more outlets. To discern whether the concept's growth is sustainable, a more important metric is looking at how stores that have been open a comparable period of time are faring.

One of the benefits of tracking a restaurant's same-store sales is that these figures provide useful early-warning signals. For example, Dave & Buster's operates large restaurant/entertainment complexes. Each complex offers a full menu of food and beverages combined with an extensive array of entertainment attractions, such as billiards, interactive games and simulators, and traditional carnival-style games of skill. Rising sales and profits helped drive these shares higher from 1996 through the first half of 1999. Interestingly, while Dave & Buster's was growing overall sales by adding outlets, same-store sales growth was steadily declining. The decline culminated with *negative* same-store sales growth of more than 2 percent in the second quarter and more than 6 percent in the third and fourth quarters of fiscal 1999. Wall Street was quick to dump these shares on the negative same-store sales figures, but a slowdown was clearly evident way before the horrible second-quarter results were announced.

To be sure, same-store sales figures, like most accounting numbers, can be manipulated. For example, since many restaurants base their same-store numbers on outlets open at least 18 months, a company can prop up its same-store numbers by closing poor-performing stores before they reach 18 months of age. Also, restaurants can keep underperforming units from hurting same-store sales numbers by selling outlets to outside entities, such as franchise operators. In this way, the company takes the costs of operating these underperformers off the books while creating a stream of franchise revenues.

Still, you should be able to garner insight into how well a retailer or restaurant chain's business is holding up by looking at same-store sales. Most retailers and restaurant chains report this information on a monthly or quarterly basis.

11. PROFIT MARGINS

A company's profitability is tied to its ability to squeeze income from revenue. Good companies have steady or rising profit margins. Bad companies usually see declining profit margins.

Monitoring profit-margin trends is easy. Two profit margins worth watching are:

- *Operating profit margin.* This ratio is determined by dividing operating profits (that's profits before interest and taxes) by revenue.

- *Net profit margin.* This ratio is determined by dividing net income by revenue.

Of these two, operating margin probably gives a truer picture of profit trends since it is less polluted by accounting items, such as amortization and depreciation.

Examining profit-margin trends provides valuable insight into the company and industry.

Let's say you own a technology company where profit margins are slipping. What you want to look at first is the level and trend of profit margins for the rest of the industry players. A good source for such comparisons is *Value Line Investment Survey,* found in most public libraries. If you see profit margins holding steady or rising for competitors, it may mean several things that need exploring:

- Are your company's costs getting out of hand?

- Is your company being forced to discount prices in order to move inventory?

- Has your company fallen behind the technology curve in its industry and is now making commodity products?

In each case, falling profit margins may be signaling fundamental shifts in the company's product portfolio or industry competitiveness. These are potential problems that will eventually show up in the bottom line.

For example, it is possible that a firm could be showing big profit gains while margins are decreasing. While the company is earning less on each unit sale, volume is so great that profits are rising. However, volume trends can change quickly, especially in technology. The risk is that when volume growth slows or reverses, the company's profits will get killed due to falling profit margins. This, essentially, is what killed the bottom lines of a lot of technology companies in recent years. Strong sales growth masked declining profit margins. When sales slowed, profits tanked.

As a rule, you don't want to own companies where profit margins are steadily declining, especially if the decline is endemic to the industry. Industry sectors that are becoming less profitable from year to year generally are not areas where Wall Street puts its dollars.

12. LONG-TERM DEBT AS A PERCENTAGE OF CAPITAL

Debt is not necessarily an evil thing. Debt can help you fund major purchases, such as automobiles and homes. Debt can help smooth out erratic cash flows. And in some cases, debt has certain tax advantages, such as interest deductions.

Too much debt, however, can bury you. Same goes for corporations. Too much debt can bankrupt a company.

Since I invest for the long term, I want companies that will be around for the long term. The quickest way to the corporate funeral home is piling up debt that the business cannot support.

An easy measure for tracking corporate debt levels is a company's *long-term debt as a percentage of total capital.* A firm's total capital is composed of shareholder equity and long-term debt. In general, companies where long-term debt is 60 percent or more of total capital are companies that are pushing the envelope when it comes to carrying debt.

To be sure, some industries are better suited for higher debt levels than others. For example, recession-resistant businesses where inventories turn over quickly can carry higher levels of debt.

Industries where debt can be a big problem are cyclical industries—autos, paper, chemicals—where economic downturns play havoc with sales and profits and make it doubly difficult to service the debt.

As is the case with most financial ratios, trends usually mean more than absolute numbers. If you own a company where long-term debt as a percentage of capital is jumping rather sharply, make sure you understand why debt levels are rising.

- Has the company made an acquisition?

- Is the firm taking on debt to maintain its dividend?

- Is the company floating more debt because it is refinancing higher-cost debt?

Few good reasons exist for a company's debt levels to be going through the roof. If a company you own is seeing its debt level skyrocket while, at the same time, profits are plummeting, that may be reason enough to dump the stock.

I've spent a fair amount of time covering these various ratios and tools, but I believe it is time well spent. Indeed, the more you can evaluate your investments on substantive criteria—as opposed to guessing at what is happening merely because the stock price is rising or falling—the better handle you'll have on whether to sell or buy more when the stock price dips.

I use these tools to give my stocks periodic "stress tests":

- Are five of the ratios turning bad?

- Ten of the ratios?

- *All* of the ratios?

Of course, you shouldn't necessarily sell a stock merely because one of these indicators has turned negative. But the beauty of having such "diagnostic" tools is that they can confirm one another. Obviously, the more of these indicators that are flashing warnings, the more likely the right decision is to sell.

Sell Rule #3: If your company goes on an acquisition spree, make sure it has a history of turning deals into dollars. If not, sell.

Any of you who have read my previous books know that I am not a big fan of companies that buy growth by buying other companies. Sure, some companies (General Electric and Tyco International come to mind) have done a good job over the years adding value to their businesses by buying and assimilating companies. In the main, however, I think you'll find plenty of evidence that indicates that making acquisitions work is extremely difficult.

Several reasons exist for the inability of companies to make deals pay off for shareholders. First, in many acquisitions, the buyer overpays. Companies pay too much for any number of reasons. Ego. A bidding war. Executive compensation tied to revenue. Fear.

That companies overpay is not a surprise. How much they overpay, however, can be staggering. Investors can gain some valuable insight into a company's success/failure in acquisitions by examining a simple component of the balance sheet—*goodwill* (also known as "intangible assets").

In a nutshell, goodwill is the excess portion of a purchase price that cannot be allocated to tangible assets. In other words, goodwill is the premium paid for buying a company's reputation, brand names, and other factors that don't carry a concrete price tag but presumably add value to the enterprise.

A good case study of a firm that overpaid dearly for acquisitions is JDS Uniphase.

While big losses were commonplace in the technology sector in 2001, JDS Uniphase's loss was one for the ages. As I noted earlier, for fiscal 2001 ended June 30, the company, a maker of fiber-optic telecom equipment, posted a loss of more than *$50 billion*. It is believed to be the largest one-year loss in the history of corporate America.

You're probably wondering how a company with revenue in fiscal 2001 of $3.2 billion could manage to lose more than $50 billion for the year.

A big reason for the bloodbath was that JDS Uniphase came to the conclusion that the firm overpaid for a slew of acquisitions over the last couple of years. Overpaid by *a lot*. About *$50 billion* worth of overpayment.

That $50 billion represents the amount of goodwill the company wrote down in fiscal 2001.

Now, you might be saying, so what? After all, the $50 billion write-down is a noncash hit to the financial statement. No big deal, right?

Actually, the write-down of goodwill is a noncash charge and doesn't impair the company's financial position. However, keep in mind that JDS Uniphase paid (or should I say overpaid, by billions of dollars) for these deals with stock. And while goodwill may disappear with the write-down, those shares don't.

In addition to share dilution (or debt service if the acquisition was a cash deal and the firm paid with borrowed money), the message a write-down sends to the financial community is not a good one.

In effect, massive goodwill write-downs show that company management is lacking in deal-making skills as well as in its ability to generate excess returns from intangible assets. If you see a company with a history of goodwill write-downs make a major acquisition, be aware that it's probably a company worth avoiding.

Sell Rule #4: If your company is accused of accounting chicanery, you better be sure you understand completely what the company is doing and whether the company's accounting practices pass the smell test.

Where there's smoke, there's usually fire. That maxim definitely applies to companies where accounting irregularities surface.

Over the years, many stocks have been devastated by issues surrounding shady accounting moves and subsequent earnings restatements. When the SEC targets a company for accounting irregularities, it is practically the kiss of death, at least in the short run. Wall Street rarely sticks around to see what happens.

You shouldn't either.

Sell Rule #5: Guard against losing your objectivity with previous winners. Bad things can and do happen to good companies.

I have been guilty of giving some of my big winners the benefit of the doubt, even when the evidence was piling up that business fundamentals were changing for the worse. I'm sure I'm not alone in this regard. That's only natural. You become attached to stocks that have been good to you in the past.

However, one lesson that comes out of the market volatility in the last three years is the following: *Bad things happen to good companies.*

Who would have ever thought that Lucent's or Cisco's business would hit the skids so badly? Yet if you looked at such things as inventory turnover and receivables turnover, you would have seen clouds forming for these and countless other companies.

Actually, many investors did see these clouds forming—heck, I wrote about these clouds in my newsletter and magazine column—but ignored them precisely because, after all, Lucent and Cisco were, well, *Lucent* and *Cisco*.

A big part of being a successful investor is maintaining objectivity about your stocks. I'm not suggesting that you sell at every sign of weakness. Again, I believe in buying right and selling sparingly.

Still, if you do your homework, run your various "stress tests" on stocks, and the preponderance of the evidence says your stock is coming up short, you should sell. And if you can't bring yourself to sell all the position, sell half.

CONCLUSION

If the volatile markets of recent years have taught us anything, it is that selling is not a four-letter word.

True, all other things equal, it is better to buy and hold stocks. Buying and holding is more tax-friendly. Buying and holding is more commission-friendly.

Nevertheless, the world changes. Industries change. Companies change.

Smart investors must be equipped to evaluate and respond to these changes. And if that means selling a stock, so be it.

The last point I want to make relates to the question on the minds of lots of investors: *Should I sell now, even if my stock has already fallen by 80 percent?*

The answer is quite simple. If you believe the stock is positioned to make you money going forward, you should hold and probably buy more. However, if after doing your homework (see our sell rules on the previous pages) the stock flunks the test, you should sell.

You shouldn't hold a stock simply because you're afraid to sell. Your fear has nothing to do with whether the stock will rise or fall in the future. And it doesn't matter whether the stock is down 80 percent or up 80 percent.

If you don't think the stock will make you money going forward, sell.

Chapter Eight

Law #8:
The Importance of Simplicity
in a Volatile World

It's a cliché, but it's true. Successful investors keep their heads when those around them are losing theirs.

Think about the craziest times in the market. What do you usually do during those times? For starters, you probably freeze up and don't do anything. That's a natural response, but it may be unproductive and certainly is not opportunistic. Or if you don't freeze, you let fear take over and you start selling investments simply because they are going down.

Successful investors, on the other hand, are organized around a simple plan. They know their investments, understand the tax ramifications of any buy/sell decisions, and predetermine at what price certain stocks are worth buying. In short, smart investors have simplified the investment process to as few key elements as possible. And, through organization and simplification, smart investors can put this plan into motion when opportunities present themselves. And the best opportunities usually occur when markets are going crazy.

Now, let me ask you:

- Do you have a plan?

- How well is your financial position organized?

- Do you know the tax implications of your investment moves?

- Have you staked out good prices for stocks if and when they pull back during market declines?

- Do you have a "watch list" of stocks for new buying?

If you are like most individual investors, your answer to all these questions is "No."

Why "no"? Because you've probably complicated your financial picture to the point that monitoring your investments is a project for NASA. You have seven different accounts with five different financial-services firms. You have IRAs, 401(k) plans, annuities, life insurance. You know you own Merck in taxable and nontaxable accounts, but you don't know what your cost basis in the stock is in the account that matters. You own some stock that you inherited from your father, but you don't know that the stock now represents more than 40 percent of your total assets. And you sure don't know what your cost basis is on the investment.

Does this mess sound familiar?

Actually, it has become easy even for relatively small investors to create incredibly complex financial positions. Think about it. Most of us have a 401(k) or 403(b) plan. Many of us have IRAs, perhaps a traditional and a Roth IRA. Many of us have at least two brokerage accounts. Layer on top a few dividend reinvestment plans, some bond and stock mutual funds, and before you know it you have more investments to track than a bounty hunter has prospects at a Harley convention.

And when you throw in that watching your investments is not your full-time job, it's no wonder you lock up when the stock market goes crazy. No wonder you miss out on great bargains created by market declines. No wonder you don't have a plan of attack when stocks decline during bear markets.

But it doesn't have to be that way.

THE BENEFITS OF SIMPLICITY

In the investment game, simplicity has many benefits. These benefits are magnified during volatile markets, when a premium is placed on wise and prompt decision making.

•   Know Your Tax Situation

One huge benefit of having a simplified, organized approach to your investments is that you are in a much better position to reap certain investment tax benefits that may present themselves during volatile markets.

Now, I don't like to make investment decisions based solely on taxes. I've seen too many instances when tax-driven investments turned out to be mistakes.

For example, in my firm's money-management business, we "inherit" a lot of portfolios from clients that have embedded capital gains. Often, these clients don't want us selling these stocks because they'll incur capital gains.

Don't get me wrong. I'm for deferring taxes as long as possible as long as it makes sense from an investment standpoint. But if you are sitting with 80 percent of your portfolio in one stock in which you have a big capital gain, you need to do what's prudent. And what's prudent is selling some of your holding, taking the tax hit, and diversifying across other investments.

So what do taxes and portfolio simplification have in common? The better you know and understand your tax position, the more you'll make investment decisions that make sense from a tax standpoint.

To get a handle on your portfolio's tax situation, you'll need to know the "cost basis" of your investments. What is cost basis? The amount of money—including commissions—that you spend to buy an investment.

For example, let's say you buy 200 shares of XYZ Corp. from your broker. The price of the stock was $20 per share, and trading fees were $30. Thus, your cost basis for XYZ stock is $4,000 ($20 times 200 shares) plus $30 (trading commissions), or $4,030.

Your cost basis comes into play when you sell an investment. Indeed, for every investment that is sold in a taxable investment account, Uncle Sam demands that you determine your capital gain or loss on that investment. And what determines whether you have a profit or loss is the cost basis and the selling price.

Return to XYZ Corp. for a moment. Let's say you sold XYZ Corp. two years later for $50 per share. Thus, the proceeds from the sale were $10,000 (200 shares times $50 per share) minus $30 (trading fee), or $9,970.

Now, what is your gain or loss on the investment? Since you invested $4,030 and received proceeds of $9,970 when you sold, your gain is $5,940. That profit will need to be recorded on your income taxes. And if you cannot offset the gain with investment losses, you have to pay taxes on the gain. (Since you owned the investment for more than 12 months, your tax rate is a maximum 20 percent. Had you owned the investment for less than 12 months, you would pay taxes at your ordinary income-tax rate.)

As you can see, cost-basis information is also essential for determining your potential tax liability in any given year. The problem with knowing your cost basis, however, is that a cost basis can sometimes be a moving target.

For example, any investor who has owned AT&T since 1983 knows that his or her original cost basis in AT&T stock has changed many times as a result of AT&T's spin-offs over the years. Indeed, when AT&T spun off the seven "Baby Bells" at the end of 1983, investors who owned AT&T and received the seven spin-offs had to adjust the cost basis on their AT&T shares accordingly. And when AT&T spun off Lucent Technologies and NCR, further adjustments to AT&T's cost basis had to occur.

Complicating cost-basis calculations even more are stock splits, reinvested dividends, and corporate restructurings and recapitalizations.

In short, determining your cost basis is not always a simple computation.

The more simplified your investment program is, however, the better your chances are of keeping track of your cost basis. And knowing your cost basis can help you maximize opportunities to save on your taxes.

For example, let's say the year is nearing an end, and throughout the year you have realized gains in some of your individual stocks. You are also sitting with substantial *unrealized* losses in a few of your mutual funds. You are going to have to pay taxes on those gains, and the tax bill is fairly substantial.

What can you do to ease your tax hit without dramatically altering the complexion of your investment portfolio?

One strategy is to sell your losing mutual funds and realize your losses for tax purposes. Those losses can be used to offset gains in your other investments.

But what if you don't want to sell your mutual funds because you believe they have good rebound potential? You still could sell those funds, realize your losses, and invest the sale proceeds in different mutual funds with similar investment objectives. In this way, you reduce your taxes without altering the allocation or investment style of your portfolio.

An alternative tax-selling approach would be to sell an investment to realize losses and buy back the same investment 31 days later. By waiting 31 days, you avoid breaking "wash sale" rules that can negate the tax benefits from a sale.

For example, let's say you own Lucent Technologies. You are sitting with a big loss in the stock, but you believe the stock has bottomed. Because of some sells you made earlier in the year, you are looking at a big tax hit if you don't reduce your capital gains. One strategy would be to sell the Lucent to book the loss. That loss will offset your investment gains and reduce your taxes. Then you buy back Lucent 31 days after the sale.

This tax arbitrage is neutral to your investment portfolio (assuming Lucent does not move up sharply in that 31-day period). You still own the same amount of Lucent you owned for the same amount of money. Yet the strategy helps you reduce taxes dramatically.

As you can see, several ways exist to lessen the tax bite in your portfolio. However, unless your portfolio is organized and simplified, chances are you'll never take advantage of these situations because you don't know your cost basis or tax situation.

Thus, one of the big reasons for portfolio simplification is to enable you to understand and react when certain tax-arbitrage situations present themselves.

And trust me—these opportunities are going to present themselves during the craziest market periods, when investment values are flying all over the place, and when you need to make decisions quickly to capture the tax benefits.

Seize the Opportunity

Great buying opportunities in stocks can happen rather suddenly. In fact, the best buying opportunities usually happen when stocks are getting clobbered, bears are running wild, and investors are selling anything and everything—even the good stuff.

Go back to the last big market calamity in September of last year. After the horrible terrorist attacks on September 11, the market closed for the next three days. When trading reopened on September 17, stocks proceeded to tank. In fact, the week of trading beginning September 17 was the worst one-week point loss in the history of the Dow Jones Industrial Average. The index fell more than 1,369 points, or roughly 14 percent.

Now think back to that time and how you were reacting. Chances are, you weren't thinking about all the great bargains being created.

I bet you weren't sitting at your desk saying, "Disney is now at $15—time to buy." Or "GE has backed off all the way to $29. According to my work, that's a great price to buy."

But you should have been.

I know hindsight is 20/20. But I also know that the best buying opportunities usually go to the best-prepared investors.

Again, it's all about having a plan, not only for the stocks you own but also for the stocks you want to own.

Right now, if I asked you about a certain stock in your portfolio, you should be able to tell me why you bought it, what you need to see from the company in order to keep holding it, and the stock price at which you would buy more if it ever got that low.

You should also be able to tell me what stocks are on your "watch list" of new buys, and at what prices you would like to buy those stocks. Putting together and monitoring a watch list of stocks can pay huge dividends over time. A watch list basically consists of those stocks that you would like to own but you deem too expensive to buy at that particular time. A good watch list contains the following ingredients:

- Stocks with strong long-term growth potential and solid financial positions. The type of stocks on my wish list are those that are industry leaders. This would include certain perpetually expensive technology stocks. For example, Applied Materials is an interesting stock to me, but it always seems to trade at a high price/earnings ratio. Having that stock on a watch list would give me a better chance of catching this stock when one of its rare buying opportunities presents itself.

- Your "buy" prices for your watch list stocks.

- If you maintain your watch list electronically (for example, via the Internet), it's nice to have various Internet links to fundamental data and news on these stocks in order to monitor their progress.

Investors should refresh their watch lists every six months or so. In this way, they are forced to keep looking for new stocks. That's important, since new opportunities may develop at any time.

Can you honestly say you have a watch list? Probably not. And the reason you don't is because you don't have a plan. And the reason you don't have a plan, in many cases, is that you have not simplified your portfolio to the point that it is easy and convenient to track and monitor your investments.

Simplicity Leads to Calmness

A big part of succeeding during volatile markets is staying calm. When you're calm, you make much better decisions. When you're calm, you don't overreact to circumstances. When you're calm, you think more clearly.

Of course, knowing you should be calm during crazy markets is one thing; actually *being* calm is quite another.

One way to ensure that you maintain a measured, calculated

approach to volatile markets is by having a clear handle on your financial position and a clear plan of attack.

And you do that through simplifying your investment approach.

Knowing When to Sell

In Chapter 7, we discussed many indicators and tools that you can use to know when to sell your investments. Admittedly, knowing when to sell requires work on your part. You have to run "stress" tests on your stocks, monitor their financials, and look at important financial ratios.

In short, successful selling requires you to be an *investor*, not merely a passive player. The problem is that being an investor takes time and energy, two commodities that we usually find in short supply.

Leading time-strapped, energy-sapping lives puts a huge premium on maintaining a simplified approach to investing. Knowing what investments you own, where those investments are held, what is happening (good or bad) to the investments, when important changes are taking place that require buy/hold/sell decisions—doing all that is necessary to be a successful investor, especially on the sell side of the equation—is much more achievable if the investment approach is simple and portfolio monitoring easy.

So what can you do to simplify and organize your investments?

THANK YOU, INTERNET

Ten years ago, keeping track of your investments was no doubt a very paper-intensive process. Paper statements. Paper journals to keep track of your cost basis. Paper folders to store your statements. Scratch paper to figure out your taxes.

Paper, paper, and more paper.

And that was if you were actually keeping track of your investments. The sad thing is that many people didn't bother with all this paper and simply did nothing in the way of maintaining records.

I know plenty of investors, for example, who started a dividend reinvestment plan 10 years ago and never bothered to keep their statements. They threw them out.

Indeed, "throwing out" *is* record keeping for many investors.

The obvious problem with shoddy record keeping, however, is that you never have a good handle on your investments, especially in the area of taxes.

Fortunately, the Internet has changed everything when it comes to simplifying your finances. Indeed, a host of Internet "portfolio trackers" and "account aggregators" gives investors many options in maintaining an organized financial picture.

PORTFOLIO TRACKERS

The first two steps in simplifying an investment program are knowing (1) what investments you own, and (2) where they are held. That means being able to combine your various investments and separate portfolios at one central record-keeping source.

The third step in the simplification process is being able to monitor what is happening to these investments on a regular basis. That means:

- Having "links" from your portfolio to various research tools.

- Having the ability to receive "e-mail alerts" on your stocks. E-mail alerts are e-mail messages automatically sent to you to alert you to changes in stock prices, news, or other events that may affect your investments.

One site that provides all of these things—and much, much more—is Quicken.

Quicken

Quicken (www.quicken.com) offers perhaps the best portfolio tracker on the Internet. Indeed, whatever you want to track, research, or compute, you can do at Quicken:

- *Track cost basis.* The tracker provides a nice and clean interface for loading important cost information on your stocks. The tracker also allows you to adjust for stock splits and other events that may affect your cost basis.

- *Customize formats to include tons of data.* You can set up your portfolio to show as much information or as little information as you want. You can customize the information to provide "at-a-glance" looks at important financial ratios and other statistics, such as market capitalization, price/earnings ratio, 52-week price range, and so forth.

- *Set up "alerts" that will automatically notify you to new information, changes in stock prices, and so on.* This is an especially useful feature. Say you want to buy more stock at a certain price. You can input that price into the tracker, and you will be automatically alerted, via e-mail, when the stock hits that price.

- *Research, research, and more research on your stocks.* Your portfolio stocks are linked to lots of research tools. Charts, insider trading data, message boards, and much more are available simply by clicking on the stock symbol.

What I like about the site is that it is incredibly user-friendly. Thus, any investor, from novice to experienced, should find this site useful, convenient, and powerful.

And the best part is that all of these services and research information are *free*.

Getting started: To get started using Quicken's portfolio tracker, simply go to the Web site—www.quicken.com. At the home page, click on "My Portfolio" near the top of the page. That link will take you to a page that asks you to input the stock symbols of your holdings. This page will help you find the symbols if you don't have the symbols handy. Once you have completed entering your portfolio, you can start customizing your portfolio page to meet your needs. The best way to see all that Quicken has to offer is by spending some time on the site and exploring. It is incredibly easy to navigate around the site, which has a wealth of available information in addition to the portfolio tracker.

Microsoft Moneycentral—CNBC

The Microsoft Moneycentral–CNBC site (www.moneycentral.com) is another very strong contender for the best portfolio tracker on the Web. This tracker offers all sorts of tools and customization features to make it easy to track your investments. The Moneycentral site has some of the best research tools on the Internet, and many of these tools are integrated into the trackers. A particularly useful tool on this tracker is the stock screener. For investors who have favorite criteria for picking stocks, this screener is especially useful. I found this site less user-friendly than the Quicken site. Still, it is extremely manageable, robust, and worth a look when shopping for a tracker. And most of the good stuff is free.

Getting started: Go to the www.moneycentral.com home page. Click on "My Money" near the top of the page. You'll be taken to a registration page. Just follow the directions.

OTHER PORTFOLIO TRACKERS

I can't imagine Quicken and Moneycentral trackers not meeting the needs of most investors. However, I also know that beauty is in the eye of the beholder. Here are other portfolio trackers worth examining:

- *Smart Money*—www.smartmoney.com. Click on the "Portfolio" link on the home page.

- *TradeTrakker*—www.tradetrakker.com. This site offers a fairly robust portfolio tracker with allocation tools. One downside: It'll cost you $19.95 if you want to continue after the free 30-day trial. Still, you might find this site is worth the price, especially for the "watch list" alerts.

- *Yahoo! Finance*—www.finance.yahoo.com. The major benefit of this portfolio tracker is that it resides on a site that has lots of great tools for investors. Indeed, the Yahoo! Finance Web site is one of the easiest and most robust financial resources on the Web.

- *Bloomberg*—www.bloomberg.com. Bloomberg is known for its analytical tools and research. To take the portfolio tracker for a spin, go to the home page and click on "Monitor" in the page's upper left-hand corner.

- *Morningstar*—www.morningstar.com. Morningstar is the leader in mutual fund information on the Web. The site's portfolio tracker is especially useful in keeping track of your mutual funds, since you can access a lot of good research information on your funds at this site.

SPECIALTY TRACKERS

Here are a few more trackers worth mentioning for their special features:

RiskGrades—www.riskgrades.com. I discuss the many powerful features of RiskGrades in Chapter 5. This site offers one of the best tools on the Internet for tracking, allocating, and optimizing portfolios.

FinPortfolio—www.finportfolio.com. For investors who are looking for fairly sophisticated asset allocation and portfolio optimization tools, FinPortfolio may fit the bill. The site offers a wealth of tools to help you make decisions about your portfolio. The site may be a little daunting for new investors, but investors who want to add more science to the study of their portfolios should find this site attractive. The site offers a free basic tracker, although to get more comprehensive services you'll need to pony up a minimum $75 per quarter. I'm including the site here because it offers some real cutting-edge tools for a fairly small amount of money.

GainsKeeper—www.gainskeeper.com. GainsKeeper is a flat-out great tool for keeping track of your investments from a tax standpoint, including accounting for investment cost-basis adjustments and capital gain/loss calculations.

Bivio—www.bivio.com. Bivio offers a very useful record-keeping tool to assist investment clubs.

Investors should note that many of these portfolio trackers (including the free ones) require users to register at the company's site. Registration is a fairly brief and painless process. If you register but don't want the company to send you marketing e-mail, choose the "Opt Out" option in the registration process.

ACCOUNT AGGREGATORS

The one problem with all portfolio trackers is that the tracking is only as good as the data you input. In other words, if you neglect to add a stock to the portfolio tracker that you've recently purchased, your portfolio tracker won't be tracking the stock.

What if a way existed for your account information to be updated automatically?

Actually, such a way exists on the Internet via "account aggregators."

Some Internet watchers believe account aggregation is the next big thing on the Internet. In its basic form, account aggregation tools take all of your financial information—checking, savings, brokerage, retirement accounts, bill payments, and credit-card balances—and "aggregate" the information on a single, personal home page.

Via this account-aggregation process, you no longer need to go to 15 different Web sites to view your accounts. All accounts may be viewed at one source.

A leader in account aggregation is Yodlee (www.yodlee.com). The firm is the engine behind the account-aggregation services offered by many leading financial-services firms, such as Charles Schwab, Citigroup, Morgan Stanley, and Quicken. Other account aggregators are ByAllAccounts (www.byallaccounts.com), CashEdge (www.cashedge.com), and uMonitor (www.umonitor.com).

Before you jump on the account-aggregation bandwagon, however, be aware of some important points.

First, in order for your accounts to be aggregated, you must turn over all pertinent PIN information for the accounts. That's how aggregators get the information. With your PIN, the aggregator goes out to the various sites and "scrapes" the information. Yodlee, for example, scrapes data from more than 2,500 sites.

Now, many investors may feel a little reluctant to give their PIN to any third party, let alone a third party in the Internet space.

Also, wherever your account is aggregated, rest assured that entity will learn a lot about your financial situation. That information can be quite useful in marketing new services.

The upshot is that with the convenience of account aggregation comes a potential loss of privacy and (albeit remote) unwanted security breaches in your account.

Would I be willing to use account aggregation? I guess the fact that I haven't signed up for aggregation services says something. Still, I've never been first into the technology pool. I generally like to see how things shake out over time, especially in the Internet world.

If you are interested in exploring account aggregation, an easy place to get started is Quicken (www.quicken.com) or Yahoo! Finance (www.finance.yahoo.com). At the Quicken home page, click on "My Finances" at the top of the page. On the linked page, scroll down until you see "My Accounts" on the left-hand sidebar. Click on "My Accounts" and follow directions. At Yahoo! Finance's home page, scroll down until you see the "Personal Finance" heading. Underneath that heading you'll see "Money Manager." Click on this link to learn about account aggregation at Yahoo!.

Also, visit the Yodlee Web site (www.yodlee.com) to see if the firm has partnered with one of your financial-services companies.

CONCLUSION

One of the best pieces of advice I've ever received when it comes to investing is the "KISS" concept—*Keep It Simple, Stupid.*

I can't think of any time when simple doesn't beat complex. That's especially the case during volatile markets.

If you have simplified your investment tracking and record keeping to a point where you can monitor portfolios easily, you will be in much better shape when market conditions require you to make the tough decisions:

- Should I sell?

- What are the tax consequences of my investment moves?

- Is it time to load up on that stock on my "watch list"?

The tools discussed in this chapter should go a long way toward allowing any investor to be better organized and prepared to take on volatile markets.

Chapter Nine

LAW #9:
STAY IN THE EYE WHEN THE
STORM MOVES—TOOLS FOR
DETECTING MARKET SHIFTS

I'VE USED THE analogy of a storm's eye throughout this book. As an investor, the place you want to be during volatile markets is in the eye. But only for so long.

Storms shift constantly. And as a storm shifts, so, too, does the storm's eye. What was once a place of safety and tranquility quickly becomes consumed by the fury.

The market's volatility to the upside in the late '90s gave way to volatility to the downside in 2000 and 2001. And with that change came a dramatic shift in the market's sweet spot. If an investor did not recognize that the storm was shifting and that the place to be safe was shifting as well, he or she was trampled. Like the weatherman who uses a variety of tools, such as barometers and wind gauges, to detect changes in weather patterns, investors need tools to determine when market volatility is rising or falling and when quantum shifts are occurring in the investment landscape.

LOOKING FOR BIG CHANGES AND SMALL VICTORIES

Before I discuss tools for detecting shifts in the investment climate, it's important you realize that what I'm trying to do here is equip you with the ability to detect *big* market shifts. It's a waste of time trying to guess market movements on a day-to-day or week-to-week basis. While short-term market movements may not always be completely random, I guarantee that if you believe you have some infallible tool for knowing market direction every 24 hours, you are mistaken. Trust me on this point. I have watched the stock market virtually every trading day for the last two decades—I've missed only one day of work in that entire time due to illness, and even when I'm on vacation you'll find a *Wall Street Journal* nearby—and what I have learned is that neither I nor anybody else can predict with any consistency short-term market moves.

In fact, it may not be all that profitable trying to figure out where the market is heading in the short term. After all, much of the gains you make with a lucky guess are pretty much taxed away (nearly 40 percent if you are in the top tax bracket).

Where the big money is made (or saved) is in anticipating major shifts in the market. Indeed, if you can dodge some of the pain when the market is tanking while capitalizing when the bullish winds are blowing, you can maintain and create plenty of wealth in the market. Of course, it seems so easy after the fact to say that stocks were overvalued or undervalued. In the midst of the buying or selling frenzy, however, it's tough to be objective. Furthermore, if it were easy to front-run quantum market shifts, everyone would do it.

The fact is that trying to time the market—which is really what we are talking about—is in most cases a loser's game, be it short-term market timing or long-term market timing.

Still, I do believe understanding the environment in which investors place their bets does have value. If you know, for example, that market risk is running at high levels, you may tweak an investment program a bit to be more defensive. If you believe volatility is on the rise, you may take measures to deal with that increased volatility. If the primary trend of the market—that's the trend that usually lasts 18 months at a minimum—has shifted from bearish to bullish, you will be in a better position to capitalize on the trend change, even if your moves are modest in scope.

Most likely, you will not be able to sidestep all of a market decline. That is, you will not be able to remain in the storm's shifting eye forever.

But remember: Small victories in the investment game have huge long-term benefits.

Do the math. If a market declines 25 percent, but your $200,000 portfolio declines, say, 10 percent, you just saved yourself 15 percentage points, or $30,000. Now, take that $30,000 savings and run it out 20 years at an annual growth rate of 9 percent. That $30,000 "save" is worth more than $168,000 over the next two decades.

Even if the "save" is just a few percentage points a year, the power of compounding can turn those small savings into big gains. For example, let's say that, using the tools I show you in this chapter, you either save yourself 1 percent a year in reduced losses or make an extra 1 percent in capital gains. On a $200,000 portfolio, that means you save $2,000 per year. (This is conservative, since you would be saving more as your $200,000 portfolio grows, but let's keep it at $2,000 per year for math's sake.)

Do you know what $2,000 per year for 20 years at 10 percent per year grows to over 20 years? $126,000.

Bottom line: You don't need big scores in the market-timing department to have a big impact on your portfolio. Lots of little saves will do quite nicely. And those saves are doable with these tools at your disposal.

REVERSION TO THE MEAN

The tools we'll be examining are effective partly because of the concept known as "reversion to the mean." While reversion to the mean is primarily a mathematical concept, it has broad applications in virtually every aspect of our lives.

For example, while some people might say that life is all about the peaks (marriage, the birth of a child, job advancement, new home) and valleys (divorce, death, financial setbacks, problem relationships), the truth is that most of the time we spend on earth huddles around the "golden mean"—that period that is characterized neither by the highs nor lows but by how we feel most days.

Our "steady state," so to speak.

True, baseline emotions may differ dramatically from person to person. Still, most of our lives center around our "normal" feeling.

In other words, although emotions and feelings may run to extremes occasionally, things usually revert to the long-run steady state.

This "mean reversion" is similar to the swinging of a pendulum. Regardless of how far a pendulum swings in one direction, it eventually swings back. That, in essence, is mean reversion—a swinging back of the pendulum after it has hit an extreme point.

Mean reversion—the swinging pendulum—has broad applications for stocks and the stock market. Indeed, while markets experience extreme valuations periodically, the market tends to revert to the mean, the center, over time. Think of reversion to the mean as the "investment law of gravity," or "Sir Isaac Newton comes to Wall Street," as former Vanguard Funds head John Bogle so aptly described it.

Of course, to use reversion to the mean, you must know the appropriate baseline measurement—that is, the "normal" or average range.

Knowing the norm was a big problem for investors who came to the stock market for the first time in the second half of the 1990s. They didn't know (or chose to ignore) the fact that the baseline return for stocks over the long run is about 11 percent per year. These investors didn't realize (or chose to ignore) the fact that when stocks were rising 30 percent or more in some years, those returns were well above the long-run average, that "golden mean."

As one mutual fund manager put it, investors' expectations as a result of the abnormal move in the market in the second half of the '90s were "like the young man whose first blind date is with a future Miss Universe—his expectations of a normal girl may be warped for the rest of his life."

Given the extreme market returns in the second half of the 1990s—market returns well above the long-run average—something would eventually have to give.

That is precisely what happened in 2000 and 2001. In fact, the stock market in 2000 and 2001 saw not only reversion *to* the mean, but *through* the mean.

The market's steep declines in 2000 and 2001 bring up an important point: When markets run to extremes for some time, the reversion process is usually severe and doesn't necessarily stop when values return to their long-run averages. As was seen with the big market declines in 2000 and 2001, stocks will revert through the mean and approach extreme levels on the other side. Think of it as the pendulum hitting an extreme level in the opposite direction.

Mean reversion can be applied not only to market returns but to a host of other investment metrics. For example, when an investor understands that the baseline price/earnings ratio for the S&P 500 Index (going all the way back to 1925) is roughly 16, it should give him or her a new appreciation for the extreme levels of price/earnings ratios of recent years. It should also give investors some pause when they hear market watchers talk about how "cheap" certain stocks are when they are trading at price/earnings ratios of 30 or more.

The last point I want to make about mean reversion is that the concept underlies a popular investment strategy called "contrarian investing." Contrarian investors go against conventional wisdom. They pride themselves on going against Wall Street's herd mentality. Contrarians sell stocks everyone loves and buy stocks everyone hates.

Actually, contrarians, whether they realize it or not, are disciples of reversion to the mean. Contrarians try to find situations where investment opinions are running to bullish or bearish extremes—where the pendulum has swung too far in one direction—and take the other side of the trade. That's what reversion to the mean is all about—stocks and the market returning to their long-run averages.

Does reversion to the mean (or contrarian investing) always work? With time, contrarians are usually proved right. Notice, however, I said "with time." That's key. Reversion to the mean doesn't happen overnight. And sometimes it doesn't happen for years.

Go back to the market period from 1995 to 1999. Throughout that period there were plenty of contrarian investors saying that these extreme valuations—this craziness in the Internet sector, the explosion in the new issues markets—couldn't last forever. Yet, contrarian investors were left in the dust in the second half of the 1990s as stocks and valuations marched higher and higher.

Yes, contrarians were finally proved right in 2000–2001 when the market went bust, but they had to endure several years where stocks didn't revert to the mean.

That's the downside of relying on indicators that depend on reversion to the mean—you will most likely be early if you act on these indicators. Indeed, as any Wall Street veteran will tell you, markets can stay at extreme levels for a while.

Because you're likely to be early when using tools based on reversion to the mean, you should never bet the farm. You should never pull all of your money out of the market because a particular tool is showing that stock prices are trading at unsustainable levels. Rather, you want to make changes in your portfolio at the margin. Instead of selling 100 percent of your stocks, perhaps you raise cash to 15 to 20 percent.

Yes, you might call that a wimpy way to invest. Still, market timing is dicey stuff. You have to make only one huge misstep to mess up your portfolio big time. Thus, any changes should be measured. Remember: You don't need to hit home runs with market timing. Small victories will do just fine.

THE FUTURES AND OPTIONS MARKETS— BAROMETERS OF SHORT-TERM MARKET VOLATILITY

It you want a surefire way to lose money in the market, "invest" (a better word is "gamble") in the futures and options markets. The futures and options markets allow investors to leverage small bets into big wins, or at least that's the bullish side for investing in these markets.

Truth be told, buying call or put options or investing in stock index futures is a tough way to make a buck. Why? For one, the options and futures markets are zero-sum games. That is, for every dollar won by someone, the money is lost by someone else.

That is different from the stock market. Indeed, winners in the stock market don't win at the expense of losers. True, for every buyer there is a seller. But my gain in a stock I buy from you doesn't come out of your hide. It's an opportunity cost for you, nothing more.

In the futures market, every dollar I win comes out of someone else's pocket. It's real money. And the fact that the options and futures markets are the domain of professional investors usually means green coats get fleeced.

I don't mean for this to be a discussion about the relative merits of investing in futures and options, however. Remember that the mission of this chapter is to provide tools to tell where markets are going in terms of volatility. To this end, the options and futures markets can be indispensable.

Without getting too technical, it's important to understand that volatility is truly the lifeblood of the options and futures markets. In fact, volatility plays a huge role in the pricing of options and futures.

Time is a crucial element in the options and futures markets. When you invest in these markets, you are making a very explicit bet on something happening in a stated period of time.

That's where volatility comes into play. Volatility compresses large price movements into shorter time periods. For an options or futures player, that is important. During volatile markets, the premium paid to play in these markets rises.

Let's use an example to explain volatility and its effects on options and futures pricing. Let's say you want to buy a call option to purchase a stock. The stock is currently trading at $20 per share. You want to buy a call option with a "strike price" of $25. The life of this particular call option is three months. What this call option gives you is the ability to buy the stock at $25 anytime within the next three months.

In this scenario, a buyer of the call option is making a bet that the stock will move to and beyond $25 within the three-month period. Indeed, if the stock stays below $25, this call option ultimately will not have any value upon expiration. That should make sense, since no investor who can buy the stock on the open market at less than $25 would want to exercise the option to buy the stock at $25.

Remember that the investor must pay something to purchase the option. Since the option in this particular example is what is referred to as "out of the money," it has no intrinsic value. Why? Because the stock is currently trading below the strike price of the option. That is, you are buying an option to buy a stock at $25 that is currently trading for $20. Obviously, the option is not a good investment, since it doesn't make sense to pay for something that allows you to buy the stock at a price higher than you could purchase it in the open market.

Now, had the strike price been below the stock price, the value of the call option would be at least the difference between the strike price and market price. If you have the option to purchase a stock at $20 that is selling at $25, the option has to be worth at least $5. From this simple example, you should be able to see that one of the factors that goes into pricing an option is the strike price of the option.

Now, let's say you buy the call option to purchase stock at $25. The current stock price is $20. Remember that all options have a finite life, usually three to nine months. You need that stock to rise to more than $25 by expiration in order for your option to have any intrinsic value.

Which option gives you a better chance to accomplish that feat: A call option that expires in one month? Or a call option that expires in nine months?

Obviously, the longer you have, the better your chances of seeing the stock rise to the needed level. What that means is that you would be willing to pay a higher price for an option that expires in nine months than you would for the option with the same $25 strike price but an expiration in one month.

Now you know the second factor influencing the price of options (and, indeed, futures): time. The more time you have on the option or future before the day of reckoning, the greater the value of the option.

At this point, you're probably wondering what all of this has to do with volatility. Well, let's go back to our example. You buy a call option with a strike price of $25 on a stock trading for $20. You buy the option that expires in three months. Since you don't have much time for the stock to rise $5 (a 25 percent gain in just 90 days), you need that underlying stock to move *fast*. Indeed, if the stock is dead for the next 90 days, your option expires worthless.

Thus, what you want as an options player is lots of volatility. You want stock prices flying all over the place. A high-volatility market represents your best chance of seeing your option investment pay off.

Now you know the third component of option prices: volatility. The more volatile the market, the higher the price you'll pay for that call option, simply because higher volatility means a higher probability that the stock will rise the required amount.

The point of this discussion is not to make you an options trader. In fact, I would argue against pursuing that line of work. Rather, I bring up the relationship between option prices and volatility for the simple reason that looking at price movements in the options market can provide useful insights into the direction of volatility.

VIX AND VIXN

The Chicago Board Options Exchange is the largest exchange in the world dedicated to options. You can buy options on various market indexes as well as options on individual stocks.

A favorite measure of options traders is the CBOE's Volatility Index, otherwise known as "the VIX." In simplest terms, the VIX reflects the implied volatilities of the market as represented by the Standard & Poor's 100. (The S&P 100 is an index composed of the 100 largest companies in the S&P 500.) The VIX attempts to decompose various options pricing on the S&P 100 to shed light on the volatility premium in the market.

A high VIX means investors believe volatility is high and will remain high in the short term (over the next 30 days or so). A low VIX indicates that the implied volatility is low.

The VIX is a nice indicator because it is easily found. You can track the VIX every day by visiting the CBOE Web site at www.cboe.com. You can also obtain a quote for the VIX at the Yahoo! Finance Web site. Enter the symbol ^VIX.

Keep in mind that the VIX reflects expectations for short-term volatility. Obviously, expectations can be wrong. That's why you don't want to place all of your faith simply in the absolute level of the VIX. What you want to see are dramatic changes in either direction.

Look at the chart of the VIX on the next page. The chart goes back to 1997. Remember: What you want to catch are potentially big changes in volatility, akin to the shifting eye of the storm. Big changes usually occur when volatility levels run to extremes.

Notice that trend lines have been drawn at the tops and bottoms of the "normal" range for the VIX. The channel created by the trend lines represents the historical VIX trading range. VIX readings in this

VIX Chart

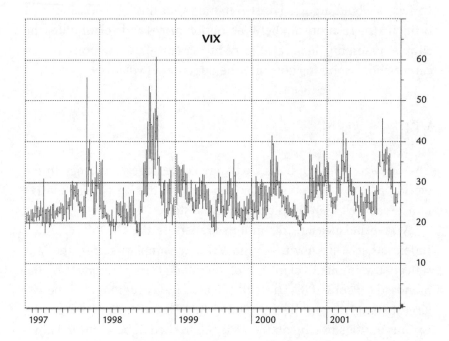

channel are well within the normal range for the index. Readings outside the channel, however, are those with the most meaning to investors searching for clues about changes in market volatility. As is the case with most sentiment indicators, their greatest value are as contrarian indicators. That's the case with the VIX. If implied market volatility, as measured by the VIX, is running at outrageously high levels, everyone believes market volatility will be high. However, it is usually at the extremes that everyone tends to be wrong. Chalk it up to the herd mentality. When a trend has become obvious to everyone, that's usually about the time the trend changes.

This also works on low VIX numbers. If the index is scraping along the bottom of its historical level, that means volatility is expected to remain extremely low. However, that also means that volatility levels have only one direction to go—up.

In other words, reversion to the mean.

A related measure of implied volatility is the Nasdaq Volatility

Index, known as "the VIXN." This indicator looks at the implied volatility of the Nasdaq 100 index. Below is a four-year chart of the VIXN, along with trend lines. The VIXN is a nice confirming indicator to the VIX in that it gives a different look at expectations for volatility in the short run.

On the next page I've overlaid the VIX chart with a chart of the S&P 100. Extreme moves in the VIX are often followed by dramatic moves in the S&P 100.

What is important to see here is that extreme levels in the VIX, either on the upside or the downside, often lead to significant short-term movements in the S&P 100. Obviously, that's significant. You want indicators to provide you lead time on changes. The VIX has done a nice job of forecasting short-term market movements.

Now look at the VIXN relative to the Nasdaq 100 index. Again, what you see are extreme levels in the VIXN foreshadowing big short-term moves in the Nasdaq 100 index.

VIXN Chart

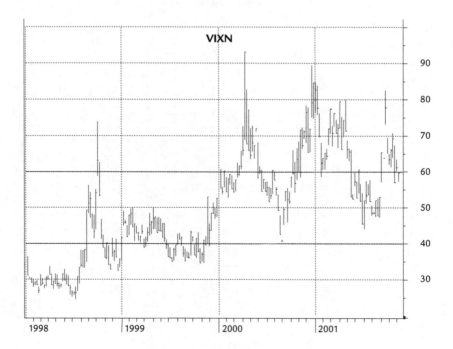

VIX/S&P Chart

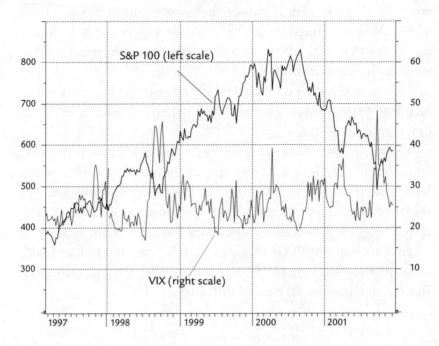

VIXN/Nasdaq Chart

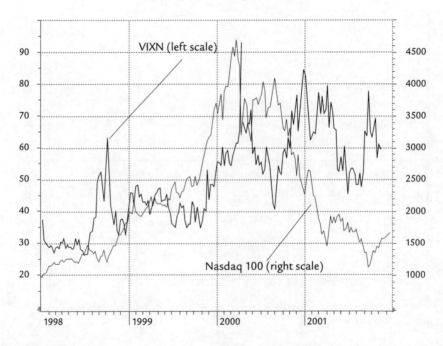

Again, I can't overemphasize the importance of considering only extreme readings when using this or any other sentiment indicator. Remember: You are looking for big shifts, potential sea-change moves in volatility and the market. Such massive shifts usually occur only when the readings run to extremes in either direction. Thus, when using this indicator to gain insight into expectations for short-term volatility—that is, volatility over the next 30 to 60 days—make sure you focus on only extreme readings. The rest is just noise around the mean.

INTERMEDIATE POTENTIAL RISK INDICATOR— A USEFUL TOOL FOR INTERMEDIATE TREND CHANGES

Longtime readers of my newsletter *DRIP Investor* know my fondness for this indicator. Indeed, in my nearly 20 years in the markets, the Intermediate Potential Risk Indicator is the single best tool I've ever seen for giving me some sense of risk and investor sentiment in the market.

The indicator looks exclusively at the percentage of stocks on the New York Stock Exchange trading above their 200-day moving average. This percentage is found every day on the "General Markets & Sectors" page of *Investor's Business Daily*. To create a 200-day moving average, you take the stock's average price over the last 200 trading days, and that is a point on the line. To get the next point, you drop a day and add a day and plot the new 200-day average price. And so on and so on. Thus, a typical 200-day moving average for a stock smooths out prices over a fairly lengthy period of time.

Over the years, my firm has quantified the percentage of NYSE stocks trading above their 200-day moving average in terms of market risk. In essence, the higher the percentage of stocks trading above their 200-day moving average, the more popular stocks are at that point in time. And the greater the popularity of stocks, the more likely you will see some reversion to the mean. Therefore, a reading of 70 percent or more of the NYSE stocks trading above their 200-day moving average constitutes "higher risk"; readings below 40 percent constitute "lower risk."

Why is a stock price's relationship to its 200-day moving average meaningful? As we've discussed, things tend to revert back to their long-run averages over time. A stock's 200-day moving average line represents a good barometer for a stock's long-run average price.

I like this tool for several reasons. First, the indicator does not depend on absolute levels of the market. Look at the Intermediate Potential Risk Chart below. According to the chart, market risk was actually lower in September 2001, when the Dow Jones Industrial Average traded for 8,300, than it was in 1996, when the Dow traded at much lower levels. The beauty of this tool is that it is a *relative* tool for that specific market period.

Keep in mind that a stock's long-run average of prices can change over time to reflect higher stock prices (which is why most 200-day moving averages trend upward). Thus, you want a tool that can adapt to changing price levels. Comparing the current stock price to its 200-day moving average level will give you some idea of how the stock is trading relative to an average level.

Intermediate Potential Risk Chart

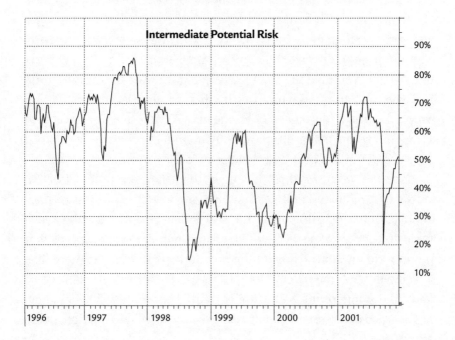

Of course, the true test of any indicator is how well it works. Fortunately, the performance of the Intermediate Potential Risk Indicator has been excellent.

My firm has done research looking at Intermediate Potential Risk levels with changes in the Dow Jones Industrial Average. What we have found is a strong correlation between risk levels (as measured by the Intermediate Potential Risk Indicator) and market returns. In fact, investors who purchased stock when the Intermediate Potential Risk Indicator fell below 30 percent did up to 4 percentage points better in return than investors who purchased stock when the Intermediate Potential Risk Indicator was not in lower-risk territory (below 40 percent). Conversely, when investors purchased stock when the Intermediate Potential Risk indicator was in high-risk territory (above 70 percent), returns were two percentage points worse than for those investors who had purchased stock when the Intermediate Potential Risk indicator was not at high-risk levels.

A recent example of the indicator's usefulness can be seen during the turbulent market period before and after the terrorist attacks of September 11, 2001. Prior to the attacks, 52 percent of NYSE stocks were trading above their 200-day moving average. That level had come down a bit in line with the market correction throughout 2001. Still, at 52 percent, the indicator was saying that there was "neutral" market risk. Based on this indicator, stocks were hardly offering screaming values.

That all changed after September 11. When the market reopened after the September 11 attacks, stocks plummeted. In fact, in the week of trading following the attack, the Dow Jones Industrial Average registered its worst one-week point decline ever.

Interestingly, had you been paying attention to the Intermediate Potential Risk Indicator throughout the market decline, what you would have seen is something rather extraordinary. That abysmal five days of trading beginning September 17 dropped the percentage of NYSE stocks trading above their 200-day moving average to just 20 percent.

In a nutshell, the battering the market took in the week after the tragedy purged 32 percentage points from the risk level in this market, putting the indicator in lower-risk territory and at its lowest level in years. To be sure, just because the market entered lower-risk territory based on this indicator didn't mean stocks couldn't get cheaper. My experience has been that it is not unusual for stocks to remain in lower-risk territory for weeks and even months.

However, what this indicator showed was that stocks had finally returned to more reasonable values. Had you put some cash to work when the risk indictor fell to such a low level, chances are good you would have made some solid profits. Indeed, after bottoming at 8,200 the week of September 17, the Dow Jones Industrial Average rose 18 percent in less than two months.

Again, when using this indicator, it's important to focus your attention on extreme levels, above 70 to 75 percent on the upside and below 30 to 40 percent on the downside. Those extremes will be much more useful in indicating possible shifts in market direction. And remember: Any changes you make to an investment program based on this tool should be made at the margin. For example, if you generally invest $500 per month, but the risk level is now in higher-risk territory, you might want to scale back that investment to perhaps $250–$350 until the risk level falls to neutral or lower risk.

The Intermediate Potential Risk Indicator is also useful for investors who buy stock on margin. When stocks are purchased on margin, it means an investor is using borrowed funds to buy stock. Obviously, buying stocks on margin is something you want to do only when stocks are offering especially compelling values; you don't want to be on margin when stocks are overvalued and poised for a tumble.

You should feel more confident buying stocks on margin when intermediate potential risk is in lower-risk territory. Conversely, if the market is in higher-risk territory, that may be a good time to lower or eliminate your margin.

Finally, if you are an investor with a shortening investment time horizon (due to age or health reasons), you may want to use this tool more aggressively in order to monitor risk in your portfolio.

For example, if your equity exposure has increased to an uncomfortable level in your portfolio (perhaps because the market has enjoyed several years of solid performance) and the intermediate risk level is now in higher-risk territory, you might want to take the opportunity to lower your equity exposure to a more acceptable level.

PREDICTING SHIFTS IN THE MARKET'S LONG-TERM TREND USING THE DOW THEORY

When it comes to market timing, the most important thing you need to know as an investor is the market's primary trend. The primary trend is the market's long-term trend. Primary market trends usually last at least 15 months.

As an investor, you need to know the following:

- Is the primary trend bearish or bullish?

- Is my investment portfolio positioned on the right side of the primary trend?

- Is the primary trend changing?

The best tool I've ever seen for answering all three of these important questions is the Dow Theory.

STILL RELEVANT AFTER ALL THESE YEARS

A perception exists in this country that new is always better than old.

In fact, what is old is often described with the worst of all possible adjectives—irrelevant.

Because the Dow Theory is more than 100 years old, many market pundits view this market-timing tool as irrelevant in this day and age of fast-moving stocks and markets.

Quite honestly, that misperception is fine by me. The fact that people ignore the Dow Theory gives its users a nice edge in looking at markets. And trust me—the Dow Theory works. Not all the time (no indicator is infallible), but enough of the time to make you plenty of money during most bull markets and save you money during bear markets.

TOOLS OF THE THEORY—
DOW INDUSTRIALS AND TRANSPORTS

The Dow Theory gets its name from Charles Dow, the founder and first editor of *The Wall Street Journal*. The genesis of the Dow Theory goes back to the late 1890s and Charles Dow's work explaining price fluctuations in the stock market. Dow determined that most stocks moved more or less in unison. This "trend" action led to the development of a "trend theory" and ultimately the Dow Theory. A protégé of Charles Dow, William Peter Hamilton, is often credited with refining the Dow Theory.

One of the reasons I like the Dow Theory is that it is relatively easy to use. Indeed, the theory looks at just two factors—the Dow Jones Industrial Average and the Dow Jones Transportation Average.

Charles Dow wanted to develop a barometer for getting a reading on the overall economy. To that end, he developed two indices. Dow's Industrial Index consisted of 12 industrial stocks (only General Electric still remains today from the original 12 Dow Industrial stocks). Dow's Rail Index consisted initially of just railroad stocks. (Obviously, the airlines, which now populate the Dow Transportation Index, were not a factor in the late 1890s.)

Dow felt that the rails, when combined with the Industrial Index, could act as "co-confirmers" of broader trends. Indeed, if the industrials—the manufacturing component of the economy—and the rails— the component that ships what the industrial firms make—were in sync (as represented by the indices moving in unison), the economy would be in sync. If these two key areas of the economy weren't in sync, that would show up in divergence in the indices.

Dow Industrials

Today, the Dow Jones Industrial Average consists of 30 companies:

AT&T	Honeywell
Alcoa	International Business Machines
American Express	Intel

Boeing	International Paper
Caterpillar	Johnson & Johnson
Citigroup	JP Morgan Chase
Coca-Cola	McDonald's
Disney (Walt)	Merck
DuPont (E.I.)	Microsoft
Eastman Kodak	Minnesota Mining and Manufacturing
Exxon Mobil	Philip Morris Companies
General Electric	Procter & Gamble
General Motors	SBC Communications
Hewlett-Packard	United Technologies
Home Depot	Wal-Mart Stores

Dow Transports

The Dow Jones Transportation Average consists of the following 20 companies:

AMR	Norfolk Southern
Airborne Freight	Northwest Air
Alexander & Baldwin	Roadway Express
Burlington Northern Santa Fe	Ryder Systems
CNF Transportation	Southwest Airlines
CSX	UAL
Delta Air Lines	Union Pacific
FedEx	US Airways
GATX	US Freight
Hunt (JB)	Yellow

To compute the respective averages, all of the closing prices of the stocks are added together and divided by a divisor. The divisor is adjusted to reflect stock splits, spin-offs, and other capitalization changes.

The Dow Averages are "price-weighted" indexes. That is, higher-priced stocks carry greater weight in the index than do lower-priced stocks.

For example, at the time of this writing, IBM is trading for $114 per share; Disney, $19 per share:

- If IBM rises 10 percent, the stock's impact on the Dow Industrials is approximately 79 points (11.40, which is 10 percent of $114, divided by the divisor, currently 0.14452124).

- If Disney rises 10 percent, the favorable impact on the Dow Industrials is just 13 points (1.9, which is 10 percent of $19, divided by 0.14452124).

As you can see, IBM's performance matters a lot more to the performance of the Dow Jones Industrial Average, by virtue of its triple-digit price tag, than does Disney's price performance.

Why are the Dow Averages price-weighted? Simple. When Charles Dow developed the Averages more than 100 years ago, the fastest computer was a brain and a pencil. Thus, the easiest way to construct and track the index was to add up the prices of the stocks each day.

The fact that the Dow Averages are price-weighted is one reason some market watchers prefer indexes, such as the S&P 500, that are weighted by market capitalizations. (Market capitalization is stock price times the number of shares outstanding.) After all, how "representative" can an index be in which the stock's per-share price is the sole determinant of its weighting in the index?

However, despite the fact that the Dow is calculated in a very different manner than the index of choice for market professionals—the S&P 500—the correlation of the two indexes is extremely high. For example, for the five-year period ended January 10, 2002, the annualized return of the Dow Jones Industrial Average is 10 percent. And for the S&P 500 Index?

Ten percent.

One reason for the close correlation between the indices is that the stocks in the Dow Industrials make up a hefty portion of the S&P 500 stocks. While some market watchers decry the Dow as being too narrow and not as representative of the overall market as, say, the S&P 500, the numbers simply do not bear this out.

Two additional points about the Dow Averages worth noting concern stock splits and the Dow's shrinking divisor.

Since higher-priced stocks carry greater weight in the index, it seems that Dow components are a bit slower to split their shares than are other issues. One reason may be that stock splits reduce the clout a company has on the index. If the market is doing well and the high-priced stocks are leading the charge, an incentive may exist for Dow stocks to remain at higher prices rather than split their shares.

Another quirk is that the divisor, because it is less than 1.0, is, in effect, a multiplier. In other words, with every adjustment in the divisor, the price movements of the Dow become more exaggerated. For example, if each Dow Industrial stock rises one point in a day, the total gain in the index is 207 points (30 divided by 0.14452124). If the divisor, perhaps because of a split, shrinks to 0.12505, a one-point advance in each Dow stock translates to an increase in the Average of 240 points (30 divided by 0.12505).

Given the drop in the Dow's divisor over the last five years, it's not surprising that the Dow Industrials have seen a significant increase in volatility, at least in terms of 100-point days to the upside and downside.

The Movement of the Industrials and Transports

Charles Dow and, later, Dow protégé William Hamilton discovered that market trends, as measured by the Dow Industrials and Transports, consisted of three movements:

1. Primary trend

2. Secondary reactions

3. Daily fluctuations

Dow and Hamilton observed that the only trend of consequence was the market's primary trend. This is the trend that extends over a comparatively long period of time. The Dow Theory believes that daily fluctuations or secondary reactions, while having value when taken as a whole over a lengthy time period, have no forecasting value when looked at individually.

Primary Trend—Bull Market

The Dow Theory defines a "bull market" as a long, broad, upward movement of prices that is interrupted at uncertain intervals by important reactions. Primary bull markets have three phases:

- The first phase is often characterized by a period of a number of weeks, and perhaps even several months, during which the Dow Averages make a succession of small movements. These viewed all together form a "saw-toothed" pattern, with rallies making successively higher tops while successive declines fail to penetrate previous lows. This pattern will normally be accompanied by small volume. This trading action is often accompanied by pessimism among market observers and the media. Yet, despite the pessimism, the Industrial and Transportation Averages refuse to retreat further. This resiliency in the face of bearish sentiment is often an indication of a market that has bottomed. What usually occurs next is that the old lows in both Dow Averages will hold, with the Industrials and Transports rallying above their previous high points. The move to new highs by both Averages signals a new bull market.

- The second phase of a bull market is often the longest. Stock prices adjust and readjust themselves to improving business and increased earnings. This is often the "gravy train" phase of bull markets, when Dow Theorists buy stocks knowing that the bullish primary trend should reward them for their courage.

- The third and final phase of a bull market is usually characterized by optimism on the part of investors. Interestingly, however, the Averages are usually telling a different story. Market reversals are followed by failed attempts to move above old highs in the Averages. These rebounds are often accompanied by diminishing market volume. Finally, after failing to move to new highs, both Averages close below their lowest points of the preceding shakeout. At this point, the market's primary trend, according to the Dow Theory, has turned bearish.

Primary Trend—Bear Market

Dow theorists define a primary bear market as a long, broad, downward movement of prices that is interrupted at irregular intervals by important reversals (rallies in this case). And, like bull markets, bear markets generally have three phases:

- The first phase of a bear market occurs after the Averages fail to go to new highs and break below important low points established during a reversal. One characteristic of the first phase of a bear market is the surrender of "get-rich-quick" hopes by late participants in the bull market, who sell aggressively.

- The second phase of a bear market is likely to be a long, drawn-out affair. The economy usually is in a recession, and corporate earnings are slipping. Interestingly, this phase usually still has investors clinging to hopes that the market is poised for a rebound, with bargains abounding in the market. These investors are usually proved wrong, however, as stocks continue to slip, even in the face of periodic good news.

- The third phase of bear markets is when things turn truly ugly. Stock prices collapse, with high-quality and speculative stocks getting creamed. However, at some point, while investor sentiment is usually at its most bearish, the Averages will refrain from retreating. Small volume, the refusal of the Averages to retreat in the face of bad news, and an all-pervading pessimism will make the Dow theorist alert for the signal—a breakout to new highs in both Averages, as discussed earlier—which will mark the coming of a new bull market.

The duration of bull and bear markets has varied significantly over the years. However, since 1897, the average bull market has lasted more than 30 months; the average bear market, approximately 15 months.

What Have You Done for Me Lately?

No market-timing tool, including the Dow Theory, is infallible. However, that the Dow Theory has stood the test of time speaks volumes about its usefulness for helping investors stay on the right side of the market's primary trend. A good example of the effectiveness of the Dow Theory can be seen in the tool's performance in the last three years.

The accompanying chart shows the performance of the Dow Industrials and Transports since the beginning of 1999. As you can see from the chart, the Dow Industrials and Transports failed to move

Dow Industrials/Transports Chart

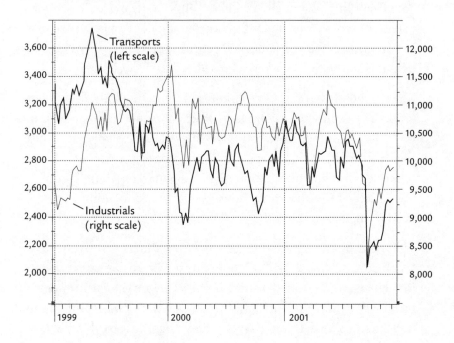

to new highs in late August 1999 and dipped below previous lows in October, thus triggering a Dow Theory bear-market signal.

Interestingly, the signal looked like a bad one as the Dow proceeded to rally strongly to all-time highs in March 2000. Then the roof fell in on the market. Indeed, both the Dow Industrials and Transports proceeded to sell off over the next 18 months, with the Dow Industrials hitting a low of 8,235 the week of September 17, 2001.

Investors who paid heed to the Dow Theory's bear-market signal would have dodged at least a portion of the market's decline in the last two years.

Of course, past performance is not indicative of future results. And the Dow Theory, like any tool, has its limitations. For example, the theory does not tell you how high or low a primary market move will carry. The theory merely tells you the direction of the primary trend. And don't expect the Dow Theory to get you in at the exact bottom of bear markets or get you out at the exact top of bull markets. The theory aims to capture the bulk, but not all, of any market move.

Nevertheless, the usefulness of the Dow Theory cannot be ignored. In fact, I would argue that the theory's effectiveness has become even greater in recent years due, in part, to its ability to keep investors focused on the market's primary trend during volatile markets.

Dow Theory Tenets

The following is a summary of the key tenets of the Dow Theory:

- The Dow Averages represent all that is known and all that can be foreseen by investors.

- Only closes in the Dow Industrials and Transports above or below old highs or old lows have value under the Dow Theory, not intraday price movements above or below critical points.

- The movements of the Dow Industrials and Transports must confirm one another in order for any signal under the Dow Theory to be authentic. Investors should think of confirmation between the two Dow Averages in terms of direction as opposed to magnitude of the move.

- Movement by one Average that is not confirmed by movement in the other Average after a reasonable period of time can often lead to a secondary reaction and, in some cases, a change in the primary trend.

- The best time to buy during primary bull markets is during secondary corrections within the primary trend. Conversely, the best time to sell stocks is during rallies within primary bear markets.

- Signals made in third phases have diminishing authority.

- Conditions that bring about bull markets and bear markets change slowly.

CONCLUSION

The last thing you want to do as an investor is get caught in the trick bag of aggressively timing the market. What is "aggressively" timing the market? I think aggressively timing the market is rotating 50 percent or more of your equity money in and out of the market.

Having said that, I also believe that investors should have a full appreciation of the risk level of the market at any point in time. Knowing, for example, that stocks are high based on the Intermediate Potential Risk Indicator—or that the Dow Theory has flashed a bear market signal . . . or that the volatility level on the VIX is indicating a potential shift in the market winds—can be useful for adjusting portfolio allocations at the margin.

What's "at the margin"? Good question. One way to tweak portfolios at the margin is to reduce equity exposure in portfolios with the shortest investment time horizon. Reduce by how much? In my mind, reducing equity exposure by 20 percent is a meaningful move "at the margin."

What do I do "at the margin"? Quite honestly, given my investment time horizon, I try to make as few changes as possible to my allocation. That is, I reduce risk using primarily "time" diversification, not asset allocation. I also try to maintain steady investment programs, even during weak markets.

However, if all three of these indicators—the VIX, Intermediate Potential Risk, and the Dow Theory—are showing high risk in the market, I might reduce equity exposure a bit (up to 20 percent or more if I'm extremely bearish).

Keep in mind, however, that the risk level must be confirmed by more than one of these indicators. That's important. Indeed, the best use of these indicators, especially since each of these tools focuses on a different time period (30 days to 60 days for the VIX, six months to 12 months for the Intermediate Potential Risk Indicator, and 12 months to 24 months for the Dow Theory), is as confirming indicators.

In other words, I am much more likely to reduce a portfolio's equity exposure at the margin if I see all three indicators flashing danger rather than a warning from just one of the indicators. Remember: Safety has its opportunity costs, especially if the market takes off and you're left holding tons of cash.

Still, if your investment time horizon is such that you cannot afford a big hit—you know, that killer crunch that wipes out 20 percent or more of your portfolio in 12 months—you do have tools at your disposal to help you know when to say when.

Ignore them at your peril.

Chapter Ten

It's Game Time

IF THERE IS a silver lining to the rocky markets of recent years, it is this: You've now had a taste of just how bad the markets can be. Actually, you've had more than a taste. You've had a pretty good gulp.

Yes, you are no doubt poorer. But while this market has bloodied you, you're still standing. You can still fight another day. And, most important, there's still plenty of time left on the clock for a big comeback.

If nothing else, you should be a lot wiser for the experience of investing during arguably some of the most difficult and volatile markets in history. And you should be able to put that wisdom to work over the next several years to make you a better investor.

My fear is that, should these difficult markets continue, many investors will leave the game. And that would be a big mistake. For the stock market, warts and all, still offers the single best path to wealth for anyone.

And I do mean *anyone.*

So what do you need to do to make sure you stay in the game? The following is a "to-do" list an investor can use to be a successful player in the volatile markets of today and tomorrow.

❑ Investor, Know Thyself

Are you a trader?
Are you a buy-and-hold investor?
What is your investment time horizon?
What is your investment objective?
How comfortable are you with risk?
Is it more important to you to create wealth or to preserve wealth?

These are the type of questions you must ask and answer if you hope to create an investment style and approach that works for you.

If you've never asked these questions, the time is now.

❑ Time to Do Your Homework

The free ride in the market is over. Don't expect to make money in the future buying just about anything. What happened in the '90s was extremely atypical for stocks. The market will likely be much more discriminating in determining whom it allows to be a "genius."

Investors will have to know what they're buying. They'll have to know how to put together diversified portfolios that match their risk profiles. They'll have to maintain good financial records. They'll have to make the tough decisions about when to sell.

Choppy markets put a premium on knowledge and information. If you want to be a player, you'll need to do your homework.

❑ No Time for Bambi Investing

Maybe your portfolio demands an overhaul. Maybe it is just fine the way it is. My point is that whether you act or sit tight should be a conscious decision, one made after evaluating your options, your investments. Unfortunately, many investors still are like deer caught in the headlights, frozen. You don't know what to do, so you do nothing.

You cannot expect to be a successful investor if you are afraid to do what's necessary for success. And that means reevaluating what you own, upgrading your portfolio if need be, rebalancing to control risk, and restructuring your portfolio to reduce volatility.

❑ Find a Way to Buy

Bear markets don't last forever. In fact they are shorter than you think. Indeed, the average bear market lasts about 15 months. That compares to an average length of bull markets of more than two years.

The upshot is that stocks generally rise two out of every three years. That means over a 30-year time frame, the market will rise in roughly 20 of the 30 years. Keep that in mind the next time you don't feel like buying stocks during market declines.

The ironic thing is that the best time to add to portfolios is not the 20 years when stocks rise, but those 10 years when stocks decline. That's when you get the best prices. Unfortunately, most people would rather buy when stocks are rising and sell when they fall.

To be a successful investor, you need to find a way to make yourself buy stocks even when you don't want to buy. It may mean investing relatively small amounts on a regular basis via DRIPs and direct-purchase plans and other dollar-based investing strategies. It may mean putting your investment program on autopilot by utilizing automatic monthly investment services.

Whatever it takes, you must find a way to add to stocks even when your head and heart tell you to do otherwise.

❑ Get Rid of the Anchors

Where your stocks traded 18 months ago is meaningless today. Just because Cisco once traded for $80 doesn't mean that it will ever trade there again.

To be sure, Cisco may trade at $80 again. But it won't be because it traded there before. If Cisco trades again at $80, it will be because its future earnings will warrant a stock price of $80.

Too many investors still anchor their decisions on stocks to the past. In essence, they are driving their portfolios looking out the rearview mirror. Don't be one of them.

❑ Create a Simple Plan

Do you have a plan as an investor?

Do you have contingencies established should certain things happen in the market?

Do you have a "watch list" of stocks and buy prices for those stocks?

Do you know what factors would determine whether you continue to hold or sell a stock?

Do you know what your cost basis is on your investments?

In short, do you have a simple plan in your investments? If you do have a plan, simplify it. If you don't have a plan, get one now.

❏ Put Away the Home-Run Swing

You don't have to swing for the fences to create wealth in the stock market. A reasonable annual return and time will do the trick. Swinging for the fences—whether it be concentrating portfolios in just a few stocks, overweighting highly volatile industry sectors, or buying penny stocks—also increases your chances for that killer loss that will take years to recover.

Indeed, investors who swung for the fences in the late '90s now wish they had choked up on the bat in the last two years and slapped some singles.

Remember: The secret of investment success is to continue to set aside money to invest over time, and to generate a reasonable rate of return each and every year while avoiding the big loss.

That alone is more than enough to make you achieve your financial dreams.

APPENDIX A: DIRECT-PURCHASE PLANS

U.S. DIRECT-PURCHASE PLANS

The following U.S. companies allow any investor to buy stock directly from the company, the first share and every share. In most cases, the minimum initial investment is $1,000 or less. Some companies will waive the minimum initial investment if an investor agrees to automatic monthly investment (via electronic debit of a bank account) of $50 to $100. To obtain enrollment information, call the toll-free number. For periodic updates of this list, visit the *DRIP Investor* newsletter Web site—www.dripinvestor.com.

Acadia Realty	($250)	800-278-4353
ADC Telecomm.	($500)	800-774-4117
Aetna	($500)	800-955-4741
AFLAC	($1,000)	800-227-4756
AGL Resources	($250)	800-774-4117
Air Products	($500)	888-694-9458
Alleg. Technologies	($1,000)	800-842-7629
Allete	($250)	800-535-3056
Alliant Energy	($250)	800-356-5343
Allstate	($500)	800-448-7007
AMB Property	($500)	800-331-9474
American Bank of CT	($250)	800-278-4353
American Elec. Power	($250)	800-955-4740
American Express	($1,000)	800-842-7629
American Home Products	($500)	800-842-7629
American States Water	($500)	888-816-6998
Ametek	($500)	800-278-4353
Anadarko Petroleum	($1,000)	800-842-7629
Annaly Mortgage	($1,000)	212-696-0100
Arch Chemicals	($500)	800-955-4735
Arrow Financial	($300)	518-745-1000
Associates First Capital	($1,000)	888-297-6879
Atmos Energy	($200)	800-774-4117
Avaya	($1,000)	866-222-8292
Avery Dennison	($500)	800-649-2291
Bank of America	($1,000)	800-642-9855
Bank of NY	($1,000)	800-727-7033
Bard (C.R.)	($250)	800-828-1639
Becton, Dickinson	($250)	800-955-4743
Bedford Properties	($1,000)	800-774-5476
BellSouth	($500)	888-266-6778
Blyth Industries	($250)	877-424-1968
Bob Evans Farms	($100)	800-272-7675
Borg-Warner Auto.	($500)	800-774-4117
Boston Beer	($500)	888-266-6780
Bowne & Co.	($500)	800-524-4458
BRE Properties	($500)	800-774-4117
Brookline Bancorp	($1,000)	800-278-4353
Calgon Carbon	($250)	888-775-2650
California Water Service	($500)	800-337-3503
Campbell Soup	($500)	800-649-2160

Caraustar Inds.	($250)	800-524-4458
Carpenter Technology	($500)	800-822-9828
Carver Bancorp	($200)	800-278-4353
Caterpillar	($250)	800-842-7629
CH Energy Group	($100)	888-280-3848
Chase Corp.	($250)	800-278-4353
ChevronTexaco	($250)	800-842-7629
Citizens & Northern Bank	($250)	800-278-4353
CMS Energy	($500)	800-774-4117
Columbus McKinnon	($250)	800-278-4353
Community Bank Sys.	($500)	800-842-7629
Compaq Computer	($250)	888-218-4373
Conectiv	($500)	800-365-6495
Conoco	($250)	800-317-4445
Consolidated Freightways	($100)	800-727-7033
Crown Am. Realty Tr.	($100)	800-774-4117
CSX	($500)	800-774-4117
Curtiss-Wright	($2,000)	888-266-6793
CVS	($100)	877-287-7526
Darden Restaurants	($1,000)	800-829-8432
Deere & Co.	($500)	800-268-7369
Delphi Automotive	($500)	800-818-6599
Delta Air Lines	($250)	201-324-1225
Diebold	($500)	800-432-0140
Disney (Walt)	($1,000)	800-948-2222
Dollar General	($50)	888-266-6785
Dominion Resources (VA)	($250)	800-552-4034
Dow Jones & Co.	($1,000)	800-842-7629
DQE	($105)	800-247-0400
DTE Energy	($100)	800-774-4117
Duke Energy	($250)	800-488-3853
Duke Realty	($250)	800-278-4353
Dynegy	($250)	800-842-7629
Eastman Kodak	($150)	800-253-6057
Electronic Data Sys.	($250)	800-278-4353
Energen	($250)	800-774-4117
Entergy	($1,000)	800-225-1721
Equifax	($500)	888-887-2971
Equity Office Prop.	($1,000)	888-752-4831
Equity Residential	($250)	800-337-5666
Essex Property	($100)	800-945-8245
Estée Lauder	($250)	800-842-7629
Exxon Mobil	($250)	800-252-1800
Fannie Mae	($250)	888-289-3266
FBL Financial	($250)	866-892-5627
FedEx	($1,000)	800-524-3120
Fifth Third Bancorp	($500)	800-837-2755
First Commonwealth Fin'l	($500)	800-727-7033
First Financial Holdings	($250)	800-998-9151
First Niagara Financial	($150)	800-842-7629
FirstEnergy	($250)	800-736-3402
Ford Motor	($1,000)	800-955-4791
Freddie Mac	($250)	888-279-4029
Frontier Insurance	($100)	888-200-3162
GenCorp	($500)	800-727-7033
General Electric	($250)	800-786-2543
General Growth Prop.	($200)	800-774-4117
Gillette	($1,000)	800-643-6989
Glenborough Realty	($250)	800-266-6785
Glimcher Realty	($100)	800-738-4931
Goodyear	($250)	800-453-2440
Granite Construction	($3,000)	888-884-5090
Gray Communications	($250)	888-835-2869
Great Atlantic & Pacific	($250)	800-278-4353
GreenPoint Financial	($2,000)	800-842-7629
Guidant	($250)	800-537-1677
Harland (John H.)	($500)	800-649-2202
Hawaiian Electric Inds.	($250)	808-543-5662
Health Care Prop. Inves.	($750)	800-524-4458
Heinz (H.J.)	($250)	800-253-3399

Hershey Foods	($500)	800-842-7629
Hillenbrand Inds.	($250)	800-774-4117
Home Depot	($250)	877-437-4273
Home Properties	($1,000)	800-774-4117
IBM	($500)	888-426-6700
Interchange Fin'l Svcs.	($100)	201-703-2265
International Paper	($500)	800-678-8715
Intimate Brands	($500)	800-955-4745
Investors Financial	($250)	888-333-5336
iStar Financial	($100)	800-756-8200
ITT Industries	($500)	800-254-2823
Jefferson Bancorp	($250)	800-278-4353
Johnson Controls	($250)	800-524-6220
JPS Industries	($250)	800-278-4353
Kaman	($250)	800-842-7629
Kansas City Power & Light	($500)	816-860-7781
Kellwood	($100)	314-576-3100
Kelly Services	($250)	800-829-8259
Kerr-McGee	($750)	800-786-2556
KeySpan	($250)	800-482-3638
Kilroy Realty	($750)	888-816-7506
Kmart	($250)	800-947-8019
Lear	($250)	800-727-7033
Lehman Brothers	($500)	800-824-5707
Lion	($150)	800-649-9895
Libbey	($100)	800-727-7033
Liberty Corp.	($250)	800-278-4353
Liberty Property Trust	($1,000)	800-944-2214
Lilly (Eli)	($1,000)	800-451-2134
Lincoln National	($2,000)	800-949-0197
Lockheed Martin	($250)	888-548-7701
Longs Drug Stores	($500)	888-213-0886
Lowe's Companies	($250)	877-282-1174
Lubrizol	($250)	800-278-4353
Lucent Technologies	($1,000)	888-582-3686
Macerich	($250)	800-567-0169
Mack-Cali Realty	($2,000)	888-632-6848
Madison Gas & Electric	($50)	800-356-6423
Mallinckrodt	($500)	800-446-2617
Manufactured Home Com.	($1,000)	800-842-7629
Marriott Int'l	($350)	800-649-2213
Mattel	($500)	888-909-9922
McCormick & Co.	($250)	800-424-5855
McDermott Int'l	($500)	800-947-4542
McDonald's	($500)	800-621-7825
McGraw-Hill	($500)	888-201-5538
MDU Resources	($50)	701-222-7991
Meadowbrook Insurance	($250)	800-649-2579
Mellon	($500)	800-842-7629
Merck	($350)	800-774-4117
Met-Pro	($1,000)	800-278-4353
Michaels Stores	($500)	800-577-4676
MidSouth Bancorp	($1,000)	800-842-7629
Mills Corp.	($250)	800-990-1010
Modine Mfg.	($500)	800-813-3324
Mony Group	($3,000)	800-608-7863
Morgan Stanley	($1,000)	800-228-0829
Motorola	($500)	800-774-4117
National Service Inds.	($600)	888-836-5069
Nationwide Financial Svcs.	($500)	800-842-7629
NCR	($500)	800-278-4353
New England Business Svc.	($250)	800-736-3001
Newell Rubbermaid	($250)	888-565-6553
Newport	($250)	888-200-3169
Newport News Shipbuilding	($500)	800-649-1861
Nike	($500)	800-401-3439
NorthWestern	($500)	800-677-6716
Office Depot	($250)	800-681-8059
OGE Energy	($250)	800-774-4117
Old National Bancorp	($500)	800-774-4117

Omnicom	($250)	800-842-7629
Oneok	($100)	800-955-4798
Owens Corning	($1,000)	800-472-2210
Pan Pacific Retail Prop.	($250)	800-524-4458
Paychex	($250)	877-814-9688
Penney (J.C.)	($250)	800-565-2576
Pennichuck	($250)	800-736-3001
Penn. Real Est. Inv.	($250)	800-278-4353
Peoples Energy	($250)	800-774-4117
PepsiAmericas	($250)	800-660-4187
PerkinElmer	($250)	800-842-7629
Pfizer	($500)	800-733-9393
Pharmacia	($250)	800-774-4117
Phelps Dodge	($1,000)	800-842-7629
Philadelphia Subrn.	($500)	800-205-8314
Phillips Petroleum	($500)	888-887-2968
Piedmont Natural Gas	($250)	800-774-4117
Pier 1 Imports	($500)	800-842-7629
Pinnacle West (AZ)	($50)	800-457-2983
PolyOne	($250)	888-767-7166
Popular	($100)	877-764-1893
Prentiss Properties	($500)	888-290-7286
Procter & Gamble	($250)	800-764-7483
ProLogis Trust	($200)	800-956-3378
Providian Financial	($500)	800-482-8690
Public Service Enterprise	($250)	800-242-0813
Public Service of New Mex.	($50)	800-545-4425
Quaker Oats	($500)	800-774-4117
Quanex	($250)	800-278-4353
Questar	($250)	800-729-6788
Radio Shack	($250)	888-218-4374
Reader's Digest	($1,000)	800-242-4653
Redwood Trust	($500)	800-774-4117
Regions Financial	($500)	800-922-3468
Reliant Energy	($250)	800-231-6406
RJR Reynolds Tobacco	($500)	800-519-3111
Roadway Express	($250)	800-774-4117
Robbins & Myers	($500)	800-622-6757
Rockwell Collins	($1,000)	888-253-4522
Rockwell Int'l	($1,000)	800-842-7629
Sanderson Farms	($500)	800-842-7629
SBC Communications	($500)	888-836-5062
SCANA	($250)	800-763-5891
Schnitzer Steel	($500)	800-727-7033
Sears, Roebuck & Co.	($500)	888-732-7788
Security Capital Pacific	($200)	800-842-7629
SEMCO Energy	($250)	800-649-1856
Sempra Energy	($500)	877-773-6772
Snap-on	($500)	800-501-9474
Sonoco Products	($250)	800-864-2246
South Jersey Industries	($100)	888-754-3100
Southern Co.	($250)	800-774-4117
Southern Union	($250)	800-793-8938
Sovran Self Storage	($250)	800-278-4353
Stanley Works	($250)	800-543-6757
Sunoco	($250)	800-888-8494
Synovus Financial	($250)	800-337-0896
Target	($500)	888-268-0203
Taubman Centers	($250)	800-774-4117
Tektronix	($500)	800-842-7629
Tenneco Automotive	($250)	800-649-9891
Thornburg Mortgage Asset	($500)	800-509-5586
Timken	($1,000)	888-347-2453
Tompkins Trustco	($100)	800-524-4458
Total System Services	($250)	800-553-0292
Transocean Sedco	($500)	800-727-7033
Tribune	($500)	800-924-1490
Tricon Global	($250)	888-439-4986
True North Comm.	($1,000)	888-347-2457
TrustCo Bank of NY	($25)	518-381-3601

Tyson Foods	($250)	800-822-7096
UAL	($250)	800-647-4488
UIL Holdings	($250)	800-278-4353
UniSource Energy	($250)	888-269-8845
United Investors Realty	($350)	800-969-3371
United National Bancorp	($100)	800-368-5948
United Wisconsin Svcs.	($100)	414-276-3737
USEC	($250)	888-485-2938
USG	($500)	877-360-5385
USX—Marathon	($500)	412-433-4801
USX—U.S. Steel	($500)	412-433-4801
UtiliCorp United	($250)	800-647-2789
Valspar	($1,000)	800-842-7629
Verizon	($1,000)	800-631-2355
Visteon	($1,000)	800-821-1403
Wal-Mart Stores	($250)	800-438-6278
Walgreen	($50)	800-286-9178
Washington REIT	($250)	877-386-8123
Waste Management	($500)	800-286-9178
Weingarten Realty	($500)	888-887-2966
Wells Fargo	($250)	800-774-4117
Western Digital	($100)	800-278-4353
Western Resources	($250)	800-774-4117
Westvaco	($250)	800-432-9874
Whirlpool	($1,000)	800-409-7442
Winston Hotels	($250)	919-510-6010
Wisconsin Energy	($50)	800-558-9663
WPS Resources	($100)	800-236-1551
Xcel Energy	($1,000)	877-778-6786
XTO Energy	($500)	800-938-6387
Yahoo!	($250)	877-946-6487
York International	($1,000)	800-774-4117

FOREIGN DIRECT-PURCHASE PLANS

One of the major developments in dividend reinvestment plans (DRIPs) in the last five years has been the growth in the number of foreign companies offering direct-purchase plans for U.S. investors. Indeed, more than 300 foreign companies allow U.S. investors to make even initial purchases directly, without a broker.

What is particularly noteworthy is that these foreign direct-purchase plans span the globe, from Argentina to the United Kingdom. Thus, a DRIP investor who wants to give a U.S. portfolio a foreign flavor has many companies and countries from which to choose.

When you purchase stock directly from foreign companies, you are actually buying American Depositary Receipts (ADRs). ADRs are securities that trade on U.S. exchanges and represent ownership in shares of the foreign company.

Investors buy and sell ADRs just as they buy and sell any security of a U.S. company. ADRs are quoted in U.S. dollars and pay dividends in U.S. dollars.

Buying ADRs directly is similar to buying stock directly from U.S. companies. To receive enrollment information, call the toll-free number. A word of caution here. When you call these transfer agents, you will likely be asked for your social security number. What I do is ignore this prompt. Eventually, you will get transferred to a live operator who can help you.

The three major transfer agents for foreign direct-purchase plans are Morgan Guaranty, Bank of New York, and Citicorp.

The terms of most foreign direct-purchase plans are similar:

- Minimum initial investment is usually $200 to $250.

- Subsequent investment minimums are usually $50 to $100.

- One-time enrollment fee is usually $10 to $15.

- Purchase fees are usually $5 plus 8 to 10 cents per share.

- Selling fees are usually $5 to $10 plus 10 to 12 cents per share.

- Shares are purchased at least twice monthly.

- In most cases, shares may be sold via the telephone.

RESEARCHING ADRs

Admittedly, finding investment opportunities among ADRs is not easy. One reason is that good information about foreign companies is not abundant, even on the Internet. One useful site is www.adr.com. The site, operated by Morgan Guaranty, provides a wealth of information on ADRs. Bank of New York operates another site— www.bankofny.com/adr.

RECOMMENDATIONS

The list below breaks down the foreign direct-purchase plans by country. While I'm sure you won't recognize all of the companies, you no doubt will be familiar with more than a few of the firms. That's because many of these companies market their goods and services in the United States. For example, several foreign drug companies make products that are popular in the United States. Two, in particular, that offer quality investments are *Elan* and *GlaxoSmithKline.*

Elan (ELN), based in Ireland, is a world leader in drug-delivery systems. The firm has been expanding its branded drug business, too. Via acquisitions and internal development, the company has carved out a niche in drugs for neurology, pain management, oncology, infectious disease, and dermatology. Elan's pioneering work in the treatment of Alzheimer's could be a real bonanza for the company down the road. Per-share profits have shown good growth over the years, and record results are expected this year and next. Long-term, further growth of its branded-products business should help drive profits. Elan is also the right size to draw takeover interest in an industry that is likely to undergo considerable consolidation over the next decade. Elan represents one of the top plays among foreign direct-purchase plans. I would have no problem owning this stock in a DRIP portfolio. Minimum initial investment is $200. There is a $10 enrollment fee. Subsequent investments may be as low as $50. Purchase and sell fees are $5 plus 10 cents per share. Bank of New York is the plan administrator. For enrollment information, call (888) 269-2377.

GlaxoSmithKline (GSK), based in the United Kingdom, is one of the largest drug companies in the world. Products include Paxil and Imigram (central nervous system), Flovent and Ventolin (respiratory), Augmentin (antibacterial), and Epivir (HIV). Glaxo's reach is huge in the drug sector. Glaxo is a leader in four of the five largest therapeutic categories. On the plus side, the firm is well protected from patent expirations relative to the rest of the industry. Research and development amounts to a hefty 15 percent of total sales. As Glaxo digests its merger with SmithKline Beecham, look for ample cost savings to help boost profits. Long term, Glaxo represents a solid blue-chip play in the drug sector. Minimum initial investment is $200. Subsequent investments may be as low as $50. There is a onetime enrollment fee of $10. Purchase and sell fees are $5 plus 10 cents per share. Bank of New York is the plan administrator. For enrollment information, call (888) 269-2377.

ARGENTINA

Banco Rio de la Plata	($200)	888-269-2377
Cresud	($200)	888-269-2377
IRSA	($200)	888-269-2377
Nortel Inversora S.A.	($250)	800-749-1687
Telecom Argentina Stet	($250)	800-749-1687
YPF Sociedad Anonima	($200)	888-269-2377

AUSTRALIA

Amcor	($250)	800-749-1687
Atlas Pacific	($200)	888-269-2377
CSR	($250)	800-749-1687
Davnet	($200)	888-269-2377
Lihir Gold	($200)	888-269-2377
National Australia Bank	($200)	888-269-2377
Novogen	($200)	888-269-2377
Orbital Engine Corp.	($200)	888-269-2377
Origin Energy	($200)	888-269-2377
Pacific Dunlop	($250)	800-749-1687
Petsec Energy	($200)	888-269-2377
Rio Tinto	($200)	888-269-2377
Santos	($250)	800-749-1687
Telstra Corp.	($200)	888-269-2377
Westpac Banking	($250)	800-749-1687
WMC Holdings	($200)	888-269-2377

BELGIUM

DELHAIZE LE LION S. A.	($200)	888-269-2377
Xeikon	($200)	888-269-2377

BRAZIL

AMBEV	($200)	888-269-2377
Aracruz Celulose S.A.	($250)	800-749-1687
Brasil Telecom	($200)	888-269-2377
Copel	($200)	888-269-2377
Companhia Brasileira	($200)	888-269-2377
Companhia Vale do Rio Doce	($250)	800-749-1687
Embraer	($250)	800-749-1687
Embratel	($200)	888-269-2377
Perdigao S. A.	($200)	888-269-2377
Tele Celular Sul	($200)	888-269-2377
Tele Centro Oeste Celular	($200)	888-269-2377
Tele Leste Celular	($200)	888-269-2377
Tele Nordeste Celular	($200)	888-269-2377
Tele Norte Celular	($200)	888-269-2377
Tele Norte Leste	($200)	888-269-2377
Telemig Celular	($200)	888-269-2377
Telesp Celular	($200)	888-269-2377
Ultrapar	($200)	888-269-2377

CHILE

AFP Provida	($200)	888-269-2377
Banco Santander Chile	($200)	888-269-2377
Banco Santiago	($250)	800-749-1687
BBV Banco BHIF	($200)	888-269-2377
Compania Cervecerias Unidas	($250)	800-749-1687
Cristalerias De Chile	($200)	888-269-2377
Embotelladora Aandina	($200)	888-269-2377
Empresas Telex-Chile	($200)	888-269-2377
Masisa	($200)	888-269-2377
Sociedad Quimica	($200)	888-269-2377
Supermercados Unimarc	($200)	888-269-2377
Vina Concha y Toro	($200)	888-269-2377

CHINA

China Eastern Airlines	($200)	888-269-2377
China Southern Airlines	($200)	888-269-2377
Guangshen Railway	($250)	800-749-1687
Huaneng Power Int'l	($250)	800-749-1687
Jilin Chemical	($200)	888-269-2377
PetroChina	($200)	888-269-2377
Sinopec Beijing Yanhua Petro.	($200)	888-269-2377
Sinopec Shanghai Petrochem.	($200)	888-269-2377
Yanzhou Coal Mining	($200)	888-269-2377

COLOMBIA

BBV Banco Ganadero—Com.	($200)	888-269-2377
BBV Banco Ganadero—Pref.	($200)	888-269-2377
Bancolombia	($200)	888-269-2377

DENMARK

Novo-Nordisk A/S	($250)	800-749-1687

DOMINICAN REPUBLIC

Tricom S.A.	($200)	888-269-2377

FINLAND

Metso	($200)	888-269-2377
Nokia	($250)	800-483-9010

FRANCE

AXA	($200)	888-269-2377
Alcatel	($200)	888-269-2377
Alstom	($200)	888-269-2377
Bouygues Offshore	($200)	888-269-2377
Dassault Systemes S.A.	($250)	800-749-1687
Elf Aquitaine	($200)	888-269-2377
Flamel Tech.	($200)	888-269-2377
France Telecom	($200)	888-269-2377
Genesys	($200)	888-269-2377
Groupe AB	($200)	888-269-2377
Groupe Danone	($250)	800-808-8010
Havas Advertising	($250)	800-749-1687
ILOG S.A.	($250)	800-749-1687
Pechiney	($200)	888-269-2377
Publicis Groupe S. A.	($200)	888-269-2377
SCOR	($200)	888-269-2377
Rhodia S.A.	($250)	800-808-8010
Thomson multimedia	($250)	800-749-1687
TotalFinaElf	($200)	888-269-2377
Vivendi Environnement	($200)	888-269-2377
Vivendi Universal	($200)	888-269-2377
Wavecom	($200)	888-269-2377

GERMANY

Allianz AG	($250)	800-749-1687
BASF AKTIENGESELLSCHAFT	($200)	888-269-2377
Deutsche Telekom AG	($250)	800-808-8010
Dialog Semiconductor	($200)	888-269-2377
Digitale Telekable AG	($200)	888-269-2377
E.ON AG	($250)	800-749-1687
Epcos AG	($250)	800-749-1687
Fresenius Medical Care AG	($250)	800-749-1687
INCAM AG	($200)	888-269-2377
New York Broker Deutschland	($200)	888-269-2377
Pfeiffer Vacuum Tech.	($200)	888-269-2377

Schering AG	($250)	800-749-1687
Siemens AG	($250)	800-749-1687

GHANA

Ashanti Goldfields	($200)	888-269-2377

GREECE

Antenna TV	($200)	888-269-2377
Hellenic Telecom.	($200)	888-269-2377
STET Hellas Telecom.	($250)	800-749-1687

HONG KONG

APT Satellite Holdings	($200)	888-269-2377
Asia Satellite Telecom.	($200)	888-269-2377
China Convergent	($200)	888-269-2377
China Mobile (H.K.)	($200)	888-269-2377
City Telecom (H.K.)	($200)	888-269-2377
CLP Holdings	($250)	800-749-1687
Zindart	($200)	888-269-2377

HUNGARY

MATAV	($250)	800-749-1687

INDIA

Mahanagar Tele. Nigam	($200)	888-269-2377

INDONESIA

P.T. Indosat	($200)	888-269-2377
P.T. Inti Indorayon Utama	($200)	888-269-2377
P.T. Pasifik Satelit Nusantara	($200)	888-269-2377
P.T. Telkom	($200)	888-269-2377
P.T. Tri Polyta Indonesia TBK	($200)	888-269-2377

IRELAND

Allied Irish Banks	($200)	888-269-2377
Bank of Ireland	($200)	888-269-2377
CRH plc	($250)	800-808-8010
Datalex	($200)	888-269-2377
Elan Corp	($200)	888-269-2377
Icon	($200)	888-269-2377
Jefferson Smurfit Group plc	($250)	800-749-1687
Ryanair	($200)	888-269-2377
SmartForce	($200)	888-269-2377
Waterford Wedgwood	($200)	888-269-2377

ISRAEL

Blue Square-Israel	($200)	888-269-2377
Delta Galil Industry	($200)	888-269-2377
Formula Systems (1985)	($200)	888-269-2377
Israel Land Develop.	($200)	888-269-2377
Koor Industries Ltd.	($200)	888-269-2377
Matav Cable Systems	($200)	888-269-2377
NICE Systems	($200)	888-269-2377
Partner Communications	($250)	800-749-1687
Super-Sol	($250)	800-749-1687
Teva Pharmaceutical Inds.	($200)	888-269-2377

ITALY

Benetton Group S.p.A.	($250)	800-749-1687
De Rigo S.p.A.	($200)	888-269-2377
Ducati Motor Holding	($200)	888-269-2377

ENI S.p.A.	($250)	800-749-1687
Fiat S.p.A.	($250)	800-749-1687
Fila Holdings S.p.A.	($200)	888-269-2377
Industrie Natuzzi S.p.A.	($200)	888-269-2377
Luxottica Group S.p.A.	($200)	888-269-2377
Sanpaolo IMI S.p.A.	($250)	800-749-1687
Telecom Italia S.p.A.	($250)	800-749-1687

JAPAN

Canon	($250)	800-749-1687
Crayfish	($200)	888-269-2377
Internet Initiative Japan	($200)	888-269-2377
Kyocera	($250)	800-808-8010
Makita Corporation	($200)	888-269-2377
Matsushita Electric Indust.	($250)	800-749-1687
Mitsubishi Tokyo Fin'l	($200)	888-269-2377
NEC Corp.	($200)	888-269-2377
Nippon Tele. & Tele.	($250)	800-749-1687
Pioneer	($250)	800-808-8010
Ricoh Company	($200)	888-269-2377
Sony	($250)	800-749-1687
TDK Corp.	($250)	800-749-1687
Toyota Motor Corp.	($200)	888-269-2377
Trend Micro	($200)	888-269-2377
Wacoal Corporation	($200)	888-269-2377

KOREA

Korea Electric Power	($200)	888-269-2377
Pohang Iron and Steel	($200)	888-269-2377

LUXEMBOURG

Anangel-American Shiphold.	($200)	888-269-2377
Transcom WorldWide S. A.	($200)	888-269-2377

MEXICO

America Movil, S.A. de C.V.	($250)	800-749-1687
Bufete Industrial	($200)	888-269-2377
Coca-Cola FEMSA	($200)	888-269-2377
Empresas ICA	($200)	888-269-2377
Grupo Casa Saba, S.A. de C.V.	($250)	800-749-1687
Grupo Elektra	($200)	888-269-2377
Grupo IMSA	($200)	888-269-2377
Grupo Industrial Durango	($200)	888-269-2377
Grupo Iusacell—Series V	($200)	888-269-2377
Grupo Tribasa	($200)	888-269-2377
Industrias Bachoco	($200)	888-269-2377
Pepsi-Gemex	($200)	888-269-2377
Savia	($200)	888-269-2377
Telefonos de Mexico	($250)	800-749-1687
Tubos de Acero de Mexico	($250)	800-749-1687
TV Azteca	($200)	888-269-2377

NETHERLANDS

ABN AMRO Holding N.V.	($250)	800-749-1687
AEGON N.V.	($250)	800-808-8010
Akzo Nobel N.V.	($250)	800-808-8010
Arcadis N.V.	($200)	888-269-2377
ASML HOLDING N.V.	($250)	800-749-1687
BE Semiconductor Inds.	($200)	888-269-2377
Chicago Bridge & Iron	($200)	888-269-2377
CNH Global N.V.	($250)	800-749-1687
Elsevier N.V.	($250)	800-808-8010
Equant N.V.	($250)	800-749-1687
HEAD N.V.	($200)	888-269-2377
ING Groep N.V.	($250)	800-749-1687

Ispat International N.V.	($200)	888-269-2377
Koninklijke Ahold N.V.	($200)	888-269-2377
KPNQwest	($200)	888-269-2377
New Skies Satellites N.V.	($200)	888-269-2377
Oce N.V.	($250)	800-749-1687
Philips Electronics	($250)	800-808-8010
Royal Dutch Petroleum	($250)	800-749-1687
ST Microelectronics N.V.	($200)	888-269-2377
Trader.com	($200)	888-269-2377
Unilever N.V.	($250)	800-749-1687
VersaTel Telecom Int'l	($200)	888-269-2377

NEW ZEALAND

Tranz Rail Holdings	($200)	888-269-2377

NORWAY

NCL Holding ASA	($200)	888-269-2377
Nera A.S.	($200)	888-269-2377
Norsk Hydro ASA	($250)	800-749-1687
Statoil Asa	($200)	888-269-2377

PERU

Compania de Minas Buen.	($200)	888-269-2377
Telefonica del Peru S.A.	($250)	800-749-1687

POLAND

Netia Holdings	($200)	888-269-2377

PORTUGAL

Espirito Santo Fin'l Group	($200)	888-269-2377
Portugal Telecom	($200)	888-269-2377

RUSSIA

OAO Rostelecom	($200)	888-269-2377
Tatneft	($200)	888-269-2377
Vimpel-Communications	($200)	888-269-2377

SINGAPORE

Asia Pulp & Paper	($200)	888-269-2377

SOUTH AFRICA

AngloGold Limited	($200)	888-269-2377
Durban Roodeport Deep	($200)	888-269-2377
Harmony Gold Mining	($200)	888-269-2377
Randgold & Exploration	($200)	888-269-2377
Sappi Limited	($200)	888-269-2377

SPAIN

Banco Bilbao Vizcaya Argen.	($200)	888-269-2377
Banco Santander	($250)	800-749-1687
Endesa S.A.	($250)	800-808-8010
Repsol S.A.	($200)	888-269-2377

SWEDEN

Biora	($200)	888-269-2377
Electrolux, AB	($250)	800-749-1687
Ericsson	($250)	800-808-8010
Modern Times Group	($200)	888-269-2377
Song Networks Holding	($250)	800-749-1687
Swedish Match	($200)	888-269-2377

Tele2 AB Class A	($200)	888-269-2377
Tele2 AB Class B	($200)	888-269-2377
Volvo	($250)	800-808-8010

SWITZERLAND

Adecco SA	($250)	800-749-1687
Logitech International	($200)	888-269-2377
Novartis	($500)	877-816-5333
Serono sa	($200)	888-269-2377
Sulzer Medica	($250)	800-808-8010

TAIWAN

Macronix	($200)	888-269-2377

UNITED KINGDOM

AMVESCAP	($200)	888-269-2377
ARM Holdings	($200)	888-269-2377
AstraZeneca PLC	($250)	800-749-1687
Baltimore Technologies PLC	($250)	800-749-1687
Barclays PLC	($250)	800-749-1687
BOC Group PLC	($250)	800-749-1687
Bookham Technology	($200)	888-269-2377
BP	($250)	877-272-2723
British Airways PLC	($250)	800-749-1687
British Energy PLC	($250)	800-749-1687
British Telecom.	($250)	800-749-1687
Bunzl	($200)	888-269-2377
Cadbury Schweppes PLC	($250)	800-749-1687
Cantab Pharmaceuticals	($200)	888-269-2377
Carlton Communications	($250)	800-749-1687
Diageo	($200)	888-269-2377
ECSOFT GROUP	($200)	888-269-2377
Eidos PLC	($250)	800-749-1687
Energis	($200)	888-269-2377
ENODIS	($200)	888-269-2377
Freeserve	($200)	888-269-2377
Galen Holdings	($200)	888-269-2377
Gallaher Group	($200)	888-269-2377
Gemini Genomics	($200)	888-269-2377
GlaxoSmithKline	($200)	888-269-2377
HSBC	($200)	888-269-2377
Huntingdon Life Sciences	($200)	888-269-2377
Imperial Chemical Inds. PLC	($250)	800-749-1687
Imperial Tobacco Group PLC	($250)	800-808-8010
Independent Energy	($200)	888-269-2377
Insignia Solutions	($200)	888-269-2377
Interactive Invest. Int'l	($200)	888-269-2377
International Power	($200)	888-269-2377
Jazztel PLC	($250)	800-749-1687
London International	($200)	888-269-2377
Marconi	($200)	888-269-2377
Merant PLC	($200)	888-269-2377
National Grid Group	($200)	888-269-2377
P&O Princess Cruises PLC	($250)	800-749-1687
Pearson	($200)	888-269-2377
Powergen	($200)	888-269-2377
Prudential PLC	($250)	800-749-1687
QXL.com	($200)	888-269-2377
Rank Group PLC	($250)	800-749-1687
Reed Int'l PLC	($250)	800-808-8010
Reuters Group PLC	($250)	800-749-1687
Rio Tinto PLC	($200)	888-269-2377
Royal Bank of Scotland	($200)	888-269-2377
Scoot.com PLC	($200)	888-269-2377
Scottish Power PLC	($250)	800-749-1687
Select Software Tools PLC	($200)	888-269-2377
Senetek PLC	($200)	888-269-2377

Shell Transport & Trading	($200)	888-269-2377
Shire Pharmaceuticals	($250)	800-749-1687
Signet Group PLC	($200)	888-269-2377
Smith & Nephew	($200)	888-269-2377
Telewest Communications	($200)	888-269-2377
Tomkins PLC	($200)	888-269-2377
Unilever PLC	($250)	800-749-1687
Vodafone Group	($200)	888-269-2377
Xenova Group PLC	($200)	888-269-2377

APPENDIX B: THE "EASY-HOLD" STOCK LIST (1,500 COMPANIES)

Appendices B through F provide "Easy-Hold" ratings on nearly 3,000 stocks and mutual funds. A number of different looks are provided for these ratings, from an alphabetical sort (Appendix B for stocks and Appendix E for mutual funds) to industry breakdowns of the top easy-hold stocks (Appendix C). Also provided are the 150 top-rated easy-hold stocks (Appendix D) and 100 top-rated easy-hold mutual funds (Appendix F).

Chapter Four discussed the various factors that went into producing the easy hold ratings for stocks and mutual funds. In a nutshell, the rating tries to capture a stock's or fund's ability to achieve decent returns during up markets and price resiliency during down markets.

When viewing the ratings, keep the following points in mind:

- When comparing easy-hold ratings for stocks or funds, slight differences in scores may not be meaningful. For example, when choosing between two stocks, don't necessarily regard the one scoring an 85 as inferior to the one scoring an 86. Rather, you want to look for substantive differences in scores. For example, consider breaking the scores in quintiles. In other words, stocks that score an 80 to 100 are in the top quintile, stocks that score 60 to 79 in the next quintile, and so on. This is probably a better way to find meaningful differences in scores.

- Remember that certain industry sectors will score better simply because these tend to be defensive holdings. Thus, electric utilities generally score better than growth stocks. That doesn't necessarily mean that utilities are better long-term investments than growth stocks. For that reason, the ratings are best used when comparing stocks within the same industry.

- Keep in mind that the rating is a percentile rank. For example, a stock that scores an 85 ranks better than 85 percent of the 1,500 stocks rated.

Also remember that no rating system is infallible. These easy-hold scores are not meant to be "buy" or "sell" recommendations. They are meant to give you some guidance on how these stocks and funds have historically behaved during up and down markets. Investors should use these scores as an additional tool in the stock/fund selection process.

	TICKER	INDUSTRY	2001 TOT. RET.	5-YR. ANN. TOT. RET.	EASY-HOLD RANK
1ST SOURCE CORP.	SRCE	Banks	21.2	8.6	94
21ST CENTURY INS GROUP	TW	Insurance (Property)	39.0	5.3	20
3D SYS CORP./DE	TDSC	Computer Systems	17.5	2.2	17
4 KIDS ENTERTAINMENT INC.	KDE	Toys	124.1	126.9	89
7-ELEVEN INC.	SE	Groceries	33.8	–4.6	36
99 CENTS ONLY STORES	NDN	Department Stores	109.6	48.8	69
AAR CORP.	AIR	Aerospace	–27.1	–13.3	30
AARON RENTS INC.	RNT	Rental	16.2	6.8	94
ABBOTT LABORATORIES	ABT	Pharmaceuticals	17.0	19.0	70
ABM INDUSTRIES INC.	ABM	Business Services	4.6	13.4	94
ACT MANUFACTURING INC.	ACTM	Printed Circuit Boards	–97.8	–57.9	31
ACTEL CORP.	ACTL	Semiconductors	–17.7	–3.5	41
ACTION PERFORMANCE COS INC.	ACTN	Toys	1188.8	11.2	13
ACTIVISION INC.	ATVI	Software	158.0	24.8	47
ACTRADE FINL TECHNOLGIES LTD	ACRT	Securities	33.5	31.2	58
ACXIOM CORP.	ACXM	Data Processing	–55.1	–6.2	44
ADC TELECOMMUNICATIONS INC.	ADCT	Phone/Network Equipment	–74.6	–10.0	25
ADOBE SYSTEMS INC.	ADBE	Software	–46.5	27.9	47
ADTRAN INC.	ADTN	Phone/Network Equipment	20.1	–9.3	67
ADV NEUROMODULATION SYS INC.	ANSI	Medical Equipment	73.0	35.4	9
ADVANCED ENERGY INDS INC.	AEIS	Electric Equipment	18.4	37.7	61
ADVANCED MARKETING SERVICES	MKT	Printing	57.7	43.8	82
ADVANTA CORP. -CL A	ADVNA	Banks	15.2	–24.0	9
ADVENT SOFTWARE INC.	ADVS	Software	24.7	37.6	73
AEROFLEX INC.	ARXX	Semiconductors	–34.3	58.4	55
AES CORP.	AES	Electric Utilities	–70.5	7.1	74
AFFILIATED COMP SVCS -CL A	ACS	Data Processing	74.9	29.0	81
AFLAC INC.	AFL	Insurance (Life)	–31.5	19.0	55
AGCO CORP.	AG	Agricultural Machinery	30.3	–11.0	6
AGL RESOURCES INC.	ATG	Natural Gas Utilities	9.6	7.5	34
AIR PRODUCTS & CHEMICALS INC.	APD	Chemicals	16.6	8.3	33
AIRGAS INC.	ARG	Chemicals	121.9	–7.2	24
AK STEEL HOLDING CORP.	AKS	Steel/Iron	31.6	–8.1	24
ALABAMA NATL BANCORP.ORATION	ALAB	Banks	53.3	16.9	96
ALBANY INTL CORP. -CL A	AIN	Machinery	61.9	0.2	36
ALBEMARLE CORP.	ALB	Chemicals	–0.7	7.8	46
ALBERTO-CULVER CO. -CL B	ACV	Household Products	5.3	14.3	68
ALCOA INC.	AA	Aluminum	7.8	19.4	64
ALEXANDER & BALDWIN INC.	ALEX	Water Transport	5.5	5.1	46
ALEXANDER'S INC.	ALX	Real Estate	–15.9	–6.4	70
ALFA CORP.	ALFA	Insurance (Property)	25.4	15.2	62
ALICO INC.	ALCO	Agriculture	97.2	14.7	53
ALLEGHENY ENERGY INC.	AYE	Electric Utilities	–21.6	9.1	76
ALLEGHENY TECHNOLOGIES INC.	ATI	Steel/Iron	10.3	–13.2	45
ALLEN TELECOM INC.	ALN	Cable/Wireless Equipment	–52.6	–17.5	9
ALLERGAN INC.	AGN	Pharmaceuticals	–22.1	34.8	61
ALLIANT ENERGY CORP.	LNT	Electric Utilities	1.8	8.7	81
ALLIANT TECHSYSTEMS INC.	ATK	Metal Products	73.5	25.9	67
ALLIED CAPITAL CP	ALD	Mortgages	35.9	20.8	93
ALLIED WASTE INDS INC.	AW	Waste	–3.5	8.7	58
ALLMERICA FINANCIAL CORP.	AFC	Insurance (Property)	–38.2	6.3	45
ALLSTATE CORP.	ALL	Insurance (Property)	–21.1	5.0	64
ALLTEL CORP.	AT	Telecommunications	1.1	17.2	91

	Ticker	Industry	2001 Tot. Ret.	5-Yr. Ann. Tot. Ret.	Easy-Hold Rank
ALPHA INDUSTRIES INC.	AHAA	Semiconductors	–41.1	52.7	35
ALPHARMA INC. -CL A	ALO	Pharmaceuticals	–39.3	13.4	80
ALTERA CORP.	ALTR	Semiconductors	–19.4	18.5	54
AMBAC FINANCIAL GP	ABK	Insurance (General)	–0.2	22.1	88
AMBASSADORS INTERNATIONL INC.	AMIE	Business Services	13.7	18.2	91
AMCORE FINL INC.	AMFI	Banks	11.4	7.5	80
AMERADA HESS CORP.	AHC	Oil/Gas	–13.0	2.7	87
AMEREN CORP.	AEE	Electric Utilities	–2.9	8.8	78
AMERICAN ELECTRIC POWER	AEP	Electric Utilities	–1.4	7.2	67
AMERICAN EXPRESS	AXP	Finance	–34.5	14.5	74
AMERICAN HEALTHWAYS INC.	AMHC	Hospitals	316.6	50.2	35
AMERICAN INTERNATIONAL GROUP	AIG	Insurance (Property)	–19.3	25.6	79
AMERICAN MANAGEMENT SYSTEMS	AMSY	Software	–8.7	–5.9	71
AMERICAN NATIONAL INSURANCE	ANAT	Insurance (Life)	19.6	6.5	51
AMERICAN PWR CNVRSION	APCC	Electric Equipment	16.8	1.2	58
AMERICAN STATES WATER CO.	AWR	Water Utilities	–1.5	15.1	49
AMERICAN WATER WORKS INC.	AWK	Water Utilities	46.4	18.9	72
AMERICAN WOODMARK CORP.	AMWD	Furniture Makers	243.8	31.5	60
AMERICREDIT CORP.	ACF	Finance	15.8	25.2	90
AMERISOURCEBERGEN CORP.	ABC	Medical Goods (Wholesale)	25.9	21.4	84
AMERISTAR CASINOS INC.	ASCA	Hotel Casinos	388.8	36.0	22
AMERN EAGLE OUTFITTERS INC.	AEOS	Clothing Stores	–7.1	86.3	69
AMERON INTERNATIONAL INC.	AMN	Building Materials	89.9	9.0	55
AMETEK INC.	AME	Electric Equipment	24.0	12.5	79
AMGEN INC.	AMGN	Biotech	–11.7	32.9	68
AMLI RESIDENTIAL PPTYS TR	AML	REITS	10.7	10.1	94
AMPHENOL CORP.	APH	Semiconductors	22.6	34.0	73
AMR CORP./DE	AMR	Air Transport	–43.1	1.2	23
ANADARKO PETROLEUM CORP.	APC	Oil/Gas	–19.7	12.5	92
ANALOG DEVICES	ADI	Semiconductors	–13.3	28.4	41
ANALOGIC CORP.	ALOG	Measuring Devices	–13.0	3.6	38
ANAREN MICROWAVE INC.	ANEN	Measuring Devices	–74.2	52.7	56
ANCHOR BANCORP. INC./WI	ABCW	Banks	13.1	16.4	93
ANCHOR GAMING	SLOT	Gambling	80.3	28.4	81
ANDREW CORP.	ANDW	Cable/Wireless Equipment	0.6	–9.2	25
ANHEUSER-BUSCH COS INC.	BUD	Alcoholic Drinks	1.0	19.9	69
ANIXTER INTL INC.	AXE	Electronics Stores	34.2	12.5	54
ANNTAYLOR STORES CORP.	ANN	Clothing Stores	40.4	14.9	40
ANSYS INC.	ANSS	Computer Systems	119.1	12.8	94
AON CORP.	AOC	Insurance (General)	6.3	7.6	30
APAC CUSTOMER SERVICES INC.	APAC	Business Services	–29.5	–41.6	21
APACHE CORP.	APA	Oil/Gas	–21.2	10.1	77
APARTMENT INVT &MGMT -CL A	AIV	REITS	–2.0	17.4	81
APOGENT TECHNOLOGIES INC.	AOT	Medical Equipment	25.9	14.7	81
APPLEBEES INTL INC.	APPB	Restaurants	63.6	13.7	71
APPLICA INC.	APN	Electric Equipment	84.8	–6.8	14
APPLIED INDUSTRIAL TECH INC.	AIT	Machinery	–6.9	2.7	61
APPLIED INNOVATION INC.	AINN	Phone/Network Equipment	–27.6	0.2	34
APRIA HEALTHCARE GROUP	AHG	Home Health	–16.0	5.9	27
APTARGROUP INC.	ATR	Machinery	20.1	15.5	89
ARCH COAL INC.	ACI	Mining	62.3	–1.7	17
ARCHER-DANIELS-MIDLAND CO.	ADM	Food Manufacturing	1.8	–2.3	31
ARCTIC CAT INC.	ACAT	Transportation Equipment	48.6	14.0	59
ARDEN GROUP INC. -CL A	ARDNA	Groceries	44.2	33.8	91
AREA BANCSHARES CORP.	AREA	Banks	19.3	8.2	91
ARKANSAS BEST CORP.	ABFS	Truck Transport	57.4	45.8	73
ARMOR HOLDINGS INC.	AH	Consultants	54.8	27.1	88
ARMSTRONG HOLDINGS INC.	ACK	Home Building	65.3	–43.3	11
ARNOLD INDUSTRIES INC.	AIND	Truck Transport	18.2	9.5	69
ARROW ELECTRONICS INC.	ARW	Office Equipment (Wholesale)	4.5	2.3	57
ARROW FINL CORP.	AROW	Banks	63.7	17.6	85
ARROW INTERNATIONAL	ARRO	Medical Equipment	6.8	7.5	74

	Ticker	Industry	2001 Tot. Ret.	5-Yr. Ann. Tot. Ret.	Easy-Hold Rank
ARTESYN TECHNOLOGIES INC.	ATSN	Electric Equipment	–41.4	–13.7	15
ASHLAND INC.	ASH	Household Products	31.8	4.8	49
ASSOCIATED BANC CORP.	ASBC	Banks	20.3	10.1	66
ASSOCIATED ESTATES RLTY CORP.	AEC	REITS	27.2	–7.3	47
ASTEC INDUSTRIES INC.	ASTE	Construction Machinery	9.6	24.9	62
ASTORIA FINL CORP.	ASFC	Savings Institutions	–0.4	9.9	79
ASYST TECHNOLOGIES INC.	ASYT	Semiconductor Equipment	–5.0	24.4	29
AT&T CORP.	T	Telecommunications	34.9	–1.5	29
ATLANTIC COAST AIRLINES HLDG	ACAI	Air Transport	14.0	50.0	53
ATLAS AIR WORLDWIDE HLDG INC.	CGO	Air Transport	–55.1	–14.4	78
ATMEL CORP.	ATML	Semiconductors	–36.6	–2.3	18
ATMI INC.	ATMI	Semiconductors	22.3	6.7	53
ATMOS ENERGY CORP.	ATO	Natural Gas Utilities	–8.1	2.3	57
ATWOOD OCEANICS	ATW	Oil/Gas	–20.5	1.9	21
AUDIOVOX CORP. -CL A	VOXX	Auto-Parts Makers	–17.1	5.6	42
AUTOMATIC DATA PROCESSING	ADP	Computer Programming	–6.2	23.3	92
AUTONATION INC.	AN	Rental	105.5	–15.4	70
AUTOZONE INC.	AZO	Auto Retail	151.9	21.2	77
AVALONBAY COMMUNITIES INC.	AVB	REITS	–0.4	11.3	89
AVANT CORP.	AVNT	Computer Programming	11.9	–8.4	87
AVERY DENNISON CORP.	AVY	Paper	5.4	11.9	75
AVID TECHNOLOGY INC.	AVID	Cable/Wireless Equipment	–33.5	3.2	13
AVISTA CORP.	AVA	Electric Utilities	–33.3	–2.8	59
AVNET INC.	AVT	Electronics Stores	20.1	–1.5	33
AVX CORP.	AVX	Semiconductors	45.2	18.1	51
AZTAR CORP.	AZR	Hotel Casinos	41.4	20.3	53
BAKER-HUGHES INC.	BHI	Oil/Gas Services	–11.1	2.6	13
BALDOR ELECTRIC	BEZ	Electric Equipment	1.4	4.7	58
BALDWIN & LYONS -CL B	BWINB	Insurance (Property)	12.1	8.9	29
BALL CORP.	BLL	Metal Products	55.3	23.9	82
BANCFIRST OHIO CORP.	BFOH	Banks	61.5	12.9	71
BANCWEST CORP.	BWE	Banks	37.3	18.6	47
BANDAG INC.	BDG	Rubber Products	–10.6	–2.8	41
BANK OF AMERICA CORP.	BAC	Banks	42.8	8.6	44
BANK OF GRANITE CORP.ORATION	GRAN	Banks	–13.1	–1.6	62
BANK OF NEW YORK CO. INC.	BK	Banks	–24.9	21.4	63
BANKATLANTIC BANCORP. -CL A	BBX	Banks	149.2	11.4	60
BANKUNITED FINANCIAL CORP.	BKUNA	Banks	74.7	8.2	43
BANNER CORP.	BANR	Savings Institutions	14.3	4.7	81
BANTA CORP.	BN	Printing	18.8	7.6	79
BARD (C.R.) INC.	BCR	Medical Equipment	40.8	20.4	49
BARNES GROUP INC.	B	Metal Products	25.3	7.3	53
BARR LABORATORIES INC.	BRL	Pharmaceuticals	8.8	47.7	49
BARRA INC.	BARZ	Software	–0.1	31.0	88
BASSETT FURNITURE INDS	BSET	Furniture Makers	31.5	–6.5	22
BAUSCH & LOMB INC.	BOL	Medical Equipment	–4.4	3.8	49
BB&T CORP.	BBT	Banks	–0.5	17.7	84
BE AEROSPACE INC.	BEAV	Aerospace	–42.7	–19.5	17
BEAR STEARNS COMPANIES INC.	BSC	Securities	16.9	21.1	39
BEAZER HOMES USA INC.	BZH	Home Building	82.9	31.7	83
BECKMAN COULTER INC.	BEC	Medical Equipment	6.5	19.6	87
BECTON DICKINSON & CO.	BDX	Medical Equipment	–3.2	10.0	71
BED BATH & BEYOND INC.	BBBY	Furniture Retail	51.5	41.1	71
BEDFORD PPTY INVS INC.	BED	Real Estate	21.5	13.9	97
BELDEN INC.	BWC	Electric Equipment	–6.4	–7.9	33
BELL MICROPRODUCTS INC.	BELM	Office Equipment (Wholesale)	–20.5	16.4	32
BELLSOUTH CORP.	BLS	Telecommunications	–5.0	15.9	89
BELO CORP. -SER A COM	BLC	Publishing	19.1	2.9	25
BEMIS CO.	BMS	Paper	50.2	8.5	66
BENCHMARK ELECTRONICS INC.	BHE	Printed Circuit Boards	–16.0	4.7	45
BERKLEY (W R) CORP.	BER	Insurance (Property)	15.1	11.4	44
BERRY PETROLEUM -CL A	BRY	Oil/Gas	20.6	4.5	85
BEST BUY CO. INC.	BBY	Electronics Stores	151.9	94.8	49
BEVERLY ENTERPRISES	BEV	Nursing	5.0	–1.4	14

	TICKER	INDUSTRY	2001 TOT. RET.	5-YR. ANN. TOT. RET.	EASY-HOLD RANK
BIO TECHNOLOGY GENERAL CORP.	BTGC	Pharmaceuticals	16.5	–8.9	19
BIOGEN INC.	BGEN	Biotech	–4.5	24.2	84
BIOMET INC.	BMET	Medical Equipment	17.1	36.2	80
BIO-RAD LABS -CL A	BIO.A	Optical Equipment	99.1	16.1	47
BISYS GROUP INC.	BSYS	Data Processing	22.8	28.1	90
BJ SERVICES CO.	BJS	Oil/Gas Services	–5.8	20.5	22
BLACK & DECKER CORP.	BDK	Machinery	–2.6	5.8	40
BLACK HILLS CORP.	BKH	Natural Gas Utilities	–22.1	17.3	98
BLOCK H & R INC.	HRB	Business Services	120.1	28.1	66
BLYTH INC.	BTH	Misc. Manufacturing	–2.7	–4.9	86
BMC INDUSTRIES INC./MN	BMM	Chemicals	–57.2	–41.5	23
BMC SOFTWARE INC.	BMC	Software	16.9	–4.6	18
BOB EVANS FARMS	BOBE	Restaurants	17.4	14.9	72
BOEING CO.	BA	Aerospace	–40.4	–4.9	53
BOISE CASCADE CORP.	BCC	Paper	3.0	3.3	47
BORDERS GROUP INC.	BGP	Stores (Misc.)	69.8	2.0	48
BORG WARNER INC.	BWA	Auto-Parts Makers	32.4	7.7	44
BOSTON BEER INC. -CL A	SAM	Alcoholic Drinks	94.6	10.8	43
BOSTON PRIVATE FINL HLDGS	BPFH	Banks	11.8	33.1	85
BOSTON SCIENTIFIC CORP.	BSX	Medical Equipment	76.2	–4.3	69
BOWATER INC.	BOW	Paper	–13.9	6.7	73
BOWNE & CO. INC.	BNE	Printing	23.5	2.3	19
BOYD GAMING CORP.	BYD	Hotel Casinos	89.1	–4.7	28
BRADY CORP.	BRC	Misc. Manufacturing	10.6	10.7	34
BRANDYWINE REALTY TRUST	BDN	REITS	10.6	9.9	61
BRE PROPERTIES -CL A	BRE	REITS	3.9	11.4	65
BRIGGS & STRATTON	BGG	Machinery	–0.7	2.1	46
BRIGHTPOINT INC.	CELL	Electronics Stores	–10.3	–23.4	26
BRINKER INTL INC.	EAT	Restaurants	5.7	22.8	92
BRISTOL MYERS SQUIBB	BMY	Pharmaceuticals	–26.2	16.3	88
BROWN & BROWN INC.	BRO	Insurance (General)	57.1	45.7	80
BROWN (TOM) INC.	TMBR	Oil/Gas	–17.8	5.3	80
BROWN-FORMAN -CL B	BF.B	Alcoholic Drinks	–3.9	8.7	80
BRUSH ENGINEERED MATERIALS	BW	Nonferrous Metals	–28.1	–0.5	39
BUCKEYE TECHNOLOGIES INC.	BKI	Chemicals	–18.2	–2.9	52
BUCKLE INC.	BKE	Clothing Stores	27.0	21.8	77
BUILDING MATERIALS HLDG CP	BMHC	Construction	27.6	–2.4	83
BURLINGTON COAT FACTORY WRHS	BCF	Clothing Stores	–11.2	9.3	60
BURLINGTON NORTHERN SANTA FE	BNI	Rail Transport	2.5	1.4	70
BURLINGTON RESOURCES INC.	BR	Oil/Gas	–24.6	–4.4	53
BURNHAM PACIFIC PPTY INC.	BPP	REITS	18.5	–12.2	46
BUSH INDUSTRIES -CL A	BSH	Furniture Makers	–5.1	–9.7	45
BUTLER MFG CO.	BBR	Metal Products	12.6	–5.1	35
C&D TECHNOLOGIES INC.	CHP	Electric Equipment	–47.0	24.8	79
CABLE DESIGN TECH CP -CL A	CDT	Electric Equipment	–18.6	–0.2	38
CABOT CORP.	CBT	Chemicals	37.2	19.9	46
CABOT OIL & GAS CORP. -CL A	COG	Oil/Gas	–22.4	8.0	43
CACI INTL INC. -CL A	CACI	Software	243.1	30.3	89
CADENCE DESIGN SYS INC.	CDN	Software	–20.3	2.1	14
CALGON CARBON CORP.	CCC	Household Products	50.5	–4.4	12
CALIFORNIA WATER SERVICE GP	CWT	Water Utilities	–0.2	8.8	47
CALLAWAY GOLF CO.	ELY	Sporting Goods	4.3	–6.3	14
CALLON PETROLEUM CO./DE	CPE	Oil/Gas	–59.0	–18.5	18
CAMBREX CORP.	CBM	Household Products	–3.4	22.1	64
CAMDEN PROPERTY TRUST	CPT	REITS	17.2	12.8	71
CAMPBELL SOUP CO.	CPB	Food Manufacturing	–11.3	–2.8	36
CAPITAL ONE FINL CORP.	COF	Finance	–17.9	35.6	88
CAPSTEAD MORTGAGE CORP.	CMO	Finance	103.5	–7.4	23
CARBO CERAMICS INC.	CRR	Clay/Glass	5.6	14.5	10
CARDINAL HEALTH INC.	CAH	Medical Goods (Wholesale)	–2.5	20.3	85
CARLISLE COS INC.	CSL	Auto-Parts Makers	–11.9	5.9	76
CARPENTER TECHNOLOGY	CRS	Nonferrous Metals	–20.1	–2.1	47
CARRAMERICA REALTY CORP.	CRE	REITS	2.3	7.7	63
CASCADE NATURAL GAS CORP.	CGC	Natural Gas Utilities	23.1	11.4	85
CASEYS GENERAL STORES INC.	CASY	Groceries	0.4	10.3	63
CASH AMERICA INTL INC.	PWN	Finance	95.6	0.5	21

	TICKER	INDUSTRY	2001 TOT. RET.	5-YR. ANN. TOT. RET.	EASY-HOLD RANK
CATALINA MARKETING CORP.	POS	Advertising	-10.9	13.6	79
CATELLUS DEVELOPMENT CORP.	CDX	Real Estate	5.1	10.1	77
CATERPILLAR INC.	CAT	Construction Machinery	13.6	9.6	36
CATHAY BANCORP.	CATY	Banks	10.4	29.3	85
CATO CORP. -CL A	CACOA	Clothing Stores	41.8	33.9	91
CBL & ASSOCIATES PPTYS INC.	CBL	REITS	33.9	12.3	98
CBRL GROUP INC.	CBRL	Restaurants	62.0	3.1	62
CCBT FINANCIAL COMPANIES INC.	CCBT	Banks	29.3	19.6	80
C-COR.NET CORP.	CCBL	Phone/Network Equipment	49.9	17.1	15
CDI CORP.	CDI	Employment	29.9	-7.7	52
CDW COMPUTER CENTERS INC.	CDWC	Electronics Stores	92.7	29.4	54
CEC ENTERTAINMENT INC.	CEC	Restaurants	27.2	29.1	84
CENDANT CORP.	CD	Business Services	103.7	-4.2	32
CENTENNIAL BANCORP.	CEBC	Banks	-1.9	12.7	93
CENTERPOINT PROPERTIES TRUST	CNT	REITS	10.2	14.5	85
CENTEX CORP.	CTX	Home Building	52.6	25.5	89
CENTRAL PARKING CORP.	CPC	Personal Svcs	-1.5	-2.3	59
CENTRAL VERMONT PUB SERV	CV	Electric Utilities	44.8	14.5	25
CENTURY ALUMINUM CO.	CENX	Aluminum	19.4	-3.3	26
CENTURYTEL INC.	CTL	Telecommunications	-7.7	19.8	69
CERNER CORP.	CERN	Computer Systems	8.0	26.4	41
CH ENERGY GROUP INC.	CHG	Electric Utilities	2.2	13.0	47
CHARMING SHOPPES	CHRS	Clothing Stores	-11.5	1.0	79
CHARTER ONE FINL INC.	CF	Banks	1.4	13.3	76
CHATEAU COMMUNITIES INC.	CPJ	REITS	5.5	12.5	68
CHECKPOINT SYSTEMS INC.	CKP	Machinery	80.2	-11.5	56
CHEESECAKE FACTORY INC.	CAKE	Restaurants	35.9	45.3	56
CHELSEA PROPERTY GROUP INC.	CPG	REITS	42.5	15.9	85
CHEMED CORP.	CHE	Waste	2.2	2.8	60
CHEMICAL FINANCIAL CORP.	CHFC	Banks	40.5	4.9	64
CHESAPEAKE CORP.	CSK	Paper	40.0	0.5	24
CHESAPEAKE ENERGY CORP.	CHK	Oil/Gas	-34.7	-24.8	51
CHEVRON TEXACO CORP.	CVX	Oil/Gas	9.3	9.9	76
CHIRON CORP.	CHIR	Pharmaceuticals	-1.5	18.7	42
CHITTENDEN CORP.	CHZ	Banks	17.4	16.3	77
CHRISTOPHER & BANKS CORP.	CHBS	Clothing Stores	173.4	96.0	43
CHUBB CORP.	CB	Insurance (Property)	-18.7	7.1	29
CHURCH & DWIGHT INC.	CHD	Chemicals	21.1	20.1	80
CHURCHILL DOWNS INC.	CHDN	Recreation	25.7	17.6	75
CIBER INC.	CBR	Computer Programming	93.8	-8.8	20
CIGNA CORP.	CI	Insurance (Life)	-29.0	17.0	61
CINCINNATI FINANCIAL CORP.	CINF	Insurance (Property)	-1.5	14.2	52
CINERGY CORP.	CIN	Electric Utilities	0.7	6.0	95
CINTAS CORP.	CTAS	Apparel Makers	-9.3	20.2	67
CIRCUIT CITY STR CRCT CTY GP	CC	Electronics Stores	126.7	11.9	4
✓ CISCO SYSTEMS INC.	CSCO	Phone/Network Equipment	-52.7	20.7	60
CITIGROUP INC.	C	Banks	0.1	28.6	51
CITIZENS BANKING CORP.	CBCF	Banks	17.7	13.3	87
CITIZENS INC.	CIA	Insurance (Life)	80.7	11.2	11
CITRIX SYSTEMS INC.	CTXS	Software	0.7	28.3	38
CITY NATIONAL CORP.	CYN	Banks	22.9	18.8	91
CLAIRES STORES INC.	CLE	Clothing Stores	-15.0	3.7	48
CLARCOR INC.	CLC	Auto-Parts Makers	33.8	15.7	83
CLAYTON HOMES INC.	CMH	Home Building	49.6	10.3	28
CLAYTON WILLIAMS ENERGY INC.	CWEI	Oil/Gas	-51.5	-5.5	15
CLECO CORP.	CNL	Electric Utilities	-16.5	15.2	73
CLOROX CO./DE	CLX	Household Products	14.1	11.5	64
CMS ENERGY CORP.	CMS	Electric Utilities	-19.8	-2.3	45
CNA FINANCIAL CORP.	CNA	Insurance (Property)	-22.9	-3.5	39
CNF INC.	CNF	Air Transport	0.5	9.9	50
COASTAL BANCORP. INC.	CBSA	Banks	22.2	15.6	55
COCA-COLA BTLNG CONS	COKE	Beverage Manufacturing	2.5	-2.9	67
COCA-COLA CO.	KO	Beverage Manufacturing	-21.4	-1.1	27
COCA-COLA ENTERPRISES	CCE	Beverage Manufacturing	0.6	3.9	38
COGNEX CORP.	CGNX	Medical Equipment	15.8	6.7	32

	TICKER	INDUSTRY	2001 TOT. RET.	5-YR. ANN. TOT. RET.	EASY-HOLD RANK
COHERENT INC.	COHR	Medical Equipment	-4.9	7.9	32
COHU INC.	COHU	Measuring Devices	43.3	12.4	16
COLE KENNETH PROD INC. -CL A	KCP	Shoes	-56.0	11.4	81
COLGATE-PALMOLIVE CO	CL	Household Products	-9.5	21.7	53
COLONIAL BANCGROUP	CNB	Banks	36.0	10.5	64
COLONIAL PROPERTIES TRUST	CLP	REITS	30.3	9.2	66
COLUMBIA BKG SYS INC.	COLB	Savings Institutions	-7.8	10.0	62
COMDISCO INC.	CDO	Rental	-95.4	-45.0	19
COMERICA INC.	CMA	Banks	-0.5	13.4	74
COMMERCE BANCSHARES INC.	CBSH	Banks	-2.0	11.8	89
COMMERCE GROUP INC./MA	CGI	Insurance (Property)	43.6	12.6	93
COMMERCIAL FEDERAL	CFB	Savings Institutions	22.5	3.1	41
COMMERCIAL METALS	CMC	Mining	60.8	5.0	41
COMML NET LEASE RLTY INC.	NNN	REITS	40.9	5.5	70
COMMONWLTH TELE ENTER	CTCO	Telecommunications	30.0	21.1	35
COMMUNITY BANKS INC. MLLRSBRG	CTY	Banks	42.1	16.7	98
COMMUNITY BK SYS INC.	CBU	Banks	10.1	9.8	86
COMMUNITY TRUST BANCORP. INC.	CTBI	Banks	65.8	9.1	56
COMPAQ COMPUTER CORP.	CPQ	Computer Equipment	-34.6	-7.7	28
COMPUTER NETWORK TECH CORP.	CMNT	Phone/Network Equipment	-38.3	28.9	11
COMPUTER SCIENCES CORP.	CSC	Computer Systems	-18.5	3.6	54
COMPUWARE CORP.	CPWR	Software	88.6	13.5	33
COMSTOCK RESOURCES INC.	CRK	Oil/Gas	-52.5	-11.6	59
CONAGRA FOODS INC.	CAG	Food Manufacturing	-4.8	2.1	37
CONCORD EFS INC.	CEFT	Finance	49.2	39.2	71
CONESTOGA ENTERPRISES	CENI	Telecommunications	91.6	18.8	49
CONMED CORP.	CNMD	Medical Equipment	74.8	7.9	59
CONSECO INC.	CNC	Insurance (Life)	-66.2	-31.8	13
CONSOLIDATED EDISON INC.	ED	Electric Utilities	10.9	13.0	75
CONSOLIDATED GRAPHICS INC.	CGX	Printing	61.3	-7.2	84
CONSTELLATION ENERGY GRP INC.	CEG	Electric Utilities	-40.2	4.5	60
CONTINENTAL AIRLS INC. -CL B	CAL	Air Transport	-49.2	-1.5	57
COOPER CAMERON CORP.	CAM	Oil/Gas Services	-38.9	1.1	8
COOPER COMPANIES INC.	COO	Medical Equipment	25.6	23.9	66
COOPER INDUSTRIES INC.	CBE	Electric Equipment	-21.5	-0.7	48
COOPER TIRE & RUBBER	CTB	Rubber Products	54.9	-1.7	49
COORS (ADOLPH) -CL B	RKY	Alcoholic Drinks	-32.5	24.8	84
COPART INC.	CPRT	Business Services	69.2	61.8	63
CORNING INC.	GLW	Communications Equipment	-83.0	-6.3	45
CORP. OFFICE PPTYS TR INC.	OFC	REITS	29.0	27.8	90
CORUS BANKSHARES INC.	CORS	Banks	-7.1	8.8	70
CORVEL CORP.	CRVL	Insurance (General)	41.9	27.6	95
COSTCO WHOLESALE CORP.	COST	Groceries	11.1	28.7	72
COUNTRYWIDE CREDIT IND INC.	CCR	Mortgages	-17.7	8.5	77
COUSINS PROPERTIES INC.	CUZ	REITS	-7.9	10.8	93
COVENANT TRANSPRT INC. -CL A	CVTI	Truck Transport	48.5	2.1	21
COVENTRY HEALTH CARE	CVH	Physicians	-25.2	16.6	74
CPB INC.	CPBI	Banks	7.9	17.5	97
CPI CORP.	CPY	Business Services	-14.5	2.4	47
CREDENCE SYSTEMS CORP.	CMOS	Measuring Devices	-19.3	13.0	45
CREDIT ACCEP CORP. MICH	CACC	Finance	48.3	-17.6	22
CREE INC.	CREE	Semiconductors	-17.1	65.9	70
CRESCENT R E EQUITIES INC.	CEI	REITS	-10.9	1.6	69
CROMPTON CORP.	CK	Rubber Products	-12.5	-13.2	34
CROSSMANN COMMUNITIES INC.	CROS	Home Building	57.9	23.9	86
CRYOLIFE INC.	CRY	Biotech	-0.8	29.2	72
CSS INDS INC.	CSS	Printing	45.5	3.5	56
CSX CORP.	CSX	Rail Transport	38.2	-0.7	21
CTS CORP.	CTS	Auto-Parts Makers	-56.1	18.1	89
CUBIC CORP.	CUB	Measuring Devices	102.8	19.2	59
CULLEN/FROST BANKERS INC.	CFR	Banks	-24.1	16.0	94
CURTISS-WRIGHT CORP.	CW	Aerospace	3.9	15.2	96
CVB FINANCIAL CORP.	CVBF	Banks	56.0	25.3	97
CVS CORP.	CVS	Stores (Misc.)	-50.3	8.1	94
CYPRESS SEMICONDUCTOR CORP.	CY	Semiconductors	1.2	7.1	46

	TICKER	INDUSTRY	2001 TOT. RET.	5-YR. ANN. TOT. RET.	EASY-HOLD RANK
CYTEC INDUSTRIES INC.	CYT	Chemicals	-32.4	-7.8	63
D R HORTON INC.	DHI	Home Building	48.7	30.3	95
DAISYTEK INTL CORP.	DZTK	Office Equipment (Wholesale)	91.6	-0.5	47
DAKTRONICS INC.	DAKT	Misc. Manufacturing	42.3	53.2	74
DANA CORP.	DCN	Auto-Parts Makers	-4.8	-12.4	11
DANAHER CORP.	DHR	Metal Products	-11.7	21.1	77
DARDEN RESTAURANTS INC.	DRI	Restaurants	55.2	32.9	77
DATASCOPE CORP.	DSCP	Medical Equipment	-0.4	11.4	91
DAVITA INC.	DVA	HMOs	42.8	2.4	14
DEAN FOODS CO.	DF	Food Manufacturing	42.1	27.5	61
DEB SHOPS INC.	DEBS	Clothing Stores	82.3	44.9	93
DEERE & CO.	DE	Agricultural Machinery	-2.5	3.7	19
DELL COMPUTER CORP.	DELL	Computer Equipment	55.9	52.3	70
DELPHI FINANCIAL GRP -CL A	DFG	Insurance (Life)	-12.8	4.7	37
DELTA & PINE LAND CO.	DLP	Agriculture	8.9	5.2	88
DELTA AIR LINES INC.	DAL	Air Transport	-41.5	-3.6	37
DELUXE CORP.	DLX	Printing	114.5	15.1	86
DENBURY RESOURCES INC.	DNR	Oil/Gas	-33.5	-13.0	53
DENDRITE INTERNATIONAL INC.	DRTE	Software	-37.3	38.5	78
DENTSPLY INTERNATL INC.	XRAY	Medical Equipment	29.1	17.1	79
DEVELOPERS DIVERSIFIED RLTY	DDR	REITS	56.1	9.3	83
DEVRY INC.	DV	Education	-24.6	19.3	72
DIAGNOSTIC PRODUCTS CORP.	DP	Diagnostics	62.0	29.6	58
DIAMOND OFFSHRE DRILLING INC.	DO	Oil/Gas Services	-22.9	2.6	9
DIANON SYSTEMS INC.	DIAN	HMOs	38.6	47.8	40
DIEBOLD INC.	DBD	Computer Equipment	23.5	1.2	49
DILLARDS INC. -CL A	DDS	Department Stores	36.8	-11.6	40
DIME BANCORP. INC.	DME	Banks	23.7	20.9	75
DIME COMMUNITY BANCSHARES	DCOM	Savings Institutions	70.9	26.2	83
DIMON INC.	DMN	Tobacco	34.3	-17.0	28
DIONEX CORP.	DNEX	Measuring Devices	-26.1	7.8	78
DISNEY (WALT) COMPANY	DIS	Broadcast TV	-27.7	-1.5	50
DOLE FOOD CO. INC.	DOL	Food Manufacturing	67.3	-3.0	38
DOLLAR TREE STORES INC.	DLTR	Department Stores	26.2	22.2	78
DOMINION RESOURCES INC.	D	Electric Utilities	-6.6	15.7	59
DONALDSON CO. INC.	DCI	Environment Control	41.0	19.6	86
DONNELLEY (R R) & SONS CO.	DNY	Printing	13.5	1.7	55
DORAL FINANCIAL CORP.	DORL	Mortgages	31.1	37.9	95
DOVER CORP.	DOV	Semiconductor Equipment	-7.4	9.3	70
DOW CHEMICAL	DOW	Chemicals	-4.1	9.2	27
DOW JONES & CO. INC.	DJ	Publishing	-1.5	12.2	20
DOWNEY FINANCIAL CORP.	DSL	Savings Institutions	-24.4	19.8	94
DPL INC.	DPL	Electric Utilities	-24.8	13.4	73
DQE INC.	DQE	Electric Utilities	-37.6	-3.7	55
DRESS BARN INC.	DBRN	Clothing Stores	-13.8	10.8	56
DREYER'S GRAND ICE CREAM INC.	DRYR	Food Manufacturing	20.4	22.4	51
DSP GROUP INC.	DSPG	Software	10.5	40.5	57
DST SYSTEMS INC.	DST	Data Processing	-25.6	26.0	84
DTE ENERGY CO.	DTE	Electric Utilities	13.0	11.4	79
DU PONT (E I) DE NEMOURS	DD	Chemicals	-9.2	0.5	36
DUKE ENERGY CORP.	DUK	Electric Utilities	-5.3	15.3	98
DUKE REALTY CORP.	DRE	REITS	6.2	11.9	97
DUPONT PHOTOMASKS INC.	DPMI	Semiconductor Equipment	-17.8	-0.9	10
DVI INC.	DVI	Finance	0.8	5.8	91
DYCOM INDUSTRIES INC.	DY	Construction	-53.5	32.4	86
DYNEGY INC.	DYN	Natural Gas Utilities	-54.2	9.1	64
EASTGROUP PROPERTIES	EGP	REITS	11.5	12.8	70
EASTMAN CHEMICAL CO.	EMN	Chemicals	-16.6	-3.3	42
EASTMAN KODAK CO.	EK	Household Products	-21.9	-15.7	76
EATON CORP.	ETN	Electric Equipment	16.8	6.6	54
EATON VANCE CORP.	EV	Money Management	11.1	44.6	92
ECOLAB INC.	ECL	Household Products	-5.6	17.9	89
EDISON INTERNATIONAL	EIX	Electric Utilities	-3.4	-2.3	28
EDO CORP.	EDO	Aerospace	267.0	31.8	39

	TICKER	INDUSTRY	2001 TOT. RET.	5-YR. ANN. TOT. RET.	EASY-HOLD RANK
EDWARDS (A G) INC.	AGE	Securities	-5.4	16.4	29
EGL INC.	EAGL	Transportation	-41.7	-4.4	29
EL PASO CORP.	EP	Natural Gas Utilities	-36.7	14.3	63
EL PASO ELECTRIC CO.	EE	Electric Utilities	9.8	17.4	63
ELANTEC SEMICONDUCTOR INC.	ELNT	Semiconductors	38.4	77.2	59
ELCOR CORP.	ELK	Oil/Gas Products	66.4	25.1	50
ELECTRO RENT CORP.	ELRC	Rental	-8.7	0.7	35
ELECTRO SCIENTIFIC INDS INC.	ESIO	Semiconductor Equipment	7.2	18.2	44
ELECTROGLAS INC.	EGLS	Semiconductor Equipment	-3.5	-1.7	9
ELECTRONIC DATA SYSTEMS CORP.	EDS	Computer Systems	19.8	11.0	56
ELECTRONICS FOR IMAGING INC.	EFII	Computer Equipment	60.1	-11.5	29
EMC CORP./MA	EMC	Computer Storage	-79.1	27.4	80
EMCOR GROUP INC.	EME	Construction	78.0	28.4	83
EMERSON ELECTRIC CO.	EMR	Electric Equipment	-25.7	5.7	88
EMPIRE DISTRICT ELECTRIC CO.	EDE	Electric Utilities	-15.0	8.6	39
EMULEX CORP.	EMLX	Phone/Network Equipment	-50.6	82.2	64
ENCORE WIRE CORP.	WIRE	Nonferrous Metals	108.2	9.6	25
ENERGEN CORP.	EGN	Natural Gas Utilities	-21.4	13.9	76
ENERGY EAST CORP.	EAS	Electric Utilities	1.0	16.9	88
ENGELHARD CORP.	EC	Chemicals	38.0	9.9	89
ENGINEERED SUPPORT SYSTEMS	EASI	Environment Control	96.8	34.4	81
ENRON CORP.	ENE	Natural Gas Utilities	-98.9	-46.4	57
ENSCO INTERNATIONAL INC.	ESV	Oil/Gas Services	-26.7	0.9	9
ENTERGY CORP.	ETR	Electric Utilities	-4.5	12.4	63
ENZO BIOCHEM INC.	ENZ	Pharmaceuticals	-0.8	7.4	41
EOG RESOURCES INC.	EOG	Oil/Gas	-28.1	9.7	79
EQUIFAX INC.	EFX	Business Services	38.6	8.8	95
EQUITABLE RESOURCES INC.	EQT	Oil/Gas	4.1	21.9	67
EQUITY INNS INC.	ENN	REITS	17.2	-1.8	55
EQUITY RESIDENTIAL PPTYS TR	EQR	REITS	10.2	13.6	90
ERIE INDEMNITY CO. -CL A	ERIE	Insurance (Property)	31.6	6.1	74
ESCO TECHNOLOGIES INC.	ESE	Measuring Devices	66.7	27.8	31
ESS TECHNOLOGY INC.	ESST	Semiconductors	329.7	-4.8	4
ESSEX PROPERTY TRUST	ESS	REITS	-4.5	17.6	69
ESTERLINE TECHNOLOGIES	ESL	Semiconductor Equipment	-39.0	4.2	54
ETHAN ALLEN INTERIORS INC.	ETH	Furniture Makers	24.7	27.1	82
EVERGREEN RESOURCES	EVG	Oil/Gas	0.0	36.2	92
EXAR CORP.	EXAR	Semiconductors	-32.7	32.2	20
EXCEL TECHNOLOGY INC.	XLTC	Medical Equipment	-12.8	16.5	45
EXPEDITORS INTL WASH INC.	EXPD	Transportation	6.5	38.2	71
EXPRESS SCRIPTS INC.	ESRX	HMOs	-8.5	39.1	86
EXTENDED STAY AMERICA INC.	ESA	Hotels	27.6	-4.0	74
EXXON MOBIL CORP.	XOM	Oil/Gas	-7.5	12.5	77
F & M BANCORP./MD	FMBN	Banks	28.6	8.2	66
F N B CORP./FL	FBAN	Banks	35.8	11.0	95
FACTSET RESEARCH SYSTEMS INC.	FDS	Online Information	-5.3	38.3	90
FAIR ISAAC & COMPANY INC.	FIC	Software	85.6	19.5	64
FAMILY DOLLAR STORES	FDO	Department Stores	41.1	36.1	89
FANNIE MAE	FNM	Finance	-7.0	18.1	96
FARMERS CAPITAL BK CORP.	FFKT	Banks	37.4	16.3	50
FASTENAL CO.	FAST	Home Supply Stores	21.2	7.9	79
FEDDERS CORP.	FJC	Environment Control	-32.4	-11.7	34
FEDERAL HOME LOAN MORTG CORP.	FRE	Finance	-3.9	20.2	95
FEDERAL REALTY INVS TRUST	FRT	REITS	32.3	5.0	79
FEDEX CORP.	FDX	Air Transport	29.8	18.4	62
FEI CO.	FEIC	Measuring Devices	38.5	27.4	17
FELCOR LODGING TR INC.	FCH	REITS	-23.4	-5.6	38
FERRO CORP.	FOE	Chemicals	15.0	8.9	61
FIDELITY BANKSHARES INC.	FFFL	Banks	102.5	22.1	63
FIDELITY NATIONAL FINL INC.	FNF	Insurance (Title)	-25.0	18.8	61
FILENET CORP.	FILE	Computer Systems	-25.5	4.9	42
FINANCIAL FEDERAL CORP.	FIF	Finance	30.9	22.9	95
FINISH LINE INC. -CL A	FINL	Shoes	158.9	-6.3	23

	TICKER	INDUSTRY	2001 TOT. RET.	5-YR. ANN. TOT. RET.	EASY-HOLD RANK
FIRST BANCORP. PR	FBP	Banks	23.0	19.0	93
FIRST BUSEY CORP. -CL A	BUSE	Banks	10.5	16.1	74
FIRST CHARTER CORP.	FCTR	Banks	18.6	2.1	60
FIRST CITIZENS BANCSH -CL A	FCNCA	Banks	22.3	6.1	99
FIRST COMMONWLTH FINL CP/PA	FCF	Banks	20.7	9.0	84
FIRST DATA CORP.	FDC	Data Processing	49.1	16.8	48
FIRST ESSEX BANCORP.	FESX	Banks	45.3	20.6	58
FIRST FED CAP CORP.	FTFC	Savings Institutions	11.8	18.0	92
FIRST FINANCIAL HOLDINGS INC.	FFCH	Savings Institutions	26.4	19.8	92
FIRST HEALTH GROUP CORP.	FHCC	Physicians	6.3	18.5	65
FIRST INDIANA CORP.	FISB	Banks	-4.2	6.7	77
FIRST INDL REALTY TRUST INC.	FR	REITS	-0.5	8.7	87
FIRST MERCHANTS CORP.	FRME	Banks	15.6	11.2	91
FIRST REPUBLIC BANK	FRC	Banks	9.8	16.7	68
FIRST SENTINEL BANCORP. INC.	FSLA	Savings Institutions	11.7	27.2	98
FIRST TENNESSEE NATL CORP.	FTN	Banks	28.6	17.3	63
FIRST VIRGINIA BANKS INC.	FVB	Banks	9.3	13.0	48
FIRSTFED FINANCIAL CORP./CA	FED	Banks	-20.7	18.4	57
FIRSTMERIT CORP.	FMER	Banks	5.1	12.4	73
FISERV INC.	FISV	Data Processing	33.8	31.2	82
FLEETBOSTON FINANCIAL CORP.	FBF	Banks	0.6	11.2	79
FLORIDA EAST COAST INDS	FLA	Rail Transport	-35.2	1.5	8
FLORIDA ROCK INDS	FRK	Building Materials	41.8	28.7	79
FLOW INTL CORP.	FLOW	Machinery	12.5	6.3	17
FLOWSERVE CORP.	FLS	Machinery	24.5	1.2	18
FLUSHING FINANCIAL CORP.	FFIC	Savings Institutions	51.9	19.3	92
FMC CORP.	FMC	Oil/Gas	-17.0	-3.2	32
FORD MOTOR CO.	F	Auto Makers	-29.8	9.8	25
FOREST CITY ENTRPRS -CL A	FCE.A	REITS	48.9	24.3	81
FOREST LABORATORIES -CL A	FRX	Pharmaceuticals	23.3	58.5	89
FOREST OIL CORP.	FST	Oil/Gas	-23.5	-4.4	59
FORTUNE BRANDS INC.	FO	Metal Products	35.5	6.3	23
FORWARD AIR CORP.	FWRD	Air Transport	-9.1	71.1	57
FOSSIL INC.	FOSL	Jewelry/Accessories	45.0	28.5	89
FPL GROUP INC.	FPL	Electric Utilities	-18.3	8.3	78
FRANKLIN ELECTRIC CO.	FELE	Machinery	21.2	13.2	69
FRANKLIN RESOURCES INC.	BEN	Money Management	-6.8	9.8	25
FREDS INC.	FRED	Department Stores	144.7	51.1	57
FRIEDMANS INC. -CL A	FRDM	Jewelry/Accessories	83.7	-10.1	44
FRONTIER OIL CORP.	FTO	Oil/Gas Products	144.4	40.0	94
FST FINL CORP. IND	THFF	Banks	40.7	6.9	88
FTI CONSULTING INC.	FCN	Business Services	220.0	27.5	57
FULLER (H. B.) CO.	FULL	Chemicals	48.6	5.9	39
FURNITURE BRANDS INTL INC.	FBN	Furniture Makers	52.0	18.0	47
FYI INC.	FYII	Data Processing	-9.2	9.9	94
G&K SERVICES INC. -CL A	GKSRA	Personal Svcs	15.2	-2.9	68
GABLES RESIDENTIAL TRUST	GBP	REITS	14.3	8.8	93
GALLAGHER (ARTHUR J.) & CO.	AJG	Insurance (General)	10.3	38.5	81
GANNETT CO.	GCI	Publishing	8.1	13.9	88
GAP INC.	GPS	Clothing Stores	-45.1	9.8	66
GARAN INC.	GAN	Apparel Makers	91.6	24.2	95
GARDNER DENVER INC.	GDI	Machinery	4.8	14.3	44
GATEWAY INC.	GTW	Computer Equipment	-55.3	-9.7	18
GBC BANCORP./CA	GBCB	Banks	-21.9	17.9	95
GENCORP. INC.	GY	Aerospace	48.1	8.4	67
GENERAL DYNAMICS CORP.	GD	Transportation Equipment	3.6	20.0	97
GENERAL ELECTRIC CO.	GE	Electric Equipment	-15.0	21.1	85
GENERAL GROWTH PPTYS INC.	GGP	REITS	13.9	9.7	94
GENERAL MOTORS CORP.	GM	Auto Makers	-1.0	5.4	28
GENESCO INC.	GCO	Shoes	-15.0	17.5	43
GENLYTE GROUP INC.	GLYT	Electric Equipment	25.3	18.9	97
GENTEX CORP.	GNTX	Auto-Parts Makers	43.5	21.6	51
GENUINE PARTS CO.	GPC	Auto-Parts Makers	45.4	8.2	84
GENZYME GENERAL	GENZ	Biotech	33.1	42.0	64
GERMAN AMERICAN BANCORP.	GABC	Savings Institutions	43.8	4.5	52
GIBRALTAR STEEL CORP.	ROCK	Steel/Iron	0.6	-7.4	74

	TICKER	INDUSTRY	2001 TOT. RET.	5-YR. ANN. TOT. RET.	EASY-HOLD RANK
GILLETTE CO.	G	Household Products	-5.5	-1.6	18
GLATFELTER (P H) CO.	GLT	Paper	31.4	2.2	49
GLENBOROUGH REALTY TRUST INC.	GLB	REITS	22.1	11.2	57
GLIMCHER REALTY TRUST	GRT	REITS	68.5	8.7	75
GOLDEN WEST FINANCIAL CORP.	GDW	Savings Institutions	-12.4	23.5	83
GOODRICH CORP.	GR	Aerospace	-24.3	-5.2	34
GORMAN-RUPP CO.	GRC	Machinery	53.6	18.4	77
GRACO INC.	GGG	Machinery	43.3	31.0	79
GRAINGER (W W) INC.	GWW	Electronics Stores	33.7	5.2	38
GRANITE CONSTRUCTION INC.	GVA	Construction	26.5	25.2	76
GREAT AMERN FINL RESOURCES	GFR	Insurance (Life)	-1.4	6.4	67
GREAT LAKES CHEMICAL CORP.	GLK	Household Products	-33.9	-8.8	42
GREAT SOUTHERN BANCORP.	GSBC	Savings Institutions	99.2	13.9	98
GREATER BAY BANCORP.	GBBK	Banks	-29.1	38.2	94
GREEN MTN COFFEE INC.	GMCR	Food Wholesale	9.6	55.0	68
GREENPOINT FINANCIAL CORP.	GPT	Savings Institutions	-10.3	11.5	57
GREIF BROS CORP. -CL A	GBCOA	Paper	17.9	4.9	91
GREY GLOBAL GROUP INC.	GREY	Advertising	3.2	22.5	51
GRIFFON CORP.	GFF	Metal Products	109.5	6.1	47
GTECH HOLDINGS CORP.	GTK	Online Information	120.3	7.2	55
GUIDANT CORP.	GDT	Medical Equipment	-7.7	28.5	96
HALLIBURTON CO.	HAL	Oil/Gas Services	-63.2	-14.2	16
HANCOCK FABRICS INC.	HKF	Stores (Misc.)	289.4	8.6	34
HANCOCK HLDG CO.	HBHC	Banks	15.5	3.8	80
HANDLEMAN CO.	HDL	Stores (Misc.)	98.0	11.5	55
HARBOR FLORIDA BANCSHARES	HARB	Savings Institutions	16.6	26.7	97
HARLAND (JOHN H.) CO.	JH	Printing	58.8	-6.1	50
HARLEY-DAVIDSON INC.	HDI	Transportation Equipment	37.0	36.3	76
HARLEYSVILLE GROUP INC.	HGIC	Insurance (Property)	-16.4	12.2	41
HARLEYSVILLE NATL CORP./PA	HNBC	Banks	40.0	21.2	92
HARMAN INTERNATIONAL INDS	HAR	Audio/Video Equipment	23.9	10.6	27
HARRAHS ENTERTAINMENT INC.	HET	Hotel Casinos	40.3	13.2	49
HARRIS CORP.	HRS	Cable/Wireless Equipment	0.3	2.3	27
HARSCO CORP.	HSC	Waste	43.6	2.7	40
HARTE HANKS INC.	HHS	Advertising	19.5	15.6	81
HARTFORD FINL SVCS GRP INC.	HIG	Insurance (Property)	-9.6	15.3	32
HAVERTY FURNITURE	HVT	Furniture Retail	70.1	26.0	77
HAWAIIAN ELECTRIC INDS	HE	Electric Utilities	15.6	9.5	37
HCA INC.	HCA	Hospitals	-12.3	0.3	21
HCC INS HLDGS INC.	HCC	Insurance (Property)	3.0	3.7	40
HEALTH CARE PPTYS INVEST INC.	HCP	REITS	32.5	10.0	80
HEALTH CARE REIT INC.	HCN	REITS	65.9	10.6	65
HEALTH MANAGEMNT ASSC	HMA	Hospitals	-11.3	13.0	78
HEALTH NET INC. - CL A	HNT	Physicians	-16.8	-2.5	42
HEALTHCARE REALTY TRUST	HR	REITS	44.4	11.7	78
HEALTHSOUTH CORP.	HRC	Physicians	-9.1	-5.2	21
HEARTLAND EXPRESS INC.	HTLD	Truck Transport	52.2	7.3	62
HEICO CORP.	HEI	Aerospace	6.4	11.7	93
HEINZ (H J) CO.	HNZ	Food Manufacturing	-9.9	6.1	64
HELIX TECHNOLOGY CORP.	HELX	Semiconductor Equipment	-3.0	12.3	38
HELMERICH & PAYNE	HP	Oil/Gas Services	-23.3	6.2	39
HENRY (JACK) & ASSOCIATES	JKHY	Computer Systems	-29.3	30.5	90
HERBALIFE INTL INC. -CL A	HERBA	Food Manufacturing	98.9	-11.3	32
HERSHEY FOODS CORP.	HSY	Food Manufacturing	7.1	11.1	58
HEXCEL CORP.	HXL	Metal Products	-65.5	-28.3	10
HIBERNIA CORP. -CL A	HIB	Banks	44.2	9.3	79
HICKORY TECH CORP.	HTCO	Telecommunications	-15.0	17.4	38
HIGHWOODS PROPERTIES INC.	HIW	REITS	14.2	3.0	65
HILB ROGAL & HAMILTON CO.	HRH	Insurance (Property)	42.8	37.1	86
HILLENBRAND INDUSTRIES	HB	Medical Equipment	9.0	10.7	46
HILTON HOTELS CORP.	HLT	Hotels	4.7	-8.8	47
HISPANIC BROADCASTING -CL A	HSP	Radio	0.0	26.5	56
HNC SOFTWARE INC.	HNCS	Software	-30.6	22.8	49
HOLLINGER INTL INC. -CL A	HLR	Publishing	-23.0	4.3	45

	TICKER	INDUSTRY	2001 TOT. RET.	5-YR. ANN. TOT. RET.	EASY-HOLD RANK
HOLLY CORP.	HOC	Oil/Gas Products	110.3	11.4	60
HOME DEPOT INC.	HD	Home Supply Stores	12.1	36.0	85
HOME PROPERTIES NEW YORK INC.	HME	REITS	22.2	15.3	93
HON INDUSTRIES	HNI	Furniture Makers	10.5	12.6	49
HONEYWELL INTERNATIONAL INC.	HON	Aerospace	−27.1	1.7	44
HOOPER HOLMES INC.	HH	Physicians	−18.8	33.2	72
HORACE MANN EDUCATORS CORP.	HMN	Insurance (Property)	1.4	2.7	20
HORMEL FOODS CORP.	HRL	Food Manufacturing	46.7	17.1	78
HOSPITALITY PROPERTIES TRUST	HPT	REITS	45.0	10.4	71
HOST MARRIOTT CORP.	HMT	REITS	−24.7	−3.1	50
HOUSEHOLD INTERNATIONAL INC.	HI	Finance	6.8	15.2	87
HOVNANIAN ENTRPRS INC. -CL A	HOV	Home Building	127.0	23.2	88
HRPT PPTYS TRUST	HRP	REITS	25.9	−2.7	68
HUBBELL INC. -CL B	HUB.B	Electric Equipment	16.3	−3.9	40
HUGHES SUPPLY INC.	HUG	Environment Control	74.8	2.9	44
HUMANA INC.	HUM	Insurance (Life)	−22.7	−9.1	15
HUNT (JB) TRANSPRT SVCS INC.	JBHT	Consultants	38.0	11.5	37
HUNTINGTON BANCSHARES	HBAN	Banks	11.0	2.5	46
IBERIABANK CORP.	IBKC	Banks	30.8	12.1	85
ICN PHARMACEUTICALS INC.	ICN	Biotech	10.4	21.9	7
ICT GROUP INC.	ICTG	Business Services	93.4	31.4	77
ICU MEDICAL INC.	ICUI	Medical Equipment	47.7	41.4	69
IDACORP. INC.	IDA	Electric Utilities	−13.1	11.3	92
IDEC PHARMACEUTICALS CORP.	IDPH	Pharmaceuticals	9.1	77.1	41
IDEX CORP.	IEX	Machinery	6.1	7.3	50
IDEXX LABS INC.	IDXX	Biotech	29.6	−4.6	30
IHOP CORP.	IHP	Restaurants	35.1	19.9	88
II-VI INC.	IIVI	Optical Equipment	13.4	6.0	28
IKON OFFICE SOLUTIONS	IKN	Office Equipment (Wholesale)	378.4	−21.1	15
ILLINOIS TOOL WORKS	ITW	Machinery	15.3	12.4	71
INDEPENDENT BANK CORP./MA	INDB	Banks	76.2	18.5	59
INDEPENDENT BANK CORP./MI	IBCP	Banks	51.8	22.1	99
INDYMAC BANCORP. INC.	NDE	Mortgages	−20.7	7.8	58
INFORMATION RESOURCES INC.	IRIC	Software	150.6	−9.9	28
INGERSOLL-RAND CO.	IR	Construction Machinery	1.4	8.7	67
INGLES MARKETS INC. -CL A	IMKTA	Groceries	25.5	4.3	50
INNKEEPERS USA TRUST	KPA	REITS	−3.6	2.6	58
INSIGHT ENTERPRISES INC.	NSIT	Electronics Stores	37.1	34.8	91
INSITUFORM TECNOL INC. -CL A	INSUA	Construction	−35.8	28.2	78
INSURANCE AUTO AUCTIONS INC.	IAAI	Auto Retail	20.9	8.8	42
INTEGRAL SYSTEMS INC./MD	ISYS	Computer Systems	37.5	32.8	51
INTEGRATED DEVICE TECH INC.	IDTI	Semiconductors	−19.7	14.3	35
INTEL CORP.	INTC	Semiconductors	4.9	14.2	46
INTERFACE INC. -CL A	IFSIA	Textiles	−33.8	−9.2	23
INTERLOGIX INC.	ILXI	Security Services	104.9	20.7	45
INTERMAGNETICS GENERAL CORP.	IMGC	Metal Products	57.7	18.7	16
INTERPOOL INC.	IPX	Water Transport	14.2	5.6	70
INTERPUBLIC GROUP OF COS	IPG	Advertising	−29.8	14.4	77
INTERSTATE BAKERIES CP	IBC	Food Manufacturing	74.6	1.0	33
INTERTAN INC.	ITN	Electronics Stores	8.0	31.0	28
INTER-TEL INC. -SER A	INTL	Phone/Network Equipment	151.0	15.4	18
INTIMATE BRANDS INC. -CL A	IBI	Clothing Stores	1.3	14.9	45
INTL BUSINESS MACHINES CORP.	IBM	Computer Equipment	43.0	26.9	52
INTL FLAVORS & FRAGRANCES	IFF	Food Manufacturing	49.7	−4.6	31
INTL GAME TECHNOLOGY	IGT	Misc. Manufacturing	42.3	30.5	72
INTL RECTIFIER CORP.	IRF	Semiconductors	16.3	18.0	23
INTL SPECIALTY PRODS INC.	ISP	Household Products	33.8	−6.1	58
INTUIT INC.	INTU	Software	8.5	32.4	60
INVACARE CORP.	IVC	Medical Equipment	−1.4	4.4	90
INVESTMENT TECHNOLOGY GP INC.	ITG	Securities	40.4	39.1	61
INVESTORS FINANCIAL SVCS CP	IFIN	Securities	−22.9	57.3	64
IOMEGA CORP.	IOM	Computer Storage	−50.1	−28.1	30
IONICS INC.	ION	Machinery	5.8	−9.0	23
IRT PROPERTY CO.	IRT	REITS	43.1	8.1	76
ISLE OF CAPRIS CASINOS INC.	ISLE	Gambling	25.9	33.2	65

	TICKER	INDUSTRY	2001 TOT. RET.	5-YR. ANN. TOT. RET.	EASY-HOLD RANK
ITT EDUCATIONAL SVCS INC.	ESI	Education	67.6	9.8	63
ITT INDUSTRIES INC.	ITT	Auto-Parts Makers	32.1	17.6	83
J & J SNACK FOODS CORP.	JJSF	Food Manufacturing	45.4	12.6	48
J JILL GROUP INC.	JILL	Stores (Misc.)	38.9	53.8	57
JABIL CIRCUIT INC.	JBL	Printed Circuit Boards	−10.5	35.4	66
JACK IN THE BOX INC.	JBX	Restaurants	−6.4	25.4	99
JACOBS ENGINEERING GROUP INC.	JEC	Engineering	42.9	22.8	83
JAKKS PACIFIC INC.	JAKK	Toys	107.7	28.9	90
JDA SOFTWARE GROUP INC.	JDAS	Computer Programming	71.1	3.3	36
JDN REALTY CORP.	JDN	REITS	28.3	0.4	63
JDS UNIPHASE CORP.	JDSU	Phone/Network Equipment	−79.2	21.5	52
JEFFERSON-PILOT CORP.	JP	Insurance (Life)	−5.0	15.4	70
JLG INDUSTRIES INC.	JLG	Machinery	0.6	−7.6	76
JOHN NUVEEN CO. -CL A	JNC	Money Management	42.7	28.2	87
JOHNSON & JOHNSON	JNJ	Household Products	14.0	20.5	78
JOHNSON CONTROLS INC.	JCI	Auto-Parts Makers	58.1	16.4	87
JONES APPAREL GROUP INC.	JNY	Apparel Makers	3.1	12.2	91
JP REALTY INC.	JPR	REITS	65.2	7.7	75
K2 INC.	KTO	Sporting Goods	−9.9	−22.6	44
KAMAN CORP. -CL A	KAMNA	Aerospace	−4.9	6.9	42
KAYDON CORP.	KDN	Metal Products	−7.0	0.7	26
KB HOME	KBH	Home Building	20.3	27.2	96
KEANE INC.	KEA	Data Processing	84.9	2.6	20
KEITHLEY INSTR INC.	KEI	Measuring Devices	−60.4	31.0	46
KELLOGG CO.	K	Food Manufacturing	18.8	1.2	37
KELLWOOD CO.	KWD	Apparel Makers	17.1	6.6	81
KELLY SERVICES INC. -CL A	KELYA	Employment	−4.1	−0.8	66
KEMET CORP.	KEM	Semiconductors	17.4	8.8	50
KENNAMETAL INC.	KMT	Machinery	40.9	2.9	24
KERR-MCGEE CORP.	KMG	Oil/Gas	−15.6	−2.2	60
KEY ENERGY SERVICES INC.	KEG	Oil/Gas Services	−11.9	−4.8	30
KEY PRODUCTION COMPANY INC.	KP	Oil/Gas	−49.3	5.9	78
KEYCORP.	KEY	Banks	−8.8	3.3	56
KEYSPAN CORP.	KSE	Natural Gas Utilities	−14.0	8.3	59
KFORCE INC.	KFRC	Consultants	105.4	−10.6	41
KIMBALL INTERNATIONAL -CL B	KBALB	Furniture Makers	9.2	−2.4	47
KIMBERLY-CLARK CORP.	KMB	Paper	−13.8	6.7	73
KIMCO REALTY CORP.	KIM	REITS	18.1	13.7	93
KINDER MORGAN INC.	KMI	Natural Gas Utilities	7.1	18.5	35
KIRBY CORP.	KEX	Water Transport	31.2	6.9	65
KLA-TENCOR CORP.	KLAC	Semiconductor Equipment	47.1	22.8	31
KNIGHT TRANSPORTATION INC.	KNGT	Truck Transport	119.5	27.2	90
KNIGHT-RIDDER INC.	KRI	Publishing	16.1	13.1	63
KOGER EQUITY INC.	KE	Real Estate	14.3	4.1	67
KOHLS CORP.	KSS	Department Stores	15.5	48.3	85
KROGER CO.	KR	Groceries	−22.9	12.4	93
KRONOS INC.	KRON	Computer Systems	134.6	27.7	43
K-SWISS INC. -CL A	KSWS	Shoes	33.3	46.9	66
KULICKE & SOFFA INDUSTRIES	KLIC	Semiconductor Equipment	52.4	12.5	20
LABOR READY INC.	LRW	Employment	54.3	5.0	55
LABORATORY CP OF AMER HLDGS.	LH	Biotech	−8.1	41.3	41
LACLEDE GROUP INC.	LG	Natural Gas Utilities	8.0	5.7	38
LAFARGE NORTH AMERICA INC.	LAF	Building Materials	61.9	15.5	52
LAM RESEARCH CORP.	LRCX	Semiconductor Equipment	60.1	19.9	19
LANCASTER COLONY CORP.	LANC	Food Manufacturing	29.4	5.0	70
LANCE INC.	LNCE	Food Manufacturing	18.6	1.0	53
LANDAMERICA FINANCIAL GP	LFG	Insurance (Title)	−28.5	8.7	31
LANDAUER INC.	LDR	Engineering	94.9	12.5	65
LANDRYS RESTAURANTS INC.	LNY	Restaurants	89.0	−2.4	40
LANDS END INC.	LE	Stores (Misc.)	99.7	13.6	12
LANDSTAR SYSTEM INC.	LSTR	Truck Transport	30.8	25.5	86
LATTICE SEMICONDUCTOR CORP.	LSCC	Semiconductors	11.9	12.3	39

	TICKER	INDUSTRY	2001 TOT. RET.	5-YR. ANN. TOT. RET.	EASY-HOLD RANK
LAUDER ESTEE COS INC. -CL A	EL	Household Products	-26.4	5.3	85
LAWSON PRODUCTS	LAWS	Machinery	-1.5	6.0	84
LA-Z-BOY INC.	LZB	Furniture Makers	41.3	19.6	77
LEAR CORP.	LEA	Auto-Parts Makers	53.7	2.2	64
LEARNING TREE INTL. INC.	LTRE	Education	-43.6	-1.1	41
LEE ENTERPRISES	LEE	Publishing	24.5	11.8	41
LEGG MASON INC.	LM	Securities	-7.5	29.2	70
LEGGETT & PLATT INC.	LEG	Furniture Makers	24.1	7.7	47
LEHMAN BROTHERS HOLDINGS INC.	LEH	Securities	-0.8	34.3	37
LENNAR CORP.	LEN	Home Building	29.3	30.7	94
LEUCADIA NATIONAL CORP.	LUK	Insurance (Property)	-17.8	13.2	42
LEXINGTON CORP. PPTYS TRUST	LXP	REITS	43.9	11.1	96
LEXMARK INTL INC. -CL A	LXK	Computer Equipment	33.1	33.7	76
LIBBEY INC.	LBY	Clay/Glass	8.5	4.2	81
LIBERTY FINANCIAL COS. INC.	L	Money Management	-23.7	6.8	46
LIBERTY PROPERTY TRUST	LRY	REITS	13.1	11.0	93
LILLY (ELI) & CO.	LLY	Pharmaceuticals	-14.4	18.1	95
LIMITED INC.	LTD	Clothing Stores	-11.8	13.7	43
LINCARE HOLDINGS INC.	LNCR	Home Health	0.4	22.8	91
LINCOLN ELECTRIC HLDGS INC.	LECO	Machinery	27.8	10.8	43
LINCOLN NATIONAL CORP.	LNC	Insurance (Life)	5.4	16.2	50
LINDSAY MANUFACTURING CO.	LNN	Agricultural Machinery	-13.8	-0.8	28
LINEAR TECHNOLOGY CORP.	LLTC	Semiconductors	-15.3	29.3	68
LIQUI-BOX CORP.	LIQB	Plastics	12.9	6.6	63
LITTELFUSE INC.	LFUS	Electric Equipment	-8.3	1.6	44
LIZ CLAIBORNE INC.	LIZ	Apparel Makers	20.6	6.3	59
LONE STAR STEAKHOUSE SALOON	STAR	Restaurants	61.5	-9.5	16
LONE STAR TECHNOLOGIES	LSS	Steel/Iron	-54.3	0.7	21
LONGS DRUG STORES INC.	LDG	Stores (Misc.)	-0.9	1.2	75
LONGVIEW FIBRE CO.	LFB	Paper	-9.6	-5.4	35
LOWES COS	LOW	Home Supply Stores	109.1	39.6	83
LSI INDS INC.	LYTS	Electric Equipment	29.6	16.5	54
LSI LOGIC CORP.	LSI	Semiconductors	-7.7	3.4	18
LTX CORP.	LTXX	Measuring Devices	61.7	28.9	32
LUBRIZOL CORP.	LZ	Oil/Gas Products	40.7	6.3	28
LUFKIN INDUSTRIES INC.	LUFK	Oil/Gas	53.6	4.9	32
M & T BANK CORP.	MTB	Savings Institutions	8.6	21.7	97
M/I SCHOTTENSTEIN HOMES INC.	MHO	Home Building	106.9	36.3	96
MACDERMID INC.	MRD	Household Products	-10.3	13.5	71
MACERICH CO.	MAC	REITS	51.8	8.9	75
MACK CALI REALTY CORP.	CLI	REITS	18.4	7.7	90
MACROMEDIA INC.	MACR	Software	-70.7	-0.2	20
MADDEN STEVEN LTD	SHOO	Shoes	84.5	22.4	88
MADISON GAS & ELECTRIC CO.	MDSN	Electric Utilities	23.5	12.2	72
MAF BANCORP. INC.	MAFB	Savings Institutions	5.4	15.4	94
MAGELLAN HEALTH SVCS	MGL	Physicians	43.1	-22.3	27
MAGNETEK INC.	MAG	Electric Equipment	-30.7	-6.9	65
MAIL-WELL INC.	MWL	Paper	-4.9	-5.6	34
MANDALAY RESORT GROUP	MBG	Hotel Casinos	-2.5	-9.0	36
MANITOWOC CO.	MTW	Environment Control	8.4	12.9	82
MANOR CARE INC.	HCR	Nursing	15.0	-3.7	15
MANPOWER INC./WI	MAN	Employment	-10.7	1.4	59
MANUFACTURED HOME CMNTYS INC.	MHC	REITS	14.4	12.6	79
MARCUS CORP.	MCS	Hotels	3.6	1.5	28
MARSH & MCLENNAN COS.	MMC	Insurance (General)	-6.3	28.3	70
MARSHALL & ILSLEY CORP.	MI	Banks	27.1	14.9	82
MARTIN MARIETTA MATERIALS	MLM	Nonmetal Mining	11.6	16.4	58
MASCO CORP.	MAS	Metal Products	-2.4	8.3	66
MASTEC INC.	MTZ	Construction	-65.3	-21.7	53
MATTEL INC.	MAT	Toys	19.4	-8.0	27
MATTHEWS INTL CORP. -CL A	MATW	Nonferrous Metals	56.6	29.2	95
MAVERICK TUBE CORP.	MVK	Steel/Iron	-42.8	15.2	15
MAXIM INTEGRATED PRODUCTS	MXIM	Semiconductors	10.7	37.4	62
MAY DEPARTMENT STORES CO.	MAY	Department Stores	16.0	6.2	86
MAYTAG CORP.	MYG	Electric Equipment	-1.8	11.6	36
MB FINANCIAL INC.	MBFI	Savings Institutions	103.3	9.7	75

	TICKER	INDUSTRY	2001 TOT. RET.	5-YR. ANN. TOT. RET.	EASY-HOLD RANK
MBIA INC.	MBI	Insurance (General)	9.8	11.1	54
MBNA CORP.	KRB	Finance	-3.7	24.7	79
MCCLATCHY CO. -CL A	MNI	Publishing	11.3	12.2	64
MCCORMICK & CO.	MKC	Food Manufacturing	18.6	14.7	86
MCDONALDS CORP.	MCD	Restaurants	-21.5	3.8	67
MCGRATH RENTCORP.	MGRC	Furniture Retail	98.7	26.9	93
MCGRAW-HILL COMPANIES	MHP	Publishing	5.7	23.8	73
MDC HOLDINGS INC.	MDC	Home Building	39.9	41.1	95
MDU RESOURCES GROUP INC.	MDU	Electric Utilities	-10.7	17.0	98
MEAD CORP.	MEA	Paper	0.7	3.4	16
MEDFORD BANCORP. INC.	MDBK	Savings Institutions	40.3	13.8	78
MEDICIS PHARMACEUT CP -CL A	MRX	Pharmaceuticals	9.2	27.0	65
MEDQUIST INC.	MEDQ	Home Health	82.8	28.8	62
MEDTRONIC INC.	MDT	Medical Equipment	-14.8	25.2	82
MELLON FINANCIAL CORP.	MEL	Banks	-21.9	18.9	65
MENTOR CORP.	MNTR	Medical Equipment	47.1	-0.2	49
MENTOR GRAPHICS CORP.	MENT	Computer Programming	-14.1	19.3	39
MERCANTILE BANKSHARES CORP.	MRBK	Banks	2.5	18.3	71
MERCK & CO.	MRK	Pharmaceuticals	-35.9	10.0	96
MERCURY GENERAL CORP.	MCY	Insurance (Property)	2.4	13.4	33
MEREDITH CORP.	MDP	Publishing	11.8	7.2	54
MERIDIAN RESOURCE CORP.	TMR	Oil/Gas Services	-53.7	-25.3	45
MERIX CORP.	MERX	Printed Circuit Boards	29.0	11.2	20
MERRILL LYNCH & CO.	MER	Securities	-22.7	22.1	56
MESA AIR GROUP INC.	MESA	Air Transport	7.4	2.2	12
MESABA HOLDINGS INC.	MAIR	Air Transport	-43.3	-6.4	78
MESTEK INC.	MCC	Measuring Devices	41.7	9.0	83
METHODE ELECTRONICS -CL A	METHA	Semiconductors	6.6	4.7	23
MGIC INVESTMENT CORP./WI	MTG	Insurance (Property)	-8.3	10.4	85
MGM MIRAGE	MGG	Hotel Casinos	2.4	10.7	74
MICHAELS STORES INC.	MIK	Toys	148.7	40.6	59
MICREL INC.	MCRL	Semiconductors	-22.1	46.0	64
MICROCHIP TECHNOLOGY INC.	MCHP	Semiconductors	76.6	20.8	38
MICRON TECHNOLOGY INC.	MU	Semiconductors	-12.7	16.3	14
MICROSEMI CORP.	MSCC	Semiconductors	113.6	33.0	16
MICROSOFT CORP.	MSFT	Software	52.7	26.2	87
MID AMERICA BANCORP./KY	MAB	Banks	50.9	18.3	66
MID ATLANTIC MEDICAL SVCS	MME	HMOs	14.6	11.2	69
MID-AMERICA APT CMNTYS INC.	MAA	REITS	31.3	8.0	43
MID-ATLANTIC REALTY TRUST	MRR	REITS	38.8	16.6	79
MIDDLESEX WATER CO.	MSEX	Water Utilities	4.3	20.5	38
MIDLAND CO.	MLAN	Insurance (Property)	59.1	29.3	94
MILACRON INC.	MZ	Machinery	0.5	-4.1	29
MILLER (HERMAN) INC.	MLHR	Furniture Makers	-17.2	11.5	69
MILLIPORE CORP.	MIL	Medical Equipment	-2.9	9.1	37
MILLS CORP.	MLS	REITS	76.4	11.6	88
MINE SAFETY APPLIANCES CO.	MSA	Machinery	62.7	20.1	55
MINERALS TECHNOLOGIES INC.	MTX	Clay/Glass	36.8	2.9	48
MINNESOTA MINING & MFG CO.	MMM	Chemicals	0.2	10.0	53
MISSISSIPPI VY BANCSHARES	MVBI	Banks	35.1	14.4	96
MOBILE MINI INC.	MINI	Metal Products	70.1	65.8	85
MODINE MFG CO.	MODI	Auto-Parts Makers	16.9	0.5	17
MODIS PROFESSIONAL SVCS INC.	MPS	Employment	73.1	-19.5	25
MOHAWK INDUSTRIES INC.	MHK	Textiles	100.5	30.2	80
MOLECULAR DEVICES CORP.	MDCC	Measuring Devices	-69.5	6.1	34
MOLEX INC.	MOLX	Semiconductors	-12.5	9.3	45
MONACO COACH CORP.	MNC	Auto Makers	85.5	46.8	73
MONDAVI ROBERT CORP. -CL A	MOND	Alcoholic Drinks	-29.8	0.8	69
MONTANA POWER CO.	MTP	Electric Utilities	-72.3	-8.7	41
MOOG INC. -CL A	MOG.A	Metal Products	12.8	6.9	77
MORGAN STANLEY DEAN WITTER	MWD	Securities	-28.4	27.9	50
MOVADO GROUP INC.	MOV	Jewelry/Accessories	26.9	6.3	49
MOVIE GALLERY INC.	MOVI	Rental	1024.3	23.0	23
MSC INDUSTRIAL DIRECT -CL A	MSM	Machinery	9.3	1.3	53
MSC SOFTWARE CORP.	MNS	Computer Systems	98.7	14.7	26
MTR GAMING GROUP INC.	MNTG	Recreation	236.8	74.1	75
MTS SYSTEMS CORP.	MTSC	Measuring Devices	42.6	2.5	43

	TICKER	INDUSTRY	2001 TOT. RET.	5-YR. ANN. TOT. RET.	EASY-HOLD RANK
MUELLER INDUSTRIES	MLI	Nonferrous Metals	24.0	11.6	59
MURPHY OIL CORP.	MUR	Oil/Gas	41.9	14.2	87
MYERS INDUSTRIES INC.	MYE	Rubber Products	5.4	4.9	65
MYLAN LABORATORIES	MYL	Pharmaceuticals	49.7	18.5	48
N B T BANCORP. INC.	NBTB	Banks	3.5	8.5	41
NABI INC.	NABI	Home Health	123.1	3.4	10
NABORS INDUSTRIES	NBR	Oil/Gas Services	−42.0	12.3	27
NACCO INDUSTRIES -CL A	NC	Machinery	31.9	2.6	46
NANOMETRICS INC.	NANO	Measuring Devices	40.5	32.5	22
NATIONAL BEVERAGE CORP.	FIZ	Beverage Manufacturing	31.7	5.7	65
NATIONAL CITY CORP.	NCC	Banks	5.9	9.6	79
NATIONAL FUEL GAS CO.	NFG	Natural Gas Utilities	−18.3	7.8	69
NATIONAL GOLF PPTYS INC.	TEE	REITS	−52.9	−16.7	80
NATIONAL HEALTH INVS INC.	NHI	REITS	106.8	−9.0	32
NATIONAL HEALTHCARE CORP.	NHC	Home Health	99.9	−10.9	35
NATIONAL INSTRUMENTS CORP.	NATI	Software	−22.9	21.4	80
NATIONAL PRESTO INDS INC.	NPK	Electric Equipment	−3.5	−0.3	51
NATIONAL SEMICONDUCTOR CORP.	NSM	Semiconductors	53.0	4.7	8
NATIONAL SERVICE INDS INC.	NSI	Electric Equipment	−41.8	−14.5	55
NATIONWIDE HEALTH PPTYS INC.	NHP	REITS	61.2	4.6	60
NATL WSTN LIFE INS CO. -CL A	NWLIA	Insurance (Life)	7.9	5.0	31
NATURES SUNSHINE PRODS INC.	NATR	Pharmaceuticals	74.4	−7.2	61
NAUTICA ENTERPRISES INC.	NAUT	Apparel Makers	−16.0	−12.7	57
NAVISTAR INTERNATIONL	NAV	Truck Makers	50.9	34.1	24
NBTY INC.	NBTY	Diagnostics	146.3	13.1	67
NCH CORP.	NCH	Household Products	41.2	−0.2	43
NCI BUILDING SYSTEMS INC.	NCS	Metal Products	−5.9	0.5	71
NEIMAN-MARCUS GROUP INC.	NMG.A	Department Stores	−12.6	4.0	58
NEW ENGLAND BUSINESS SVC INC.	NEB	Printing	9.4	1.1	92
NEW HORIZONS WORLDWIDE INC.	NEWH	Education	−17.1	0.5	78
NEW JERSEY RESOURCES	NJR	Natural Gas Utilities	12.6	14.8	91
NEW PLAN EXCEL REALTY TR	NXL	REITS	60.0	3.1	84
NEW YORK CMNTY BANCORP. INC.	NYCB	Savings Institutions	43.5	33.4	73
NEW YORK TIMES CO. -CL A	NYT	Publishing	9.2	19.3	67
NEWELL RUBBERMAID INC.	NWL	Metal Products	25.3	−0.2	50
NEWFIELD EXPLORATION CO.	NFX	Oil/Gas	−25.1	6.4	84
NEWMONT MINING CORP.	NEM	Gold/Silver	12.7	−15.1	13
NEWPARK RESOURCES	NR	Engineering	−17.4	−3.2	10
NEWPORT CORP.	NEWP	Medical Equipment	−75.5	45.7	56
NICOR INC.	GAS	Natural Gas Utilities	0.8	7.5	50
NIKE INC. -CL B	NKE	Shoes	1.8	−0.3	15
NISOURCE INC.	NI	Electric Utilities	−21.7	7.6	69
NN INC.	NNBR	Metal Products	24.8	−2.5	52
NOBLE AFFILIATES INC.	NBL	Oil/Gas	−23.0	−5.4	47
NOBLE DRILLING CORP.	NE	Oil/Gas Services	−21.6	11.4	19
NORDSON CORP.	NDSN	Machinery	5.8	−1.9	52
NORDSTROM INC.	JWN	Department Stores	13.4	4.1	17
NORFOLK SOUTHERN CORP.	NSC	Rail Transport	39.5	−6.3	26
NORTEK INC.	NTK	Electric Equipment	17.8	6.9	90
NORTH PITTSBURGH SYSTEMS	NPSI	Telecommunications	76.1	−1.3	27
NORTHEAST UTILITIES	NU	Electric Utilities	−25.6	7.6	45
NORTHERN TRUST CORP.	NTRS	Banks	−25.4	28.5	91
NORTHROP GRUMMAN CORP.	NOC	Aerospace	23.7	6.2	52
NORTHWEST AIRLINES CORP.	NWAC	Air Transport	−47.9	−16.7	11
NORTHWEST BANCORP. INC.	NWSB	Savings Institutions	28.9	13.4	92
NORTHWEST NATURAL GAS CO	NWN	Oil/Gas	1.4	6.4	60
NORTHWESTERN CORP.	NOR	Electric Utilities	−3.9	9.5	100
NOVELL INC.	NOVL	Software	−12.0	−13.5	4
NOVELLUS SYSTEMS INC.	NVLS	Semiconductor Equipment	9.8	34.3	35
NSTAR	NST	Electric Utilities	10.1	16.7	74
NU HORIZONS ELECTRS CORP.	NUHC	Electronics Stores	15.0	15.3	54
NUCOR CORP.	NUE	Steel/Iron	35.5	2.0	31
NUI CORP.	NUI	Natural Gas Utilities	−23.2	5.0	63
NVR INC.	NVR	Home Building	65.0	73.4	99
O'REILLY AUTOMOTIVE INC.	ORLY	Auto Retail	36.3	35.4	67
OAKLEY INC.	OO	Medical Equipment	20.4	8.1	47

	TICKER	INDUSTRY	2001 TOT. RET.	5-YR. ANN. TOT. RET.	EASY-HOLD RANK
OCCIDENTAL PETROLEUM CORP.	OXY	Oil/Gas	13.8	7.1	86
OCEAN ENERGY INC.	OEI	Oil/Gas	11.5	-2.5	36
OCEANEERING INTERNATIONAL	OII	Oil/Gas Services	13.8	6.9	19
OFFICE DEPOT INC.	ODP	Stores (Misc.)	160.2	9.2	25
OFFSHORE LOGISTICS	OLOG	Oil/Gas Services	-17.6	-1.7	24
OGE ENERGY CORP.	OGE	Electric Utilities	0.3	8.1	79
OGLEBAY NORTON CO.	OGLE	Mining	-17.9	-3.8	63
OLD REPUBLIC INTL CORP.	ORI	Insurance (Property)	-10.6	11.9	55
OLD SECOND BANCORP. INC./IL	OSBC	Savings Institutions	69.8	16.5	84
OLIN CORP.	OLN	Chemicals	-23.8	-0.7	36
OM GROUP INC.	OMG	Chemicals	22.2	20.8	78
OMEGA FINL CORP.	OMEF	Savings Institutions	23.3	9.8	60
OMNICARE INC.	OCR	Medical Goods (Wholesale)	15.5	-4.6	24
ON ASSIGNMENT INC.	ASGN	Employment	-19.4	25.5	93
ONEOK INC.	OKE	Natural Gas Utilities	-23.5	7.5	70
OPTION CARE INC.	OPTN	Physicians	212.8	24.6	48
ORACLE CORP.	ORCL	Software	-52.5	24.4	48
ORTHODONTIC CENTERS OF AMER	OCA	Physicians	-2.4	13.8	64
OSHKOSH B'GOSH INC. -CL A	GOSHA	Apparel Makers	128.4	42.2	90
OSHKOSH TRUCK CORP.	OTRKB	Auto Makers	11.7	49.7	86
OSMONICS INC.	OSM	Measuring Devices	103.9	-8.6	40
OTTER TAIL CORP.	OTTR	Electric Utilities	9.2	18.4	84
OUTBACK STEAKHOUSE INC.	OSI	Restaurants	32.4	13.9	87
OWENS & MINOR INC.	OMI	Medical Goods (Wholesale)	5.8	14.4	50
OWENS-ILLINOIS INC.	OI	Clay/Glass	75.6	-15.2	17
OXFORD HEALTH PLANS INC.	OHP	HMOs	-23.7	-12.4	20
OXFORD INDUSTRIES INC.	OXM	Apparel Makers	60.8	3.3	57
PACCAR INC.	PCAR	Truck Makers	36.9	19.1	44
PACIFIC CAPITAL BANCORP.	SABB	Banks	1.9	17.8	100
PACIFIC CENTURY FINANCIAL CP	BOH	Savings Institutions	50.9	7.8	26
PACIFIC NORTHWEST BANCORP.	PNWB	Savings Institutions	52.3	1.7	62
PACIFIC SUNWEAR CALIF INC.	PSUN	Clothing Stores	-20.3	21.8	89
PACIFICARE HEALTH SYS	PHSY	HMOs	6.7	-28.4	30
PALL CORP.	PLL	Measuring Devices	16.3	1.7	47
PALM HARBOR HOMES INC.	PHHM	Home Building	52.1	6.0	9
PANERA BREAD CO.	PNRA	Restaurants	128.1	51.6	50
PAPA JOHNS INTERNATIONAL INC.	PZZA	Restaurants	23.5	-4.0	85
PARAMETRIC TECHNOLOGY CORP.	PMTC	Computer Systems	-41.9	-21.2	13
PAREXEL INTERNATIONAL CORP.	PRXL	Biotech	32.7	-11.1	11
PARK ELECTROCHEMICAL CORP.	PKE	Printed Circuit Boards	-13.1	13.0	24
PARKER DRILLING CO.	PKD	Oil/Gas Services	-27.1	-17.4	6
PARKER-HANNIFIN CORP.	PH	Machinery	5.8	14.0	68
PARKWAY PROPERTIES INC.	PKY	Real Estate	20.5	11.5	66
PATTERSON DENTAL CO.	PDCO	Medical Goods (Wholesale)	20.8	34.2	93
PATTERSON-UTI ENERGY INC.	PTEN	Oil/Gas Services	-37.4	29.3	38
PAXAR CORP.	PXR	Machinery	39.4	0.6	85
PAYCHEX INC.	PAYX	Business Services	-27.6	29.0	62
PEDIATRIX MEDICAL GROUP INC.	PDX	Physicians	41.0	-1.7	30
PENN ENGR & MFG CORP.	PNN	Electric Equipment	-3.1	12.4	79
PENN NATIONAL GAMING INC.	PENN	Recreation	197.8	16.3	82
PENN VIRGINIA CORP.	PVA	Oil/Gas	5.5	11.9	94
PENNFED FINANCIAL SVCS INC.	PFSB	Savings Institutions	46.9	20.9	66
PENNSYLVANIA RE INVS TRUST	PEI	REITS	32.8	8.5	88
PEOPLES BANK BRIDGEPORT CT	PBCT	Banks	-13.1	6.3	34
PEOPLES ENERGY CORP.	PGL	Natural Gas Utilities	-10.7	7.9	51
PEOPLESOFT INC.	PSFT	Software	8.1	11.3	29
PEPSIAMERICAS INC.	PAS	Beverage Manufacturing	-15.5	-0.2	62
PEPSICO INC.	PEP	Beverage Manufacturing	-0.5	14.1	32
PERFORMANCE TECHNOLOGIES INC.	PTIX	Phone/Network Equipment	-2.2	25.4	21
PERKINELMER INC.	PKI	Business Services	-32.7	30.5	38
PERRIGO COMPANY	PRGO	Pharmaceuticals	42.7	5.3	25
PFF BANCORP. INC.	PFB	Savings Institutions	33.6	13.8	84
PFIZER INC.	PFE	Pharmaceuticals	-12.5	24.7	83

	TICKER	INDUSTRY	2001 TOT. RET.	5-YR. ANN. TOT. RET.	EASY-HOLD RANK
PG&E CORP.	PCG	Electric Utilities	-3.8	1.9	51
PHARMACEUTICAL PROD DEV INC.	PPDI	Pharmaceuticals	30.1	20.7	85
PHARMACIA CORP.	PHA	Pharmaceuticals	-29.3	4.5	45
PHILADELPHIA CONS HLDG. CORP.	PHLY	Insurance (Property)	22.1	26.5	95
PHILADELPHIA SUBURBAN CORP.	PSC	Water Utilities	17.9	22.5	78
PHILIP MORRIS COS. INC.	MO	Tobacco	9.1	9.3	66
PHILLIPS PETROLEUM CO.	P	Oil/Gas	8.6	9.4	73
PHOENIX TECHNOLOGIES LTD.	PTEC	Software	-13.7	-6.3	13
PICO HOLDINGS INC.	PICO	Insurance (Property)	0.5	-9.5	4
PIEDMONT NATURAL GAS CO.	PNY	Natural Gas Utilities	-2.0	13.8	67
PIER 1 IMPORTS INC./DE	PIR	Furniture Retail	70.6	18.7	69
PINNACLE SYSTEMS INC.	PCLE	Cable/Wireless Equipment	7.7	24.8	35
PINNACLE WEST CAPITAL	PNW	Electric Utilities	-9.1	9.4	90
PIONEER STANDARD ELECTRONICS	PIOS	Electronics Stores	16.7	0.3	57
PITNEY BOWES INC.	PBI	Business Services	20.1	9.7	72
PITT-DES MOINES INC.	PDM	Metal Products	-3.7	20.5	15
PITTSTON COMPANY	PZB	Security Services	11.7	-3.5	50
PIXAR	PIXR	Entertainment	19.9	22.6	74
PLAINS RESOURCES INC.	PLX	Oil/Gas	16.5	9.5	81
PLANAR SYSTEMS INC.	PLNR	Computer Equipment	-15.2	12.4	42
PLANTRONICS INC.	PLT	Phone/Network Equipment	-45.4	27.9	73
PLATO LEARNING INC.	TUTR	Software	47.0	15.0	32
PLEXUS CORP.	PLXS	Printed Circuit Boards	-12.6	44.7	48
PLUM CREEK TIMBER CO. INC.	PCL	Forestry/Wood Product	20.6	10.7	32
PMC-SIERRA INC.	PMCS	Semiconductors	-73.0	41.5	48
PMI GROUP INC.	PMI	Insurance (Property)	-0.8	13.0	83
PNC FINANCIAL SVCS GROUP INC.	PNC	Banks	-20.8	11.9	61
POGO PRODUCING CO.	PPP	Oil/Gas	-15.2	-10.6	55
POLARIS INDS INC.	PII	Transportation Equipment	48.6	22.2	73
POMEROY COMPUTER RES INC.	PMRY	Office Equipment (Wholesale)	-11.5	-11.2	69
POPE & TALBOT INC.	POP	Forestry/Wood Product	-11.4	2.6	30
POPULAR INC.	BPOP	Savings Institutions	13.3	13.9	86
POST PROPERTIES INC.	PPS	REITS	2.9	4.7	70
POTOMAC ELECTRIC POWER	POM	Electric Utilities	-3.8	3.8	82
POWELL INDUSTRIES INC.	POWL	Electric Equipment	47.2	6.2	35
PPG INDUSTRIES INC.	PPG	Chemicals	15.2	1.1	46
PPL CORP.	PPL	Electric Utilities	-20.8	13.9	87
PRAXAIR INC.	PX	Chemicals	26.3	5.0	33
PRECISION CASTPARTS CORP.	PCP	Steel/Iron	-32.6	3.1	72
PREPAID LEGAL SERVICES INC.	PPD	Business Services	-14.1	3.7	74
PRESIDENTIAL LIFE CORP.	PLFE	Insurance (Life)	40.5	13.4	42
PRESSTEK INC.	PRST	Computer Systems	-12.7	-23.8	12
PRICE (T. ROWE) GROUP	TROW	Money Management	-16.3	11.2	74
PRIDE INTERNATIONAL INC.	PDE	Oil/Gas Services	-38.7	-8.3	7
PRIMA ENERGY CORP.	PENG	Oil/Gas	-37.9	26.7	75
PRIME HOSPITALITY CORP.	PDQ	Hotels	-4.9	-7.3	59
PROASSURANCE CORP.	PRA	Insurance (Property)	5.3	5.9	33
PROCTER & GAMBLE CO.	PG	Household Products	3.0	9.8	66
PROGRESS ENERGY INC.	PGN	Electric Utilities	-3.8	9.8	59
PROGRESS SOFTWARE CORP.	PRGS	Software	19.7	21.0	57
PROGRESSIVE CORP.-OHIO	PGR	Insurance (Property)	44.4	17.5	36
PROLOGIS TRUST	PLD	REITS	3.0	9.0	77
PROMISTAR FINANCIAL CORP.	PRFC	Banks	46.7	11.3	70
PROTECTIVE LIFE CORP.	PL	Insurance (Life)	-8.6	9.5	75
PROVIDENT BANKSHARES CORP.	PBKS	Savings Institutions	26.5	12.9	88
PROXIM INC.	PROX	Cable/Wireless Equipment	-76.9	-2.9	35
PS BUSINESS PARKS	PSB	REITS	18.6	14.9	92
PUBLIC SERVICE ENTRP	PEG	Electric Utilities	-8.9	15.8	83
PUBLIC STORAGE INC.	PSA	REITS	44.8	6.5	88
PUGET ENERGY INC.	PSD	Electric Utilities	-14.7	5.8	94
PULTE HOMES INC.	PHM	Home Building	6.3	24.5	92
QLOGIC CORP.	QLGC	Semiconductors	-42.2	69.1	62

	Ticker	Industry	2001 Tot. Ret.	5-Yr. Ann. Tot. Ret.	Easy-Hold Rank
QUAKER CHEMICAL CORP.	KWR	Oil/Gas Products	14.6	9.5	76
QUAKER CITY BANCORP. INC.	QCBC	Savings Institutions	17.6	19.7	99
QUAKER FABRIC CORP.	QFAB	Textiles	107.8	−2.3	54
QUALCOMM INC.	QCOM	Cable/Wireless Equipment	−38.6	59.6	47
QUANEX CORP.	NX	Steel/Iron	44.6	3.5	39
QUESTAR CORP.	STR	Natural Gas Utilities	−14.4	10.0	72
QUIKSILVER INC.	ZQK	Apparel Makers	−11.2	19.3	82
QUINTILES TRANSNATIONAL CORP.	QTRN	Biotech	−23.3	−13.5	65
RADIAN GROUP INC.	RDN	Insurance (General)	14.7	18.8	89
RADIOSHACK CORP.	RSH	Electronics Stores	−29.3	23.2	63
RADISYS CORP.	RSYS	Semiconductors	−24.0	−9.6	17
RAINBOW TECHNOLOGIES INC.	RNBO	Software	−53.2	3.6	16
RALCORP. HOLDINGS INC.	RAH	Food Manufacturing	38.6	17.6	52
RALSTON PURINA CO.	RAL	Food Manufacturing	29.4	16.1	38
RANGE RESOURCES CORP.	RRC	Oil/Gas	−33.8	−22.8	21
RARE HOSPITALITY INTL INC.	RARE	Restaurants	1.0	12.4	68
RAYMOND JAMES FINANCIAL CORP.	RJF	Securities	3.1	23.0	67
RAYONIER INC.	RYN	Forestry/Wood Product	30.9	8.9	34
RAYTHEON CO.	RTN	Measuring Devices	6.6	−5.6	17
READERS DIGEST ASSN -CL A	RDA	Publishing	−40.5	−8.8	39
REALTY INC.OME CORP.	O	REITS	28.1	13.4	91
RECKSON ASSOCS RLTY CORP.	RA	REITS	0.1	9.2	86
REDWOOD TRUST INC.	RWT	REITS	52.5	−2.2	37
REEBOK INTERNATIONAL LTD.	RBK	Shoes	−3.1	−8.8	22
REGAL BELOIT	RBC	Electric Equipment	31.0	4.4	40
REGENCY CENTERS CORP.	REG	REITS	26.9	9.4	79
REGIONS FINL CORP.	RGBK	Banks	13.8	6.4	91
REGIS CORP./MN	RGIS	Personal Svcs	78.9	19.6	87
REHABCARE GROUP INC.	RHB	Physicians	−42.4	34.6	84
REINSURANCE GROUP AMER INC.	RGA	Reinsurance	−5.6	10.4	59
RELIANCE STEEL & ALUMINUM CO.	RS	Aluminum	7.0	12.0	83
RELIANT ENERGY INC.	REI	Electric Utilities	−36.0	8.9	86
RENAL CARE GROUP INC.	RCI	HMOs	17.1	18.0	82
RENT-A-CENTER INC.	RCII	Rental	−2.7	18.3	96
REPUBLIC BANCORP. INC.	RBNC	Banks	44.5	20.1	70
RESMED INC.	RMD	Medical Equipment	35.2	57.9	74
RESOURCE AMERICA INC.	REXI	Oil/Gas	−17.8	10.1	27
RESPIRONICS INC.	RESP	Medical Equipment	21.5	14.8	19
REYNOLDS & REYNOLDS -CL A	REY	Printing	22.1	0.5	33
RFS HOTEL INVESTORS INC.	RFS	REITS	−4.7	−0.8	57
RGS ENERGY GROUP INC.	RGS	Electric Utilities	21.6	22.1	71
RICHARDSON ELEC LTD.	RELL	Electronics Stores	−10.8	9.8	56
RIGGS NATL CORP. WASH. D. C.	RIGS	Banks	1.5	−3.0	12
RIGHT MANAGEMENT CONSULTANTS	RMCI	Employment	147.1	11.8	32
RIGHTCHOICE MGD CARE	RIT	Insurance (Life)	101.0	45.8	66
RIVIANA FOODS INC.	RVFD	Food Manufacturing	−6.2	3.4	61
RLI CORP.	RLI	Insurance (Property)	2.2	12.7	37
ROADWAY CORPORATION	ROAD	Truck Transport	74.5	14.7	81
ROANOKE ELECTRIC STEEL CORP.	RESC	Steel/Iron	37.0	7.2	36
ROBBINS & MYERS INC.	RBN	Machinery	−2.2	−0.5	27
ROBERT HALF INTL INC.	RHI	Employment	0.8	18.6	92
ROCK-TENN COMPANY	RKT	Paper	99.0	−3.9	34
ROCKWELL INTL. CORP.	ROK	Machinery	−4.6	2.3	51
ROGERS CORP.	ROG	Machinery	−26.2	17.4	66
ROHM & HAAS CO.	ROH	Chemicals	−2.5	7.2	31
ROHN INDUSTRIES INC.	ROHN	Cable/Wireless Equipment	−46.0	−18.9	48
ROLLINS INC.	ROL	Business Services	0.7	1.8	60
ROPER INDUSTRIES INC./DE	ROP	Machinery	50.8	21.5	54
ROSS STORES INC.	ROST	Clothing Stores	91.0	21.5	68
ROWAN COS INC.	RDC	Oil/Gas Services	−28.3	−3.1	14
ROYAL BANCSHARES/PA -CL A	RBPAA	Banks	57.9	22.7	54
RPC INC.	RES	Oil/Gas Services	50.3	25.1	73
RPM INC.-OHIO	RPM	Paints/Coatings	77.6	5.0	63
RSA SECURITY INC.	RSAS	Computer Systems	−50.5	−3.6	37

	Ticker	Industry	2001 Tot. Ret.	5-Yr. Ann. Tot. Ret.	Easy-Hold Rank
RTI INTL METALS INC.	RTI	Aerospace	-30.5	-18.8	14
RUBY TUESDAY INC.	RI	Restaurants	35.6	35.0	90
RUDDICK CORP.	RDK	Groceries	43.1	5.0	57
RUSS BERRIE & CO. INC.	RUS	Clay/Glass	49.5	15.0	52
RUSSELL CORP.	RML	Apparel Makers	-0.2	-10.5	35
RYAN'S FAMILY STK HOUSES INC.	RYAN	Restaurants	129.4	25.8	92
RYDER SYSTEM INC.	R	Rental	37.0	-2.3	26
RYLAND GROUP INC.	RYL	Home Building	80.2	41.5	88
S & T BANCORP. INC.	STBA	Banks	16.6	13.4	63
S Y BANCORP. INC.	SYI	Banks	66.8	19.8	95
SAFEWAY INC.	SWY	Groceries	-33.2	14.3	91
SAGA COMMUNICATIONS -CL A	SGA	Radio	39.2	15.7	90
SAKS INC.	SKS	Department Stores	-6.6	-12.7	17
SALTON INC.	SFP	Electric Equipment	-8.7	32.3	93
SANDERSON FARMS INC.	SAFM	Food Manufacturing	189.3	6.9	67
SANDISK CORP.	SNDK	Computer Storage	-48.1	24.2	65
SANDY SPRING BANCORP. INC.	SASR	Banks	115.5	27.8	96
SAPIENT CORP.	SAPE	Consultants	-35.3	8.0	33
SARA LEE CORP.	SLE	Food Manufacturing	-7.0	6.0	65
SBC COMMUNICATIONS INC.	SBC	Telecommunications	-16.0	11.1	78
SBS TECHNOLOGIES INC.	SBSE	Measuring Devices	-51.3	-4.7	73
SCANA CORP.	SCG	Electric Utilities	-1.6	5.9	67
SCANSOURCE INC.	SCSC	Office Equipment (Wholesale)	22.1	25.4	93
SCHAWK INC. -CL A	SGK	Printing	27.4	6.7	67
SCHEIN HENRY INC.	HSIC	Medical Goods (Wholesale)	6.9	1.5	40
SCHERING-PLOUGH	SGP	Pharmaceuticals	-35.9	18.7	90
SCHOLASTIC CORP.	SCHL	Publishing	13.6	8.4	46
SCHULER HOMES INC. -CL A	SHLR	Home Building	120.6	26.0	99
SCHULMAN (A.) INC.	SHLM	Chemicals	24.1	-8.2	22
SCHWAB (CHARLES) CORP.	SCH	Securities	-45.3	27.1	56
SCHWEITZER-MAUDUIT INTL INC.	SWM	Paper	27.5	-2.6	48
SCI SYSTEMS INC.	SCI	Printed Circuit Boards	25.9	24.4	39
SCIENTIFIC-ATLANTA INC.	SFA	Cable/Wireless Equipment	-26.4	26.4	61
SCOTTS COMPANY	SMG	Agrochemicals	28.9	19.1	80
SCP POOL CORP.	POOL	Sporting Goods	37.0	46.3	91
SEACOAST BANKING CORP./FL	SBCFA	Banks	80.5	15.8	72
SEACOR SMIT INC.	CKH	Oil/Gas Services	-11.8	2.0	15
SEALED AIR CORP.	SEE	Plastics	33.8	-0.4	25
SEARS ROEBUCK & CO.	S	Department Stores	40.1	2.9	64
SECOND BANCORP. INC.	SECD	Banks	54.5	9.6	68
SEI INVESTMENTS CO.	SEIC	Business Services	-19.3	65.5	75
SEITEL INC.	SEI	Engineering	-26.2	-7.4	19
SELECTIVE INS GROUP INC.	SIGI	Insurance (Property)	-8.1	5.7	56
SEMCO ENERGY INC.	SEN	Natural Gas Utilities	-26.6	-3.4	29
SEMITOOL INC.	SMTL	Semiconductor Equipment	18.5	19.3	37
SEMPRA ENERGY	SRE	Natural Gas Utilities	9.9	9.9	91
SEMTECH CORP.	SMTC	Semiconductors	61.8	75.6	53
SENSIENT TECHNOLOGIES CORP.	SXT	Food Manufacturing	-6.1	6.1	42
SEQUA CORP. -CL A	SQA.A	Aerospace	30.6	3.9	26
SEROLOGICALS CORP.	SERO	Pharmaceuticals	42.7	6.5	23
SERVICE CORP. INTERNATIONAL	SRV	Personal Svcs	185.1	-28.6	12
SERVICEMASTER CO.	SVM	Business Services	24.3	6.2	87
SHAW GROUP INC.	SGR	Metal Products	-53.0	15.0	25
SHERWIN-WILLIAMS CO.	SHW	Paints/Coatings	7.1	1.6	27
SHUFFLE MASTER INC.	SHFL	Machinery	48.1	31.8	69
SHURGARD STORAGE CTRS -CL A	SHU	REITS	40.8	9.6	66
SIERRA HEALTH SERVICES	SIE	HMOs	113.2	-13.2	33
SILICON VY BANCSHARES	SIVB	Savings Institutions	-22.7	27.1	87
SILICONIX INC.	SILI	Semiconductors	21.9	28.5	61
SIMMONS FIRST NATL. CP -CL A	SFNCA	Savings Institutions	46.6	6.1	86
SIMON PROPERTY GROUP INC.	SPG	REITS	31.7	6.1	66
SIMPSON MANUFACTURING INC.	SSD	Metal Products	12.4	20.0	85
SIPEX CORP.	SIPX	Semiconductors	-46.3	-4.4	4

	TICKER	INDUSTRY	2001 TOT. RET.	5-YR. ANN. TOT. RET.	EASY-HOLD RANK
SITEL CORP.	SWW	Business Services	−16.5	−30.0	25
SJW CORP.	SJW	Water Utilities	−13.7	16.6	21
SKY FINANCIAL GROUP INC.	SKYF	Savings Institutions	26.2	13.9	76
SKYLINE CORP.	SKY	Home Building	75.0	8.3	27
SKYWEST INC.	SKYW	Air Transport	−11.2	49.8	69
SLI INC.	SLI	Electric Equipment	−58.5	−36.8	51
SMART & FINAL INC.	SMF	Groceries	22.8	−13.0	33
SMITH (A O) CORP.	AOS	Electric Equipment	17.8	1.9	62
SMITH INTERNATIONAL INC.	SII	Machinery	−28.1	3.6	21
SMITHFIELD FOODS INC.	SFD	Food Manufacturing	45.0	18.3	69
SMUCKER (JM) CO.	SJM	Food Manufacturing	29.5	18.0	61
SMURFIT-STONE CONTAINER CORP.	SSCC	Paper	6.9	−0.1	53
SNAP-ON INC.	SNA	Metal Products	24.9	1.7	44
SOLECTRON CORP.	SLR	Printed Circuit Boards	−66.7	11.1	72
SONIC CORP.	SONC	Restaurants	54.4	26.0	66
SONOCO PRODUCTS CO.	SON	Paper	27.0	5.6	39
SOUTH FINANCIAL GROUP INC.	TSFG	Banks	37.7	4.0	27
SOUTH JERSEY INDUSTRIES	SJI	Natural Gas Utilities	14.9	11.8	73
SOUTHERN CO.	SO	Electric Utilities	27.9	18.3	68
SOUTHERN PERU COPPER	PCU	Mining	−4.5	−0.4	31
SOUTHERN UNION CO.	SUG	Natural Gas Utilities	−25.3	10.4	36
SOUTHTRUST CORP.	SOTR	Banks	24.2	19.2	76
SOUTHWEST AIRLINES	LUV	Air Transport	−17.2	33.7	80
SOUTHWEST GAS CORP.	SWX	Natural Gas Utilities	6.1	7.1	63
SOUTHWEST SECURITIES GROUP	SWS	Securities	10.3	22.6	49
SOUTHWESTERN ENERGY CO.	SWN	Oil/Gas	0.2	−5.5	31
SOVEREIGN BANCORP. INC.	SOV	Savings Institutions	52.2	7.0	63
SOVRAN SELF STORAGE INC.	SSS	REITS	72.0	9.3	76
SPEEDWAY MOTORSPORTS INC.	TRK	Recreation	5.3	3.8	73
SPHERION CORP.	SFN	Employment	−13.7	−11.3	71
SPS TECHNOLOGIES INC.	ST	Steel/Iron	−36.3	1.7	84
SPSS INC.	SPSS	Software	−19.5	−8.6	30
SPX CORP.	SPW	Metal Products	26.5	18.5	30
ST. FRANCIS CAP CORP.	STFR	Savings Institutions	80.1	14.3	83
ST. JOE CO.	JOE	Real Estate	26.6	16.9	77
ST. JUDE MEDICAL INC.	STJ	Medical Equipment	26.4	12.9	49
ST. MARY LAND & EXPLOR CO.	MARY	Oil/Gas	−36.1	12.0	41
ST. PAUL COS	SPC	Insurance (General)	−17.0	11.4	23
STANDARD COMMERCIAL CORP.	STW	Tobacco	145.2	−1.5	20
STANDARD MOTOR PRODS	SMP	Truck Makers	94.1	2.3	29
STANDARD PACIFIC CP	SPF	Home Building	5.6	34.5	87
STANDEX INTERNATIONAL CORP.	SXI	Machinery	9.4	−3.5	56
STANLEY FURNITURE CO. INC.	STLY	Furniture Makers	−1.5	19.1	86
STANLEY WORKS	SWK	Metal Products	53.0	14.5	39
STAPLES INC.	SPLS	Stores (Misc.)	58.3	18.4	41
STARBUCKS CORP.	SBUX	Restaurants	−13.9	21.6	71
STATE AUTO FINL CORP.	STFC	Insurance (Property)	−8.4	13.5	77
STATE STREET CORP.	STT	Securities	−15.2	27.5	66
STATION CASINOS INC.	STN	Gambling	−25.1	10.6	41
STEAK N SHAKE CO.	SNS	Restaurants	60.6	1.4	78
STEIN MART INC.	SMRT	Clothing Stores	−28.1	−3.8	46
STEPAN CO.	SCL	Household Products	5.7	6.3	64
STERIS CORP.	STE	Medical Equipment	13.3	−3.4	13
STERLING BANCORP./NY	STL	Banks	50.5	23.2	87
STERLING BANCSHRS/TX	SBIB	Banks	−3.8	19.1	94
STEWART & STEVENSON SERVICES	SSSS	Machinery	−15.8	−6.5	21
STEWART ENTERPRISES -CL A	STEI	Personal Svcs	214.2	−18.4	25
STEWART INFO SVCS	STC	Insurance (Title)	−11.0	14.3	39
STILLWATER MINING CO.	SWC	Mining	−53.0	8.9	86
STONE ENERGY CORP.	SGY	Oil/Gas Services	−38.8	5.7	89
STORAGE TECHNOLOGY CP	STK	Computer Storage	129.7	−2.9	9
STORAGE USA INC.	SUS	REITS	43.0	10.5	58
STRIDE RITE CORP.	SRR	Shoes	−4.0	−5.9	39
STRYKER CORP.	SYK	Medical Equipment	15.6	31.6	72
STUDENT LOAN CORP.	STU	Finance	54.1	20.6	93
STURM RUGER & CO. INC.	RGR	Metal Products	37.2	−2.8	42
SUFFOLK BANCORP.	SUBK	Banks	81.3	26.8	88

	Ticker	Industry	2001 Tot. Ret.	5-Yr. Ann. Tot. Ret.	Easy-Hold Rank
SUMMIT PROPERTIES INC.	SMT	REITS	3.7	11.1	98
SUN COMMUNITIES INC.	SUI	REITS	18.3	7.8	83
SUNGARD DATA SYSTEMS INC.	SDS	Computer Systems	22.8	24.0	90
SUNOCO INC.	SUN	Oil/Gas Products	13.9	12.3	91
SUNRISE ASSISTED LIVING INC.	SRZ	Nursing	16.4	0.9	88
SUNTRUST BANKS INC.	STI	Banks	2.0	7.1	72
SUPERIOR ENERGY SERVICES INC.	SPN	Oil/Gas Services	−24.8	23.6	77
SUPERIOR INDUSTRIES INTL.	SUP	Auto-Parts Makers	29.0	13.0	59
SUPERTEX INC.	SUPX	Semiconductors	−11.4	5.9	10
SUPERVALU INC.	SVU	Food Wholesale	64.5	12.3	58
SUSQUEHANNA BANCSHARES INC.	SUSQ	Banks	31.5	10.1	91
SWIFT ENERGY CO.	SFY	Oil/Gas	−46.3	−5.7	65
SWIFT TRANSPORTATION CO. INC.	SWFT	Truck Transport	8.6	15.5	50
SYKES ENTERPRISES INC.	SYKE	Computer Systems	110.5	−17.9	24
SYMANTEC CORP.	SYMC	Software	98.7	35.5	39
SYMBOL TECHNOLOGIES	SBL	Computer Equipment	−33.8	22.3	52
SYMMETRICOM INC.	SYMM	Phone/Network Equipment	−21.9	−10.5	13
SYNCOR INTL CORP./DE	SCOR	Medical Goods (Wholesale)	−21.3	33.8	68
SYSCO CORP.	SYY	Food Wholesale	−11.7	27.9	84
SYSTEMS & COMPUTER TECH. CORP.	SCTC	Computer Programming	−16.0	5.3	14
TALBOTS INC.	TLB	Clothing Stores	−19.9	21.9	47
TANGER FACTORY OUTLET CTRS.	SKT	REITS	2.2	4.6	33
TARGET CORP.	TGT	Department Stores	28.0	34.2	78
TBC CORP.	TBCC	Auto-Parts Makers	193.5	12.3	51
TECH DATA CORP.	TECD	Office Equipment (Wholesale)	60.0	9.6	54
TECHNE CORP.	TECH	Diagnostics	2.2	41.5	74
TECHNITROL INC.	TNL	Phone/Network Equipment	−32.5	24.4	74
TECO ENERGY INC.	TE	Electric Utilities	−15.0	7.1	73
TECUMSEH PRODUCTS CO. -CL A	TECUA	Environment Control	23.9	0.0	33
TEJON RANCH CO.	TRC	Agriculture	24.3	10.9	29
TEKELEC	TKLC	Cable/Wireless Equipment	−39.6	35.7	47
TEKTRONIX INC.	TEK	Measuring Devices	−23.5	9.6	20
TELEFLEX INC.	TFX	Aerospace	8.6	14.2	88
TELLABS INC.	TLAB	Phone/Network Equipment	−73.5	−4.5	81
TEMPLE-INLAND INC.	TIN	Paper	8.3	3.3	52
TENET HEALTHCARE CORP.	THC	Hospitals	32.1	21.8	55
TENNANT CO.	TNC	Machinery	−21.1	8.4	85
TERADYNE INC.	TER	Measuring Devices	−19.1	19.9	64
TEREX CORP.	TEX	Construction Machinery	8.4	11.6	91
TESORO PETROLEUM CORP.	TSO	Oil/Gas Products	12.8	−1.3	62
TETRA TECH INC.	TTEK	Engineering	−21.9	19.7	81
TEXAS INDUSTRIES INC.	TXI	Steel/Iron	24.1	8.8	25
TEXTRON INC.	TXT	Aerospace	−8.2	−0.5	60
THERAGENICS CORP.	TGX	Diagnostics	97.2	−2.7	72
THERMO ELECTRON CORP.	TMO	Medical Equipment	−7.1	−7.7	16
THOMAS INDUSTRIES INC.	TII	Machinery	8.9	14.1	60
THOR INDUSTRIES INC.	THO	Truck Makers	88.1	17.5	75
THORNBURG MORTGAGE INC.	TMA	REITS	145.2	8.9	27
THQ INC.	THQI	Software	98.9	63.4	58
THREE-FIVE SYSTEMS INC.	TFS	Semiconductors	−11.6	19.8	13
TIDEWATER INC.	TDW	Oil/Gas Services	−22.3	−4.0	11
TIFFANY & CO.	TIF	Jewelry/Accessories	0.1	28.7	58
TIMBERLAND CO. -CL A	TBL	Shoes	−44.6	31.3	86
TIMKEN CO.	TKR	Metal Products	11.6	−3.3	8
TITAN CORP.	TTN	Computer Systems	53.5	49.2	56
TJX COMPANIES INC.	TJX	Clothing Stores	44.4	28.2	72
TOLL BROTHERS INC.	TOL	Home Building	7.4	17.6	99
TOLLGRADE COMMUNICATIONS INC.	TLGD	Measuring Devices	−8.6	16.6	66
TOMPKINSTRUSTCO INC.	TMP	Savings Institutions	48.5	16.4	99
TOOTSIE ROLL INDUSTRIES INC.	TR	Food Manufacturing	−12.0	18.7	71
TORCHMARK CORP.	TMK	Insurance (Life)	3.3	13.9	71

	Ticker	Industry	2001 Tot. Ret.	5-Yr. Ann. Tot. Ret.	Easy-Hold Rank
TORO CO.	TTC	Agricultural Machinery	24.0	5.7	68
TOTAL SYSTEM SERVICES INC.	TSS	Data Processing	–5.1	3.6	87
TOWER AUTOMOTIVE INC.	TWR	Metal Products	0.3	–10.4	42
TOWN & COUNTRY TRUST	TCT	REITS	17.9	18.2	89
TOYS R US INC.	TOY	Toys	24.3	–7.0	12
TRANS WORLD ENTMT CORP.	TWMC	Stores (Misc.)	–15.0	26.1	76
TRANSATLANTIC HOLDINGS INC.	TRH	Reinsurance	29.5	21.2	64
TRC COS INC.	TRR	Engineering	158.1	61.9	59
TREDEGAR CORP.	TG	Aluminum	9.9	8.1	62
TREMONT CORP.	TRE	Nonferrous Metals	–8.7	–3.6	25
TRIAD GUARANTY INC.	TGIC	Insurance (Property)	9.5	20.3	98
TRIARC COS INC. -CL A	TRY	Beverage Manufacturing	0.2	16.1	71
TRIBUNE CO.	TRB	Publishing	–10.4	14.9	46
TRIMBLE NAVIGATION LTD	TRMB	Cable/Wireless Equipment	–32.5	7.1	26
TRIQUINT SEMICONDUCTOR INC.	TQNT	Semiconductors	–71.9	22.8	60
TRNSACTN SYS ARCHTCTS -CL A	TSAI	Software	6.0	–18.1	10
TRUST CO NJ JERSEY CITY	TCNJ	Banks	106.1	15.5	77
TRUSTCO BANK CORP./NY	TRST	Banks	24.1	20.8	54
TRUSTMARK CORP.	TRMK	Banks	18.2	16.2	70
TRW INC.	TRW	Auto-Parts Makers	–1.4	–3.0	38
TUPPERWARE CORP.	TUP	Plastics	–1.9	–15.1	23
TXU CORP.	TXU	Electric Utilities	12.1	9.1	81
TYSON FOODS INC. -CL A	TSN	Food Manufacturing	–8.2	–11.9	15
U S B HOLDING INC.	UBH	Banks	37.2	20.8	96
U S BANCORP.	USB	Banks	–6.9	18.2	79
U S INDUSTRIES INC.	USI	Metal Products	–68.0	–34.9	21
U S PHYSICAL THERAPY INC.	USPH	Physicians	104.1	37.8	64
UGI CORP.	UGI	Natural Gas Utilities	26.5	13.1	56
UICI	UCI	Insurance (Property)	127.4	–16.1	13
UIL HOLDINGS CORP.	UIL	Electric Utilities	9.3	17.8	31
ULTRAMAR DIAMOND SHAMROCK	UDS	Oil/Gas Products	62.7	13.4	96
UMB FINANCIAL CORP.	UMBF	Banks	14.6	5.7	91
UNIFIRST CORP.	UNF	Personal Svcs	121.9	2.1	58
UNION PACIFIC CORP.	UNP	Rail Transport	14.0	0.8	53
UNION PLANTERS CORP.	UPC	Savings Institutions	32.6	7.7	65
UNIONBANCAL CORP.	UB	Banks	62.7	19.7	67
UNISOURCE ENERGY CORP.	UNS	Electric Utilities	–1.2	2.8	60
UNIT CORP.	UNT	Oil/Gas	–31.9	5.5	51
UNITED BANKSHARES INC./WV	UBSI	Banks	40.6	15.8	69
UNITED DOMINION REALTY TRUST	UDR	REITS	44.7	7.1	44
UNITED FIRE & CAS CO.	UFCS	Insurance (Property)	48.9	–1.6	49
UNITED INDUSTRIAL CORP.	UIC	Measuring Devices	54.5	27.9	23
UNITED NATIONAL BANCORP./NJ	UNBJ	Banks	29.8	14.2	75
UNITED STATIONERS INC.	USTR	Office Equipment (Wholesale)	35.3	28.1	89
UNITED TECHNOLOGIES CORP.	UTX	Aerospace	–16.8	15.9	75
UNITEDHEALTH GROUP INC.	UNH	Physicians	15.4	25.8	55
UNITRIN INC.	UTR	Insurance (Life)	8.9	13.4	41
UNIVERSAL AMERICAN FINL CP	UHCO	Insurance (Life)	72.4	24.7	97
UNIVERSAL CORP./VA	UVV	Tobacco	8.8	6.9	56
UNIVERSAL ELECTRONICS INC.	UEIC	Communications Equipment	11.5	44.3	36
UNIVERSAL FOREST PRODS INC.	UFPI	Forestry/Wood Product	58.7	10.1	74
UNIVERSAL HEALTH RLTY INCOME	UHT	REITS	28.5	12.6	67
UNIVERSAL HEALTH SVCS. -CL B	UHS	Hospitals	–23.4	24.5	67
UNOCAL CORP.	UCL	Oil/Gas	–4.6	–0.2	73
UNUMPROVIDENT CORP.	UNM	Insurance (Life)	0.8	–4.4	33
URBAN OUTFITTERS INC.	URBN	Clothing Stores	203.9	13.2	21
URS CORP.	URS	Engineering	86.6	24.9	96
US CELLULAR CORP.	USM	Wireless Communications	–24.9	10.2	72
US ONCOLOGY INC.	USON	HMOs	19.4	–6.0	49
USA EDUCATION INC.	SLM	Finance	24.7	27.6	46
USFREIGHTWAYS CORP.	USFC	Truck Transport	5.7	4.0	75
USG CORP.	USG	Clay/Glass	–74.5	–29.5	30
UST INC.	UST	Tobacco	32.1	8.2	55

	Ticker	Industry	2001 Tot. Ret.	5-Yr. Ann. Tot. Ret.	Easy-Hold Rank
USX-MARATHON GROUP	MRO	Oil/Gas	11.5	7.8	60
UTILICORP. UNITED INC.	UCU	Electric Utilities	-15.6	12.6	98
VALHI INC.	VHI	Chemicals	12.6	17.0	65
VALMONT INDUSTRIES	VALM	Electric Equipment	-20.0	-5.5	42
VALSPAR CORP.	VAL	Paints/Coatings	25.0	8.5	66
VALUE LINE INC.	VALU	Publishing	43.8	13.3	61
VANS INC.	VANS	Shoes	-24.8	0.4	52
VARCO INTERNATIONAL INC.	VRC	Oil/Gas Services	-31.1	-0.7	11
VARIAN MEDICAL SYTEMS INC.	VAR	Measuring Devices	4.9	25.9	39
VERITAS DGC INC.	VTS	Oil/Gas Services	-42.7	0.0	8
VERITAS SOFTWARE CO.	VRTS	Software	-48.8	55.6	69
VERIZON COMMUNICATIONS	VZ	Telecommunications	-2.6	11.3	93
VESTA INSURANCE GROUP INC.	VTA	Insurance (Property)	59.7	-23.4	15
VF CORP.	VFC	Apparel Makers	10.6	5.4	63
VIAD CORP.	VVI	Business Services	4.6	9.3	77
VICOR CORP.	VICR	Measuring Devices	-46.7	-0.6	18
VINTAGE PETROLEUM INC.	VPI	Oil/Gas	-32.3	-3.0	53
VISHAY INTRTECHNOLOGY	VSH	Semiconductors	28.9	11.6	76
VISX INC./DE	EYE	Medical Equipment	26.9	19.1	54
VITAL SIGNS INC.	VITL	Medical Equipment	9.2	6.8	70
VITESSE SEMICONDUCTOR CORP.	VTSS	Semiconductors	-77.5	10.4	41
VOLT INFO SCIENCES INC.	VOL	Employment	-17.6	-10.1	13
VORNADO REALTY TRUST	VNO	REITS	16.1	15.7	80
VULCAN MATERIALS CO.	VMC	Nonmetal Mining	2.1	21.1	71
W HOLDING COMPANY INC.	WHI	Banks	42.0	27.7	98
WACHOVIA CORP.	WB	Banks	16.1	0.5	46
WACKENHUT CORP. -SER A	WAK	Security Services	83.7	8.2	86
WACKENHUT CORRECTIONS CORP.	WHC	Business Services	87.9	-7.1	80
WALGREEN CO.	WAG	Stores (Misc.)	-19.2	28.1	93
WALLACE COMPUTER SVCS INC.	WCS	Printing	16.0	-8.2	38
WAL-MART STORES	WMT	Department Stores	8.9	39.0	80
WASHINGTON FED INC.	WFSL	Savings Institutions	3.6	11.8	55
WASHINGTON MUTUAL INC.	WM	Savings Institutions	-5.3	14.0	87
WASHINGTON POST -CL B	WPO	Publishing	-13.2	10.7	52
WASHINGTON REIT	WRE	REITS	11.3	14.3	91
WASHINGTON TR BANCORP. INC.	WASH	Banks	39.6	9.2	95
WASTE MANAGEMENT INC.	WMI	Waste	15.0	0.1	17
WATERS CORP.	WAT	Measuring Devices	-53.6	38.5	79
WATSCO INC.	WSO	Electronics Stores	24.2	-5.3	52
WATTS INDUSTRIES -CL A	WTS	Metal Products	9.8	-0.9	45
WAUSAU-MOSINEE PAPER CORP.	WMO	Paper	23.0	-6.1	13
WD-40 CO.	WDFC	Oil/Gas Products	44.7	6.3	43
WEATHERFORD INTL INC.	WFT	Oil/Gas Services	-21.1	16.4	16
WEBSTER FINL CORP. WATERBURY	WBST	Savings Institutions	13.8	13.6	69
WEIS MARKETS INC.	WMK	Groceries	-24.6	0.3	55
WELLMAN INC.	WLM	Chemicals	12.2	0.3	13
WELLPOINT HLTH NETWRK -CL A	WLP	Physicians	1.4	27.7	87
WELLS FARGO & CO.	WFC	Banks	-20.2	17.2	76
WENDY'S INTERNATIONAL INC.	WEN	Restaurants	12.1	8.4	62
WERNER ENTERPRISES INC.	WERN	Truck Transport	43.7	11.5	43
WESBANCO INC.	WSBC	Banks	-6.1	3.0	34
WESCO FINANCIAL CORP.	WSC	Reinsurance	12.2	11.4	95
WEST COAST BANCORP./OR	WCBO	Savings Institutions	46.1	10.6	68
WEST PHARMACEUTICAL SVSC INC.	WST	Plastics	11.4	1.1	29
WESTAMERICA BANCORP.ORATION	WABC	Banks	-6.0	17.8	47
WESTCORP.	WES	Savings Institutions	27.4	-1.0	57
WESTERN GAS RESOURCES INC.	WGR	Oil/Gas	-3.4	12.3	39
WESTVACO CORP.	W	Paper	0.8	3.0	28
WESTWOOD ONE INC.	WON	Radio	55.6	29.3	40
WET SEAL INC. -CL A	WTSLA	Clothing Stores	71.8	10.6	42
WEYERHAUSER CO.	WY	Forestry/Wood Product	9.8	5.9	58
WFS FINANCIAL INC.	WFSI	Finance	29.8	3.9	60
WGL HOLDINGS INC.	WGL	Natural Gas Utilities	-0.1	10.2	49
WHIRLPOOL CORP.	WHR	Electric Equipment	57.2	12.2	60
WHITNEY HOLDING CORP.	WTNY	Banks	25.1	7.8	61
WHOLE FOODS MARKET INC.	WFMI	Groceries	42.5	31.1	42
WILEY (JOHN) & SONS -CL A	JW.A	Publishing	8.0	24.4	87

	TICKER	INDUSTRY	2001 TOT. RET.	5-YR. ANN. TOT. RET.	EASY-HOLD RANK
WILLAMETTE INDUSTRIES	WLL	Paper	13.2	10.6	78
WILLIAMS COS. INC.	WMB	Oil/Gas	−29.4	10.1	50
WILLIAMS-SONOMA INC.	WSM	Furniture Retail	114.5	18.7	49
WILMINGTON TRUST CORP.	WL	Banks	5.3	13.3	76
WINN-DIXIE STORES INC.	WIN	Groceries	−23.9	−11.7	38
WINNEBAGO INDUSTRIES	WGO	Truck Makers	111.6	40.4	84
WINSTON HOTELS INC.	WXH	REITS	21.6	0.0	39
WISCONSIN ENERGY CORP.	WEC	Electric Utilities	3.5	2.1	85
WMS INDUSTRIES INC.	WMS	Misc. Manufacturing	−0.6	47.9	43
WOLVERINE TUBE INC.	WLV	Nonferrous Metals	−5.3	−20.3	46
WOLVERINE WORLD WIDE	WWW	Shoes	−0.3	−4.0	15
WOODHEAD INDUSTRIES INC.	WDHD	Electric Equipment	−17.3	5.3	43
WOODWARD GOVERNOR CO.	WGOV	Aerospace	32.1	15.4	54
WORLD ACCEPTANCE CP/DE	WRLD	Finance	32.7	1.2	93
WORLDCOM INC.-WORLDCOM GROUP	WCOM	Telecommunications	5.4	−3.1	55
WORTHINGTON INDUSTRIES	WOR	Steel/Iron	85.9	−0.4	37
WPS RESOURCES CORP.	WPS	Electric Utilities	5.5	12.2	76
WRIGLEY (WM) JR. CO.	WWY	Food Manufacturing	8.9	14.7	75
WSFS FINL CORP.	WSFS	Savings Institutions	36.1	12.1	65
XANSER CORP.	XNR	Oil/Gas	−8.3	10.6	97
XCEL ENERGY INC.	XEL	Electric Utilities	0.6	10.0	82
XILINX INC.	XLNX	Semiconductors	−15.3	33.5	26
X-RITE INC.	XRIT	Measuring Devices	10.3	−11.5	34
XTO ENERGY INC.	XTO	Oil/Gas	−5.2	29.5	85
YELLOW CORP.	YELL	Truck Transport	23.3	11.8	60
YORK INTL.	YRK	Environment Control	26.6	−5.8	50
ZEBRA TECHNOLOGIES CP -CL A	ZBRA	Computer Equipment	36.1	18.9	70
ZIONS BANCORP.ORATION	ZION	Banks	−14.5	16.8	90
ZOLL MEDICAL CORP.	ZOLL	Medical Equipment	11.1	29.4	71
ZORAN CORP.	ZRAN	Semiconductors	110.6	12.6	6
ZYGO CORP.	ZIGO	Optical Equipment	−43.8	−9.4	6

APPENDIX C: "EASY-HOLD" STOCKS BY INDUSTRY

	Ticker	Industry	Easy-Hold Rank
HARTE HANKS INC.	HHS	Advertising	81
CATALINA MARKETING CORP.	POS	Advertising	79
INTERPUBLIC GROUP OF COS.	IPG	Advertising	77
GREY GLOBAL GROUP INC.	GREY	Advertising	51
CURTISS-WRIGHT CORP.	CW	Aerospace	96
HEICO CORP.	HEI	Aerospace	93
TELEFLEX INC.	TFX	Aerospace	88
UNITED TECHNOLOGIES CORP.	UTX	Aerospace	75
GENCORP. INC.	GY	Aerospace	67
TEXTRON INC.	TXT	Aerospace	60
WOODWARD GOVERNOR CO.	WGOV	Aerospace	54
BOEING CO.	BA	Aerospace	53
NORTHROP GRUMMAN CORP.	NOC	Aerospace	52
HONEYWELL INTERNATIONAL INC.	HON	Aerospace	44
TORO CO.	TTC	Agricultural Machinery	68
LINDSAY MANUFACTURING CO.	LNN	Agricultural Machinery	28
DEERE & CO.	DE	Agricultural Machinery	19
AGCO CORP.	AG	Agricultural Machinery	6
DELTA & PINE LAND CO.	DLP	Agriculture	88
ALICO INC.	ALCO	Agriculture	53
TEJON RANCH CO.	TRC	Agriculture	29
SCOTTS COMPANY	SMG	Agrochemicals	80
SOUTHWEST AIRLINES	LUV	Air Transport	80
MESABA HOLDINGS INC.	MAIR	Air Transport	78
ATLAS AIR WORLDWIDE HLDG INC.	CGO	Air Transport	78
SKYWEST INC.	SKYW	Air Transport	69
FEDEX CORP.	FDX	Air Transport	62
CONTINENTAL AIRLS INC. -CL B	CAL	Air Transport	57
FORWARD AIR CORP.	FWRD	Air Transport	57
ATLANTIC COAST AIRLINES HLDG	ACAI	Air Transport	53
CNF INC.	CNF	Air Transport	50
DELTA AIR LINES INC.	DAL	Air Transport	37
COORS (ADOLPH) -CL B	RKY	Alcoholic Drinks	84
BROWN-FORMAN -CL B	BF.B	Alcoholic Drinks	80
MONDAVI ROBERT CORP. -CL A	MOND	Alcoholic Drinks	69
ANHEUSER-BUSCH COS. INC.	BUD	Alcoholic Drinks	69
BOSTON BEER INC. -CL A	SAM	Alcoholic Drinks	43
RELIANCE STEEL & ALUMINUM CO.	RS	Aluminum	83
ALCOA INC.	AA	Aluminum	64
TREDEGAR CORP.	TG	Aluminum	62
CENTURY ALUMINUM CO.	CENX	Aluminum	26
GARAN INC.	GAN	Apparel Makers	95
JONES APPAREL GROUP INC.	JNY	Apparel Makers	91
OSHKOSH B'GOSH INC. -CL A	GOSHA	Apparel Makers	90
QUIKSILVER INC.	ZQK	Apparel Makers	82
KELLWOOD CO.	KWD	Apparel Makers	81
CINTAS CORP.	CTAS	Apparel Makers	67
VF CORP.	VFC	Apparel Makers	63
LIZ CLAIBORNE INC.	LIZ	Apparel Makers	59
OXFORD INDUSTRIES INC.	OXM	Apparel Makers	57
NAUTICA ENTERPRISES INC.	NAUT	Apparel Makers	57
RUSSELL CORP.	RML	Apparel Makers	35
HARMAN INTERNATIONAL INDS	HAR	Audio/Video Equipment	27
OSHKOSH TRUCK CORP.	OTRKB	Auto Makers	86
MONACO COACH CORP.	MNC	Auto Makers	73
GENERAL MOTORS CORP.	GM	Auto Makers	28
FORD MOTOR CO.	F	Auto Makers	25
AUTOZONE INC.	AZO	Auto Retail	77

	Ticker	Industry	Easy-Hold Rank
O'REILLY AUTOMOTIVE INC.	ORLY	Auto Retail	67
INSURANCE AUTO AUCTIONS INC.	IAAI	Auto Retail	42
CTS CORP.	CTS	Auto-Parts Makers	89
JOHNSON CONTROLS INC.	JCI	Auto-Parts Makers	87
GENUINE PARTS CO.	GPC	Auto-Parts Makers	84
CLARCOR INC.	CLC	Auto-Parts Makers	83
ITT INDUSTRIES INC.	ITT	Auto-Parts Makers	83
CARLISLE COS. INC.	CSL	Auto-Parts Makers	76
LEAR CORP.	LEA	Auto-Parts Makers	64
SUPERIOR INDUSTRIES INTL	SUP	Auto-Parts Makers	59
GENTEX CORP.	GNTX	Auto-Parts Makers	51
TBC CORP.	TBCC	Auto-Parts Makers	51
PACIFIC CAPITAL BANCORP.	SABB	Banks	100
INDEPENDENT BANK CORP./MI	IBCP	Banks	99
FIRST CITIZENS BANCSH -CL A	FCNCA	Banks	99
COMMUNITY BANKS INC. MLLRSBRG	CTY	Banks	98
W HOLDING COMPANY INC.	WHI	Banks	98
CVB FINANCIAL CORP.	CVBF	Banks	97
CPB INC.	CPBI	Banks	97
ALABAMA NATL BANCORP.ORATION	ALAB	Banks	96
MISSISSIPPI VY BANCSHARES	MVBI	Banks	96
U S B HOLDING INC.	UBH	Banks	96
TRIARC COS. INC. -CL A	TRY	Beverage Manufacturing	71
COCA-COLA BTLNG CONS	COKE	Beverage Manufacturing	67
NATIONAL BEVERAGE CORP.	FIZ	Beverage Manufacturing	65
PEPSIAMERICAS INC.	PAS	Beverage Manufacturing	62
COCA-COLA ENTERPRISES	CCE	Beverage Manufacturing	38
PEPSICO INC.	PEP	Beverage Manufacturing	32
COCA-COLA CO.	KO	Beverage Manufacturing	27
BIOGEN INC.	BGEN	Biotech	84
CRYOLIFE INC.	CRY	Biotech	72
AMGEN INC.	AMGN	Biotech	68
QUINTILES TRANSNATIONAL CORP.	QTRN	Biotech	65
GENZYME GENERAL	GENZ	Biotech	64
LABORATORY CP OF AMER HLDGS	LH	Biotech	41
IDEXX LABS INC.	IDXX	Biotech	30
PAREXEL INTERNATIONAL CORP.	PRXL	Biotech	11
ICN PHARMACEUTICALS INC.	ICN	Biotech	7
DISNEY (WALT) COMPANY	DIS	Broadcast TV	50
FLORIDA ROCK INDS	FRK	Building Materials	79
AMERON INTERNATIONAL INC.	AMN	Building Materials	55
LAFARGE NORTH AMERICA INC.	LAF	Building Materials	52
EQUIFAX INC.	EFX	Business Services	95
ABM INDUSTRIES INC.	ABM	Business Services	94
AMBASSADORS INTERNATIONL INC.	AMIE	Business Services	91
SERVICEMASTER CO.	SVM	Business Services	87
WACKENHUT CORRECTIONS CORP.	WHC	Business Services	80
VIAD CORP.	VVI	Business Services	77
ICT GROUP INC.	ICTG	Business Services	77
SEI INVESTMENTS CO.	SEIC	Business Services	75
PREPAID LEGAL SERVICES INC.	PPD	Business Services	74
PITNEY BOWES INC.	PBI	Business Services	72
SCIENTIFIC-ATLANTA INC.	SFA	Cable/Wireless Equipment	61
ROHN INDUSTRIES INC.	ROHN	Cable/Wireless Equipment	48
TEKELEC	TKLC	Cable/Wireless Equipment	47
QUALCOMM INC.	QCOM	Cable/Wireless Equipment	47
PINNACLE SYSTEMS INC.	PCLE	Cable/Wireless Equipment	35
PROXIM INC.	PROX	Cable/Wireless Equipment	35
HARRIS CORP.	HRS	Cable/Wireless Equipment	27
TRIMBLE NAVIGATION LTD	TRMB	Cable/Wireless Equipment	26
ANDREW CORP.	ANDW	Cable/Wireless Equipment	25
AVID TECHNOLOGY INC.	AVID	Cable/Wireless Equipment	13
ENGELHARD CORP.	EC	Chemicals	89
CHURCH & DWIGHT INC.	CHD	Chemicals	80
OM GROUP INC.	OMG	Chemicals	78
VALHI INC.	VHI	Chemicals	65
CYTEC INDUSTRIES INC.	CYT	Chemicals	63
FERRO CORP.	FOE	Chemicals	61

	TICKER	INDUSTRY	EASY-HOLD RANK
MINNESOTA MINING & MFG CO.	MMM	Chemicals	53
BUCKEYE TECHNOLOGIES INC.	BKI	Chemicals	52
CABOT CORP.	CBT	Chemicals	46
ALBEMARLE CORP.	ALB	Chemicals	46
DEB SHOPS INC.	DEBS	Clothing Stores	93
CATO CORP. -CL A	CACOA	Clothing Stores	91
PACIFIC SUNWEAR CALIF INC.	PSUN	Clothing Stores	89
CHARMING SHOPPES	CHRS	Clothing Stores	79
BUCKLE INC.	BKE	Clothing Stores	77
TJX COMPANIES INC.	TJX	Clothing Stores	72
AMERN EAGLE OUTFITTERS INC.	AEOS	Clothing Stores	69
ROSS STORES INC.	ROST	Clothing Stores	68
GAP INC.	GPS	Clothing Stores	66
BURLINGTON COAT FACTORY WRHS	BCF	Clothing Stores	60
CORNING INC.	GLW	Communications Equipment	45
UNIVERSAL ELECTRONICS INC.	UEIC	Communications Equipment	36
LEXMARK INTL INC. -CL A	LXK	Computer Equipment	76
DELL COMPUTER CORP.	DELL	Computer Equipment	70
ZEBRA TECHNOLOGIES CP -CL A	ZBRA	Computer Equipment	70
SYMBOL TECHNOLOGIES	SBL	Computer Equipment	52
INTL BUSINESS MACHINES CORP.	IBM	Computer Equipment	52
DIEBOLD INC.	DBD	Computer Equipment	49
PLANAR SYSTEMS INC.	PLNR	Computer Equipment	42
ELECTRONICS FOR IMAGING INC.	EFII	Computer Equipment	29
COMPAQ COMPUTER CORP.	CPQ	Computer Equipment	28
GATEWAY INC.	GTW	Computer Equipment	18
AUTOMATIC DATA PROCESSING	ADP	Computer Programming	92
AVANT CORP.	AVNT	Computer Programming	87
MENTOR GRAPHICS CORP.	MENT	Computer Programming	39
JDA SOFTWARE GROUP INC.	JDAS	Computer Programming	36
CIBER INC.	CBR	Computer Programming	20
SYSTEMS & COMPUTER TECH CORP.	SCTC	Computer Programming	14
EMC CORP./MA	EMC	Computer Storage	80
SANDISK CORP.	SNDK	Computer Storage	65
IOMEGA CORP.	IOM	Computer Storage	30
STORAGE TECHNOLOGY CP	STK	Computer Storage	9
ANSYS INC.	ANSS	Computer Systems	94
HENRY (JACK) & ASSOCIATES	JKHY	Computer Systems	90
SUNGARD DATA SYSTEMS INC.	SDS	Computer Systems	90
TITAN CORP.	TTN	Computer Systems	56
ELECTRONIC DATA SYSTEMS CORP.	EDS	Computer Systems	56
COMPUTER SCIENCES CORP.	CSC	Computer Systems	54
INTEGRAL SYSTEMS INC./MD	ISYS	Computer Systems	51
KRONOS INC.	KRON	Computer Systems	43
FILENET CORP.	FILE	Computer Systems	42
CERNER CORP.	CERN	Computer Systems	41
DYCOM INDUSTRIES INC.	DY	Construction	86
BUILDING MATERIALS HLDG CP	BMHC	Construction	83
EMCOR GROUP INC.	EME	Construction	83
INSITUFORM TECNOL INC. -CL A	INSUA	Construction	78
GRANITE CONSTRUCTION INC.	GVA	Construction	76
MASTEC INC.	MTZ	Construction	53
TEREX CORP.	TEX	Construction Machinery	91
INGERSOLL-RAND CO.	IR	Construction Machinery	67
ASTEC INDUSTRIES INC.	ASTE	Construction Machinery	62
CATERPILLAR INC.	CAT	Construction Machinery	36
ARMOR HOLDINGS INC.	AH	Consultants	88
KFORCE INC.	KFRC	Consultants	41
HUNT (JB) TRANSPRT SVCS INC.	JBHT	Consultants	37
SAPIENT CORP.	SAPE	Consultants	33
FYI INC.	FYII	Data Processing	94
BISYS GROUP INC.	BSYS	Data Processing	90
TOTAL SYSTEM SERVICES INC.	TSS	Data Processing	87
DST SYSTEMS INC.	DST	Data Processing	84
FISERV INC.	FISV	Data Processing	82
AFFILIATED COMP SVCS -CL A	ACS	Data Processing	81
FIRST DATA CORP.	FDC	Data Processing	48
ACXIOM CORP.	ACXM	Data Processing	44

	TICKER	INDUSTRY	EASY-HOLD RANK
KEANE INC.	KEA	Data Processing	20
FAMILY DOLLAR STORES	FDO	Department Stores	89
MAY DEPARTMENT STORES CO.	MAY	Department Stores	86
KOHLS CORP.	KSS	Department Stores	85
WAL-MART STORES	WMT	Department Stores	80
TARGET CORP.	TGT	Department Stores	78
DOLLAR TREE STORES INC.	DLTR	Department Stores	78
99 CENTS ONLY STORES	NDN	Department Stores	69
SEARS ROEBUCK & CO.	S	Department Stores	64
NEIMAN-MARCUS GROUP INC.	NMG.A	Department Stores	58
FREDS INC.	FRED	Department Stores	57
TECHNE CORP.	TECH	Diagnostics	74
THERAGENICS CORP.	TGX	Diagnostics	72
NBTY INC.	NBTY	Diagnostics	67
DIAGNOSTIC PRODUCTS CORP.	DP	Diagnostics	58
NEW HORIZONS WORLDWIDE INC.	NEWH	Education	78
DEVRY INC.	DV	Education	72
ITT EDUCATIONAL SVCS INC.	ESI	Education	63
LEARNING TREE INTL INC.	LTRE	Education	41
GENLYTE GROUP INC.	GLYT	Electric Equipment	97
SALTON INC.	SFP	Electric Equipment	93
NORTEK INC.	NTK	Electric Equipment	90
EMERSON ELECTRIC CO.	EMR	Electric Equipment	88
GENERAL ELECTRIC CO.	GE	Electric Equipment	85
C&D TECHNOLOGIES INC.	CHP	Electric Equipment	79
PENN ENGR & MFG CORP.	PNN	Electric Equipment	79
AMETEK INC.	AME	Electric Equipment	79
MAGNETEK INC.	MAG	Electric Equipment	65
SMITH (A O) CORP.	AOS	Electric Equipment	62
NORTHWESTERN CORP.	NOR	Electric Utilities	100
MDU RESOURCES GROUP INC.	MDU	Electric Utilities	98
UTILICORP. UNITED INC.	UCU	Electric Utilities	98
DUKE ENERGY CORP.	DUK	Electric Utilities	98
CINERGY CORP.	CIN	Electric Utilities	95
PUGET ENERGY INC.	PSD	Electric Utilities	94
IDACORP. INC.	IDA	Electric Utilities	92
PINNACLE WEST CAPITAL	PNW	Electric Utilities	90
ENERGY EAST CORP.	EAS	Electric Utilities	88
PPL CORP.	PPL	Electric Utilities	87
INSIGHT ENTERPRISES INC.	NSIT	Electronics Stores	91
RADIOSHACK CORP.	RSH	Electronics Stores	63
PIONEER STANDARD ELECTRONICS	PIOS	Electronics Stores	57
RICHARDSON ELEC LTD	RELL	Electronics Stores	56
CDW COMPUTER CENTERS INC.	CDWC	Electronics Stores	54
ANIXTER INTL INC.	AXE	Electronics Stores	54
NU HORIZONS ELECTRS CORP.	NUHC	Electronics Stores	54
WATSCO INC.	WSO	Electronics Stores	52
BEST BUY CO. INC.	BBY	Electronics Stores	49
GRAINGER (W W) INC.	GWW	Electronics Stores	38
ON ASSIGNMENT INC.	ASGN	Employment	93
ROBERT HALF INTL INC.	RHI	Employment	92
SPHERION CORP.	SFN	Employment	71
KELLY SERVICES INC. -CL A	KELYA	Employment	66
MANPOWER INC./WI	MAN	Employment	59
LABOR READY INC.	LRW	Employment	55
CDI CORP.	CDI	Employment	52
RIGHT MANAGEMENT CONSULTANTS	RMCI	Employment	32
MODIS PROFESSIONAL SVCS INC.	MPS	Employment	25
VOLT INFO SCIENCES INC.	VOL	Employment	13
URS CORP.	URS	Engineering	96
JACOBS ENGINEERING GROUP INC.	JEC	Engineering	83
TETRA TECH INC.	TTEK	Engineering	81
LANDAUER INC.	LDR	Engineering	65
TRC COS. INC.	TRR	Engineering	59
SEITEL INC.	SEI	Engineering	19
NEWPARK RESOURCES	NR	Engineering	10
PIXAR	PIXR	Entertainment	74
DONALDSON CO. INC.	DCI	Environment Control	86
MANITOWOC CO.	MTW	Environment Control	82

	TICKER	INDUSTRY	EASY-HOLD RANK
ENGINEERED SUPPORT SYSTEMS	EASI	Environment Control	81
YORK INTL	YRK	Environment Control	50
HUGHES SUPPLY INC.	HUG	Environment Control	44
FEDDERS CORP.	FJC	Environment Control	34
TECUMSEH PRODUCTS CO. -CL A	TECUA	Environment Control	33
FANNIE MAE	FNM	Finance	96
FINANCIAL FEDERAL CORP.	FIF	Finance	95
FEDERAL HOME LOAN MORTG CORP.	FRE	Finance	95
WORLD ACCEPTANCE CP/DE	WRLD	Finance	93
STUDENT LOAN CORP.	STU	Finance	93
DVI INC.	DVI	Finance	91
AMERICREDIT CORP.	ACF	Finance	90
CAPITAL ONE FINL CORP.	COF	Finance	88
HOUSEHOLD INTERNATIONAL INC.	HI	Finance	87
MBNA CORP.	KRB	Finance	79
MCCORMICK & CO.	MKC	Food Manufacturing	86
HORMEL FOODS CORP.	HRL	Food Manufacturing	78
WRIGLEY (WM) JR CO.	WWY	Food Manufacturing	75
TOOTSIE ROLL INDUSTRIES INC.	TR	Food Manufacturing	71
LANCASTER COLONY CORP.	LANC	Food Manufacturing	70
SMITHFIELD FOODS INC.	SFD	Food Manufacturing	69
SANDERSON FARMS INC.	SAFM	Food Manufacturing	67
SARA LEE CORP.	SLE	Food Manufacturing	65
HEINZ (H J) CO.	HNZ	Food Manufacturing	64
SYSCO CORP.	SYY	Food Wholesale	84
GREEN MTN COFFEE INC.	GMCR	Food Wholesale	68
SUPERVALU INC.	SVU	Food Wholesale	58
UNIVERSAL FOREST PRODS INC.	UFPI	Forestry/Wood Product	74
WEYERHAUSER CO.	WY	Forestry/Wood Product	58
RAYONIER INC.	RYN	Forestry/Wood Product	34
PLUM CREEK TIMBER CO. INC.	PCL	Forestry/Wood Product	32
POPE & TALBOT INC.	POP	Forestry/Wood Product	30
STANLEY FURNITURE CO. INC.	STLY	Furniture Makers	86
ETHAN ALLEN INTERIORS INC.	ETH	Furniture Makers	82
LA-Z-BOY INC.	LZB	Furniture Makers	77
MILLER (HERMAN) INC.	MLHR	Furniture Makers	69
AMERICAN WOODMARK CORP.	AMWD	Furniture Makers	60
HON INDUSTRIES	HNI	Furniture Makers	49
KIMBALL INTERNATIONAL -CL B	KBALB	Furniture Makers	47
LEGGETT & PLATT INC.	LEG	Furniture Makers	47
FURNITURE BRANDS INTL INC.	FBN	Furniture Makers	47
BUSH INDUSTRIES -CL A	BSH	Furniture Makers	45
MCGRATH RENTCORP.	MGRC	Furniture Retail	93
HAVERTY FURNITURE	HVT	Furniture Retail	77
BED BATH & BEYOND INC.	BBBY	Furniture Retail	71
PIER 1 IMPORTS INC./DE	PIR	Furniture Retail	69
WILLIAMS-SONOMA INC.	WSM	Furniture Retail	49
ANCHOR GAMING	SLOT	Gambling	81
ISLE OF CAPRIS CASINOS INC.	ISLE	Gambling	65
STATION CASINOS INC.	STN	Gambling	41
NEWMONT MINING CORP.	NEM	Gold/Silver	13
KROGER CO.	KR	Groceries	93
ARDEN GROUP INC. -CL A	ARDNA	Groceries	91
SAFEWAY INC.	SWY	Groceries	91
COSTCO WHOLESALE CORP.	COS.T	Groceries	72
CASEYS GENERAL STORES INC.	CASY	Groceries	63
RUDDICK CORP.	RDK	Groceries	57
WEIS MARKETS INC.	WMK	Groceries	55
INGLES MARKETS INC. -CL A	IMKTA	Groceries	50
WHOLE FOODS MARKET INC.	WFMI	Groceries	42
WINN-DIXIE STORES INC.	WIN	Groceries	38
EXPRESS SCRIPTS INC.	ESRX	HMOs	86
RENAL CARE GROUP INC.	RCI	HMOs	82
MID ATLANTIC MEDICAL SVCS	MME	HMOs	69
US ONCOLOGY INC.	USON	HMOs	49
DIANON SYSTEMS INC.	DIAN	HMOs	40
SIERRA HEALTH SERVICES	SIE	HMOs	33
PACIFICARE HEALTH SYS	PHSY	HMOs	30

	TICKER	INDUSTRY	EASY-HOLD RANK
OXFORD HEALTH PLANS INC.	OHP	HMOs	20
DAVITA INC.	DVA	HMOs	14
SCHULER HOMES INC. -CL A	SHLR	Home Building	99
TOLL BROTHERS INC.	TOL	Home Building	99
NVR INC.	NVR	Home Building	99
KB HOME	KBH	Home Building	96
M/I SCHOTTENSTEIN HOMES INC.	MHO	Home Building	96
MDC HOLDINGS INC.	MDC	Home Building	95
D R HORTON INC.	DHI	Home Building	95
LENNAR CORP.	LEN	Home Building	94
PULTE HOMES INC.	PHM	Home Building	92
CENTEX CORP.	CTX	Home Building	89
LINC.ARE HOLDINGS INC.	LNCR	Home Health	91
MEDQUIST INC.	MEDQ	Home Health	62
NATIONAL HEALTHCARE CORP.	NHC	Home Health	35
APRIA HEALTHCARE GROUP	AHG	Home Health	27
NABI INC.	NABI	Home Health	10
HOME DEPOT INC.	HD	Home Supply Stores	85
LOWES COS.	LOW	Home Supply Stores	83
FASTENAL CO.	FAST	Home Supply Stores	79
HEALTH MANAGEMNT ASSC	HMA	Hospitals	78
UNIVERSAL HEALTH SVCS -CL B	UHS	Hospitals	67
TENET HEALTHCARE CORP.	THC	Hospitals	55
AMERICAN HEALTHWAYS INC.	AMHC	Hospitals	35
HCA INC.	HCA	Hospitals	21
MGM MIRAGE	MGG	Hotel Casinos	74
AZTAR CORP.	AZR	Hotel Casinos	53
HARRAHS ENTERTAINMENT INC.	HET	Hotel Casinos	49
MANDALAY RESORT GROUP	MBG	Hotel Casinos	36
BOYD GAMING CORP.	BYD	Hotel Casinos	28
AMERISTAR CASINOS INC.	ASCA	Hotel Casinos	22
EXTENDED STAY AMERICA INC.	ESA	Hotels	74
PRIME HOSPITALITY CORP.	PDQ	Hotels	59
HILTON HOTELS CORP.	HLT	Hotels	47
MARCUS CORP.	MCS	Hotels	28
ECOLAB INC.	ECL	Household Products	89
LAUDER ESTEE COS. INC. -CL A	EL	Household Products	85
JOHNSON & JOHNSON	JNJ	Household Products	78
EASTMAN KODAK CO.	EK	Household Products	76
MACDERMID INC.	MRD	Household Products	71
ALBERTO-CULVER CO. -CL B	ACV	Household Products	68
PROCTER & GAMBLE CO.	PG	Household Products	66
CLOROX CO./DE	CLX	Household Products	64
STEPAN CO.	SCL	Household Products	64
CAMBREX CORP.	CBM	Household Products	64
CORVEL CORP.	CRVL	Insurance (General)	95
RADIAN GROUP INC.	RDN	Insurance (General)	89
AMBAC FINANCIAL GP	ABK	Insurance (General)	88
GALLAGHER (ARTHUR J.) & CO.	AJG	Insurance (General)	81
BROWN & BROWN INC.	BRO	Insurance (General)	80
MARSH & MCLENNAN COS.	MMC	Insurance (General)	70
MBIA INC.	MBI	Insurance (General)	54
AON CORP.	AOC	Insurance (General)	30
ST PAUL COS.	SPC	Insurance (General)	23
UNIVERSAL AMERICAN FINL CP	UHCO	Insurance (Life)	97
PROTECTIVE LIFE CORP.	PL	Insurance (Life)	75
TORCHMARK CORP.	TMK	Insurance (Life)	71
JEFFERSON-PILOT CORP.	JP	Insurance (Life)	70
GREAT AMERN FINL RESOURCES	GFR	Insurance (Life)	67
RIGHTCHOICE MGD CARE	RIT	Insurance (Life)	66
CIGNA CORP.	CI	Insurance (Life)	61
AFLAC INC.	AFL	Insurance (Life)	55
AMERICAN NATIONAL INSURANCE	ANAT	Insurance (Life)	51
LINC.O.LN NATIONAL CORP.	LNC	Insurance (Life)	50
TRIAD GUARANTY INC.	TGIC	Insurance (Property)	98
PHILADELPHIA CONS HLDG CORP.	PHLY	Insurance (Property)	95
MIDLAND CO.	MLAN	Insurance (Property)	94
COMMERCE GROUP INC./MA	CGI	Insurance (Property)	93
HILB ROGAL & HAMILTON CO.	HRH	Insurance (Property)	86

	TICKER	INDUSTRY	EASY-HOLD RANK
MGIC INVESTMENT CORP./WI	MTG	Insurance (Property)	85
PMI GROUP INC.	PMI	Insurance (Property)	83
AMERICAN INTERNATIONAL GROUP	AIG	Insurance (Property)	79
STATE AUTO FINL CORP.	STFC	Insurance (Property)	77
ERIE INDEMNITY CO. -CL A	ERIE	Insurance (Property)	74
FIDELITY NATIONAL FINL INC.	FNF	Insurance (Title)	61
STEWART INFO SVCS	STC	Insurance (Title)	39
LANDAMERICA FINANCIAL GP	LFG	Insurance (Title)	31
FOSSIL INC.	FOSL	Jewelry/Accessories	89
TIFFANY & CO.	TIF	Jewelry/Accessories	58
MOVADO GROUP INC.	MOV	Jewelry/Accessories	49
FRIEDMANS INC. -CL A	FRDM	Jewelry/Accessories	44
APTARGROUP INC.	ATR	Machinery	89
PAXAR CORP.	PXR	Machinery	85
TENNANT CO.	TNC	Machinery	85
LAWSON PRODUCTS	LAWS	Machinery	84
GRACO INC.	GGG	Machinery	79
GORMAN-RUPP CO.	GRC	Machinery	77
JLG INDUSTRIES INC.	JLG	Machinery	76
ILLINOIS TOOL WORKS	ITW	Machinery	71
SHUFFLE MASTER INC.	SHFL	Machinery	69
FRANKLIN ELECTRIC CO.	FELE	Machinery	69
MESTEK INC.	MCC	Measuring Devices	83
WATERS CORP.	WAT	Measuring Devices	79
DIONEX CORP.	DNEX	Measuring Devices	78
SBS TECHNOLOGIES INC.	SBSE	Measuring Devices	73
TOLLGRADE COMMUNICATIONS INC.	TLGD	Measuring Devices	66
TERADYNE INC.	TER	Measuring Devices	64
CUBIC CORP.	CUB	Measuring Devices	59
ANAREN MICROWAVE INC.	ANEN	Measuring Devices	56
PALL CORP.	PLL	Measuring Devices	47
KEITHLEY INSTR INC.	KEI	Measuring Devices	46
GUIDANT CORP.	GDT	Medical Equipment	96
DATASCOPE CORP.	DSCP	Medical Equipment	91
INVACARE CORP.	IVC	Medical Equipment	90
BECKMAN COULTER INC.	BEC	Medical Equipment	87
MEDTRONIC INC.	MDT	Medical Equipment	82
APOGENT TECHNOLOGIES INC.	AOT	Medical Equipment	81
BIOMET INC.	BMET	Medical Equipment	80
DENTSPLY INTERNATL INC.	XRAY	Medical Equipment	79
RESMED INC.	RMD	Medical Equipment	74
ARROW INTERNATIONAL	ARRO	Medical Equipment	74
PATTERSON DENTAL CO.	PDCO	Medical Goods (Wholesale)	93
CARDINAL HEALTH INC.	CAH	Medical Goods (Wholesale)	85
AMERISOURCEBERGEN CORP.	ABC	Medical Goods (Wholesale)	84
SYNCOR INTL CORP./DE	SCOR	Medical Goods (Wholesale)	68
OWENS & MINOR INC.	OMI	Medical Goods (Wholesale)	50
SCHEIN HENRY INC.	HSIC	Medical Goods (Wholesale)	40
OMNICARE INC.	OCR	Medical Goods (Wholesale)	24
MOBILE MINI INC.	MINI	Metal Products	85
SIMPSON MANUFACTURING INC.	SSD	Metal Products	85
BALL CORP.	BLL	Metal Products	82
DANAHER CORP.	DHR	Metal Products	77
MOOG INC. -CL A	MOG.A	Metal Products	77
NCI BUILDING SYSTEMS INC.	NCS	Metal Products	71
ALLIANT TECHSYSTEMS INC.	ATK	Metal Products	67
MASCO CORP.	MAS	Metal Products	66
BARNES GROUP INC.	B	Metal Products	53
NN INC.	NNBR	Metal Products	52
STILLWATER MINING CO.	SWC	Mining	86
OGLEBAY NORTON CO.	OGLE	Mining	63
COMMERCIAL METALS	CMC	Mining	41
SOUTHERN PERU COPPER	PCU	Mining	31
ARCH COAL INC.	ACI	Mining	17
BLYTH INC.	BTH	Misc. Manufacturing	86
DAKTRONICS INC.	DAKT	Misc. Manufacturing	74
INTL GAME TECHNOLOGY	IGT	Misc. Manufacturing	72
WMS INDUSTRIES INC.	WMS	Misc. Manufacturing	43
BRADY CORP.	BRC	Misc. Manufacturing	34

	TICKER	INDUSTRY	EASY-HOLD RANK
EATON VANCE CORP.	EV	Money Management	92
JOHN NUVEEN CO. -CL A	JNC	Money Management	87
PRICE (T. ROWE) GROUP	TROW	Money Management	74
LIBERTY FINANCIAL COS. INC.	L	Money Management	46
FRANKLIN RESOURCES INC.	BEN	Money Management	25
DORAL FINANCIAL CORP.	DORL	Mortgages	95
ALLIED CAPITAL CP	ALD	Mortgages	93
COUNTRYWIDE CREDIT IND INC.	CCR	Mortgages	77
INDYMAC BANCORP. INC.	NDE	Mortgages	58
BLACK HILLS CORP.	BKH	Natural Gas Utilities	98
NEW JERSEY RESOURCES	NJR	Natural Gas Utilities	91
SEMPRA ENERGY	SRE	Natural Gas Utilities	91
CASCADE NATURAL GAS CORP.	CGC	Natural Gas Utilities	85
ENERGEN CORP.	EGN	Natural Gas Utilities	76
SOUTH JERSEY INDUSTRIES	SJI	Natural Gas Utilities	73
QUESTAR CORP.	STR	Natural Gas Utilities	72
ONEOK INC.	OKE	Natural Gas Utilities	70
NATIONAL FUEL GAS CO.	NFG	Natural Gas Utilities	69
PIEDMONT NATURAL GAS CO.	PNY	Natural Gas Utilities	67
MATTHEWS INTL CORP. -CL A	MATW	Nonferrous Metals	95
MUELLER INDUSTRIES	MLI	Nonferrous Metals	59
CARPENTER TECHNOLOGY	CRS	Nonferrous Metals	47
WOLVERINE TUBE INC.	WLV	Nonferrous Metals	46
BRUSH ENGINEERED MATERIALS	BW	Nonferrous Metals	39
TREMONT CORP.	TRE	Nonferrous Metals	25
ENCORE WIRE CORP.	WIRE	Nonferrous Metals	25
VULCAN MATERIALS CO.	VMC	Nonmetal Mining	71
MARTIN MARIETTA MATERIALS	MLM	Nonmetal Mining	58
SUNRISE ASSISTED LIVING INC.	SRZ	Nursing	88
MANOR CARE INC.	HCR	Nursing	15
BEVERLY ENTERPRISES	BEV	Nursing	14
SCANSOURCE INC.	SCSC	Office Equipment (Wholesale)	93
UNITED STATIONERS INC.	USTR	Office Equipment (Wholesale)	89
POMEROY COMPUTER RES INC.	PMRY	Office Equipment (Wholesale)	69
ARROW ELECTRONICS INC.	ARW	Office Equipment (Wholesale)	57
TECH DATA CORP.	TECD	Office Equipment (Wholesale)	54
DAISYTEK INTL CORP.	DZTK	Office Equipment (Wholesale)	47
BELL MICROPRODUCTS INC.	BELM	Office Equipment (Wholesale)	32
IKON OFFICE SOLUTIONS	IKN	Office Equipment (Wholesale)	15
XANSER CORP.	XNR	Oil/Gas	97
PENN VIRGINIA CORP.	PVA	Oil/Gas	94
✔ANADARKO PETROLEUM CORP.	APC	Oil/Gas	92
EVERGREEN RESOURCES	EVG	Oil/Gas	92
AMERADA HESS CORP.	AHC	Oil/Gas	87
MURPHY OIL CORP.	MUR	Oil/Gas	87
OCCIDENTAL PETROLEUM CORP.	OXY	Oil/Gas	86
XTO ENERGY INC.	XTO	Oil/Gas	85
BERRY PETROLEUM -CL A	BRY	Oil/Gas	85
NEWFIELD EXPLORATION CO.	NFX	Oil/Gas	84
ULTRAMAR DIAMOND SHAMROCK	UDS	Oil/Gas Products	96
FRONTIER OIL CORP.	FTO	Oil/Gas Products	94
SUNOCO INC.	SUN	Oil/Gas Products	91
QUAKER CHEMICAL CORP.	KWR	Oil/Gas Products	76
TESORO PETROLEUM CORP.	TSO	Oil/Gas Products	62
HOLLY CORP.	HOC	Oil/Gas Products	60
ELCOR CORP.	ELK	Oil/Gas Products	50
WD-40 CO.	WDFC	Oil/Gas Products	43
LUBRIZOL CORP.	LZ	Oil/Gas Products	28
STONE ENERGY CORP.	SGY	Oil/Gas Services	89
FACTSET RESEARCH SYSTEMS INC.	FDS	Online Information	90
GTECH HOLDINGS CORP.	GTK	Online Information	55
BIO-RAD LABS -CL A	BIO.A	Optical Equipment	47
II-VI INC.	IIVI	Optical Equipment	28
ZYGO CORP.	ZIGO	Optical Equipment	6
VALSPAR CORP.	VAL	Paints/Coatings	66
RPM INC.-OHIO	RPM	Paints/Coatings	63
SHERWIN-WILLIAMS CO.	SHW	Paints/Coatings	27
GREIF BROS CORP. -CL A	GBCOA	Paper	91
WILLAMETTE INDUSTRIES	WLL	Paper	78

	TICKER	INDUSTRY	EASY-HOLD RANK
AVERY DENNISON CORP.	AVY	Paper	75
KIMBERLY-CLARK CORP.	KMB	Paper	73
BOWATER INC.	BOW	Paper	73
BEMIS CO.	BMS	Paper	66
SMURFIT-STONE CONTAINER CORP.	SSCC	Paper	53
TEMPLE-INLAND INC.	TIN	Paper	52
GLATFELTER (P H) CO.	GLT	Paper	49
SCHWEITZER-MAUDUIT INTL INC.	SWM	Paper	48
REGIS CORP./MN	RGIS	Personal Services	87
G&K SERVICES INC. -CL A	GKSRA	Personal Services	68
CENTRAL PARKING CORP.	CPC	Personal Services	59
UNIFIRST CORP.	UNF	Personal Services	58
STEWART ENTERPRISES -CL A	STEI	Personal Services	25
SERVICE CORP. INTERNATIONAL	SRV	Personal Services	12
MERCK & CO.	MRK	Pharmaceuticals	96
LILLY (ELI) & CO.	LLY	Pharmaceuticals	95
SCHERING-PLOUGH	SGP	Pharmaceuticals	90
FOREST LABORATORIES -CL A	FRX	Pharmaceuticals	89
BRISTOL MYERS SQUIBB	BMY	Pharmaceuticals	88
PHARMACEUTICAL PROD DEV INC.	PPDI	Pharmaceuticals	85
PFIZER INC.	PFE	Pharmaceuticals	83
ALPHARMA INC. -CL A	ALO	Pharmaceuticals	80
ABBOTT LABORATORIES	ABT	Pharmaceuticals	70
MEDICIS PHARMACEUT CP -CL A	MRX	Pharmaceuticals	65
TELLABS INC.	TLAB	Phone/Network Equipment	81
TECHNITROL INC.	TNL	Phone/Network Equipment	74
PLANTRONICS INC.	PLT	Phone/Network Equipment	73
ADTRAN INC.	ADTN	Phone/Network Equipment	67
EMULEX CORP.	EMLX	Phone/Network Equipment	64
CISCO SYSTEMS INC.	CSCO	Phone/Network Equipment	60
JDS UNIPHASE CORP.	JDSU	Phone/Network Equipment	52
APPLIED INNOVATION INC.	AINN	Phone/Network Equipment	34
ADC TELECOMMUNICATIONS INC.	ADCT	Phone/Network Equipment	25
PERFORMANCE TECHNOLOGIES INC.	PTIX	Phone/Network Equipment	21
WELLPOINT HLTH NETWRK -CL A	WLP	Physicians	87
REHABCARE GROUP INC.	RHB	Physicians	84
COVENTRY HEALTH CARE	CVH	Physicians	74
HOOPER HOLMES INC.	HH	Physicians	72
FIRST HEALTH GROUP CORP.	FHCC	Physicians	65
ORTHODONTIC CENTERS OF AMER	OCA	Physicians	64
U S PHYSICAL THERAPY INC.	USPH	Physicians	64
UNITEDHEALTH GROUP INC.	UNH	Physicians	55
OPTION CARE INC.	OPTN	Physicians	48
HEALTH NET INC. - CL A	HNT	Physicians	42
LIQUI-BOX CORP.	LIQB	Plastics	63
WEST PHARMACEUTICAL SVSC INC.	WST	Plastics	29
SEALED AIR CORP.	SEE	Plastics	25
TUPPERWARE CORP.	TUP	Plastics	23
SOLECTRON CORP.	SLR	Printed Circuit Boards	72
JABIL CIRCUIT INC.	JBL	Printed Circuit Boards	66
PLEXUS CORP.	PLXS	Printed Circuit Boards	48
BENCHMARK ELECTRONICS INC.	BHE	Printed Circuit Boards	45
SCI SYSTEMS INC.	SCI	Printed Circuit Boards	39
ACT MANUFACTURING INC.	ACTM	Printed Circuit Boards	31
PARK ELECTROCHEMICAL CORP.	PKE	Printed Circuit Boards	24
MERIX CORP.	MERX	Printed Circuit Boards	20
NEW ENGLAND BUSINESS SVC INC.	NEB	Printing	92
DELUXE CORP.	DLX	Printing	86
CONSOLIDATED GRAPHICS INC.	CGX	Printing	84
ADVANCED MARKETING SERVICES	MKT	Printing	82
BANTA CORP.	BN	Printing	79
SCHAWK INC. -CL A	SGK	Printing	67
CSS INDS INC.	CSS	Printing	56
DONNELLEY (R R) & SONS CO.	DNY	Printing	55
HARLAND (JOHN H.) CO.	JH	Printing	50
WALLACE COMPUTER SVCS INC.	WCS	Printing	38
GANNETT CO.	GCI	Publishing	88
WILEY (JOHN) & SONS -CL A	JW.A	Publishing	87
MCGRAW-HILL COMPANIES	MHP	Publishing	73

	Ticker	Industry	Easy-Hold Rank
NEW YORK TIMES CO. -CL A	NYT	Publishing	67
MCCLATCHY CO. -CL A	MNI	Publishing	64
KNIGHT-RIDDER INC.	KRI	Publishing	63
VALUE LINE INC.	VALU	Publishing	61
MEREDITH CORP.	MDP	Publishing	54
WASHINGTON POST -CL B	WPO	Publishing	52
SCHOLASTIC CORP.	SCHL	Publishing	46
SAGA COMMUNICATIONS -CL A	SGA	Radio	90
HISPANIC BROADCASTING -CL A	HSP	Radio	56
WESTWOOD ONE INC.	WON	Radio	40
BURLINGTON NORTHERN SANTA FE	BNI	Rail Transport	70
UNION PACIFIC CORP.	UNP	Rail Transport	53
NORFOLK SOUTHERN CORP.	NSC	Rail Transport	26
CSX CORP.	CSX	Rail Transport	21
FLORIDA EAST COAST INDS	FLA	Rail Transport	8
BEDFORD PPTY INVS INC.	BED	Real Estate	97
CATELLUS DEVELOPMENT CORP.	CDX	Real Estate	77
ST. JOE CO.	JOE	Real Estate	77
ALEXANDER'S INC.	ALX	Real Estate	70
KOGER EQUITY INC.	KE	Real Estate	67
PARKWAY PROPERTIES INC.	PKY	Real Estate	66
PENN NATIONAL GAMING INC.	PENN	Recreation	82
MTR GAMING GROUP INC.	MNTG	Recreation	75
CHURCHILL DOWNS INC.	CHDN	Recreation	75
SPEEDWAY MOTORSPORTS INC.	TRK	Recreation	73
WESCO FINANCIAL CORP.	WSC	Reinsurance	95
TRANSATLANTIC HOLDINGS INC.	TRH	Reinsurance	64
REINSURANCE GROUP AMER INC.	RGA	Reinsurance	59
SUMMIT PROPERTIES INC.	SMT	REITS	98
CBL & ASSOCIATES PPTYS INC.	CBL	REITS	98
DUKE REALTY CORP.	DRE	REITS	97
LEXINGTON CORP. PPTYS TRUST	LXP	REITS	96
AMLI RESIDENTIAL PPTYS TR	AML	REITS	94
GENERAL GROWTH PPTYS INC.	GGP	REITS	94
KIMCO REALTY CORP.	KIM	REITS	93
LIBERTY PROPERTY TRUST	LRY	REITS	93
GABLES RESIDENTIAL TRUST	GBP	REITS	93
RENT-A-CENTER INC.	RCII	Rental	96
AARON RENTS INC.	RNT	Rental	94
AUTONATION INC.	AN	Rental	70
ELECTRO RENT CORP.	ELRC	Rental	35
RYDER SYSTEM INC.	R	Rental	26
MOVIE GALLERY INC.	MOVI	Rental	23
COMDISCO INC.	CDO	Rental	19
JACK IN THE BOX INC.	JBX	Restaurants	99
BRINKER INTL INC.	EAT	Restaurants	92
RYAN'S FAMILY STK HOUSES INC.	RYAN	Restaurants	92
RUBY TUESDAY INC.	RI	Restaurants	90
IHOP CORP.	IHP	Restaurants	88
OUTBACK STEAKHOUSE INC.	OSI	Restaurants	87
PAPA JOHNS INTERNATIONAL INC.	PZZA	Restaurants	85
CEC ENTERTAINMENT INC.	CEC	Restaurants	84
STEAK N SHAKE CO.	SNS	Restaurants	78
DARDEN RESTAURANTS INC.	DRI	Restaurants	77
MYERS INDUSTRIES INC.	MYE	Rubber Products	65
COOPER TIRE & RUBBER	CTB	Rubber Products	49
BANDAG INC.	BDG	Rubber Products	41
CROMPTON CORP.	CK	Rubber Products	34
QUAKER CITY BANCORP. INC.	QCBC	Savings Institutions	99
TOMPKINSTRUSTCO INC.	TMP	Savings Institutions	99
FIRST SENTINEL BANCORP. INC.	FSLA	Savings Institutions	98
GREAT SOUTHERN BANCORP.	GSBC	Savings Institutions	98
M & T BANK CORP.	MTB	Savings Institutions	97
HARBOR FLORIDA BANCSHARES	HARB	Savings Institutions	97
MAF BANCORP. INC.	MAFB	Savings Institutions	94
DOWNEY FINANCIAL CORP.	DSL	Savings Institutions	94
FLUSHING FINANCIAL CORP.	FFIC	Savings Institutions	92
FIRST FED CAP CORP.	FTFC	Savings Institutions	92

	Ticker	Industry	Easy-Hold Rank
LEGG MASON INC.	LM	Securities	70
RAYMOND JAMES FINANCIAL CORP.	RJF	Securities	67
STATE STREET CORP.	STT	Securities	66
INVESTORS FINANCIAL SVCS CP	IFIN	Securities	64
INVESTMENT TECHNOLOGY GP INC.	ITG	Securities	61
ACTRADE FINL TECHNOLGIES LTD	ACRT	Securities	58
SCHWAB (CHARLES) CORP.	SCH	Securities	56
MERRILL LYNCH & CO.	MER	Securities	56
MORGAN STANLEY DEAN WITTER	MWD	Securities	50
SOUTHWEST SECURITIES GROUP	SWS	Securities	49
WACKENHUT CORP. -SER A	WAK	Security Services	86
PITTSTON COMPANY	PZB	Security Services	50
INTERLOGIX INC.	ILXI	Security Services	45
DOVER CORP.	DOV	Semiconductor Equipment	70
ESTERLINE TECHNOLOGIES	ESL	Semiconductor Equipment	54
ELECTRO SCIENTIFIC INDS INC.	ESIO	Semiconductor Equipment	44
HELIX TECHNOLOGY CORP.	HELX	Semiconductor Equipment	38
SEMITOOL INC.	SMTL	Semiconductor Equipment	37
NOVELLUS SYSTEMS INC.	NVLS	Semiconductor Equipment	35
KLA-TENCOR CORP.	KLAC	Semiconductor Equipment	31
ASYST TECHNOLOGIES INC.	ASYT	Semiconductor Equipment	29
KULICKE & SOFFA INDUSTRIES	KLIC	Semiconductor Equipment	20
LAM RESEARCH CORP.	LRCX	Semiconductor Equipment	19
VISHAY INTRTECHNOLOGY	VSH	Semiconductors	76
AMPHENOL CORP.	APH	Semiconductors	73
CREE INC.	CREE	Semiconductors	70
LINEAR TECHNOLOGY CORP.	LLTC	Semiconductors	68
MICREL INC.	MCRL	Semiconductors	64
QLOGIC CORP.	QLGC	Semiconductors	62
MAXIM INTEGRATED PRODUCTS	MXIM	Semiconductors	62
SILICONIX INC.	SILI	Semiconductors	61
TRIQUINT SEMICONDUCTOR INC.	TQNT	Semiconductors	60
ELANTEC SEMICONDUCTOR INC.	ELNT	Semiconductors	59
MADDEN STEVEN LTD	SHOO	Shoes	88
TIMBERLAND CO. -CL A	TBL	Shoes	86
COLE KENNETH PROD INC. -CL A	KCP	Shoes	81
K-SWISS INC. -CL A	KSWS	Shoes	66
VANS INC.	VANS	Shoes	52
GENESCO INC.	GCO	Shoes	43
STRIDE RITE CORP.	SRR	Shoes	39
FINISH LINE INC. -CL A	FINL	Shoes	23
REEBOK INTERNATIONAL LTD	RBK	Shoes	22
NIKE INC. -CL B	NKE	Shoes	15
CACI INTL INC. -CL A	CACI	Software	89
BARRA INC.	BARZ	Software	88
MICROSOFT CORP.	MSFT	Software	87
NATIONAL INSTRUMENTS CORP.	NATI	Software	80
DENDRITE INTERNATIONAL INC.	DRTE	Software	78
ADVENT SOFTWARE INC.	ADVS	Software	73
AMERICAN MANAGEMENT SYSTEMS	AMSY	Software	71
VERITAS SOFTWARE CO.	VRTS	Software	69
FAIR ISAAC & COMPANY INC.	FIC	Software	64
INTUIT INC.	INTU	Software	60
SCP POOL CORP.	POOL	Sporting Goods	91
K2 INC.	KTO	Sporting Goods	44
CALLAWAY GOLF CO.	ELY	Sporting Goods	14
SPS TECHNOLOGIES INC.	ST	Steel/Iron	84
GIBRALTAR STEEL CORP.	ROCK	Steel/Iron	74
PRECISION CASTPARTS CORP.	PCP	Steel/Iron	72
ALLEGHENY TECHNOLOGIES INC.	ATI	Steel/Iron	45
QUANEX CORP.	NX	Steel/Iron	39
WORTHINGTON INDUSTRIES	WOR	Steel/Iron	37
ROANOKE ELECTRIC STEEL CORP.	RESC	Steel/Iron	36
NUCOR CORP.	NUE	Steel/Iron	31
TEXAS INDUSTRIES INC.	TXI	Steel/Iron	25
AK STEEL HOLDING CORP.	AKS	Steel/Iron	24
CVS CORP.	CVS	Stores (Misc.)	94
WALGREEN CO.	WAG	Stores (Misc.)	93

	TICKER	INDUSTRY	EASY-HOLD RANK
TRANS WORLD ENTMT CORP.	TWMC	Stores (Misc.)	76
LONGS DRUG STORES INC.	LDG	Stores (Misc.)	75
J JILL GROUP INC.	JILL	Stores (Misc.)	57
HANDLEMAN CO.	HDL	Stores (Misc.)	55
BORDERS GROUP INC.	BGP	Stores (Misc.)	48
STAPLES INC.	SPLS	Stores (Misc.)	41
HANCOCK FABRICS INC.	HKF	Stores (Misc.)	34
OFFICE DEPOT INC.	ODP	Stores (Misc.)	25
VERIZON COMMUNICATIONS	VZ	Telecommunications	93
ALLTEL CORP.	AT	Telecommunications	91
BELLSOUTH CORP.	BLS	Telecommunications	89
SBC COMMUNICATIONS INC.	SBC	Telecommunications	78
CENTURYTEL INC.	CTL	Telecommunications	69
WORLDCOM INC.-WORLDCOM GROUP	WCOM	Telecommunications	55
CONESTOGA ENTERPRISES	CENI	Telecommunications	49
HICKORY TECH CORP.	HTCO	Telecommunications	38
COMMONWLTH TELE ENTER	CTCO	Telecommunications	35
AT&T CORP.	T	Telecommunications	29
MOHAWK INDUSTRIES INC.	MHK	Textiles	80
QUAKER FABRIC CORP.	QFAB	Textiles	54
INTERFACE INC. -CL A	IFSIA	Textiles	23
PHILIP MORRIS COS. INC.	MO	Tobacco	66
UNIVERSAL CORP./VA	UVV	Tobacco	56
UST INC.	UST	Tobacco	55
DIMON INC.	DMN	Tobacco	28
STANDARD COMMERCIAL CORP.	STW	Tobacco	20
JAKKS PACIFIC INC.	JAKK	Toys	90
4 KIDS ENTERTAINMENT INC.	KDE	Toys	89
MICHAELS STORES INC.	MIK	Toys	59
MATTEL INC.	MAT	Toys	27
ACTION PERFORMANCE COS. INC.	ACTN	Toys	13
TOYS R US INC.	TOY	Toys	12
EXPEDITORS INTL WASH INC.	EXPD	Transportation	71
EGL INC.	EAGL	Transportation	29
GENERAL DYNAMICS CORP.	GD	Transportation Equipment	97
HARLEY-DAVIDSON INC.	HDI	Transportation Equipment	76
POLARIS INDS INC.	PII	Transportation Equipment	73
ARCTIC CAT INC.	ACAT	Transportation Equipment	59
WINNEBAGO INDUSTRIES	WGO	Truck Makers	84
THOR INDUSTRIES INC.	THO	Truck Makers	75
PACCAR INC.	PCAR	Truck Makers	44
STANDARD MOTOR PRODS	SMP	Truck Makers	29
NAVISTAR INTERNATIONL	NAV	Truck Makers	24
KNIGHT TRANSPORTATION INC.	KNGT	Truck Transport	90
LANDSTAR SYSTEM INC.	LSTR	Truck Transport	86
ROADWAY CORP.ORATION	ROAD	Truck Transport	81
USFREIGHTWAYS CORP.	USFC	Truck Transport	75
ARKANSAS BEST CORP.	ABFS	Truck Transport	73
ARNOLD INDUSTRIES INC.	AIND	Truck Transport	69
HEARTLAND EXPRESS INC.	HTLD	Truck Transport	62
YELLOW CORP.	YELL	Truck Transport	60
SWIFT TRANSPORTATION CO. INC.	SWFT	Truck Transport	50
WERNER ENTERPRISES INC.	WERN	Truck Transport	43
CHEMED CORP.	CHE	Waste	60
ALLIED WASTE INDS INC.	AW	Waste	58
HARSCO CORP.	HSC	Waste	40
WASTE MANAGEMENT INC.	WMI	Waste	17
INTERPOOL INC.	IPX	Water Transport	70
KIRBY CORP.	KEX	Water Transport	65
ALEXANDER & BALDWIN INC.	ALEX	Water Transport	46
PHILADELPHIA SUBURBAN CORP.	PSC	Water Utilities	78
AMERICAN WATER WORKS INC.	AWK	Water Utilities	72
AMERICAN STATES WATER CO.	AWR	Water Utilities	49
CALIFORNIA WATER SERVICE GP	CWT	Water Utilities	47
MIDDLESEX WATER CO.	MSEX	Water Utilities	38
SJW CORP.	SJW	Water Utilities	21
US CELLULAR CORP.	USM	Wireless Communications	72

APPENDIX D: THE TOP 150 "EASY-HOLD" STOCKS

	Ticker	Easy-Hold Rank
NORTHWESTERN CORP.	NOR	100
PACIFIC CAPITAL BANCORP.	SABB	100
SCHULER HOMES INC. -CL A	SHLR	99
TOLL BROTHERS INC.	TOL	99
INDEPENDENT BANK CORP./MI	IBCP	99
QUAKER CITY BANCORP. INC.	QCBC	99
JACK IN THE BOX INC.	JBX	99
TOMPKINSTRUSTCO. INC.	TMP	99
FIRST CITIZENS BANCSH -CL A	FCNCA	99
NVR INC.	NVR	99
FIRST SENTINEL BANCORP. INC.	FSLA	98
BLACK HILLS CORP.	BKH	98
MDU RESOURCES GROUP INC.	MDU	98
UTILICORP. UNITED INC.	UCU	98
COMMUNITY BANKS INC. MLLRSBRG	CTY	98
SUMMIT PROPERTIES INC.	SMT	98
GREAT SOUTHERN BANCORP.	GSBC	98
W HOLDING COMPANY INC.	WHI	98
CBL & ASSOCIATES PPTYS INC.	CBL	98
DUKE ENERGY CORP.	DUK	98
TRIAD GUARANTY INC.	TGIC	98
M & T BANK CORP.	MTB	97
HARBOR FLORIDA BANCSHARES	HARB	97
CVB FINANCIAL CORP.	CVBF	97
XANSER CORP.	XNR	97
DUKE REALTY CORP.	DRE	97
BEDFORD PPTY INVS INC.	BED	97
GENLYTE GROUP INC.	GLYT	97
GENERAL DYNAMICS CORP.	GD	97
UNIVERSAL AMERICAN FINL CP	UHCO	97
CPB INC.	CPBI	97
ALABAMA NATL BANCORP.ORATION	ALAB	96
MISSISSIPPI VY BANCSHARES	MVBI	96
RENT-A-CENTER INC.	RCII	96
KB HOME	KBH	96
LEXINGTON CORP. PPTYS TRUST	LXP	96
MERCK & CO.	MRK	96
U S B HOLDING INC.	UBH	96
GUIDANT CORP.	GDT	96
ULTRAMAR DIAMOND SHAMROCK	UDS	96
URS CORP.	URS	96
SANDY SPRING BANCORP. INC.	SASR	96
CURTISS-WRIGHT CORP.	CW	96
M/I SCHOTTENSTEIN HOMES INC.	MHO	96
FANNIE MAE	FNM	96
DORAL FINANCIAL CORP.	DORL	95
GARAN INC.	GAN	95
S Y BANCORP. INC.	SYI	95
EQUIFAX INC.	EFX	95
PHILADELPHIA CONS HLDG CORP.	PHLY	95
F N B CORP./FL	FBAN	95
MDC HOLDINGS INC.	MDC	95
WASHINGTON TR BANCORP. INC.	WASH	95
MATTHEWS INTL CORP. -CL A	MATW	95
CORVEL CORP.	CRVL	95
FINANCIAL FEDERAL CORP.	FIF	95
WESCO FINANCIAL CORP.	WSC	95

	TICKER	EASY-HOLD RANK
FEDERAL HOME LOAN MORTG CORP.	FRE	95
LILLY (ELI) & CO.	LLY	95
D R HORTON INC.	DHI	95
GBC BANCORP./CA	GBCB	95
CINERGY CORP.	CIN	95
AARON RENTS INC.	RNT	94
1ST SOURCE CORP.	SRCE	94
FYI INC.	FYII	94
CVS CORP.	CVS	94
ANSYS INC.	ANSS	94
MAF BANCORP. INC.	MAFB	94
DOWNEY FINANCIAL CORP.	DSL	94
FRONTIER OIL CORP.	FTO	94
CULLEN/FROST BANKERS INC.	CFR	94
GREATER BAY BANCORP.	GBBK	94
PUGET ENERGY INC.	PSD	94
AMLI RESIDENTIAL PPTYS TR	AML	94
GENERAL GROWTH PPTYS INC.	GGP	94
LENNAR CORP.	LEN	94
MIDLAND CO.	MLAN	94
STERLING BANCSHRS/TX	SBIB	94
ABM INDUSTRIES INC.	ABM	94
PENN VIRGINIA CORP.	PVA	94
KIMCO REALTY CORP.	KIM	93
VERIZON COMMUNICATIONS	VZ	93
ANCHOR BANCORP. INC./WI	ABCW	93
WORLD ACCEPTANCE CP/DE	WRLD	93
LIBERTY PROPERTY TRUST	LRY	93
STUDENT LOAN CORP.	STU	93
ALLIED CAPITAL CP	ALD	93
HEICO CORP.	HEI	93
MCGRATH RENTCORP.	MGRC	93
DEB SHOPS INC.	DEBS	93
CENTENNIAL BANCORP.	CEBC	93
COMMERCE GROUP INC./MA	CGI	93
KROGER CO.	KR	93
ON ASSIGNMENT INC.	ASGN	93
GABLES RESIDENTIAL TRUST	GBP	93
HOME PROPERTIES NEW YORK INC.	HME	93
COUSINS PROPERTIES INC.	CUZ	93
FIRST BANCORP. P R	FBP	93
WALGREEN CO.	WAG	93
PATTERSON DENTAL CO.	PDCO	93
SCANSOURCE INC.	SCSC	93
SALTON INC.	SFP	93
FLUSHING FINANCIAL CORP.	FFIC	92
HARLEYSVILLE NATL CORP./PA	HNBC	92
PULTE HOMES INC.	PHM	92
ROBERT HALF INTL INC.	RHI	92
AUTOMATIC DATA PROCESSING	ADP	92
NEW ENGLAND BUSINESS SVC INC.	NEB	92
IDACORP. INC.	IDA	92
BRINKER INTL INC.	EAT	92
FIRST FED CAP CORP.	FTFC	92
ANADARKO PETROLEUM CORP.	APC	92
FIRST FINANCIAL HOLDINGS INC.	FFCH	92
PS BUSINESS PARKS	PSB	92
EATON VANCE CORP.	EV	92
RYAN'S FAMILY STK HOUSES INC.	RYAN	92
EVERGREEN RESOURCES	EVG	92
NORTHWEST BANCORP. INC.	NWSB	92
AMBASSADORS INTERNATIONL INC.	AMIE	91
JONES APPAREL GROUP INC.	JNY	91
LINCARE HOLDINGS INC.	LNCR	91
ARDEN GROUP INC. -CL A	ARDNA	91
ALLTEL CORP.	AT	91
REGIONS FINL CORP.	RGBK	91
TEREX CORP.	TEX	91

	Ticker	Easy-Hold Rank
AREA BANCSHARES CORP.	AREA	91
DVI INC.	DVI	91
NEW JERSEY RESOURCES	NJR	91
SAFEWAY INC.	SWY	91
UMB FINANCIAL CORP.	UMBF	91
CATO CORP. -CL A	CACOA	91
DATASCOPE CORP.	DSCP	91
INSIGHT ENTERPRISES INC.	NSIT	91
SUSQUEHANNA BANCSHARES INC.	SUSQ	91
NORTHERN TRUST CORP.	NTRS	91
REALTY INC.O.ME CORP.	O	91
SUNOCO INC.	SUN	91
FIRST MERCHANTS CORP.	FRME	91
SCP POOL CORP.	POOL	91
WASHINGTON REIT	WRE	91
GREIF BROS CORP. -CL A	GBCOA	91
CITY NATIONAL CORP.	CYN	91
SEMPRA ENERGY	SRE	91
NORTEK INC.	NTK	90
JAKKS PACIFIC INC.	JAKK	90
BISYS GROUP INC.	BSYS	90
ZIONS BANCORP.ORATION	ZION	90
AMERICREDIT CORP.	ACF	90
HENRY (JACK) & ASSOC.	JKHY	90
SUNGARD DATA SYSTEMS	SDS	90

APPENDIX E: THE "EASY-HOLD"

MUTUAL FUND LIST (1,200 FUNDS)

Fund Name	Style	Ticker	Phone Number	Easy-Hold Rank
AAL Capital Growth A	Large Blend	AALGX	800-553-6319	62
AAL Equity Income A	Large Value	AAUTX	800-553-6319	80
AAL Mid Cap Stock A	Mid-Cap Growth	AASCX	800-553-6319	50
AAL Small Cap Stock A	Small Growth	AASMX	800-553-6319	54
Advance Capital I Eqty Grth	Mid-Cap Growth	ADEGX	800-345-4783	41
Advantus Horizon A	Large Growth	ADIOX	800-665-6005	2
Advantus Horizon B	Large Growth	ADHBX	800-665-6005	0
Advantus Horizon C	Large Growth	-	800-665-6005	1
Advantus Spectrum A	Domestic Hybrid	ADAAX	800-665-6005	39
Advantus Spectrum B	Domestic Hybrid	ADSBX	800-665-6005	29
Advantus Spectrum C	Domestic Hybrid	-	800-665-6005	30
Aetna Growth A	Large Growth	AEGAX	800-367-7732	9
Aetna Small Company A	Small Blend	AESAX	800-367-7732	66
AIM Adv Flex C	Large Value	IAFCX	800-959-4246	52
AIM Aggressive Growth A	Small Growth	AAGFX	800-959-4246	27
AIM Blue Chip A	Large Blend	ABCAX	800-959-4246	15
AIM Capital Development A	Small Growth	ACDAX	800-959-4246	43
AIM Charter A	Large Blend	CHTRX	800-959-4246	15
AIM Charter B	Large Blend	BCHTX	800-959-4246	8
AIM Constellation A	Large Growth	CSTGX	800-959-4246	14
AIM Global Health Care A	Specialty-Health	GGHCX	800-959-4246	88
AIM Global Health Care B	Specialty-Health	GTHBX	800-959-4246	84
AIM Global Utilities A	Specialty-Utilities	AUTLX	800-959-4246	64
AIM Global Utilities B	Specialty-Utilities	AUTBX	800-959-4246	53
AIM Mid Cap Equity A	Mid-Cap Growth	GTAGX	800-959-4246	65
AIM Mid Cap Equity B	Mid-Cap Growth	GTABX	800-959-4246	61
AIM Real Estate C	Specialty-Real Estate	IARCX	800-959-4246	88
AIM Summit	Large Growth	SMMIX	800-959-4246	11
AIM Value A	Large Blend	AVLFX	800-959-4246	33
AIM Value B	Large Blend	AVLBX	800-959-4246	21
AIM Weingarten A	Large Growth	WEINX	800-959-4246	6
AIM Weingarten B	Large Growth	BWEIX	800-959-4246	2
Alger Capital Apprec Retire	Large Growth	ALARX	800-992-3362	38
Alger Capital Appreciation B	Large Growth	ACAPX	800-992-3863	12
Alger Growth Retirement	Large Growth	ALGRX	800-992-3362	34
Alger Large Cap Growth B	Large Growth	AFGPX	800-992-3863	16
Alger Mid Cap Growth B	Mid-Cap Growth	AMCGX	800-992-3863	40
Alger Mid Cap Growth Retire	Mid-Cap Growth	ALMRX	800-992-3362	52
Alger Small Cap Retirement	Mid-Cap Growth	ALSRX	800-992-3362	8
Alger Small Capitalization B	Mid-Cap Growth	ALSCX	800-992-3863	0
Alleghany/Montag&Cald Gr N	Large Growth	MCGFX	800-992-8151	36
Alliance Growth & Income A	Large Value	CABDX	800-227-4618	87
Alliance Growth & Income B	Large Value	CBBDX	800-227-4618	75
Alliance Growth & Income C	Large Value	CBBCX	800-227-4618	76
Alliance Growth Investors A	Domestic Hybrid	AGIAX	800-227-4618	66
Alliance Growth Investors B	Domestic Hybrid	AGIBX	800-227-4618	59
Alliance Growth Investors C	Domestic Hybrid	AGICX	800-227-4618	60
Alliance Premier Growth A	Large Growth	APGAX	800-227-4618	3
Alliance Premier Growth B	Large Growth	APGBX	800-227-4618	2
Alliance Premier Growth C	Large Growth	APGCX	800-227-4618	2
Alliance Technology A	Specialty-Technology	ALTFX	800-227-4618	9
Alliance Technology B	Specialty-Technology	ATEBX	800-227-4618	7
Alliance Technology C	Specialty-Technology	ATECX	800-227-4618	7
AllianceBernstein Utility A	Specialty-Utilities	AUIAX	800-227-4618	93
AllianceBernstein Utility B	Specialty-Utilities	AUIBX	800-227-4618	88
AllianceBernstein Utility C	Specialty-Utilities	AUICX	800-227-4618	92
Alpine U.S. Real Estate Eq B	Specialty-Real Estate	AUEBX	888-785-5578	43
Alpine U.S. Real Estate Eq Y	Specialty-Real Estate	EUEYX	888-785-5578	47

Fund Name	Style	Ticker	Phone Number	Easy-Hold Rank
Amana Income	Large Value	AMANX	800-728-8762	63
American Capital Exchange	Large Growth	ACEHX	713-993-0500	61
American Cent Equity Gr Inv	Large Blend	BEQGX	800-345-2021	45
American Cent Equity Inc Inv	Mid-Cap Value	TWEIX	800-345-2021	100
American Cent Growth Inv	Large Growth	TWCGX	800-345-2021	17
American Cent Inc & Grow Inv	Large Value	BIGRX	800-345-2021	61
American Cent Ultra Inv	Large Growth	TWCUX	800-345-2021	18
American Cent Utilities Inv	Specialty-Utilities	BULIX	800-345-2021	85
American Cent Value Inv	Mid-Cap Value	TWVLX	800-345-2021	95
American Funds Amcap A	Large Growth	AMCPX	800-421-4120	86
American Funds Amer Mutual A	Large Value	AMRMX	800-421-4120	95
American Funds Fdmntl Invs A	Large Value	ANCFX	800-421-4120	84
American Funds Growth Fund A	Large Growth	AGTHX	800-421-4120	68
American Funds Inv Co Amer A	Large Value	AIVSX	800-421-4120	89
American Funds New Economy A	Large Blend	ANEFX	800-421-4120	40
American Funds Smcap World A	Small Growth	SMCWX	800-421-4120	24
American Funds Wash Mutual A	Large Value	AWSHX	800-421-4120	90
American Gas Index	Specialty-Utilities	GASFX	800-343-3355	98
American Heritage Growth	Mid-Cap Blend	AHEGX	800-828-5050	4
American Perform Balanced	Domestic Hybrid	APBAX	800-762-7085	74
American Perform Equity	Large Blend	APEQX	800-762-7085	42
Ameristock	Large Value	AMSTX	800-394-5064	97
AmSouth Capital Growth A	Large Growth	ICGAX	800-451-8379	22
AmSouth Large Cap A	Large Growth	ILCAX	800-451-8379	49
Aon REIT Index	Specialty-Real Estate	AREYX	800-266-3637	99
Apex Mid Cap Growth	Small Growth	BMCGX	877-593-8637	0
Aquila Cascadia Equity A	Mid-Cap Value	CASAX	800-228-7496	22
Aquila Cascadia Equity C	Mid-Cap Value	CASCX	212-697-6666	17
Aquila Cascadia Equity Y	Mid-Cap Value	ACEYX	212-697-6666	28
Ariel	Small Blend	ARGFX	800-292-7435	96
Ariel Appreciation	Mid-Cap Blend	CAAPX	800-292-7435	94
ARK Balanced A	Domestic Hybrid	ARBAX	800-275-3863	88
ARK Blue Chip Equity A	Large Value	ARBCX	800-275-3863	54
ARK Small Cap Equity A	Small Growth	ARPAX	800-275-3863	50
Artisan Small Cap	Small Growth	ARTSX	800-344-1770	40
Atlas Growth & Income A	Large Growth	ASGIX	800-933-2852	53
Avondale Hester Total Return	Large Blend	AHTRX	800-282-2340	71
AXP New Dimensions A	Large Blend	INNDX	800-328-8300	45
AXP New Dimensions B	Large Blend	INDBX	800-328-8300	26
AXP Research Opportunities A	Large Blend	IRDAX	800-328-8300	22
AXP Research Opportunities B	Large Blend	IROBX	800-328-8300	15
AXP Small Company Index A	Small Blend	ISIAX	800-328-8300	63
AXP Small Company Index B	Small Blend	ISIBX	800-328-8300	54
AXP Stock A	Large Blend	INSTX	800-328-8300	46
AXP Stock B	Large Blend	IDSBX	800-328-8300	35
AXP Strategy Aggressive A	Mid-Cap Growth	ISAAX	800-328-8300	10
AXP Strategy Aggressive B	Mid-Cap Growth	INAGX	800-328-8300	7
AXP Utilities Income A	Specialty-Utilities	INUTX	800-328-8300	88
AXP Utilities Income B	Specialty-Utilities	IUTBX	800-328-8300	81
Babson Enterprise II	Small Blend	BAETX	800-422-2766	78
Babson Growth	Large Growth	BABSX	800-422-2766	13
Baron Asset	Mid-Cap Growth	BARAX	800-992-2766	19
Baron Growth	Small Growth	BGRFX	800-992-2766	55
BB&T Balanced A	Domestic Hybrid	BBBAX	800-228-1872	68
BB&T Balanced B	Domestic Hybrid	BBBCX	800-228-1872	59
BB&T Balanced Tr	Domestic Hybrid	BBBBX	800-228-1872	75
BB&T Capital Appreciation B	Large Growth	OVCBX	800-228-1872	15
BB&T Large Company Value A	Large Value	BBTGX	800-228-1872	72
BB&T Large Company Value B	Large Value	BGISX	800-228-1872	60
BB&T Large Company Value Tr	Large Value	BBISX	800-228-1872	82
BB&T Mid-Cap Value B	Large Value	-	800-228-1872	90
BB&T Small Company Growth A	Small Growth	BBBSX	800-228-1872	14
BB&T Small Company Growth B	Small Growth	BSCGX	800-228-1872	10
BB&T Small Company Growth Tr	Small Growth	BBCGX	800-228-1872	18
Bear Stearns Insiders Sel A	Large Value	BSIAX	800-766-4111	73
Bear Stearns Insiders Sel C	Large Value	BSICX	800-766-4111	71
Berger Small Cap Value Inst	Small Value	BSVIX	800-333-1001	100
Berwyn	Small Value	BERWX	800-992-6757	63

Fund Name	Style	Ticker	Phone Number	Easy-Hold Rank
BlackRock Balanced Inv A	Domestic Hybrid	PCBAX	800-441-7762	58
BlackRock Balanced Inv B	Domestic Hybrid	CBIBX	800-441-7762	50
BlackRock Balanced Svc	Domestic Hybrid	PCBSX	800-441-7762	63
BlackRock Small Cap Grth IvA	Mid-Cap Growth	CSGEX	800-441-7762	24
BlackRock Small Cap Grth Svc	Mid-Cap Growth	PCGEX	800-441-7762	29
Bonnel Growth	Mid-Cap Growth	ACBGX	800-873-8637	20
Bramwell Growth	Large Growth	BRGRX	800-272-6227	35
Bridges Investment	Large Blend	BRGIX	402-397-4700	51
Bridgeway Aggressive Growth	Mid-Cap Growth	BRAGX	800-661-3550	44
Brinson Tactical Alloc A	Large Blend	PWTAX	800-647-1568	66
Brinson Tactical Alloc B	Large Blend	PWTBX	800-647-1568	55
Brinson Tactical Alloc C	Large Blend	KPAAX	800-647-1568	57
Brown Capital Balanced Instl	Large Growth	BCBIX	800-525-3863	51
Brown Capital Equity Instl	Large Growth	BCEIX	800-525-3863	22
Brown Capital Small Co Instl	Small Growth	BCSIX	800-525-3863	57
Buffalo Balanced	Domestic Hybrid	BUFBX	800-492-8332	84
Buffalo Equity	Large Blend	BUFEX	800-492-8332	71
Buffalo USA Global	Large Blend	BUFGX	800-492-8332	62
Burnham A	Large Blend	BURHX	800-874-3863	52
Burnham B	Large Blend	BURIX	800-874-3863	37
Calamos Growth A	Mid-Cap Growth	CVGRX	800-823-7386	47
Calamos Growth C	Mid-Cap Growth	CVGCX	800-823-7386	43
Caldwell & Orkin Market Opp	Domestic Hybrid	COAGX	800-237-7073	92
California Invmt S&P 500 Idx	Large Blend	SPFIX	800-225-8778	57
California Invmt S&P MidCap	Mid-Cap Blend	SPMIX	800-225-8778	87
Calvert Capital Accumulate A	Mid-Cap Growth	CCAFX	800-368-2748	26
Calvert Capital Accumulate C	Mid-Cap Growth	CCACX	800-368-2748	21
Calvert Large Cap Growth I	Large Growth	CLCIX	800-368-2748	19
Calvert Social Inv Equity A	Large Blend	CSIEX	800-368-2748	63
Calvert Social Inv Equity C	Large Blend	CSECX	800-368-2748	54
Capital Management MidCap Iv	Mid-Cap Blend	CMCIX	800-525-3863	64
Capital Value Inv	Domestic Hybrid	CAPVX	800-525-3863	36
Capstone Growth	Large Blend	TRDFX	800-262-6631	35
Carl Domino Equity Income	Mid-Cap Value	CDEIX	800-506-9922	82
CCMI Equity	Large Blend	COEFX	800-422-2080	52
CDC Nvest Capital Growth A	Large Growth	NEFCX	800-225-5478	5
CDC Nvest Capital Growth B	Large Growth	NECBX	800-225-5478	2
CDC Nvest Capital Growth C	Large Growth	NECGX	800-225-5478	2
CDC Nvest Growth A	Large Value	NEFGX	800-225-5478	46
CDC Nvest Growth and Inc A	Large Value	NEFOX	800-225-5478	34
CDC Nvest Growth and Inc B	Large Value	NEGBX	800-225-5478	29
CDC Nvest Growth and Inc C	Large Value	NECOX	800-225-5478	30
Centura Mid Cap Equity A	Mid-Cap Growth	CMEAX	800-442-3688	62
Centura Mid Cap Equity B	Mid-Cap Growth	CMEBX	800-442-3688	50
Centura Mid Cap Equity C	Mid-Cap Growth	CEGCX	800-442-3688	69
Century Shares Trust	Specialty-Financial	CENSX	800-321-1928	80
CGM Capital Development	Mid-Cap Value	LOMCX	800-345-4048	35
CGM Mutual	Domestic Hybrid	LOMMX	800-345-4048	61
CGM Realty	Specialty-Real Estate	CGMRX	800-345-4048	99
Chesapeake Aggressive Growth	Mid-Cap Growth	CPGRX	800-525-3863	13
Cincinnati	Mid-Cap Value	CINFX	800-354-5525	70
Citizens Core Growth Stndrd	Large Growth	WAIDX	800-223-7010	7
Citizens Emerg Growth Stndrd	Mid-Cap Growth	WAEGX	800-223-7010	29
Clipper	Large Value	CFIMX	800-776-5033	100
CMC Small Cap	Small Blend	COSCX	800-547-1707	48
Cohen & Steers Realty Shr	Specialty-Real Estate	CSRSX	800-437-9912	99
Columbia Growth	Large Growth	CLMBX	800-547-1707	13
Columbia Real Estate Equity	Specialty-Real Estate	CREEX	800-547-1707	99
Columbia Special	Mid-Cap Growth	CLSPX	800-547-1707	42
Commerce Balanced Instl	Domestic Hybrid	CFBLX	800-305-2140	59
Commerce Growth Instl	Large Blend	CFGRX	800-305-2140	12
Commerce Mid Cap Growth Instl	Mid-Cap Growth	CFAGX	800-305-2140	9
Concorde Value	Mid-Cap Value	CONVX	972-387-8258	82
Consulting Grp Lrg Cap Val	Large Value	TLVUX	212-816-8725	82
Consulting Grp Sm Cap Grth	Small Growth	TSGUX	212-816-8725	29
Consulting Grp Sm Cap Val	Small Value	TSVUX	212-816-8725	97
Copley	Large Value	COPLX	800-424-8570	73
Country Asset Allocation	Domestic Hybrid	CTYAX	800-245-2100	93

Fund Name	Style	Ticker	Phone Number	Easy-Hold Rank
Country Growth	Large Blend	CTYGX	800-245-2100	72
Credit Suisse Inst Sm Co Gr	Small Growth	WISCX	800-927-2874	23
CRM Small Cap Value Inv	Small Blend	CRMSX	800-276-2883	92
Croft-Leominster Value	Mid-Cap Value	CLVFX	800-551-0990	70
CS Warburg Pincus Bl Chp A	Large Blend	WIGRX	800-225-8011	35
CS Warburg Pincus Bl Chp B	Large Blend	WGRBX	800-225-8011	26
CS Warburg Pincus Cp Apr Adv	Large Growth	WCATX	800-927-2874	25
CS Warburg Pincus Cp Apr Com	Large Growth	CUCAX	800-927-2874	35
CS Warburg Pincus Emg Gr Adv	Mid-Cap Growth	WEGTX	800-927-2874	4
CS Warburg Pincus Emg Gr Com	Mid-Cap Growth	CUEGX	800-927-2874	7
CS Warburg Pincus SmCo VI A	Small Blend	WFAGX	800-225-8011	90
CS Warburg Pincus SmCo VI B	Small Blend	WSCBX	800-225-8011	77
Davis Financial A	Specialty-Financial	RPFGX	800-279-0279	57
Davis Financial B	Specialty-Financial	DFIBX	800-279-0279	48
Davis NY Venture A	Large Value	NYVTX	800-279-0279	71
Davis NY Venture B	Large Value	NYVBX	800-279-0279	52
Davis NY Venture C	Large Value	NYVCX	800-279-0279	53
Davis Real Estate A	Specialty-Real Estate	RPFRX	800-279-0279	94
Davis Real Estate B	Specialty-Real Estate	DREBX	800-279-0279	87
Delafield	Small Value	DEFIX	800-221-3079	96
Delaware Decatur Eq Inc A	Large Value	DELDX	800-523-4640	67
Delaware Decatur Eq Inc B	Large Value	DEIBX	800-523-4640	59
Delaware Decatur Eq Inc C	Large Value	DECCX	800-523-4640	61
Delaware Growth & Income A	Large Value	DEDTX	800-523-4640	56
Delaware Growth & Income B	Large Value	DEOBX	800-523-4640	48
Delaware Growth & Income C	Large Value	DTRCX	800-523-4640	50
Delaware Growth Opport A	Mid-Cap Growth	DFCIX	800-523-4640	27
Delaware Growth Opport B	Mid-Cap Growth	DFBIX	800-523-4640	19
Delaware Growth Opport C	Mid-Cap Growth	DEEVX	800-523-4640	20
Delaware REIT A	Specialty-Real Estate	DPREX	800-523-4640	98
Delaware Small Cap Value A	Small Value	DEVLX	800-523-4640	80
Delaware Small Cap Value B	Small Value	DEVBX	800-523-4640	64
Delaware Small Cap Value C	Small Value	DEVCX	800-523-4640	66
Delaware Trend A	Mid-Cap Growth	DELTX	800-523-4640	33
Delaware Trend B	Mid-Cap Growth	DERBX	800-523-4640	26
Delaware Trend C	Mid-Cap Growth	DETCX	800-523-4640	27
Deutsche Emerging Gr A	Small Growth	FLEGX	800-730-1313	22
Deutsche Emerging Gr B	Small Growth	FLEBX	800-730-1313	16
Deutsche Flag Communic A	Specialty-Communication	TISHX	800-730-1313	8
Deutsche Flag Communic B	Specialty-Communication	FTEBX	800-730-1313	4
Deutsche Flag Eq Partners A	Large Value	FLEPX	800-730-1313	73
Deutsche Flag Eq Partners B	Large Value	FEPBX	800-730-1313	56
Deutsche Flag Value Bldr A	Domestic Hybrid	FLVBX	800-730-1313	93
Deutsche Flag Value Bldr B	Domestic Hybrid	FVBBX	800-730-1313	83
Deutsche Real Estate Secs A	Specialty-Real Estate	FLREX	800-730-1313	95
Deutsche Real Estate Secs B	Specialty-Real Estate	FLRBX	800-730-1313	90
DFA U.S. Large Cap Value III	Mid-Cap Value	DFUVX	310-395-8005	93
Dodge & Cox Stock	Large Value	DODGX	800-621-3979	99
Domini Social Equity	Large Blend	DSEFX	800-762-6814	40
Dresdner RCM MidCap	Mid-Cap Growth	DRMCX	800-726-7240	31
Dresdner RCM Small Cap	Small Growth	DRSCX	800-726-7240	6
Dreyfus Appreciation	Large Blend	DGAGX	800-373-9387	61
Dreyfus Balanced	Domestic Hybrid	DRBAX	800-373-9387	88
Dreyfus Disc Stock	Large Blend	DDSTX	800-373-9387	38
Dreyfus Emerging Leaders	Small Growth	DRELX	800-373-9387	60
Dreyfus Founders Discovery F	Small Growth	FDISX	800-525-2440	33
Dreyfus Founders Growth F	Large Growth	FRGRX	800-525-2440	5
Dreyfus Growth & Income	Large Value	DGRIX	800-373-9387	69
Dreyfus LifeTime Growth Inv	Domestic Hybrid	DLGIX	800-373-9387	66
Dreyfus LifeTime Growth R	Domestic Hybrid	DLGRX	800-373-9387	71
Dreyfus New Leaders	Mid-Cap Growth	DNLDX	800-373-9387	55
Dreyfus Premier Balanced B	Domestic Hybrid	PRBBX	888-338-8084	65
Dreyfus Premier Balanced C	Domestic Hybrid	DPBCX	888-338-8084	67
Dreyfus Premier Core Val A	Large Value	DCVIX	888-338-8084	81
Dreyfus Premier Core Val Is	Large Value	DCVFX	888-338-8084	87
Dreyfus Premier Core Val R	Large Value	DTCRX	888-338-8084	89
Dreyfus Premier Grth & Inc A	Large Value	PEGAX	888-338-8084	47
Dreyfus Premier Grth & Inc B	Large Value	PEGBX	888-338-8084	41

Fund Name	Style	Ticker	Phone Number	Easy-Hold Rank
Dreyfus Premier Grth & Inc C	Large Value	DGICX	888-338-8084	43
Dreyfus Premier Grth & Inc R	Large Value	DRERX	888-338-8084	53
Dreyfus Premier Lrg Co Stk A	Large Blend	DRDEX	888-338-8084	22
Dreyfus Premier Lrg Co Stk R	Large Blend	DEIRX	888-338-8084	30
Dreyfus Premier Mid cap Stk A	Mid-Cap Blend	DPMAX	800-554-4611	48
Dreyfus Premier Mid cap Stk R	Mid-Cap Blend	DDMRX	800-554-4611	55
Dreyfus Premier Sm Co Stk A	Mid-Cap Growth	DPSAX	800-554-4611	37
Dreyfus Premier Sm Co Stk B	Mid-Cap Growth	DPSBX	800-554-4611	33
Dreyfus Premier Sm Co Stk C	Mid-Cap Growth	DPSCX	800-554-4611	36
Dreyfus Premier Sm Co Stk R	Mid-Cap Growth	DPSRX	800-554-4611	43
Dreyfus Premier Third Cent Z	Large Growth	DRTHX	800-373-9387	26
Dreyfus Small Company Value	Small Value	DSCVX	800-373-9387	71
Eagle Growth	Mid-Cap Blend	EGRWX	800-749-9933	83
Eastcliff Growth	Large Growth	EASGX	800-595-5519	13
Eastcliff Total Return	Large Growth	EATRX	800-595-5519	22
Eaton Vance Spec Equities A	Small Growth	EVSEX	800-225-6265	11
Eaton Vance Spec Equities B	Small Growth	EMSEX	800-225-6265	7
Eaton Vance Spec Equities C	Small Growth	ECSEX	800-225-6265	8
Eaton Vance Tax-Mgd Gr 1.0	Large Blend	CAPEX	800-225-6265	73
Eaton Vance Tax-Mgd Gr 1.1 A	Large Blend	ETTGX	800-225-6265	57
Eaton Vance Tax-Mgd Gr 1.1 B	Large Blend	EMTGX	800-225-6265	47
Eaton Vance Tax-Mgd Gr 1.1 C	Large Blend	ECTGX	800-225-6265	48
Eaton Vance Wldwd Health A	Specialty-Health	ETHSX	800-225-6265	70
Eclipse Growth Equity	Large Growth	NIGEX	770-631-0414	16
Eclipse Growth Equity Svc	Large Growth	MAGSX	770-631-0414	12
Eclipse Mid Cap Value	Mid-Cap Value	ECGIX	770-631-0414	75
Eclipse Small Cap Value	Small Value	EEQFX	770-631-0414	55
Elfun Trusts	Large Blend	ELFNX	800-242-0134	83
Elite Growth & Income	Large Blend	ELGIX	800-423-1068	75
Emerald Growth A	Small Growth	HSPGX	800-232-0224	44
Enterprise Equity Income A	Large Value	ENGIX	800-432-4320	62
Enterprise Equity Income B	Large Value	ENIBX	800-432-4320	56
Enterprise Growth A	Large Growth	ENGRX	800-432-4320	25
Enterprise Growth B	Large Growth	ENGBX	800-432-4320	19
Enterprise Small Co Value A	Small Blend	ENSPX	800-432-4320	79
Enterprise Small Co Value B	Small Blend	ESCBX	800-432-4320	74
EquiTrust Blue Chip	Large Value	FBBLX	800-247-4170	41
Evergreen Blue Chip B	Large Blend	EKNBX	800-343-2898	20
Evergreen Growth A	Small Growth	EGWAX	800-343-2898	29
Evergreen Growth C	Small Growth	EGRTX	800-343-2898	27
Evergreen Large Company Gr B	Large Growth	EKJBX	800-343-2898	14
Evergreen Omega A	Large Growth	EKOAX	800-343-2898	29
Evergreen Omega B	Large Growth	EKOBX	800-343-2898	20
Evergreen Omega C	Large Growth	EKOCX	800-343-2898	22
Evergreen Small Co Growth B	Mid-Cap Growth	EKABX	800-343-2898	17
Evergreen Util & Telecomm A	Specialty-Utilities	EVUAX	800-343-2898	75
Evergreen Util & Telecomm B	Specialty-Utilities	EVUBX	800-343-2898	65
Evergreen Util & Telecomm C	Specialty-Utilities	EVUCX	800-343-2898	60
Evergreen Util & Telecomm I	Specialty-Utilities	EVUYX	800-343-2898	82
Excelsior Blended Equity	Large Blend	UMEQX	800-446-1012	41
Excelsior Engy & Nat Resrc	Specialty-Natural Res	UMESX	800-446-1012	85
Excelsior Equity Instl	Large Growth	EXEQX	800-446-1012	31
Excelsior Value & Restruct	Large Value	UMBIX	800-446-1012	83
Excelsior Value Equity	Mid-Cap Value	UMVEX	800-446-1012	87
Excelsior Value Equity Instl	Mid-Cap Value	EXVAX	800-446-1012	90
Fairmont	Mid-Cap Value	FAIMX	800-262-9936	39
FAM Equity-Income	Small Blend	FAMEX	800-932-3271	95
FAM Value	Small Value	FAMVX	800-932-3271	96
Federated Capital Apprec A	Large Blend	FEDEX	800-341-7400	63
Federated Capital Apprec B	Large Blend	CPABX	800-341-7400	47
Federated Capital Apprec C	Large Blend	CPACX	800-341-7400	49
Federated Equity-Income A	Large Value	LEIFX	800-341-7400	47
Federated Equity-Income B	Large Value	LEIBX	800-341-7400	38
Federated Equity-Income C	Large Value	LEICX	800-341-7400	40
Federated Equity-Income F	Large Value	LFEIX	800-341-7400	44
Federated Growth Strat A	Large Growth	FGSAX	800-341-7400	21
Federated Growth Strat B	Large Growth	FGSBX	800-341-7400	15
Federated Growth Strat C	Large Growth	FGSCX	800-341-7400	17

Fund Name	Style	Ticker	Phone Number	Easy-Hold Rank
Federated Kaufmann K	Mid-Cap Growth	KAUFX	800-341-7400	51
Fidelity Adv Eqty Grth A	Large Growth	EPGAX	800-522-7297	27
Fidelity Adv Eqty Grth Instl	Large Growth	EQPGX	800-522-7297	35
Fidelity Adv Eqty Grth T	Large Growth	FAEGX	800-522-7297	24
Fidelity Adv Eqty Inc A	Large Value	FEIAX	800-522-7297	83
Fidelity Adv Eqty Inc B	Large Value	FEIBX	800-522-7297	72
Fidelity Adv Eqty Inc Instl	Large Value	EQPIX	800-522-7297	91
Fidelity Adv Eqty Inc T	Large Value	FEIRX	800-522-7297	81
Fidelity Adv Large Cap A	Large Growth	FALAX	800-522-7297	20
Fidelity Adv Large Cap B	Large Growth	FALHX	800-522-7297	13
Fidelity Adv Large Cap Instl	Large Growth	FALIX	800-522-7297	31
Fidelity Adv Large Cap T	Large Growth	FALGX	800-522-7297	19
Fidelity Adv Val Strat A	Small Blend	FSOAX	800-522-7297	76
Fidelity Adv Val Strat B	Small Blend	FASBX	800-522-7297	67
Fidelity Adv Val Strat Init	Small Blend	FSLSX	800-522-7297	90
Fidelity Adv Val Strat Instl	Small Blend	FASOX	800-522-7297	89
Fidelity Adv Val Strat T	Small Blend	FASPX	800-522-7297	74
Fidelity Asset Manager: Grth	Large Growth	FASGX	800-544-8888	66
Fidelity Blue Chip Growth	Large Growth	FBGRX	800-544-8888	23
Fidelity Capital Apprec	Large Blend	FDCAX	800-544-8888	57
Fidelity Congress Street	Large Blend	CNGRX	800-544-8888	84
Fidelity Contrafund	Large Growth	FCNTX	800-544-8888	59
Fidelity Dividend Growth	Large Blend	FDGFX	800-544-8888	82
Fidelity Equity-Income	Large Value	FEQIX	800-544-8888	88
Fidelity Exchange	Large Blend	FDLEX	800-544-8888	65
Fidelity Growth & Income	Large Blend	FGRIX	800-544-8888	65
Fidelity Growth Company	Large Growth	FDGRX	800-544-8888	41
Fidelity Independence	Large Growth	FDFFX	800-544-8888	44
Fidelity Large Cap Stock	Large Growth	FLCSX	800-544-8888	39
Fidelity Low-Priced Stock	Small Value	FLPSX	800-544-8888	99
Fidelity Magellan	Large Blend	FMAGX	800-544-8888	50
Fidelity New Millennium	Mid-Cap Growth	FMILX	800-544-8888	40
Fidelity Real Estate Invmnt	Specialty-Real Estate	FRESX	800-544-8888	100
Fidelity Value	Mid-Cap Value	FDVLX	800-544-8888	95
Fiduciary Capital Growth	Small Blend	FCGFX	800-338-1579	90
Fifth Third Balanced A	Domestic Hybrid	FSBFX	800-334-0483	64
Fifth Third Balanced C	Domestic Hybrid	FTBCX	888-799-5353	60
Fifth Third Mid Cap A	Mid-Cap Growth	FSMCX	800-334-0483	32
Fifth Third Mid Cap C	Mid-Cap Growth	FCMCX	888-799-5353	27
Fifth Third Multicap Val Adv	Mid-Cap Value	MXSEX	800-334-0483	87
Fifth Third Pinnacle A	Large Blend	FSPIX	800-334-0483	11
Fifth Third Quality Grth A	Large Blend	FSQGX	800-334-0483	33
Fifth Third Quality Grth C	Large Blend	FSQCX	888-799-5353	27
First American Equity Indx A	Large Blend	FAEIX	800-637-2548	45
First American Equity Indx B	Large Blend	FAEQX	800-637-2548	34
First American Equity-Inc A	Large Value	FFEIX	800-637-2548	89
First American Equity-Inc B	Large Value	FAEBX	800-637-2548	79
First American Health Sci A	Specialty-Health	FHSAX	800-637-2548	65
First American Health Sci B	Specialty-Health	FHSBX	800-637-2548	58
First American Lrg Cap Gr A	Large Growth	FFDGX	800-637-2548	4
First American Lrg Cap Gr B	Large Growth	FDGBX	800-637-2548	2
First American Lrg Cap Val A	Large Value	FASKX	800-637-2548	59
First American Lrg Cap Val B	Large Value	FATBX	800-637-2548	48
First American Mid Cap Val A	Mid-Cap Value	FASEX	800-637-2548	70
First American Mid Cap Val B	Mid-Cap Value	FAESX	800-637-2548	59
First American Real Estate A	Specialty-Real Estate	FREAX	800-637-2548	98
First American Real Estate B	Specialty-Real Estate	FREBX	800-637-2548	93
First American Sm Cap Grth A	Small Growth	FEGAX	800-637-2548	40
First American Sm Cap Val A	Small Blend	FSCAX	800-637-2548	83
First American Technology A	Specialty-Technology	FATAX	800-637-2548	7
First American Technology B	Specialty-Technology	FITBX	800-637-2548	4
First Eagle Fund of Amer Y	Mid-Cap Blend	FEAFX	800-451-3623	78
First Eagle SoGen Global A	International Hybrid	SGENX	800-334-2143	98
First Funds Growth & Inc II	Large Blend	FFGIX	800-442-1941	69
First Funds Growth & Inc III	Large Blend	FTREX	800-442-1941	62
First Invest Blue Chip A	Large Blend	FIBCX	800-423-4026	35
First Invest Blue Chip B	Large Blend	FBCBX	800-423-4026	18
First Invest Growth & Inc A	Large Blend	FGINX	800-423-4026	45

Fund Name	Style	Ticker	Phone Number	Easy-Hold Rank
First Invest Growth & Inc B	Large Blend	FGIBX	800-423-4026	30
First Invest Mid-Cap A	Mid-Cap Growth	FIUSX	800-423-4026	44
First Invest Special Sit A	Small Growth	FISSX	800-423-4026	15
First Invest Special Sit B	Small Growth	FISBX	800-423-4026	11
First Invest Utilities Inc A	Specialty-Utilities	FIUTX	800-423-4026	57
First Invest Utilities Inc B	Specialty-Utilities	FIUBX	800-423-4026	49
First Mutual	Large Growth	FMFDX	800-257-4414	15
Firsthand Technology Value	Specialty-Technology	TVFQX	888-884-2675	17
FirstMerit Equity	Large Growth	FMEFX	800-627-1289	7
Flex-funds Highlands Growth	Large Blend	FLCGX	800-325-3539	26
Flex-funds Total Return Util	Specialty-Utilities	FLRUX	800-325-3539	93
FMC Select	Mid-Cap Blend	-	800-932-7781	98
FPA Capital	Small Value	FPPTX	800-982-4372	74
FPA Perennial	Small Blend	FPPFX	800-982-4372	77
Franklin Bal Sheet Invmt A	Small Value	FRBSX	800-342-5236	97
Franklin CA Growth A	Mid-Cap Growth	FKCGX	800-342-5236	47
Franklin CA Growth C	Mid-Cap Growth	FCIIX	800-342-5236	28
Franklin Equity Income A	Large Value	FISEX	800-342-5236	93
Franklin Equity Income C	Large Value	FRETX	800-342-5236	85
Franklin Global Health A	Specialty-Health	FKGHX	800-342-5236	75
Franklin Global Health C	Specialty-Health	FGIIX	800-342-5236	59
Franklin Growth A	Large Blend	FKGRX	800-342-5236	78
Franklin Growth and Inc A	Large Growth	FKREX	800-342-5236	42
Franklin Growth and Inc C	Large Growth	FREQX	800-342-5236	24
Franklin Growth C	Large Blend	FRGSX	800-342-5236	64
Franklin MicroCap Value A	Small Value	FRMCX	800-342-5236	94
Franklin Rising Dividends A	Mid-Cap Value	FRDPX	800-342-5236	90
Franklin Rising Dividends C	Mid-Cap Value	FRDTX	800-342-5236	87
Franklin Small Cap Grth I A	Mid-Cap Growth	FRSGX	800-342-5236	45
Franklin Small Cap Grth I C	Mid-Cap Growth	FRSIX	800-342-5236	24
Franklin Utilities A	Specialty-Utilities	FKUTX	800-342-5236	92
Franklin Utilities C	Specialty-Utilities	FRUSX	800-342-5236	86
Franklin Value A	Small Value	FRVLX	800-342-5236	79
Franklin Value C	Small Value	FRVFX	800-342-5236	75
Fremont Structured Core	Large Blend	FEQFX	800-548-4539	45
Fremont U.S. Micro-Cap	Small Growth	FUSMX	800-548-4539	48
Frontier Equity	Small Growth	FEFPX	800-231-2901	1
Gabelli Asset	Mid-Cap Blend	GABAX	800-422-3554	94
Gabelli Equity-Income	Large Value	GABEX	800-422-3554	94
Gabelli Glob Telecommun	Specialty-Communication	GABTX	800-422-3554	46
Gabelli Growth	Large Blend	GABGX	800-422-3554	26
Gabelli Small Cap Growth	Small Blend	GABSX	800-422-3554	90
Gabelli Value	Mid-Cap Blend	GABVX	800-422-3554	72
Gabelli Westwood Bal Ret	Domestic Hybrid	WEBAX	800-937-8966	95
Gabelli Westwood Bal Svc	Domestic Hybrid	WEBCX	800-937-8966	91
Gabelli Westwood Equity Ret	Large Value	WESWX	800-937-8966	78
Gabelli Westwood Equity Svc	Large Value	WEECX	800-937-8966	63
Galaxy Equity Growth Ret A	Large Blend	GAEGX	800-628-0414	34
Galaxy Equity Growth Ret B	Large Blend	GBEGX	800-628-0414	25
Galaxy Equity Growth Tr	Large Blend	GEGTX	800-628-0414	41
Galaxy Equity Income Ret A	Large Value	GAEIX	800-628-0414	65
Galaxy Equity Income Tr	Large Value	GEITX	800-628-0414	79
Galaxy Equity Value Ret A	Large Value	GALEX	800-628-0414	48
Galaxy Equity Value Ret B	Large Value	GEVBX	800-628-0414	41
Galaxy Equity Value Tr	Large Value	GEVTX	800-628-0414	58
Galaxy Growth & Inc Ret A	Large Value	SGIEX	800-628-0414	60
Galaxy Growth & Inc Ret B	Large Value	GGRBX	800-628-0414	43
Galaxy Growth & Inc Tr	Large Value	SMGIX	800-628-0414	62
Galaxy Growth II Tr	Mid-Cap Growth	SEGRX	800-628-0414	46
Galaxy II Large Co Index Ret	Large Blend	ILCIX	800-628-0414	51
Galaxy II Small Co Index Ret	Small Blend	ISCIX	800-628-0414	82
Galaxy II Utility Index Ret	Specialty-Utilities	IUTLX	800-628-0414	93
Galaxy Large Cap Value Ret A	Large Value	GALVX	800-628-0414	48
Galaxy Large Cap Value Tr	Large Value	GTLVX	800-628-0414	55
Galaxy Small Cap Value Ret A	Small Blend	SSCEX	800-628-0414	95
Galaxy Small Cap Value Tr	Small Blend	SMCEX	800-628-0414	99
Galaxy Small Co Equity Ret A	Small Growth	GASEX	800-628-0414	37
Galaxy Small Co Equity Ret B	Small Growth	GERBX	800-628-0414	28

Fund Name	Style	Ticker	Phone Number	Easy-Hold Rank
Galaxy Small Co Equity Tr	Small Growth	GSETX	800-628-0414	44
Gartmore Total Return D	Large Blend	MUIFX	800-848-0920	46
Gateway	Domestic Hybrid	GATEX	800-354-6339	90
GE U.S. Equity A	Large Blend	GEEQX	800-735-4547	67
GE U.S. Equity B	Large Blend	GEEBX	800-735-4547	47
GE Value Equity A	Large Value	ITVAX	800-735-4547	59
GE Value Equity B	Large Value	ITVBX	800-735-4547	51
General Elec S&S Program	Large Value	GESSX	800-242-0134	81
Glenmede Large Cap Value	Large Value	GTMEX	800-442-8299	73
Glenmede Small Cap Value	Small Blend	GTCSX	800-442-8299	92
Glenmede Strategic Equity	Large Blend	GTCEX	800-442-8299	55
Golden Oak Growth A	Large Growth	GOGRX	800-545-6331	8
Goldman Sachs Cap Grth A	Large Blend	GSCGX	800-526-7384	30
Goldman Sachs Cap Grth B	Large Blend	GSCBX	800-526-7384	23
Goldman Sachs Core US Eq A	Large Blend	GSSQX	800-526-7384	37
Goldman Sachs Core US Eq B	Large Blend	GSSBX	800-526-7384	32
Goldman Sachs Core US Eq Svc	Large Blend	GSESX	800-526-7384	39
Government Street Equity	Large Blend	GVEQX	866-738-1125	54
Green Century Balanced	Small Growth	GCBLX	800-934-7336	45
Green Century Equity	Large Blend	GCEQX	800-934-7336	21
Growth Fund of Washington	Large Value	GRWAX	800-622-4273	51
Hancock Balanced A	Domestic Hybrid	SVBAX	800-225-5291	68
Hancock Balanced B	Domestic Hybrid	SVBBX	800-225-5291	60
Hancock Core Equity A	Large Blend	JHDCX	800-225-5291	25
Hancock Core Equity B	Large Blend	JHIDX	800-225-5291	18
Hancock Fincl Indust A	Specialty-Financial	FIDAX	800-225-5291	40
Hancock Health Sci A	Specialty-Health	JHGRX	800-225-5291	63
Hancock Health Sci B	Specialty-Health	JHRBX	800-225-5291	58
Hancock Regional Bank A	Specialty-Financial	FRBAX	800-225-5291	66
Hancock Regional Bank B	Specialty-Financial	FRBFX	800-225-5291	58
Hancock Small Cap Growth A	Small Growth	TAEMX	800-225-5291	23
Hancock Small Cap Growth B	Small Growth	TSEGX	800-225-5291	16
Hancock Sovereign Investor A	Large Value	SOVIX	800-225-5291	74
Hancock Sovereign Investor B	Large Value	SOVBX	800-225-5291	62
Hancock Technology A	Specialty-Technology	NTTFX	800-225-5291	14
Hancock Technology B	Specialty-Technology	FGTBX	800-225-5291	9
Harbor Capital Appreciation	Large Growth	HACAX	800-422-1050	25
Harbor Growth	Mid-Cap Growth	HAGWX	800-422-1050	39
Harbor Value	Large Value	HAVLX	800-422-1050	89
Harris Bretall Growth Equity	Large Growth	HBSSX	800-385-7003	4
Harris Ins Equity Instl	Large Value	HEQIX	800-982-8782	67
Harris Ins Equity N	Large Value	HIEQX	800-982-8782	65
Harris Ins Equity-Inc Instl	Large Value	HEIIX	800-982-8782	60
Harris Ins Equity-Inc N	Large Value	HENAX	800-982-8782	55
Hartford Cap Apprec A	Mid-Cap Growth	ITHAX	888-843-7824	56
Hartford Cap Apprec B	Mid-Cap Growth	IHCAX	888-843-7824	51
Hartford Dividend & Gr A	Large Value	IHGIX	888-843-7824	80
Hartford Dividend & Gr B	Large Value	ITDGX	888-843-7824	70
Hartford Stock A	Large Blend	IHSTX	888-843-7824	32
Hartford Stock B	Large Blend	ITSBX	888-843-7824	24
Haven	Mid-Cap Blend	HAVEX	800-844-4836	79
Heartland Value	Small Value	HRTVX	800-432-7856	87
Heartland Value Plus	Small Value	HRVIX	800-432-7856	73
Henlopen	Small Growth	HENLX	800-922-0224	28
Heritage Capital Apprec A	Large Blend	HRCPX	800-421-4184	50
Heritage Capital Apprec C	Large Blend	HRCCX	800-421-4184	46
Heritage Small Cap Stock A	Small Growth	HRSCX	800-421-4184	39
Heritage Small Cap Stock C	Small Growth	HSCCX	800-421-4184	34
Hibernia Capital Appr A	Large Blend	TWRSX	800 999-0124	36
HighMark Balanced Fid	Domestic Hybrid	HMBAX	800-433-6884	71
HighMark Balanced Ret A	Domestic Hybrid	HMBRX	800-433-6884	64
HighMark Growth Fiduciary	Large Growth	HMGRX	800-433-6884	4
HighMark Growth Ret A	Large Growth	HMRGX	800-433-6884	3
HighMark Large Cap Val Fid	Large Value	HMIEX	800-433-6884	60
HighMark Large Cap Val Ret A	Large Value	HMERX	800-433-6884	53
HighMark Val Momentum Fid	Large Value	HMVMX	800-433-6884	74
HighMark Val Momentum Ret A	Large Value	HMVLX	800-433-6884	64
Hodges	Mid-Cap Blend	HDPMX	877-232-1222	6

Fund Name	Style	Ticker	Phone Number	Easy-Hold Rank
Holland Balanced	Domestic Hybrid	HOLBX	800-304-6552	71
Homestead Value	Mid-Cap Value	HOVLX	800-258-3030	89
HSBC Growth & Income	Large Blend	MTREX	800-634-2536	21
Huntington Growth Inv A	Large Growth	HGWIX	800-253-0412	26
Huntington Growth Tr	Large Growth	HGWTX	800-253-0412	34
Huntington Income-Eq Tr	Large Value	HIEFX	800-253-0412	81
ICAP Discretionary Equity	Large Value	ICDEX	888-221-4227	92
ICAP Equity	Large Value	ICAEX	888-221-4227	92
IDEX Alger Aggressive Gr A	Large Growth	IAGAX	888-233-4339	10
IDEX Alger Aggressive Gr B	Large Growth	IAGBX	888-233-4339	8
IDEX Alger Aggressive Gr M	Large Growth	IAGCX	888-233-4339	9
IDEX Janus Capital Apprec A	Mid-Cap Growth	ICAPX	888-233-4339	5
IDEX Janus Capital Apprec B	Mid-Cap Growth	ICABX	888-233-4339	5
IDEX Janus Capital Apprec M	Mid-Cap Growth	ICACX	888-233-4339	4
IDEX Janus Growth A	Large Growth	IDETX	888-233-4339	7
IDEX Janus Growth B	Large Growth	IDEWX	888-233-4339	4
IDEX Janus Growth M	Large Growth	IDEUX	888-233-4339	5
IDEX LKCM Strategic TotRet A	Domestic Hybrid	IEQIX	888-233-4339	63
IDEX LKCM Strategic TotRet B	Domestic Hybrid	IEQBX	888-233-4339	56
IDEX LKCM Strategic TotRet M	Domestic Hybrid	IEQCX	888-233-4339	58
IMS Capital Value	Mid-Cap Value	IMSCX	800-934-5550	61
Independence One Eqty Pl Tr	Large Blend	IOEPX	800-334-2292	47
INVESCO Balanced Inv	Domestic Hybrid	IMABX	800-525-8085	72
INVESCO Blue Chip Growth Inv	Large Growth	FLRFX	800-525-8085	2
INVESCO Dynamics Inv	Mid-Cap Growth	FIDYX	800-525-8085	26
INVESCO Energy Inv	Specialty-Natural Res	FSTEX	800-525-8085	65
INVESCO Equity Income Inv	Large Blend	FIIIX	800-525-8085	68
INVESCO Leisure Inv	Mid-Cap Blend	FLISX	800-525-8085	68
INVESCO Small Company Gr Inv	Small Growth	FIEGX	800-525-8085	34
INVESCO Telecomm Inv	Specialty-Communication	ISWCX	800-525-8085	16
INVESCO Utilities Inv	Specialty-Utilities	FSTUX	800-525-8085	58
IPS Millennium	Large Growth	IPSMX	800-249-6927	32
Ivy Global Science & Tech A	Specialty-Technology	IVTAX	800-456-5111	1
Ivy Global Science & Tech B	Specialty-Technology	IVTBX	800-456-5111	0
Ivy Global Science & Tech C	Specialty-Technology	IVTCX	800-456-5111	0
Ivy Growth A	Large Growth	IVYFX	800-456-5111	4
Ivy Growth B	Large Growth	IVYBX	800-456-5111	1
Ivy Growth C	Large Growth	IVYCX	800-456-5111	1
Ivy US Emerging Growth A	Mid-Cap Growth	IVEGX	800-456-5111	7
Ivy US Emerging Growth B	Mid-Cap Growth	IVEBX	800-456-5111	4
Ivy US Emerging Growth C	Mid-Cap Growth	IVGEX	800-456-5111	5
Jamestown Balanced	Domestic Hybrid	JAMBX	866-738-1126	77
Jamestown Equity	Large Blend	JAMEX	866-738-1126	32
Janus Enterprise	Mid-Cap Growth	JAENX	800-525-8983	22
Janus Growth & Income	Large Growth	JAGIX	800-525-8983	62
Janus Mercury	Large Growth	JAMRX	800-525-8983	52
Janus Olympus	Large Growth	JAOLX	800-525-8983	44
Janus Venture	Small Growth	JAVTX	800-525-8983	30
Jefferson Growth & Income A	Mid-Cap Value	JEFAX	800-216-9785	43
Jensen	Large Growth	JENSX	800-221-4384	93
Jundt Growth A	Large Growth	JGFHX	800-370-0612	11
Jundt Growth B	Large Growth	JGFBX	800-370-0612	9
Jundt Growth C	Large Growth	JGFCX	800-370-0612	9
Jundt Growth I	Large Growth	JGFIX	800-370-0612	13
Jundt U.S. Emerging Growth A	Small Growth	JEGHX	800-370-0612	17
Jundt U.S. Emerging Growth B	Small Growth	JEGBX	800-370-0612	12
Jundt U.S. Emerging Growth C	Small Growth	JEGCX	800-370-0612	14
Kayne Anderson Rudnick Lg Cp	Large Blend	KARDX	310-556-2721	55
Keeley Small Cap Value	Small Value	KSCVX	800-533-5344	77
Kenilworth	Large Blend	-	312-236-5388	17
Kent Index Equity Invmt	Large Blend	KNIDX	800-633-5368	49
Kent Small Co Growth Invmt	Small Growth	KNEMX	800-633-5368	34
Kenwood Growth & Income	Mid-Cap Value	KNWDX	312-368-1666	84
Lake Forest Core Equity	Large Blend	LFCEX	800-592-7722	34
LEADER Growth & Income Instl	Large Blend	MAGIX	800-219-4182	50
Legg Mason Amer Leading Pr	Large Value	LMALX	800-577-8589	49
Legg Mason Focus	Large Blend	FOCTX	800-822-5544	14
Legg Mason Value Pr	Large Value	LMVTX	800-577-8589	54

Fund Name	Style	Ticker	Phone Number	Easy-Hold Rank
Leonetti Balanced	Domestic Hybrid	LEONX	800-282-2340	71
Liberty Acorn Z	Small Growth	ACRNX	800-322-2847	96
Liberty Contrarian Equity A	Mid-Cap Value	CHEYX	800-322-2847	67
Lighthouse Contrarian	Small Blend	LGFTX	800-282-2340	43
LKCM Equity	Large Blend	LKEQX	800-688-5526	83
LKCM Small Cap Equity	Small Blend	LKSCX	817-332-3235	95
Longleaf Partners	Mid-Cap Value	LLPFX	800-445-9469	98
Longleaf Partners Realty	Specialty-Real Estate	LLREX	800-445-9469	95
Longleaf Partners Small Cap	Small Value	LLSCX	800-445-9469	96
Lord Abbett Affiliated A	Large Value	LAFFX	800-201-6984	94
Lord Abbett Affiliated B	Large Value	LAFBX	800-201-6984	87
Lord Abbett Affiliated C	Large Value	LAFCX	800-201-6984	88
Lord Abbett All Value A	Large Value	LDFVX	800-201-6984	86
Lord Abbett All Value C	Large Value	GILAX	800-201-6984	82
Lord Abbett Developing Gr A	Small Growth	LAGWX	800-201-6984	25
Lord Abbett Developing Gr B	Small Growth	LADBX	800-201-6984	18
Lord Abbett Developing Gr C	Small Growth	LADCX	800-201-6984	20
Lord Abbett Growth Opport A	Mid-Cap Growth	LMGAX	800-201-6984	45
Lord Abbett Large-Cap Res A	Large Value	LRLCX	800-201-6984	80
Lord Abbett Large-Cap Res B	Large Value	LARBX	800-201-6984	64
Lord Abbett Mid-Cap Value A	Mid-Cap Value	LAVLX	800-201-6984	97
Lord Abbett Small-Cap Val A	Small Blend	LRSCX	800-201-6984	81
Lou Holland Growth	Large Blend	LHGFX	800-295-9779	40
Lutheran Brotherhood A	Large Blend	LUBRX	800-990-6290	36
MainStay Capital Apprec A	Large Growth	MCSAX	800-624-6782	10
MainStay Capital Apprec B	Large Growth	MCSCX	800-624-6782	8
Mairs & Power Balanced	Domestic Hybrid	MAPOX	800-304-7404	98
Mairs & Power Growth	Mid-Cap Blend	MPGFX	800-304-7404	99
Managers Special Equity	Small Growth	MGSEX	800-835-3879	42
Managers Value	Large Value	MGIEX	800-835-3879	82
Marshall Equity-Income Inv	Large Value	MREIX	800-236-8560	80
Marshall Lg-Cap Gr & Inc Inv	Large Blend	MASTX	800-236-8560	45
Marshall Mid-Cap Value Inv	Mid-Cap Value	MRVEX	800-236-8560	94
MassMutual Instl Balanced S	Domestic Hybrid	MBLDX	413-788-8411	78
Matrix Advisors Value	Mid-Cap Value	MAVFX	800-366-6223	89
Matrix Emerging Growth	Mid-Cap Growth	MEGFX	800-576-8229	2
Matrix Growth	Large Blend	GATGX	800-366-6223	18
Matterhorn Growth	Large Blend	FWLEX	800-637-3901	25
Matthew 25	Mid-Cap Blend	MXXVX	888-625-3863	79
Maxim Ariel SmallCap Value	Small Blend	-	800-338-4015	96
Maxim INVESCO SmallCap Gr	Small Growth	-	800-338-4015	33
MegaTrends	Large Value	MEGAX	800-873-8637	54
Mercury Growth Opportunity A	Large Growth	MROAX	800-995-6526	19
Mercury Growth Opportunity B	Large Growth	MROBX	888-763-2260	12
Mercury Growth Opportunity C	Large Growth	MROCX	800-995-6526	14
Mercury Growth Opportunity I	Large Growth	MROIX	800-995-6526	23
Mercury HW Large Cap Value I	Large Value	MCPIX	888-763-2260	88
Mercury HW Small Cap Value I	Small Value	MMAIX	888-763-2260	85
Merger	Domestic Hybrid	MERFX	800-343-8959	98
Meridian Growth	Small Growth	MERDX	800-446-6662	96
Meridian Value	Small Blend	MVALX	800-446-6662	98
Merrill Lynch Equity Inc A	Large Value	MADVX	800-995-6526	84
Merrill Lynch Equity Inc B	Large Value	MBDVX	800-995-6526	68
Merrill Lynch Equity Inc C	Large Value	MCDVX	800-995-6526	70
Merrill Lynch Equity Inc D	Large Value	MDDVX	800-995-6526	79
Merrill Lynch Focus Value A	Mid-Cap Blend	MAPNX	800-995-6526	80
Merrill Lynch Focus Value B	Mid-Cap Blend	MBPNX	800-995-6526	73
Merrill Lynch Focus Value C	Mid-Cap Blend	MCPNX	800-995-6526	68
Merrill Lynch Focus Value D	Mid-Cap Blend	MDPNX	800-995-6526	75
Merrill Lynch Fundmntl GrthA	Large Growth	MAFGX	800-995-6526	36
Merrill Lynch Fundmntl GrthB	Large Growth	MBFGX	800-995-6526	21
Merrill Lynch Fundmntl GrthC	Large Growth	MCFGX	800-995-6526	23
Merrill Lynch Fundmntl GrthD	Large Growth	MDFGX	800-995-6526	31
Merrill Lynch Healthcare A	Specialty-Health	MAHCX	800-995-6526	80
Merrill Lynch Healthcare B	Specialty-Health	MBHCX	800-995-6526	75
Merrill Lynch Healthcare C	Specialty-Health	MCHCX	800-995-6526	76
Merrill Lynch Healthcare D	Specialty-Health	MDHCX	800-995-6526	77
Merrill Lynch Natural Res A	Specialty-Natural Res	MAGRX	800-995-6526	77

Fund Name	Style	Ticker	Phone Number	Easy-Hold Rank
Merrill Lynch Natural Res B	Specialty-Natural Res	MBGRX	800-995-6526	56
Merrill Lynch Natural Res C	Specialty-Natural Res	MCGRX	800-995-6526	56
Merrill Lynch Natural Res D	Specialty-Natural Res	MDGRX	800-995-6526	61
Merrill Lynch Sm Cap Val A	Small Blend	MASPX	800-995-6526	83
Merrill Lynch Sm Cap Val B	Small Blend	MBSPX	800-995-6526	73
Merrill Lynch Sm Cap Val C	Small Blend	MCSPX	800-995-6526	73
Merrill Lynch Sm Cap Val D	Small Blend	MDSPX	800-995-6526	80
Meyers Pride Value	Mid-Cap Value	MYPVX	800-410-3337	65
MFS Core Growth A	Large Blend	MFCAX	800-225-2606	39
MFS Emerging Growth A	Large Growth	MFEGX	800-637-2929	7
MFS Emerging Growth B	Large Growth	MEGBX	800-637-2929	2
MFS Growth Opportunities A	Large Growth	MGOFX	800-637-2929	17
MFS Growth Opportunities B	Large Growth	MGOBX	800-637-2929	6
MFS Massachusetts Inv A	Large Blend	MITTX	800-637-2929	47
MFS Massachusetts Inv B	Large Blend	MITBX	800-637-2929	26
MFS Massachusetts Inv C	Large Blend	MITCX	800-637-2929	28
MFS Mid-Cap Growth A	Mid-Cap Growth	OTCAX	800-637-2929	37
MFS Mid-Cap Growth B	Mid-Cap Growth	OTCBX	800-637-2929	30
MFS Mid-Cap Growth C	Mid-Cap Growth	OTCCX	800-637-2929	31
MFS Utilities A	Specialty-Utilities	MMUFX	800-637-2929	87
MFS Utilities B	Specialty-Utilities	MMUBX	800-637-2929	77
MFS Utilities C	Specialty-Utilities	MMUCX	800-637-2929	78
MFS Value A	Large Value	MEIAX	800-637-2929	92
Monetta	Small Growth	MONTX	800-666-3882	20
Monetta Large-Cap Equity	Large Growth	MLCEX	800-666-3882	1
Monterey Murphy Technology	Specialty-Technology	MNWTX	800-251-1970	0
Montgomery Balanced P	Domestic Hybrid	MAAPX	800-572-3863	74
Montgomery Balanced R	Domestic Hybrid	MNAAX	800-572-3863	76
Montgomery Small Cap P	Small Growth	MNSPX	800-572-3863	11
Montgomery Small Cap R	Small Growth	MNSCX	800-572-3863	13
Morgan Keegan Select Cap Gr	Mid-Cap Blend	MKCGX	800-366-7426	11
Morgan Stan Inst SmCp Val	Small Blend	MPSCX	800-548-7786	78
Morgan Stanley Amer Opp B	Large Growth	AMOBX	800-869-6397	24
Morgan Stanley Cap Gr Secs B	Large Growth	CAPBX	800-869-3863	29
Morgan Stanley Dividend Gr B	Large Value	DIVBX	800-869-3863	60
Morgan Stanley Global Util B	Specialty-Utilities	GUTBX	800-869-3863	75
Morgan Stanley Mid-Cap Eq B	Mid-Cap Growth	MCFBX	800-869-3863	17
Morgan Stanley Nat Res Dev B	Specialty-Natural Res	NREBX	800-869-6397	42
Morgan Stanley Sm Cap Gr B	Mid-Cap Growth	SMPBX	800-869-3863	12
Morgan Stanley Total Ret B	Large Blend	TRFBX	800-869-3863	18
Morgan Stanley Utilities B	Specialty-Utilities	UTLBX	800-869-3863	66
Morgan Stanley Val-Add Mkt B	Mid-Cap Value	VADBX	800-869-3863	81
Mosaic Investors	Large Value	MINVX	800-368-3195	86
Mosaic Mid-Cap Growth	Mid-Cap Blend	GTSGX	800-368-3195	92
MSB	Large Blend	MSBFX	800-661-3938	61
Muhlenkamp	Mid-Cap Value	MUHLX	800-860-3863	70
Munder Index 500 A	Large Blend	MUXAX	800-468-6337	48
Munder Index 500 B	Large Blend	MUXBX	800-468-6337	44
Munder Index 500 K	Large Blend	MUXKX	800-468-6337	49
Munder Multi-Season Growth A	Large Blend	MUSAX	800-468-6337	19
Munder Multi-Season Growth B	Large Blend	MUSGX	800-468-6337	16
Munder Multi-Season Growth C	Large Blend	MUSCX	800-468-6337	14
Munder Multi-Season Growth K	Large Blend	MUSKX	800-468-6337	21
Munder Real Estate Eq Invt A	Specialty-Real Estate	MURAX	800-468-6337	91
Munder Real Estate Eq Invt B	Specialty-Real Estate	MURBX	800-468-6337	83
Munder Real Estate Eq Invt C	Specialty-Real Estate	MURCX	800-468-6337	85
Mutual Shares Z	Mid-Cap Value	MUTHX	800-553-3014	100
Nations Blue Chip Inv A	Large Blend	PHBCX	800-321-7854	31
Navellier Aggr Growth	Small Growth	NPFGX	800-887-8671	44
Navellier Aggr Small Cap Eq	Small Growth	NASCX	800-887-8671	2
Needham Growth	Mid-Cap Growth	NEEGX	800-625-7071	48
Neuberger Berman Fasciano	Small Growth	NBFSX	800-877-9700	70
Neuberger Berman Focus Adv	Large Value	NBFAX	800-877-9700	46
Neuberger Berman Focus Inv	Large Value	NBSSX	800-877-9700	54
Neuberger Berman Focus Tr	Large Value	NBFCX	800-877-9700	51
Neuberger Berman Genesis Inv	Small Blend	NBGNX	800-877-9700	89
Neuberger Berman Genesis Tr	Small Blend	NBGEX	800-877-9700	89
Neuberger Berman Guard Adv	Large Value	NBGUX	800-877-9700	42

Fund Name	Style	Ticker	Phone Number	Easy-Hold Rank
Neuberger Berman Guard Inv	Large Value	NGUAX	800-877-9700	54
Neuberger Berman Guard Tr	Large Value	NBGTX	800-877-9700	52
Neuberger Berman Manhatt Adv	Mid-Cap Growth	NBMBX	800-877-9700	8
Neuberger Berman Manhatt Inv	Mid-Cap Growth	NMANX	800-877-9700	14
Neuberger Berman Manhatt Tr	Mid-Cap Growth	NBMTX	800-877-9700	12
Neuberger Berman Part Adv	Large Value	NBPBX	800-877-9700	55
Neuberger Berman Part Inv	Large Value	NPRTX	800-877-9700	66
Neuberger Berman Part Tr	Large Value	NBPTX	800-877-9700	64
Neuberger Berman Soc Resp In	Large Value	NBSRX	800-877-9700	50
New Alternatives	Small Blend	NALFX	800-423-8383	87
Nicholas	Large Blend	NICSX	800-227-5987	42
Nicholas Equity Income	Mid-Cap Value	NSEIX	800-227-5987	74
Nicholas II	Mid-Cap Growth	NCTWX	800-227-5987	28
Nicholas Limited Edition	Small Growth	NCLEX	800-227-5987	29
Nicholas-Apple Grth Eq A	Mid-Cap Growth	NAPGX	800-225-1852	14
Nicholas-Apple Grth Eq B	Mid-Cap Growth	NAGBX	800-551-8643	9
Nicholas-Apple Grth Eq C	Mid-Cap Growth	PNACX	800-551-8643	10
Noah	Large Growth	NOAHX	800-794-6624	1
North American Gr & Inc A	Large Blend	NAIAX	800-872-8037	23
North American Gr & Inc B	Large Blend	NARBX	800-872-8037	20
North American Gr & Inc C	Large Blend	NAGIX	800-872-8037	23
North American Large Cp Gr A	Large Growth	NAEAX	800-872-8037	3
North American Large Cp Gr B	Large Growth	NAYBX	800-872-8037	1
North American Large Cp Gr C	Large Growth	NGECX	800-872-8037	1
North Track Achievers A	Large Blend	PDAPX	800-826-4600	15
North Track PSE Tec 100 Id A	Specialty-Technology	PPTIX	800-826-4600	30
North Track S&P 100 Plus A	Large Blend	PPSPX	800-826-4600	31
Northern Growth Equity	Large Growth	NOGEX	800-595-9111	38
Northern Select Equity	Large Growth	NOEQX	800-595-9111	39
Northern Technology	Specialty-Technology	NTCHX	800-595-9111	18
Nuveen Large-Cap Value A	Large Value	NNGAX	800-351-4100	80
Nuveen Large-Cap Value B	Large Value	NNGBX	800-621-7227	69
Nuveen Large-Cap Value C	Large Value	NNGCX	800-621-7227	71
Nuveen Large-Cap Value R	Large Value	NNGRX	800-621-7227	89
Oak Ridge Small Cap Equity	Mid-Cap Growth	ORIGX	800-407-7298	37
Oak Value	Mid-Cap Blend	OAKVX	800-622-2474	68
Oakmark Equity & Income I	Domestic Hybrid	OAKBX	800-625-6275	100
Oberweis Emerging Growth	Small Growth	OBEGX	800-323-6166	33
Oberweis Micro-Cap	Small Growth	OBMCX	800-323-6166	34
Old Dominion Investors'	Large Value	ODIFX	757-539-2396	51
Olstein Financial Alert C	Mid-Cap Value	OFALX	800-799-2113	70
ONE Fund Growth	Large Blend	ONGRX	800-578-8078	9
ONE Fund Income & Growth	Large Blend	ONIGX	800-578-8078	41
ONE Fund Small Cap	Small Growth	-	800-578-8078	7
One Group Divers Eq A	Large Blend	PAVGX	800-480-4111	39
One Group Divers Eq B	Large Blend	OVBGX	800-480-4111	24
One Group Equity Income A	Large Value	OIEIX	800-480-4111	67
One Group Equity Income B	Large Value	OGIBX	800-480-4111	56
One Group Equity Index A	Large Blend	OGEAX	800-480-4111	46
One Group Equity Index B	Large Blend	OGEIX	800-480-4111	24
One Group Large Cap Grth A	Large Growth	OLGAX	800-480-4111	7
One Group Large Cap Grth B	Large Growth	OGLGX	800-480-4111	3
One Group Large Cap Value A	Large Value	OLVAX	800-480-4111	67
One Group Large Cap Value B	Large Value	OLVBX	800-480-4111	49
One Group Mid Cap Growth A	Mid-Cap Growth	OSGIX	800-480-4111	40
One Group Mid Cap Growth B	Mid-Cap Growth	OGOBX	800-480-4111	33
One Group Mid Cap Value A	Mid-Cap Value	OGDIX	800-480-4111	90
One Group Mid Cap Value B	Mid-Cap Value	OGDBX	800-480-4111	72
One Group Small Cap Growth A	Small Growth	PGSGX	800-480-4111	41
One Group Small Cap Growth B	Small Growth	OGFBX	800-480-4111	36
Oppenheimer Capital Ap A	Large Growth	OPTFX	800-525-7048	42
Oppenheimer Capital Ap B	Large Growth	OTGBX	800-525-7048	36
Oppenheimer Capital Ap C	Large Growth	OTFCX	800-525-7048	37
Oppenheimer Growth A	Large Growth	OPPSX	800-525-7048	9
Oppenheimer Growth B	Large Growth	OPSBX	800-525-7048	5
Oppenheimer Growth C	Large Growth	OGRCX	800-525-7048	6
Oppenheimer Growth Y	Large Growth	OGRYX	800-525-7048	14
Oppenheimer Main St Gr&Inc A	Large Blend	MSIGX	800-525-7048	43

Fund Name	Style	Ticker	Phone Number	Easy-Hold Rank
Oppenheimer Main St Gr&Inc B	Large Blend	OMSBX	800-525-7048	23
Oppenheimer Main St Gr&Inc C	Large Blend	MIGCX	800-525-7048	25
Oppenheimer Quest Opport A	Large Value	QVOPX	800-525-7048	84
Oppenheimer Quest Opport B	Large Value	QOPBX	800-525-7048	79
Oppenheimer Quest Opport C	Large Value	QOPCX	800-525-7048	81
Oppenheimer Total Return A	Large Blend	OPTRX	800-525-7048	49
Oppenheimer Total Return B	Large Blend	OTRBX	800-525-7048	37
Oppenheimer Total Return C	Large Blend	OTRCX	800-525-7048	39
Oppenheimer Total Return Y	Large Blend	OTRYX	800-525-7048	54
Pacific Advisors Small Cap A	Small Blend	PASMX	800-989-6693	41
PaineWebber Pace Lg Gr Eq P	Large Growth	PCLCX	800-647-1568	6
PaineWebber Pace Sm/Med Gr P	Mid-Cap Growth	PCSGX	800-647-1568	38
Papp America-Abroad	Large Blend	PAAFX	800-421-4004	19
Papp Stock	Large Growth	LRPSX	800-421-4004	17
Parnassus Income Equity Inc	Large Value	PRBLX	800 999-3505	96
Payson Balanced	Large Value	PBFDX	800-805-8285	85
Payson Value	Large Value	PVFDX	800-805-8285	56
PBHG Growth	Mid-Cap Growth	PBHGX	800-433-0051	16
PBHG Growth Tr	Mid-Cap Growth	PBGWX	800-433-0051	12
PBHG Limited	Small Growth	PBLDX	800-433-0051	32
Pennsylvania Mutual Inv	Small Value	PENNX	800-221-4268	100
Performance Large Cap Eq A	Large Blend	PFECX	800-737-3676	38
Performance Mid Cap Eq A	Mid-Cap Blend	PCGCX	800-737-3676	45
Perkins Opportunity	Small Growth	POFDX	800-998-3190	30
Permanent Port Aggr Growth	Large Blend	PAGRX	800-531-5142	51
Phoenix-Duff Real Est A	Specialty-Real Estate	PHRAX	800-243-4361	98
Phoenix-Duff Real Est B	Specialty-Real Estate	PHRBX	800-243-4361	95
Phoenix-Seneca Growth A	Large Blend	SGCRX	860-403-5000	28
Phoenix-Seneca Mid-Cap Edg A	Mid-Cap Growth	EDGEX	860-403-5000	36
Phoenix-Seneca Real Estate A	Specialty-Real Estate	REALX	860-403-5000	86
Pilgrim Growth Opp A	Large Growth	NGRAX	800-334-3444	14
Pilgrim Growth Opp B	Large Growth	NGRBX	800-334-3444	10
Pilgrim Growth Opp C	Large Growth	NGRCX	800-334-3444	11
Pilgrim Growth Opp T	Large Growth	ADGRX	800-334-3444	11
Pilgrim Small Cap Opp A	Small Growth	NSPAX	800-334-3444	37
Pilgrim Small Cap Opp B	Small Growth	NSPBX	800-334-3444	30
Pilgrim Small Cap Opp C	Small Growth	NSPCX	800-334-3444	31
Pilgrim Small Cap Opp T	Small Growth	ADSPX	800-334-3444	31
PIMCO Innovation A	Specialty-Technology	PIVAX	888-877-4626	15
PIMCO Innovation B	Specialty-Technology	PIVBX	888-877-4626	12
PIMCO Innovation C	Specialty-Technology	PIVCX	888-877-4626	13
Pin Oak Aggressive Stock	Large Growth	POGSX	888-462-5386	25
Pioneer A	Large Value	PIODX	800-225-6292	67
Pioneer B	Large Value	PBODX	800-225-6292	48
Pioneer C	Large Value	PCODX	800-225-6292	49
Pioneer Equity-Income A	Large Value	PEQIX	800-225-6292	86
Pioneer Equity-Income B	Large Value	PBEQX	800-225-6292	74
Pioneer Equity-Income C	Large Value	PCEQX	800-225-6292	76
Pioneer Mid-Cap Value A	Mid-Cap Value	PCGRX	800-225-6292	81
Pioneer Mid-Cap Value B	Mid-Cap Value	PBCGX	800-225-6292	77
Pioneer Mid-Cap Value C	Mid-Cap Value	PCCGX	800-225-6292	77
Pioneer Value A	Large Value	PIOTX	800-225-6292	72
Pioneer Value B	Large Value	PBOTX	800-225-6292	52
Pioneer Value C	Large Value	PCOTX	800-225-6292	61
Polynous Growth A	Small Value	PAGFX	800-924-3863	20
Preferred Large Cap Value	Large Value	PFVLX	800-662-4769	80
Primary Trend	Large Value	PTFDX	800-443-6544	88
Principal Utilities A	Specialty-Utilities	PUTLX	800-451-5447	79
Principal Utilities B	Specialty-Utilities	PRUBX	800-451-5447	68
Prudential Natural Res A	Specialty-Natural Res	PGNAX	800-225-1852	62
Prudential Natural Res B	Specialty-Natural Res	PRGNX	800-225-1852	57
Prudential Natural Res C	Specialty-Natural Res	PNRCX	800-225-1852	58
Prudential Stock Index Z	Large Blend	PSIFX	800-225-1852	53
Prudential Utility A	Specialty-Utilities	PRUAX	800-225-1852	97
Prudential Utility B	Specialty-Utilities	PRUTX	800-225-1852	91
Prudential Utility C	Specialty-Utilities	PCUFX	800-225-1852	91
Putnam Fund for Grth & Inc A	Large Value	PGRWX	800-225-1581	78
Putnam Fund for Grth & Inc B	Large Value	PGIBX	800-225-1581	65

Fund Name	Style	Ticker	Phone Number	Easy-Hold Rank
Putnam Fund for Grth & Inc M	Large Value	PGRMX	800-225-1581	69
Putnam Global Growth & Inc A	World Stock	PUTIX	800-225-1581	72
Putnam Growth Opport A	Large Growth	POGAX	800-225-1581	5
Putnam Health Sciences A	Specialty-Health	PHSTX	800-225-1581	64
Putnam Health Sciences B	Specialty-Health	PHSBX	800-225-1581	56
Putnam Health Sciences M	Specialty-Health	PHLMX	800-225-1581	58
Putnam Investors A	Large Growth	PINVX	800-225-1581	9
Putnam Investors B	Large Growth	PNVBX	800-225-1581	5
Putnam Investors M	Large Growth	PNVMX	800-225-1581	6
Putnam New Opportunities A	Large Growth	PNOPX	800-225-1581	10
Putnam New Opportunities B	Large Growth	PNOBX	800-225-1581	6
Putnam New Opportunities M	Large Growth	PNOMX	800-225-1581	6
Putnam New Value A	Large Value	PANVX	800-225-1581	93
Putnam New Value B	Large Value	PBNVX	800-225-1581	85
Putnam New Value M	Large Value	PMNVX	800-225-1581	88
Putnam OTC Emerging Growth A	Mid-Cap Growth	POEGX	800-225-1581	3
Putnam OTC Emerging Growth B	Mid-Cap Growth	POTBX	800-225-1581	0
Putnam OTC Emerging Growth M	Mid-Cap Growth	POEMX	800-225-1581	1
Putnam Voyager II A	Mid-Cap Growth	PVIIX	800-225-1581	6
Putnam Voyager II B	Mid-Cap Growth	PVYBX	800-225-1581	2
Putnam Voyager II M	Mid-Cap Growth	PVYMX	800-225-1581	3
Pzena Focused Value	Mid-Cap Value	PZFVX	800-385-7003	84
Quantitative Mid Cap Ord	Mid-Cap Growth	QNIIX	800-326-2151	36
Quantitative Small Cap Ord	Small Growth	USBNX	800-326-2151	47
Regional Opportunity B	Large Growth	ROFBX	513-721-4800	6
Regions Value B	Large Value	FPEIX	800-433-2829	59
Reserve Informed Investors R	Large Growth	RIGAX	800-637-1700	27
Reserve Small-Cap Growth R	Small Growth	REGAX	800-637-1700	33
Reynolds Blue Chip Growth	Large Growth	RBCGX	800-773-9665	3
Reynolds Opportunity	Large Growth	ROPPX	800-773-9665	3
Rightime Blue Chip	Large Blend	RTBCX	800-242-1421	21
Rightime MidCap	Mid-Cap Growth	RTMCX	800-242-1421	33
Royce Low-Priced Stock	Small Value	RYLPX	800-221-4268	85
Royce Micro-Cap Inv	Small Value	RYOTX	800-221-4268	86
Royce Premier	Small Blend	RYPRX	800-221-4268	93
Royce Total Return	Small Value	RYTRX	800-221-4268	98
Royce Trust & GiftShares Inv	Small Value	RGFAX	800-221-4268	81
RS Contrarian	World Stock	RSCOX	800-766-3863	64
RS Diversified Growth	Small Growth	RSDGX	800-766-3863	38
RS Emerging Growth	Mid-Cap Growth	RSEGX	800-766-3863	32
RS MidCap Opportunities	Mid-Cap Growth	RSMOX	800-766-3863	50
RSI Retrmnt Core Equity	Large Blend	RSICX	800-772-3615	27
RSI Retrmnt Emerging Growth	Small Growth	RSIGX	800-772-3615	21
SAFECO Equity	Large Value	SAFQX	800-426-6730	51
SAFECO Growth Opp	Small Blend	SAFGX	800-426-6730	46
SAFECO Northwest	Mid-Cap Blend	SFNWX	800-426-6730	38
SAFECO Small Co Value	Small Blend	SFSCX	800-426-6730	44
Salomon Bros Capital O	Mid-Cap Value	SACPX	800-725-6666	96
Salomon Bros Investors Val 2	Large Value	SINOX	800-725-6666	73
Salomon Bros Investors Val A	Large Value	SINAX	800-725-6666	85
Salomon Bros Investors Val B	Large Value	SBINX	800-725-6666	72
Salomon Bros Investors Val O	Large Value	SAIFX	800-725-6666	91
Salomon Bros Opportunity	Large Value	SAOPX	800-725-6666	91
Schroder U.S. Smaller Co Inv	Small Growth	SCUIX	800-464-3108	76
Schwab 1000 Inv	Large Blend	SNXFX	800-435-4000	52
Schwab Analytics	Large Blend	SWANX	800-435-4000	49
Schwab MarketTrack Growth	Large Blend	SWHGX	800-435-4000	71
Schwab S&P 500 e.Sh	Large Blend	SWPEX	800-435-4000	53
Schwab S&P 500 Inv	Large Blend	SWPIX	800-435-4000	52
Schwab Small Cap Index Inv	Small Blend	SWSMX	800-435-4000	79
Schwartz Value	Small Value	RCMFX	888-726-0753	66
Scudder Blue Chip A	Large Blend	KBCAX	800-621-1048	28
Scudder Blue Chip B	Large Blend	KBCBX	800-621-1048	19
Scudder Blue Chip C	Large Blend	KBCCX	800-621-1048	23
Scudder Blue Chip I	Large Blend	-	800-621-1048	40
Scudder Capital Growth AARP	Large Blend	ACGFX	800-322-2282	28
Scudder Contrarian A	Large Value	KDCAX	800-621-1048	78
Scudder Contrarian B	Large Value	KDCBX	800-621-1048	67

Fund Name	Style	Ticker	Phone Number	Easy-Hold Rank
Scudder Contrarian C	Large Value	KDCCX	800-621-1048	69
Scudder Dreman Hi Ret Eq A	Large Value	KDHAX	800-621-1048	93
Scudder Dreman Hi Ret Eq B	Large Value	KDHBX	800-621-1048	84
Scudder Dreman Hi Ret Eq C	Large Value	KDHCX	800-621-1048	85
Scudder Dreman Hi Ret Eq I	Large Value	-	800-621-1048	97
Scudder Large Co Val S	Large Value	SCDUX	800-621-1048	85
Security Equity A	Large Blend	SECEX	800-888-2461	22
Security Equity B	Large Blend	SEQBX	800-888-2461	12
Security Ultra A	Mid-Cap Growth	SECUX	800-888-2461	49
Security Ultra B	Mid-Cap Growth	SEUBX	800-888-2461	40
Selected American	Large Value	SLASX	800-243-1575	79
Seligman Capital A	Mid-Cap Growth	SCFIX	800-221-2783	40
Seligman Capital B	Mid-Cap Growth	SLCBX	800-221-2783	31
Seligman Capital D	Mid-Cap Growth	SLCDX	800-221-2783	32
Seligman Common Stock A	Large Value	SCSFX	800-221-2783	42
Seligman Common Stock B	Large Value	SBCSX	800-221-2783	37
Seligman Common Stock D	Large Value	SCSDX	800-221-2783	38
Seligman Communicate&Info A	Specialty-Technology	SLMCX	800-221-2783	16
Seligman Communicate&Info B	Specialty-Technology	SLMBX	800-221-2450	13
Seligman Communicate&Info D	Specialty-Technology	SLMDX	800-221-2783	11
Seligman Global Technology A	Specialty-Technology	SHGTX	800-221-2450	13
Seligman Global Technology B	Specialty-Technology	SHTBX	800-221-2450	10
Seligman Global Technology D	Specialty-Technology	SHTDX	800-221-2450	11
Seligman Growth A	Large Growth	SGRFX	800-221-2783	8
Seligman Growth B	Large Growth	SGBTX	800-221-2783	5
Seligman Growth D	Large Growth	SGRDX	800-221-2783	6
Sentinel Common Stock A	Large Value	SENCX	800-282-3863	70
Sentinel Common Stock B	Large Value	SNCBX	800-282-3863	57
Sentinel Mid-Cap Growth A	Mid-Cap Growth	SNTNX	800-282-3863	20
Sentinel Small Company A	Small Growth	SAGWX	800-282-3863	74
Sentinel Small Company B	Small Growth	SESBX	800-282-3863	66
Sentry	Large Blend	SNTRX	800-533-7827	43
Sequoia	Large Value	SEQUX	800-686-6884	84
Sextant Growth	Large Growth	SSGFX	800-728-8762	58
SG Cowen Income+Growth A	Mid-Cap Value	COIGX	800-262-7116	97
SG Cowen Income+Growth B	Mid-Cap Value	-	800-262-7116	91
SG Cowen Income+Growth I	Mid-Cap Value	CIGCX	800-262-7116	98
SG Cowen Opportunity A	Small Blend	CWNOX	800-262-7116	74
SG Cowen Opportunity B	Small Blend	-	800-262-7116	69
SG Cowen Opportunity I	Small Blend	COPCX	800-262-7116	80
SIFE Trust A-I	Specialty-Financial	SIFEX	800-524-7433	63
SIFE Trust A-II	Specialty-Financial	SFIIX	800-524-7433	59
Sit Large Cap Growth	Large Growth	SNIGX	800-332-5580	8
Sit Mid Cap Growth	Mid-Cap Growth	NBNGX	800-332-5580	18
Sit Small Cap Growth	Mid-Cap Growth	SSMGX	800-332-5580	34
SM&R Equity Income T	Large Value	AMNIX	800-231-4639	64
SM&R Growth	Large Blend	AMRNX	800-231-4639	32
Smith Barney Aggr Growth A	Large Growth	SHRAX	800-451-2010	54
Smith Barney Aggr Growth B	Large Growth	SAGBX	800-451-2010	46
Smith Barney Aggr Growth L	Large Growth	SAGCX	800-451-2010	47
Smith Barney Appreciation A	Large Value	SHAPX	800-347-1123	82
Smith Barney Appreciation B	Large Value	SAPBX	800-347-1123	67
Smith Barney Appreciation L	Large Value	SAPCX	800-347-1123	68
Smith Barney Divers Lg Gr A	Large Growth	CFLGX	800-347-1123	10
Smith Barney Fundmntl Val A	Large Value	SHFVX	800-451-2010	77
Smith Barney Fundmntl Val B	Large Value	SFVBX	800-451-2010	68
Smith Barney Fundmntl Val L	Large Value	SFVCX	800-451-2010	69
Smith Barney Large Cp Core 1	Large Blend	CSGWX	800-451-2010	53
Smith Barney Large Cp Core A	Large Blend	GROAX	800-544-5445	42
Smith Barney Large Cp Core B	Large Blend	GROBX	800-451-2010	33
Smith Barney Peachtree Gr A	Large Growth	SBOAX	800-451-2010	3
Smith Barney Peachtree Gr B	Large Growth	SBOBX	800-451-2010	1
Smith Barney Peachtree Gr L	Large Growth	SBOLX	800-451-2010	1
Smith Barney Sm Cap Core A	Small Growth	SBDSX	800-451-2010	45
Smith Barney Soc Awareness A	Large Blend	SSIAX	800-451-2010	72
Smith Barney Soc Awareness L	Large Blend	SESLX	800-451-2010	61
Smith Barney Social Aware B	Large Blend	SESIX	800-451-2010	60
Smith Barney Telecomm Income	Specialty-Communication	ATINX	800-451-2010	38

Fund Name	Style	Ticker	Phone Number	Easy-Hold Rank
Sound Shore	Mid-Cap Value	SSHFX	800-551-1980	94
SouthTrust Value	Large Value	STREX	800-225-5782	79
Spectra N	Large Growth	SPECX	800-711-6141	15
SSgA Growth & Income	Large Blend	SSGWX	800-647-7327	52
SSgA S&P 500 Index	Large Blend	SVSPX	800-647-7327	54
SSgA Small Cap	Small Blend	SVSCX	800-647-7327	46
State Farm Balanced	Domestic Hybrid	STFBX	800-447-0740	83
State Farm Growth	Large Blend	STFGX	800-447-0740	59
State St Exchange	Large Blend	STSEX	800-562-0032	61
State St Res Glb Resource A	Specialty-Natural Res	SSGRX	800-882-0052	63
State St Res Glb Resource B	Specialty-Natural Res	SSBGX	800-882-0052	62
State St Res Glb Resource C	Specialty-Natural Res	SSGDX	800-882-0052	63
State St Res Glb Resource S	Specialty-Natural Res	-	800-882-0052	67
State St Res Invmnt Tr A	Large Blend	SITAX	800-882-0052	27
State St Res Invmnt Tr B	Large Blend	SITBX	800-882-0052	23
State St Res Invmnt Tr C	Large Blend	SITDX	800-882-0052	19
State St Res Invmnt Tr S	Large Blend	STSTX	800-882-0052	35
State St Res Large Growth A	Large Growth	SGFAX	800-882-0052	8
State St Res Large Growth B	Large Growth	SGFBX	800-882-0052	3
State St Res Large Growth C	Large Growth	SGFDX	800-882-0052	3
State St Res Large Growth S	Large Growth	STSGX	800-882-0052	10
State St Res Large Value A	Large Value	SSAVX	800-882-0052	64
State St Res Large Value B	Large Value	SSBIX	800-882-0052	56
State St Res Large Value C	Large Value	SSDVX	800-882-0052	57
State St Res Large Value S	Large Value	SSVCX	800-882-0052	76
Stein Roe Growth Stock	Large Growth	SRFSX	800-338-2550	16
Stein Roe Young Investor	Large Growth	SRYIX	800-338-2550	18
STI Classic Gr and I Flex	Large Value	CVIBX	800-428-6970	55
STI Classic Gr and I Inv	Large Value	CFVIX	800-428-6970	72
STI Classic Val Inc Stk Flex	Large Value	SVIFX	800-428-6970	60
STI Classic Val Inc Stk Inv	Large Value	SVIIX	800-428-6970	70
STI Classic Val Inc Stk Tr	Large Value	STVTX	800-428-6970	81
Stonebridge Aggressive Grth	Mid-Cap Growth	SBAGX	800-639-3935	43
Stratton Growth	Large Value	STRGX	800-634-5726	86
Stratton Monthly Div REIT	Specialty-Real Estate	STMDX	800-634-5726	99
Strong Advisor Common Stk Z	Mid-Cap Blend	STCSX	800-368-1030	72
Strong American Utilities	Specialty-Utilities	SAMUX	800-368-1030	96
Strong Growth & Inc Inv	Large Blend	SGRIX	800-368-1030	32
Strong Growth Inv	Large Growth	SGROX	800-368-1030	28
Strong Large Cap Growth	Large Growth	STRFX	800-368-1030	20
Strong Opportunity Inv	Mid-Cap Value	SOPFX	800-368-1030	86
Strong Value	Large Value	STVAX	800-368-1030	75
SunAmerica Blue Chip Grth A	Large Blend	SVLAX	800-858-8850	23
SunAmerica Blue Chip Grth B	Large Blend	SVLBX	800-858-8850	17
SunAmerica Growth & Income A	Large Blend	SEIAX	800-858-8850	22
SunAmerica Growth & Income B	Large Blend	SEIBX	800-858-8850	16
SunAmerica Growth Opp A	Mid-Cap Growth	SGWAX	800-858-8850	24
SunAmerica Growth Opp B	Mid-Cap Growth	SGWBX	800-858-8850	18
SunAmerica New Century A	Mid-Cap Growth	SEGAX	800-858-8850	18
SunAmerica New Century B	Mid-Cap Growth	SEGBX	800-858-8850	15
T. Rowe Price Blue Chip	Large Blend	TRBCX	800-638-5660	38
T. Rowe Price Capital Opport	Large Blend	PRCOX	800-638-5660	27
T. Rowe Price Equity-Inc	Large Value	PRFDX	800-638-5660	96
T. Rowe Price Growth Stock	Large Blend	PRGFX	800-638-5660	56
T. Rowe Price Mid-Cap Gr	Mid-Cap Growth	RPMGX	800-638-5660	57
T. Rowe Price New Era	Specialty-Natural Res	PRNEX	800-638-5660	86
T. Rowe Price New Horizons	Small Growth	PRNHX	800-638-5660	41
T. Rowe Price Sci & Tech	Specialty-Technology	PRSCX	800-638-5660	11
T. Rowe Price Sm-Cp Stk	Small Blend	OTCFX	800-638-5660	90
T. Rowe Price Sm-Cp Val	Small Value	PRSVX	800-638-5660	99
T. Rowe Price Value	Mid-Cap Value	TRVLX	800-638-5660	95
Texas Capital Value & Growth	Small Value	TCVGX	800-880-0324	50
Thompson Plumb Balanced	Domestic Hybrid	THPBX	800-356-1260	97
Thompson Plumb Growth	Large Blend	THPGX	800-356-1260	84
Thornburg Value A	Large Blend	TVAFX	800-847-0200	77
Thornburg Value C	Large Blend	TVCFX	800-847-0200	69
Timothy Plan Small Value A	Small Blend	TPLNX	800-846-7526	62
Timothy Plan Small Value B	Small Blend	TIMBX	800-846-7526	58
Tocqueville	Mid-Cap Value	TOCQX	800-697-3863	73

Fund Name	Style	Ticker	Phone Number	Easy-Hold Rank
Tocqueville Small Cap Value	Small Blend	TSCVX	800-697-3863	76
Torray	Large Value	TORYX	800-443-3036	74
Touchstone Aggressive Grth A	Large Growth	TAGAX	800-638-8194	10
Touchstone Growth/Value A	Large Growth	TGVFX	800-638-8194	32
Transamerica Prem Equity Inv	Large Growth	TEQUX	800-892-7587	13
Trent Equity	Large Blend	TREFX	336-282-9302	26
Turner Midcap Value	Mid-Cap Blend	CCEVX	800-224-6312	94
Turner Small Cap Value	Small Value	TCSVX	800-224-6312	94
Tweedy, Browne American Val	Mid-Cap Value	TWEBX	800-432-4789	91
U.S. Global Leaders Growth	Large Growth	USGLX	800-282-2340	50
UAM Analytic Defens Eq Instl	Large Blend	ANDEX	877-826-5465	83
UAM Analytic Enhanced Eq Ins	Large Blend	ANEEX	877-826-5465	60
UAM C&B Equity Inst	Mid-Cap Value	CBEQX	877-826-5465	97
UAM Chicago Asset Val/Cont	Large Value	CAMEX	877-826-5465	62
UAM FMA Small Co Instl	Small Blend	FMACX	877-826-5465	95
UAM Rice Hall James Sm Cap	Small Blend	RHJSX	877-826-5465	73
UAM Sirach Equity Instl	Large Growth	SIEQX	877-826-5465	8
UAM Sirach Growth Instl	Large Growth	SGRWX	877-826-5465	13
UAM Sirach Spec Eqty Instl	Mid-Cap Growth	SSEPX	877-826-5465	39
UAM TJ Core Equity Instl Svc	Large Value	TJCEX	877-826-5465	53
UAM TS&W Equity	Large Value	TSWEX	877-826-5465	75
USAA Aggressive Growth	Mid-Cap Growth	USAUX	800-382-8722	28
USAA Balanced Strategy	Domestic Hybrid	USBSX	800-382-8722	97
USAA Growth & Income	Large Value	USGRX	800-382-8722	77
USAA Growth Strategy	Large Growth	USGSX	800-382-8722	35
USAA Income Stock	Large Value	USISX	800-382-8722	89
Van Eck Global Hard Assets A	Specialty-Natural Res	GHAAX	800-826-1115	33
Van Eck Global Hard Assets B	Specialty-Natural Res	GHABX	800-826-1115	31
Van Eck Global Hard Assets C	Specialty-Natural Res	GHACX	800-826-1115	31
Van Eck/Chubb Growth & Incom	Large Blend	CHGIX	800-452-4822	13
Van Kampen Aggr Grow A	Mid-Cap Growth	VAGAX	800-421-5666	32
Van Kampen Aggr Grow B	Mid-Cap Growth	VAGBX	800-421-5666	24
Van Kampen Aggr Grow C	Mid-Cap Growth	VAGCX	800-421-5666	34
Van Kampen Amer Value A	Mid-Cap Blend	MSAVX	800-421-5666	41
Van Kampen Amer Value B	Mid-Cap Blend	MGAVX	800-421-5666	36
Van Kampen Amer Value C	Mid-Cap Blend	MSVCX	800-421-5666	37
Van Kampen Comstock A	Large Value	ACSTX	800-421-5666	97
Van Kampen Comstock B	Large Value	ACSWX	800-421-5666	91
Van Kampen Comstock C	Large Value	ACSYX	800-421-5666	92
Van Kampen Emerg Growth A	Large Growth	ACEGX	800-421-5666	37
Van Kampen Emerg Growth B	Large Growth	ACEMX	800-421-5666	27
Van Kampen Emerg Growth C	Large Growth	ACEFX	800-421-5666	27
Van Kampen Enterprise A	Large Growth	ACENX	800-421-5666	9
Van Kampen Enterprise B	Large Growth	ACEOX	800-421-5666	4
Van Kampen Enterprise C	Large Growth	ACEPX	800-421-5666	5
Van Kampen Growth & Income A	Large Value	ACGIX	800-421-5666	93
Van Kampen Growth & Income B	Large Value	ACGJX	800-421-5666	83
Van Kampen Growth & Income C	Large Value	ACGKX	800-421-5666	85
Van Kampen Growth A	Mid-Cap Growth	VGRAX	800-421-5666	26
Van Kampen Growth B	Mid-Cap Growth	VGRBX	800-421-5666	20
Van Kampen Growth C	Mid-Cap Growth	VGRCX	800-421-5666	21
Van Kampen Real Estate Sec A	Specialty-Real Estate	ACREX	800-421-5666	94
Van Kampen Real Estate Sec B	Specialty-Real Estate	ACRBX	800-421-5666	91
Van Kampen Real Estate Sec C	Specialty-Real Estate	ACRCX	800-421-5666	91
Van Kampen Utility A	Specialty-Utilities	VKUAX	800-421-5666	87
Van Kampen Utility B	Specialty-Utilities	VKUBX	800-421-5666	78
Van Kampen Utility C	Specialty-Utilities	VKUCX	800-421-5666	78
Van Wagoner Emerging Growth	Mid-Cap Growth	VWEGX	800-228-2121	19
Van Wagoner Mid-Cap Growth	Mid-Cap Growth	VWMDX	800-228-2121	3
Vanguard 500 Index	Large Blend	VFINX	800-662-7447	54
Vanguard Energy	Specialty-Natural Res	VGENX	800-662-7447	91
Vanguard Equity-Income	Large Value	VEIPX	800-662-7447	94
Vanguard Explorer	Small Growth	VEXPX	800-662-7447	69
Vanguard Ext Mkt Idx	Mid-Cap Blend	VEXMX	800-662-7447	47
Vanguard Growth Equity	Large Growth	VGEQX	800-662-7447	12
Vanguard Growth Idx	Large Growth	VIGRX	800-662-7447	25
Vanguard Morgan Growth	Large Blend	VMRGX	800-662-7447	51
Vanguard REIT Index	Specialty-Real Estate	VGSIX	800-662-7447	99
Vanguard Sm Cp Index	Small Blend	NAESX	800-662-7447	76

Fund Name	Style	Ticker	Phone Number	Easy-Hold Rank
Vanguard Strategic Equity	Mid-Cap Value	VSEQX	800-662-7447	96
Vanguard Tax-Mgd Cap App	Large Growth	VMCAX	800-662-7447	44
Vanguard Tax-Mgd Gr&Inc	Large Blend	VTGIX	800-662-7447	53
Vanguard Tot Stk Idx	Large Blend	VTSMX	800-662-7447	53
Vanguard Utilities Income	Specialty-Utilities	VGSUX	800-662-7447	87
Vanguard Value Index	Large Value	VIVAX	800-662-7447	82
Vanguard Windsor	Large Value	VWNDX	800-662-7447	92
Vanguard Windsor II	Large Value	VWNFX	800-662-7447	89
Victory Diversified Stock A	Large Value	SRVEX	800-539-3863	76
Victory Established Value G	Mid-Cap Value	GETGX	800-539-3863	88
Victory Growth A	Large Blend	SGRSX	800-539-3863	20
Victory Small Company Opp G	Small Value	GOGFX	800-539-3863	68
Victory Special Value A	Mid-Cap Value	SSVSX	800-539-3863	78
Victory Value A	Large Value	SVLSX	800-539-3863	69
Vintage Aggressive Growth	Large Growth	AVAGX	800-438-6375	12
Vintage Balanced	Domestic Hybrid	AMBFX	800-438-6375	70
Vintage Equity S	Large Blend	VEQSX	800-438-6375	24
Vontobel U.S. Value	Mid-Cap Value	VUSVX	800-527-9500	71
W&R Core Equity C	Large Blend	WTRCX	800-366-5465	36
W&R Core Equity Y	Large Blend	WCEYX	800-366-5465	42
W&R Small Cap Growth C	Small Growth	WRGCX	800-366-5465	38
Wachovia Equity A	Large Blend	BTEFX	800-994-4414	35
Wachovia Equity B	Large Blend	WEFBX	800-994-4414	15
Wachovia Equity Index A	Large Blend	BTEIX	800-994-4414	46
Wachovia Equity Index Y	Large Blend	BEIYX	800-994-4414	53
Wachovia Equity Y	Large Blend	BTEYX	800-994-4414	43
Wachovia Growth and Income A	Large Blend	CFEQX	800-994-4414	16
Wachovia Special Values A	Small Value	BTSVX	800-994-4414	97
Wachovia Special Values Y	Small Value	BSPYX	800-994-4414	99
Waddell & Reed Accumul A	Large Blend	UNACX	800-366-5465	80
Waddell & Reed Adv Accumul Y	Large Blend	WAAYX	800-366-5465	86
Waddell & Reed Adv Cont A	Domestic Hybrid	UNCIX	800-366-5465	84
Waddell & Reed Adv Vangrd A	Large Growth	UNVGX	800-366-5465	30
Wall Street	Mid-Cap Growth	WALLX	800-443-4693	29
Wasatch Core Growth	Small Blend	WGROX	800-551-1700	81
Wasatch Micro Cap	Small Growth	WMICX	800-551-1700	73
Wasatch Small Cap Growth	Small Growth	WAAEX	800-551-1700	57
Wasatch Ultra Growth	Small Growth	WAMCX	800-551-1700	45
Wayne Hummer Growth	Large Growth	WHGRX	800-621-4477	69
Weitz Hickory	Small Blend	WEHIX	800-232-4161	39
Wells Fargo Asset Alloc A	Domestic Hybrid	SFAAX	800-222-8222	76
Wells Fargo Asset Alloc B	Domestic Hybrid	SASBX	800-222-8222	66
Wells Fargo Divr Equity A	Large Blend	NVDAX	800-222-8222	53
Wells Fargo Divr Equity B	Large Blend	NVDBX	800-222-8222	35
Wells Fargo Equity Income A	Large Value	NVAEX	800-222-8222	67
Wells Fargo Equity Income B	Large Value	NVBEX	800-222-8222	58
Wells Fargo Growth A	Large Blend	SFGRX	800-222-8222	16
Wells Fargo Growth B	Large Blend	SBGWX	800-222-8222	10
Wells Fargo Growth Eq A	Large Growth	NVEAX	800-222-8222	29
Wells Fargo Growth Eq B	Large Growth	NVEBX	800-222-8222	21
Westcore Growth & Income	Large Growth	WTEIX	800-392-2673	52
Westcore Midco Growth	Mid-Cap Growth	WTMGX	800-392-2673	30
White Oak Growth Stock	Large Growth	WOGSX	888-462-5386	17
Whitehall Growth	Large Blend	WHGFX	800-994-2533	49
William Blair Growth N	Large Growth	WBGSX	800-742-7272	22
Wilshire Target Lrg Gr Inv	Large Growth	DTLGX	888-200-6796	19
Wilshire Target Lrg Val Inv	Large Value	DTLVX	888-200-6796	82
Wilshire Target Sm Gr Inv	Small Growth	DTSGX	888-200-6796	28
Wilshire Target Sm Val Inv	Small Value	DTSVX	888-200-6796	86
WM Growth A	Large Growth	SRGFX	800-222-5852	42
WM Growth B	Large Growth	SQGRX	800-222-5852	33
WM Small Cap Stock A	Small Growth	SREMX	800-222-5852	29
WM Small Cap Stock B	Small Growth	SQEMX	800-222-5852	25
WPG Large Cap Growth	Large Blend	WPGFX	800-223-3332	21
Wright Major Blue Chip Eqty	Large Blend	WQCEX	800-888-9471	25
Wright Selected Blue Chip Eq	Mid-Cap Blend	WSBEX	800-888-9471	44
WWW Internet	Specialty-Technology	WWIFX	606-263-2204	5
Yacktman	Mid-Cap Blend	YACKX	800-525-8258	76

APPENDIX F: THE TOP 100 "EASY-HOLD"
MUTUAL FUNDS

Fund Name	Ticker	Easy-Hold Rank
Clipper	CFIMX	100
Mutual Shares Z	MUTHX	100
Oakmark Equity & Income I	OAKBX	100
Berger Small Cap Value Inst	BSVIX	100
Pennsylvania Mutual Inv	PENNX	100
Fidelity Real Estate Invmnt	FRESX	100
American Cent Equity Inc Inv	TWEIX	100
Vanguard REIT Index	VGSIX	99
Fidelity Low-Priced Stock	FLPSX	99
Stratton Monthly Div REIT	STMDX	99
Dodge & Cox Stock	DODGX	99
Wachovia Special Values Y	BSPYX	99
Mairs & Power Growth	MPGFX	99
CGM Realty	CGMRX	99
Cohen & Steers Realty Shr	CSRSX	99
Aon REIT Index	AREYX	99
T. Rowe Price Sm-Cp Val	PRSVX	99
Galaxy Small Cap Value Tr	SMCEX	99
Columbia Real Estate Equity	CREEX	99
Meridian Value	MVALX	98
Delaware REIT A	DPREX	98
Royce Total Return	RYTRX	98
American Gas Index	GASFX	98
Mairs & Power Balanced	MAPOX	98
SG Cowen Income+Growth I	CIGCX	98
FMC Select	-	98
Phoenix-Duff Real Est A	PHRAX	98
First American Real Estate A	FREAX	98
Merger	MERFX	98
First Eagle SoGen Global A	SGENX	98
Longleaf Partners	LLPFX	98
Scudder Dreman Hi Ret Eq I	-	97
Van Kampen Comstock A	ACSTX	97
Thompson Plumb Balanced	THPBX	97
Prudential Utility A	PRUAX	97
Franklin Bal Sheet Invmt A	FRBSX	97
Consulting Grp Sm Cap Val	TSVUX	97
Wachovia Special Values A	BTSVX	97
UAM C&B Equity Inst	CBEQX	97
USAA Balanced Strategy	USBSX	97
SG Cowen Income+Growth A	COIGX	97
Lord Abbett Mid-Cap Value A	LAVLX	97
Ameristock	AMSTX	97
Meridian Growth	MERDX	96
Strong American Utilities	SAMUX	96
Longleaf Partners Small-Cap	LLSCX	96
Parnassus Income Equity Inc	PRBLX	96
Vanguard Strategic Equity	VSEQX	96
Maxim Ariel SmallCap Value	-	96
Delafield	DEFIX	96
FAM Value	FAMVX	96
T. Rowe Price Equity-Inc	PRFDX	96
Ariel	ARGFX	96
Liberty Acorn Z	ACRNX	96
Salomon Bros Capital O	SACPX	96
LKCM Small Cap Equity	LKSCX	95
Gabelli Westwood Bal Ret	WEBAX	95
FAM Equity-Income	FAMEX	95

Fund Name	Ticker	Easy-Hold Rank
Phoenix-Duff Real Est B	PHRBX	95
Deutsche Real Estate Secs A	FLREX	95
Fidelity Value	FDVLX	95
American Cent Value Inv	TWVLX	95
Longleaf Partners Realty	LLREX	95
American Funds Amer Mutual A	AMRMX	95
T. Rowe Price Value	TRVLX	95
Galaxy Small Cap Value Ret A	SSCEX	95
UAM FMA Small Co Instl	FMACX	95
Davis Real Estate A	RPFRX	94
Lord Abbett Affiliated A	LAFFX	94
Turner Midcap Value	CCEVX	94
Marshall Mid-Cap Value Inv	MRVEX	94
Franklin MicroCap Value A	FRMCX	94
Van Kampen Real Estate Sec A	ACREX	94
Gabelli Equity-Income	GABEX	94
Gabelli Asset	GABAX	94
Ariel Appreciation	CAAPX	94
Sound Shore	SSHFX	94
Vanguard Equity-Income	VEIPX	94
Turner Small Cap Value	TCSVX	94
DFA U.S. Large Cap Value III	DFUVX	93
First American Real Estate B	FREBX	93
Flex-funds Total Return Util	FLRUX	93
Van Kampen Growth & Income A	ACGIX	93
AllianceBernstein Utility A	AUIAX	93
Scudder Dreman Hi Ret Eq A	KDHAX	93
Royce Premier	RYPRX	93
Putnam New Value A	PANVX	93
Galaxy II Utility Index Ret	IUTLX	93
Deutsche Flag Value Bldr A	FLVBX	93
Jensen	JENSX	93
Country Asset Allocation	CTYAX	93
Franklin Equity Income A	FISEX	93
Vanguard Windsor	VWNDX	92
CRM Small Cap Value Inv	CRMSX	92
Mosaic Mid-Cap Growth	GTSGX	92
MFS Value A	MEIAX	92
Glenmede Small Cap Value	GTCSX	92
ICAP Equity	ICAEX	92
ICAP Discretionary Equity	ICDEX	92
Van Kampen Comstock C	ACSYX	92

INDEX

Page numbers of charts appear in italics.

A

Account aggregators, 203–4
Accounts receivable turnover, 168–71
  BMC Software example, 168–70,
    170
Acquisitions
  goodwill/intangible assets and, 186
  JDS Uniphase fiasco, 186–87
  review of company's and sell
    decision, 186–87
  tech companies and, 167
Airline stocks, 15
  easy-hold recommendation, 85
Alltel, 76–77
  dividend growth, 38
  ultimate all-weather portfolio pick,
    117
Alpha, 89
Amazon, 21
American Century Equity Income
    Fund, 91
Amgen, 181
AOL Time Warner, 31
Applied Materials, 32, 197
Asset allocation, 104
  aggressive growth, 106
  all-weather allocation, 106
  considering all assets and portfolios,
    107
  current income and, 105
  formula for percentage of portfolio
    in stocks, 104–5
  income and growth investments, 105
  long-term growth, 105
  preservation of capital, 105
  risk tolerance and, 104, 106
  time horizon and, 104
  tool for, SmartMoney.com, 106
Asset classes
  cash/fixed-income investments,
    50–51
  hard assets, 51

  real estate, 51
  stocks/stock mutual funds, 50
Asset correlation, 116
AT&T, 31
  tax liabilities and, 194
Athey, Preston, 95
Automatic Data Processing (ADP), 77,
    93
  ultimate all-weather portfolio pick,
    117
Average daily trading volume, 29–30
  source for statistics, 30

B

Banks, regional, 23
Barron's, finding yields of market
    indexes in, 37
Basic materials sector, 41
Berkshire Hathaway, 56
Beta, 19
  evaluating easy-hold mutual funds,
    89
  evaluating easy-hold stocks, 73
Bethlehem Steel, 56
Bid-ask spread, 30–31
Biotechnology sector
  easy-hold recommendation, 87
  long-term growth potential, 88
BISYS Group, 77
Bivio, 203
Bloomberg
  Personal Finance, 165–66, 172
  portfolio tracking, 202
  Web site, 166
BMC Software, 168–70, *170*
Bonds, 23
  corporate, 33, 39, 51
  credit risk (defaults), 95–96
  exotic investments, 33, 34
  foreign, 44
  401(k) plan allocation, 138
  high-coupon-paying, 44, 96
  illiquidity and, 33
  inflation risk, 97
  interest income, 36

Bonds *(continued)*
  interest-rate risk, 96
  junk, 96
  laddering, 97
  low-coupon-paying, 44, 96
  long-term, 44, 96
  low volatility, 44
  municipal, 39
  portfolio recommendations, 108
  ratings, 96, 108
  reinvestment risk, 96
  risk/return comparison, 51
  short-term, 44, 96
  treasury securities, 36, 39, 51
  types of (list), 50–51
  zero-coupon, 96
  See also Mutual funds (bonds).
Bogle, John, 210
Book value
  growth, 176–78
  per share, 177
Bristol-Myers Squibb, 21
Brokers
  Folio*fn*, 154–55
  Monthly Investment Plan, 153–54
  Sharebuilder, 154
  SIPC insurance, 156–58
Buffett, Warren, 56, 110
Burlington Northern Santa Fe, 179
Buy-and-hold investing
  "buy more over time" aspect, 66–67
  selling stocks and, 65–66
  volatility and, 17–18
Buying stock. *See* Dollar-based
  investing; Direct investments;
  DRIPs; Planning; Portfolio
  creation.
Buying Stock Without a Broker
  (Carlson), 145
ByAllAccounts, 203

C
Campbell Soup, 177
Capital expenditure ratio, 178–79
Capital gains. *See* Taxes.
Capital goods sector, 41
Carlson, Charles B.
  company's 401(k) plan and, 136
  company's managed account
    portfolios, 111
  diversification of own portfolio, 4

dividends received by, 36
DRIPs and, 145–47
early investing of, 146
newsletter, *DRIP Investor*, 291
"Stock Selector" columns, 165
tech stock holdings, 4
Cash burn, 173
CashEdge, 203
Cash flow, 168, 171. *See also* Accounts
  receivable turnover; Cash ratio.
Cash investments
  bull market in, 23
  liquidity and, 32, 33
  types of investments (list), 50–51
  ultimate all-weather portfolio
    component, 119
  Vanguard Money Market Fund, 119
Cash ratio, 171–72
  Palm example, 172–73
Charles Schwab
  account aggregator, 203
  per-trade charges online, 132
Cisco, 17, 32, 110, 165
  buying spree, 175–76
  decline, 126, 159, 188
  stock price, 65
Citigroup, 31
  account aggregator, 203
Clipper mutual fund, 91
Clorox, 93
Coca-Cola, 175
Commerce Group, dividend growth, 38
Communications services sector, 41
  easy-hold recommendation, 76–77
  telecom stocks, 77
Compaq, 180
Consumer cyclicals sector
  performance, 41
  volatility of, 43
Consumer staples sector
  performance, 41, 42
  weathering volatility and, 43
Contrarian investing, 211–12
"Cost basis" of investments, 193–94
CSX, 179
Cullen/Frost Bankers, dividend
  growth, 38

D
Datascope, 78
Dave & Busters's, 182

Day trader, 8, 67–68
Days payable, 174–75
Debt (of companies)
  interest coverage, 174
  long-term as a percentage of capital,
    184–85
Dell Computer, 32
  fixed-asset leverage ratio, 180
Direct-purchase plans, 145, 149–50
  easy-hold stock recommendations,
    78, 79–81, 82, 84, 85, 87
  recommended stocks, 151–53
Disney Corp., 196, 225–26
Diversification, 47–64
  across asset classes, 52–55
  age of investor and, 49–50
  asset classes, 50–51
  Carlson's portfolio, 4
  dollar-cost averaging, 57–60
  lack of, consequences, 3
  reason for, 48–49
  risk tolerance and, 53
  time, 57–63, *63*
  time horizon and asset classes, 53
  value averaging, 60–61
  weighting and rebalancing assets,
    55–57
  within asset classes, 49–52, 110, 111
Dividends
  companies with five-year dividend
    growth over ten percent, 38–39
  evaluating easy holds and, 73
  generating portfolio returns with,
    35
  growth, 37–39
  high-yield stocks, 37
  reinvesting, power of, 35
  S&P 500, annualized returns since
    1926, 35
  taxing of, 36
  volatile markets and, 34–36
  yield vs. growth, 37
Dodge & Cox Stock mutual fund, 92
Dollar-based investing, 129–31
  benefits, 130–31
  buying easier with, 128
  buying in volatile markets, 127, 196,
    236–37
  dollar-based brokers, 153–55
  DRIPs and direct-purchase plans,
    145–53

401(k) plans, 134–41
  mutual funds, 131–34
Dollar-cost averaging (DCA), 57–59
  lump-sum investing vs., 59–60
  tips for, 58–59
  value averaging vs., 61
Dow, Charles, 224, 226, 227
Dow Jones Industrial Average
  chart, *230*
  companies composing, 224–25
  decline, 2000, 4, 20, 52
  decline, 2001, 4
  gains, pre-2000, 7
  as price weighted, 225–26
  risk levels correlated with market
    returns, 221
  September 17, 2001, point drop, 15,
    221
Dow Jones Transportation Index, 224
  chart, *230*
  companies composing, 225
Dow Jones Utility Average
  gain, 2000, 4, 21
Dow Theory, 223–31
  chart, *230*
  primary trend, bear market, 228–29
  primary trend, bull market, 227–28
  tenets, 231
Dreyfus Appreciation Fund, 134
DRIP Investor, 291
DRIPs (dividend reinvestment plans),
    59, 145–47
  nuts and bolts of, 147–49
  recommended stocks, 151–53
  record-keeping, 151
  shortcomings, 150–51
  telephone redemption, 150
  ultimate all-weather portfolio picks,
    120
Duke Energy, 78, 117
Duke Realty, 78–79, 117

E
Earnings before interest and taxes
    (EBIT), 174
Earnings growth variability, 73
Eastman Kodak, 181
Easy holds, 69–71
  dollar-cost averaging and, 59
  fifteen "easy hold" criteria for
    evaluating stocks, 72–76

Easy holds *(continued)*
  finding, 71–72
  fixed-income investments
    recommended, 95–100
  health care sector, 43
  mutual funds recommended, 88–95
  stocks recommended, 76–88
Energy sector
  easy-hold recommendation, 79–80
  performance, 41
Equifax, 79, 93, 117
Equities. *See* Stocks.
Equity per share (book value per
  share), 73
Exotic investments, 33, 34
Expenses, dollar-cost averaging and,
  59
Exxon Mobil, 31, 79–80, 147
  direct-purchase and DRIP
    recommended, 152
  dividend growth, 38
  dividends, 36
  IRA option, 152
  ultimate all-weather portfolio pick,
    117

F
Fidelity Low-Price Stock mutual fund,
  92
Financial services sector
  easy hold recommendations, 77–78,
    79–80
  performance, 41
  weathering volatility and, 43
FinPortfolio, 202
First Midwest Bancorp, 38
First Virginia Banks, 38
Fixed-asset leverage ratio, 179–80
  railroads vs. software, 179–80
Fixed-income investments
  assets included in, 50–51
  I Bonds, 99–100
  mutual funds, 100
  risk measures to consider, 95–97
  TIPS (Treasury inflation-protected
    securities), 97–99
Float, 28–29
  finding at Yahoo! Finance, 28–29
Folio*fn*, 154–55
Foreign stocks and bonds
  bonds, 44

401(k) plan allocation, 138
  illiquidity and, 33
401(k) plan
  all-weather portfolio allocation,
    137–41
  asset allocation and, 107
  benefits, 135
  changing jobs and, 140–41
  contribution schedule, 137
  rebalancing, 140
  qualifier before maxing out,
    136
  regular investing and, 127
403(b) plan, 135, 137. *See also* 401(k)
  plan.
Futures markets, 212–15

G
Gainskeeper, 202
Gannett publishing company, 79
Gates, Bill, 56
Gateway, 180
GE, 31, 80–81, 196
  ultimate all-weather portfolio
    pick, 117
Globalization, 11–12
Gross profit margins, 167–68
Growth investing style, 65, 71,
  164–65
Growth stocks
  capital gains on, 35
  cash ratio, monitoring, 173
  late '90s and, 164
Guidant, 81
  ultimate all-weather portfolio
    pick, 117

H
Hamilton, William, 227
Harley-Davidson, 81–82
  ultimate all-weather portfolio
    pick, 117
Health care stocks, 23
  as "easy hold," 43
  easy-hold recommendations, 78,
    81, 82
  growth investors and, 71
  low volatility, 44
  as recession fighter, 42, 43
  sector performance, 41, 42
  spread of returns, 42, 43

I

I Bonds, 99–100
  Web site, 100
IBM, 31
  average daily trading volume, 29
  bid-ask spread, 31
  Dow Jones Industrial Average and,
    225–26
  market capitalization, 33
  outstanding shares, 28
Inflation
  bond risk and, 97
  index for measuring (CPI-U), 98
Information services, growth investors
    and, 71
Insider buying and selling, 29
Intel, 32
Interest coverage, 174
Intermediate Potential Risk Indicator,
    219–22, *220*
Internet
  account aggregators, 203–4
  dollar-based brokers on, 153–55
  portfolio trackers, 198–202
  retailing and, 19
  specialty trackers, 202–3
  stock information and stock
    volatility, 12–14, 28–30
  See also Yahoo! Finance; *specific sites.*
Internet (dot.com) stocks
  cause of extinction, 171
  overvaluation of, 8
  patterns of, 8
  price-earnings ratio of, 39
  volatility of, 19, 70
Inventory turnover ratio, 166–68
Invesco Fund, 132
  Dynamics, 134
Investor nation, 9–10
IRAs, traditional and Roth, 141–44
  asset allocation and, 107
  contribution limits, 144
  converting traditional to Roth,
    143–44
  investment options, 145
  SEP, 144–45
  taxes, 141, 142–43

J

JDS Uniphase, 32
  acquisitions, 175–76

loss, record-setting, 40, 186–87
stock price and earnings, 39–40,
    162
Jefferson-Pilot, 38
Jensen mutual fund, 92–93
John Nuveen, 38
Johnson & Johnson, 21, 82
  ultimate all-weather portfolio pick,
    117
Johnson Controls, 82
JPS industries
  average daily trading volume, 29–30
  bid-ask spread, 31
  outstanding shares (float), 28, 31

K

KEOGH, 145

L

Laddering, 97
Large-cap stocks
  annual returns since 1926, 62–63,
    63
  category defined, 33
  401(k) plan allocation, 138
  liquidity and, 33
  risk/return, 51
Lehman Brothers Aggregate Bond
    Index, 100
Limit orders, 163
Limited partnerships, 33
Lincoln National, 38
Liquidity, 26–31
  average daily trading volume and,
    29–30
  bid-ask spread and, 30–31
  company's, monitoring, 171–73
  float and, 28–29
  illiquid markets, 33–34
  maximizing, things to do, 33–34
  most liquid markets, 32–33
  quick escape route in volatile
    markets, 29
  safe vs. liquid, 32
  volume leaders and, 31–32
Long-Term Capital Management,
    32
Lucent Technologies, 4, 17, 31, 188,
    194
  red flags of decline, 166–67
  stock prices, 167

M

MacKinnon, Ian, 100
Mairs & Power Growth fund, 93
Margin, buying on, 222
Market timing, 227–31
    aggressive, 232
Marsh & McLennan, 38
Mayo, Grantham, 20
McGraw-Hill, 38
McGregor, Clyde, 94
Mercantile Bankshares, 38
Merck & Co., 21, 38
Meridian Value mutual fund, 93–94
    ultimate all-weather portfolio pick,
        118
Metrics (used in company analysis)
    accounts receivable turnover,
        168–71, *170*
    book value growth, 176–78
    capital expenditure ratio, 178–79
    cash ratio, 171–73
    days payable, 174–75
    deterioration of earnings and sales,
        165
    fixed-asset leverage ratio, 179–80
    inventory turnover ratio, 166–68
    long-term debt as a percentage of
        capital, 184–85
    profit margins, 183–84
    R&D as percentage of sales, 180–82
    sales per employee, 175–76
    same-store sales comparisons,
        182–83
Micro cap stocks
    category defined, 33, 94
    illiquidity and, 33
Microsoft, 32, 56, 83
    dividends, lack of, 36
    fixed-asset leverage ratio, 179–80
    Moneycentral-CNBC, 201
    ultimate all-weather portfolio pick,
        118
Mid-cap stocks, 401(k) plan allocation,
    138–39
Morgan Stanley, account aggregator,
    203
Morningstar, 113
    portfolio tracking, 202
Motorola, 31
Moving average, calculating, 219
Mutual funds (equity)

advantages for investors, 132
bear market performance, 90
correlations, 116
easy-hold criteria for, 88–90
expense ratio, 90
fees, 133
first, 131
401(k) plan allocation, 138
index funds, 133, 138
load-adjusted returns, 89
no-load, 59, 132
recommendations, 134
risk assessment, 116
Sharpe ratio and, 89
small initial investment, 132
taxes, 133
top ten easy holds, 91–95
ultimate all-weather portfolio picks,
    118
volatility of, 44
yield, 90
Mutual funds (fixed income/bonds),
    100
diversification, 116
portfolio recommendations, 108–9

N

Nasdaq Composite
    average daily move, 20
    decline, 2000, record of, 4, 20, 21, 52
    decline, 2001, 4
    gains, pre-2000, 7
    gains, record, 20
    most actives, 32
    VIXN, 216–18, *217, 218*
New Economy, 16
New York Stock Exchange
    Intermediate Potential Risk
        Indicator and, 219–22, *220*
    most actives, 31
    moving average, calculating, 219
No-Load Stocks (Carlson), 145
Norfolk Southern railroad, 179
Nortel Networks, 31

O

Oakmark Equity & Income mutual
    fund, 94
Old Republic International, 38
Operating profit margins, 86
Oracle, 32, 110, 179

P

Palm, 172–73

Patterson Dental, 83

Pennsylvania Mutual fund, 94
  ultimate all-weather portfolio pick,
    118

PeopleSoft, 179

Pets.com, 17

Pfizer, 31, 83–84
  direct-purchase and DRIP
    recommended, 152
  R&D, 181–82
  ultimate all-weather portfolio pick,
    118

Pharmaceuticals
  easy-hold recommendation, 83–84
  ultimate all-weather portfolio pick,
    118

Philadelphia Suburban, 84
  ultimate all-weather portfolio pick,
    118

Philip Morris, 38

Planning, 237–38
  buy opportunity or "watch list," 192,
    196–97
  calmness during volatile markets,
    197–98
  KISS, 204
  market timing and, 232–33
  organizing investments, 191
  sell decisions, 192, 198
  tax implications, 192, 193–96
  three factors, 205
  See also Account aggregators;
    Portfolio trackers.

Popular, 84–85
  direct-purchase and DRIP
    recommended, 152–53
  dividends, 36
  ultimate all-weather portfolio pick,
    118
  Web site, 85, 153

Portfolio creation
  account aggregators, 203–4
  all-weather allocation, 106
  asset allocation, 104–7
  asset correlation, 116
  benchmarking with S&P 500,
    112–13
  bonds/bond mutual funds, 108–9
  diversification across asset classes,

52–55
  diversification within asset classes,
    49–52, 110, 112
  dollar-cost averaging, 57–60
  easy holds (fixed-income
    investments), 95–100
  easy holds (mutual funds), 88–95
  easy holds (stocks), 69–88
  extending investment holding
    periods, 61–63, *63*
  401(k) plan allocation, 137–39
  how many stocks and mutual funds
    in, 111
  "Instant X-Ray" of, 113
  mutual fund diversification, 116
  questions to ask yourself, 122–23
  RiskGrades and, 114–15, 116
  risk lowering, 109–11
  sectors chosen for, 112–13
  single stock weightings, 112
  stock selection, 114–15
  time diversification, 57
  types of, 107
  upgrading during volatile markets,
    127–28
  value averaging, 60–61
  volatile stocks in, 69
  weighting and rebalancing assets,
    55–57. 112–13
  See also Planning; Portfolio:
    Ultimate All-Weather.

Portfolio tracking, 198–203
  Microsoft Moneycentral, 201
  Quicken, 199–200
  specialty trackers, 202–3

Portfolio: ultimate all-weather
  bond fund picks, 118–19
  cash component, 119
  mutual fund picks, 118
  number of investments, 119
  risk profile, 120–22
  start-up costs, 119–20
  stock allocation, 119
  stock picks, 117–18
  taxes and, 119

Price/earnings ratio, 164–65
  evaluating easy holds and, 75
  late '90s and, 164

Private equity, 33

Procter & Gamble, 147

Profit margins, 183–84

Public Storage, 38
Publishing, easy-hold
    recommendation, 80

Q

Quaker Horizon Dow 30 Plus Fund, 57
QUALCOMM, 32
Quicken
    account aggregator, 203, 204
    portfolio tracker, 199–200
    Web site, 200

R

Real estate
    diversification and, 53
    easy-hold recommendations, 78–79
    investment trusts (REITs), 23, 79
    types of investment, 51
Recession fighting stocks, 39–43
Reports, annual or quarterly
    company's outstanding shares
        listed, 28
    source for, SEC Web site, 28
    10-Q and 10-K, 166, 169, 174
Research & development (R&D)
    as percentage of sales, 180–82
    Pfizer, 181–82
    spending as "tiebreaker," 181
Retail industry, 19
    easy-hold recommendation, 86–87
Retirement, dollar-based investments,
    134
    401(k) plans, 134–41
    IRAs, traditional and Roth, 141–44
    KEOGH, 145
    SEP IRA, 144–45
Return on Equity (ROE), 74
    evaluating easy holds and, 74, 86
Revenue growth
    evaluating easy holds and, 73, 74
    variability, 74
Reverse stock split, 130
Reversion to mean, 209–12
Risk
    bond exposure to, 95–97
    diversification and, 53
    eye-of-the-hurricane investing
        (conservative growth), 25
    finding the eye of the hurricane, 26
    Intermediate Potential Risk
        Indicator, 219–22, *220*

large-cap vs. small-cap stocks, 51
    measuring, RiskGrades and, 114–15,
        116
    systematic (overall market),
        109–110
    tolerance for, 44, 53–55, 104, 106
    unsystematic (company), 109,
        110–11
    See also Asset allocation; Liquidity;
        Volatility.
RiskGrades, 202
    how to use, 114–15
    mutual funds and, 116
Roth Conversion Calculators, 143–44
Russell 2000
    decline 2000, 4, 20
Russell 3000
    evaluating easy holds and, 72–73

S

Sales
    per employee, 175–76
    R&D as percentage of, 180–82
    same-store comparisons, 182–83
Santayana, George, 1
SBC Communications, 38
Scudder, 131
SEC (Securities and Exchange
    Commission)
    company 10-Q and 10-Ks and, 166
    Regulation FD (Fair Disclosure),
        12–14
Sectors, 40–43
    best/worst returns, 43
    performance, 40–41
    See also specific sectors.
Selling stock
    accounting chicanery, finding, 187
    avoiding the big loser, 160–61
    deterioration of earnings and sales,
        165
    limit orders, 163
    market timing, 227–31, 232
    metrics to analyze company's
        health, 165–86
    objectivity with previous winners
        and, 187–88
    reinvestment risk, 159–60
    stop order, 163
    stress tests to review stocks,
        185–86

taxes, 159, 188
transaction fees, 160
volatile markets and, 161
when to sell, 161–63
See also Metrics.
SEP IRA, 144–45
Sharebuilder, 154
Sharpe ratio, 89
Siebel Systems, 179
Siegel, Jeremy, 18–19
SIPC insurance, 156–58
Web site, 158
Small-cap stocks
decline 2000, 4
401(k) plan allocation, 139
risk/return vs. large-cap, 51, 139
SmartMoney.com, 106
information on fund correlation,
116
portfolio tracking, 201
Southwest Airlines, 85
ultimate all-weather portfolio pick,
118
Standard & Poor's (S&P) 100
VIX and, 215–17, *216, 218*
Standard & Poor's (S&P) 500
average daily move, 20
benchmarking with, 112–13, 226
decline, 2000, 4, 20
gains, pre-2000, 7
returns, percent annualized since
1926, 35
Standard deviation of returns
best/worst, 43
biggest spread, 42
evaluating easy-hold mutual funds
and, 89
evaluating easy-hold stocks and, 75
large-cap vs. small-cap stocks, 51
Stock market
average daily trading volume, 29–30
bear market, 74, 127–28, 228–29,
236
bull market, 23, 227–28
decline, 2000–2001, 4
declines, cause, 40
detecting market shifts, tools for,
208–27
Dow Theory to predict shifts,
223–31
downturn, criteria for, 74

earnings volatility leads to equity
volatility, 15–16
emotion, impact of, 8, 9
frictionless movement in, 10–11
globalization of, 11–12
high-yield stocks in bull or bear
markets, 37
Internet and movement of
information, 12–14
investors, identity of, 9–10
most active stocks, 31–32
pendulum effect, 7–9, 62–63, *63*
reversion to mean, 209–12
sector performance, 1985–2001, 41
sweet spot, finding, 23
tech stock crash, 1, 3
terrorism, impact of, 14–15
upside volatility, 1995-1999, 7
See also individual indexes.
Stock options (puts and calls), 146,
212–15
Stocks
average daily trading volume, 29
bid-ask spread, 31
common, 44
dividend yield, 34–36
exotic, 34
float, 28–29
formula for percent of portfolio,
104–5
growth, 35
low volatility, 44
matching style and selection, 67–69
preferred, 39, 44
prices linked to earnings, 39
top ten easy holds, 76–88
types of (list), 50
ultimate all-weather portfolio picks,
118
volatility of, 44, 110–11
See also Easy holds; Large-cap
stocks; Micro-cap stocks; Mid-cap
stocks; Portfolio: Ultimate All
Weather; Small-cap stocks.
Stocks for the Long Run (Siegel),
18–19
Stock splits, 226–27
Stop order, 163
Studzinski, Edward, 94
SunGard Data Systems, 85
Sun Microsystems, 32

Synovus Financial, 38
Sysco, 85
  ultimate all-weather portfolio pick,
    118

T
T. Rowe Price, 132
  dividend growth, 38
  Price Growth Stock fund, 134
  Small-Cap Value fund, 95
Taxes
  arbitrage, 195–96
  capital gains, 34, 36, 133, 195–96
  "cost basis" of investments and,
    193–94
  dividend income, 36
  Folio*fn*, 155
  Gainskeeper tool, 202
  holding stocks to avoid, 56
  I Bonds, 100
  IRAs, traditional and Roth, 141,
    142–43
  mutual funds, 133, 155
  planning for, 193–96
  selling stocks and, 159, 188
  TIPS, 99, 100
  wash sale, 195
Technology stocks
  acquisitions and, 167
  crash of, 1, 3–4, 39
  easy-hold recommendations,
    76–77, 85–86
  future prediction for, 5
  growth investors and, 71
  not "easy hold," 43
  product obsolescence and, 167
  sector performance, 41
  spread of returns, best/worst, 42, 43
  volatility of, 43, 44, 68
Telecom stocks
  receivables turnover and red flag
    for problems, 170–71
  volatility, 44
Terrorism
  impact on stocks, 14–15
  September 11, 1–3, 196, 221
Time diversification, 57–64
  dollar-cost averaging, 57–60
  extending holding periods, 61–62
  laddering, 97
  value averaging, 60–61

Time horizon (for investments)
  age of investor and asset
    diversification, 49–50
  Intermediate Potential Risk
    indicator, and shortened, 222
  market volatility and, 44
TIPS (Treasury inflation-protected
  securities), 97–99
"To-do" investor list, 236–38
TradeTrakker, 201
Transportation sector performance, 41
Treasury securities, 36, 39
  I Bonds, 99–100
  risk/return, 51
  TIPS (Treasury inflation-protected
    securities), 97–99

U
UMB Scout WorldWide mutual fund
  ultimate all-weather portfolio pick,
    118
uMonitor, 203
Union Pacific railroad, 179
Utilities/Utility stocks
  easy-hold recommendations, 78, 84
  gain, 2000–2001, 4, 23
  low volatility, 44
  sector performance, 41

V
Value averaging, 60–61
Value investing, 65, 71, 94
Vanguard
  High-Yield Corporate Fund, 108,
    109, 118
  Money Market Fund, 119
  Short Term Corporate Bond Fund,
    100, 108, 109, 118
  Total Bond Market Index fund, 100,
    108, 109, 118
  ultimate all-weather portfolio picks,
    118
Van Wagoner Micro-Cap Fund, 133
Venture capital, 33
Veritas Software, 177
VIX and VIXN, 215–19, *216, 217, 218*
Volatility
  beta and, 19
  buy-and-hold investing and, 17–18
  buying during volatile markets,
    127–28, 196, 236–37

detecting market shifts, tools for, 208–27
dividend yield to cushion, 34–36
earnings volatility leads to equity volatility, 15–16
firm-level increase, 110
flexibility and liquidity, need for and, 27
foreign markets and globalization, 11–12
frequency of market swings, 7, 9–16
frictionless markets and, 10–11
futures and options markets and, 212–15
gains and profits, 21
historical prices and, 19–20
impermanence of, 6–7
indexes of (VIX and VIXN), 215–19, *216, 218*
individual or retail vs. institutional investors and, 9–10
Internet and movement of information, 12–14
liquidity, need for, 29–30
low, investments, 44
neutral nature of, 16–17
selective, 20–21
short-term time horizons vs. long-term time horizons, 18–19
standard deviation of returns and, 42
stocks, increase in volatility for individual, 110–11
terrorism and, 14–15
uncertainty and, 26
upside and downside of (pendulum), 7–9, 62–63, *63*
See also Diversification; Portfolio, all-weather.
Volume leaders (most actively traded stocks), 31–32

W
Wal-Mart Stores, 85
ultimate all-weather portfolio pick, 118
Walgreen, 87
ultimate all-weather portfolio pick, 118
Wall Street Journal, test for exotic investments and, 34
"Wash sale" rules, 195
"Watch list," 192, 196–97
ingredients in, 197
Waters, 87–88
ultimate all-weather portfolio pick, 118
Westamerica Bancorp, 38
WorldCom, 32
Wright, David, 72, 76, 88, 90

X
Xerox, 56

Y
Yahoo! stock price fluctuations, 65, 159
Yahoo! Finance
account aggregator, 204
average daily trading volume statistics, 30
float statistics, 28–29
historical daily trading volumes, 30
insider buying and selling tracked, 29
portfolio tracking, 201–2
stock-charting service, 8
Yield, 90
Yodlee, 204

ABOUT THE AUTHOR

Charles Carlson is Chief Executive Officer of Horizon Publishing. He is also Chief Executive Officer of Horizon Investment Services, a money management concern. Mr. Carlson is editor of "DRIP Investor" investment newsletter, is a contributing editor of "Dow Theory Forecasts" investment newsletter, and is the co-portfolio manager of the Quaker-Horizon Dow 30 Plus Fund. Mr. Carlson, who is a Chartered Financial Analyst (CFA), holds an undergraduate degree in journalism from Northwestern University (1982) and an MBA from the University of Chicago (1993). He is a regular contributor to *Bloomberg Personal Finance* magazine and is the author of seven books, including the best-selling *Eight Steps to Seven Figures* (Doubleday), *Buying Stocks Without a Broker* (McGraw-Hill), *Individual Investor Revolution* (McGraw-Hill), and *No-Load Stocks* (McGraw-Hill). Mr. Carlson's comments appear in such newspapers and magazines as *The Wall Street Journal, The New York Times, USA Today, Newsweek, U.S. News & World Report, The Washington Post, Money, BusinessWeek, Forbes, Barron's,* and *Kiplinger's Personal Finance.* Mr. Carlson also appears frequently on television and radio shows, including CNBC, CNN, NBC's *Today Show,* and Business Radio Network. He lives in Valparaiso, Indiana.

Mr. Carlson can be reached at (219) 852-3220, ext. 326, or ccarlson @horizonpublishing.com.